UNDERSTANDING NEW MEDIA

Eugenia
Siapera

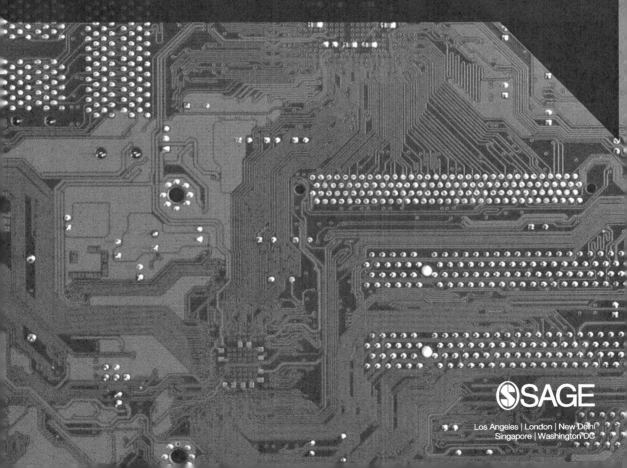

UNDERSTANDING
NEW MEDIA

Eugenia
Siapera

⑤SAGE

Los Angeles | London | New Delhi
Singapore | Washington DC

First published 2012
Reprinted 2013

SAGE Publications Ltd
1 Oliver's Yard
55 City Road
London EC1Y 1SP

SAGE Publications Inc.
2455 Teller Road
Thousand Oaks, California 91320

SAGE Publications India Pvt Ltd
B 1/I 1, Mohan Cooperative Industrial Area
Mathura Road
New Delhi 110 044

SAGE Publications Asia-Pacific Pte Ltd
3 Church Street
#10-04 Samsung Hub
Singapore 049483

Library of Congress Control Number: 2011926279

British Library Cataloguing in Publication data

A catalogue record for this book is available from the British Library

ISBN 978-1-84860-778-1
ISBN 978-1-84860-779-8 (pbk)

Typeset by C&M Digitals (P) Ltd, Chennai, India
Printed and bound by MPG Pringroup, UK
Printed on paper from sustainable resources

TABLE OF CONTENTS

CHAPTER 1

UNDERSTANDING NEW MEDIA

Learning Objectives

- To understand the relevant terminology
- To learn about different approaches to the study of the new media
- To critically apprehend the relationship between technology, new media and society
- To learn the main positions of important theorists of technology and media
- To understand and explore the role of e-tivities

Introduction – Why Study the New Media?

> Today, after more than a century of electric technology, we have extended our central nervous system itself in a global embrace, abolishing both space and time […]. Rapidly, we approach the final phase […] when the creative process of knowing will be collectively and corporately extended to the whole of human society […].

Marshall McLuhan, *Understanding Media: The Extensions of Man*, 1964: 3

> The media determine our situation.

Friedrich Kittler, *Gramophone, Film, Typewriter*, 1999: xxxix

The excerpt above, from the introduction of *Understanding Media*, reveals McLuhan's vision of the electronic media world: through the media, humanity, fully connected, will collaboratively build and share a global world. The fragmentation and alienation associated with the 'mechanical age', or the age of the industrial revolution, is now replaced with a compulsion to participate and become involved. Kittler's statement is more succinct: all that we are, he claims, is determined by the media. The crucial argument in both theorists is that the media play a central explanatory role in the shifts and transformations in human history. Understanding media therefore means understanding humanity. We shall examine McLuhan's and Kittler's work in more detail later, but for now, the important issue is that understanding media brings not only an insight into the technologies or devices themselves, but also into societal changes. Understanding new media is expected to lead to an understanding of changes and transformations in social processes, norms, ideas and practices. The media are inextricably bound to society: the study of one requires the study of the other. This book is therefore concerned with tracking and critically examining the changes in society associated with the new media.

The exact nature of the relationship between the media and society is a subject of much debate as we shall see in the relevant section below. But even without reaching any definite conclusions, the increasing centrality of the media, and especially of the *new* media, is clear to all of us. Televisions and radio sets have had a long presence in households in at least the developed world. But the rise of the new media is associated with their ubiquity; they are found everywhere: in living rooms, offices and schools, in the streets, in playrooms and bedrooms. And what's more they are found not only in the so-called developed world, but in developing countries as well. A recent report puts the number of mobile phone users in Africa to 37% of the continent's population, with an annual growth rate of 49% (IT News Africa, 2009). This spread poses a series of important questions regarding society, but also about economic, political and cultural institutions, as well as our experiences. We may want to see these as increasingly, or perhaps even inevitably, mediated (Livingstone, 2009). In other words, the involvement of the new media in society, the economy, politics, culture, the self and experiences is such that none of these escape unscathed. Our goal in this book is to show how all these aspects of life have been articulated with the new media. Understanding new media, in this sense, means understanding how they interact with a series of social, economic, political, cultural and psychological processes, giving rise to a new kind of world. As we shall see, this world may not resemble very closely the one in McLuhan's vision, but it can nevertheless be thought of as a new media world.

What is meant, however, by the term 'new media'? As a first step in the quest for understanding, we need to discuss terms: why new media? Why not digital or online media? The first section of this chapter will discuss terminology. Different terms, we will argue, prioritize different elements and construct different versions, perhaps to the exclusion of some aspects. We will examine the various synonyms and explain why this book decided to adopt the term new media even though they already now have a history of at least 30 years.

Terminology, however, is only part of the story: how and in what ways are the (new) media connected (sometimes quite literally) to society? What is the relationship between the media and society in broader, more theoretical terms? Do they determine society much in the way argued by McLuhan? Or are the media as well as society determined by economic processes, as Marx would argue? These and other hypotheses will be critically examined in the second section of this chapter. The perspective assumed here is that is perhaps better understood as mediation (Silverstone, 2005; 2006), which assumes a dialectical relationship between the media and society.

An explanation of the structure of the book will follow the discussions of terms and theories concerning the new media. The various chapters that make up the book, the reasons underlying their choice, and their main arguments will be summarized in the third section of this chapter. This section will also introduce the concept of the e-tivity (Salmon, 2002). E-tivities form an important part of this book, as they enable readers to acquire a hands-on understanding of some of the issues examined in each chapter.

Why *New* Media?

'What's in a name?' wondered Shakespeare's Juliet. 'A rose by any other name would smell as sweet' (Romeo and Juliet, II, ii, 1–2). Indeed, although we use several names, the question remains: does anything change if we call them new media, online, or digital media? Do they not refer to the same media? Well, Juliet may actually be wrong: different names bring to the fore different attributes, and by prioritizing different elements, they focus attention on some aspects and overlook others. The result is that for all intents and purposes they end up 'smelling differently', to use Shakespeare's analogy. In other words, their outlook, attributes and uses, shift as a result of the names used to apprehend them. In this manner, names do not merely describe them, but construct them as particular kinds of media. A decision on which name to use is therefore quite an important one. In this section we will explain why the term new media was adopted in this book, by discussing the two main alternative terms: digital media and online media.

Digital Media

One of the defining characteristic of the kinds of media under study is that they are digital (Lister, Dovey, Giddings, Grant and Kelly, 2009). This means that all the information or data in these media is encoded in numbers. The most common numerical system used is the binary code of 0 and 1: all information is therefore converted in a series of 0s and 1s. Information such as, for instance, a name, can be represented by any arbitrary combination of numbers. From this point of view, the interpretation of the digital code is independent of its representation. On the other hand, analogue media encode and store information in corresponding physical objects. Thus, sound, text and images elicit analogous responses in vinyl, paper or film. This is a relationship of more or less direct correspondence of encoded information and physical objects, in which information is interpreted in an equally direct manner. For example, words are encoded in a book by pressing metallic letters on paper, and once printed they cannot change. Recorded music is encoded by carving grooves in vinyl.

Lister et al. (2009: 18) refer to four main outcomes of the turn towards digital media. First, media texts become de-linked from particular media. We can now read books on the internet or on Kindle, watch television or films online or on our mobiles, and upload photographs on our blog or hang them on digital frames. This attribute leads to the much talked about media convergence (e.g. Jenkins, 2006b). Secondly, information can be compressed and fit in very small spaces: there are USB flash drives, for instance, that fit 464 gigabytes (GB) – and there is even a device (E-Disk® Altima™ flash drive) measuring 3.5" that can store up to 1 terabyte (1,000 GB). To understand the magnitude of these measures, 1 gigabyte contains about 4,500 books of 200 pages each, and 1 terabyte can contain more than 4.5 million books! A third outcome of digitalization is that access to data can be very fast and also that it does not have to be linear. Imagine that you have stored all your books in a flash drive or on your computer's hard disk. You can access any book in this collection in a matter of seconds, and also information within this book without having to flip through all the pages one by one. Finally, a more ambivalent outcome of digitalization is that data can be manipulated in ways unimaginable in the analogue media age. In the Stalinist Soviet Union, disgraced Party members would disappear from official photographs and records through painstaking retouching by photography experts (see King, 1997). Careful examination could easily reveal the falsification of the photographs. Digital photographs have reversed the situation: retouching is available to all of us at a click of a few buttons. While this may be a useful tool for removing 'red eyes' from pictures, it can clearly have more sinister uses.

There is no doubt that the process of digitalizing the media has had profound effects. In the EU, the 2012 digital switchover puts a formal end to analogue media. Soon, the process of digitalization will turn all media into digital media. But how does this term fare when it comes to understanding the media? With its emphasis on the mode of encoding and converting data and information, the term digital media seems to focus primarily on the technological element of the media. To talk of digital media therefore appears to prioritize aspects that relate to the technology that made them possible. While the technological element is without doubt important, we have to ask here whether it is the defining characteristic of these media. A possible objection concerns the implicit technological determinism associated with such a position. To posit that the technology is the defining dimension of the media overlooks the ways in which users shape them, or the broader socio-cultural and economic environment which produced them in the first place. We can therefore keep from the term digital the importance of technological attributes, but we also need to add other elements as well.

Online Media

A second term for apprehending the media is to refer or construct them as online media. This is a direct reference to the internet, which is in many ways the prototypical new medium. The term online media prioritizes the element of connectivity, or the ways in which they connect with other media, mainly computers, but also more recently mobile telephones. Connectivity is certainly a crucial attribute of the media under study: the ability to link to distant, and sometimes near, others, one or many at the same time, has had wide consequences. For one, it introduces a shift within modernity, which is typically associated with isolation and individuation (see Giddens, 1991). In addition, it introduces, or perhaps continues and accelerates, shifts in the relatively separate and distinct socio-cultural and politico-economic organization of the nation-state; such shifts are associated with the process of globalization (see Robertson, 1992; c.f. Chapter 2). To refer to the media under study as online media constructs them as primarily connected media. But is this attribute the defining characteristic of the media? To be sure, connectivity is a crucial element, but focusing on it overlooks the other ways in which we relate to the media. Moreover, connections to distant others were already possible with the telegraph and later the telephone. Online connectivity does not seem to point to a kind of replacement or rupture in the same way that the digital replaced analogue, and from this point of view, the shifts it introduces are more in terms of the quality and degree of connection. In short, the term online media captures another important dimension, but which needs to be thought alongside others.

New Media

We therefore end up with the term new media. There are a lot of issues with this term: it introduces a somewhat arbitrary split between 'old' and 'new' media, it overlooks that 'new' media such as the internet already have a 40 year history, while it also fails to denote any of the dimensions along which the 'new' differ from the 'old' other than their age difference. Yet, these problems, especially the failure to specify what may qualify as a new medium, actually allow us to include attributes such as digital, online and others as well without limiting or prioritizing any single one. In addition, although for some critics the reference to 'new' may appear to disregard the ways in which more mature media have evolved in recent years (Bell, 2009), it denotes a dynamism and penchant for constant change. The term can therefore include all kinds of media formats as long as they are indeed evolving.

But the term new media further signifies a shift in media logic, which denotes a certain degree of novelty. Discussing the new media, Lev Manovich (2001) argued that thinking of them as digital and/or is only half the story: for Manovich these elements may be present in older media forms as well. The new element that points to a significant change in the media is that they are the result of a convergence between the computational logic characteristic of the computers and the communicative logic characteristic of the media. While for Manovich this has the result of the dominance of a specific logic, that of the database, over the communicative logic of the media, we would like here to leave open the question of a dominant logic. We can retain Manovich's idea of the convergence between computational and communicative logic as characteristic of the new media, as this shows the uniqueness of these kinds of media. On the other hand, while to be sure, the database is one kind of logic found in these media, it may be too early to think of it as the prevailing one. Rather, we would like to point out, as argued above, that the term new signifies precisely this openness and struggle between different ideas, users, logics and so on, which seem to be part and parcel of the new media, at least at this, relatively early stage of their existence.

From this point of view, the use of the term new media constructs them as novel, innovative and dynamic. Furthermore, its reluctance to commit to any single attribute or logic as the defining one means that they can all be included as necessary but not sufficient criteria for understanding the new media. At the same time, it recognizes the specificity and uniqueness of the type of media we are looking at. The choice of this term is therefore more appropriate for a book that seeks to outline the dynamic introduced by these kinds of media and the wider consequences they may have for everyday life. But this presupposes a relationship between the media and society. The next section will examine the theories, suppositions and arguments regarding this complex relationship.

Technologies, Media and Society

The central question regarding (new) media and technology concerns the nature of their relationship with people and society. Do they determine, shape or otherwise influence them? Conversely, do individuals and societal structures produce, use and give meaning to media and technological artefacts? Both sides make convincing arguments supporting their main tenets, but they also share something important: their focus on the pivotal or fundamental role of communication media and the technologies that support them. In this section we will examine the work of four important thinkers of the relationship between humanity and technology: McLuhan, Kittler, Stiegler and Castells. This rather eclectic decision is based on notions of origin and original: McLuhan was the first to prioritize the study of media and technologies, and his work, notwithstanding its many openings, presages some of the more recent developments. On the other hand, the approaches of Friedrich Kittler and Bernard Stiegler are stunningly original and as such especially fruitful in rethinking this relationship in different terms, as well as in developing a coherent and consistent politics of technology, that will then allow us to actively criticize contemporary developments. Finally, the work of Manuel Castells offers an especially useful empirical grounding of some of the more fanciful claims made by theorists of technology.

The focus on these theorists does not mean to imply that they are the only or main ones. The field of knowledge is such that it cannot be conceived or shaped by a few individuals, no matter how gifted they are. Thus theorists such as Lev Manovich, who discussed the logic of the database, Geert Lovink, McKenzie Wark and many others, have made important contributions to our understanding of technology and (new) media. Some of this work will be discussed in other chapters in this book, whose remit is to look into detail in specific areas of mediated life. But this section needs to address the fundamentals of the relationship between technology and society or better humanity. The question here is not only what does technology do, but more fundamentally what are technology and media, and why are they so important for us? For Mark Hansen (2006), the importance of the (new) media does not lie in their attributes, on whether they are digital or analogue, new or old and so on. Rather the crucial issue regarding the media is that they are at the same time artefacts or material devices, as well as 'transcendental', that is, they exist and do things beyond and above their material use. Thinking of the media as material artefacts that not only enable but condition and circumscribe communication raises important questions regarding the mediation of life. With this in mind we can examine the ideas of four major thinkers of new media and technologies.

McLuhan

As with this chapter, a theoretical interrogation of the relationship between the media and society typically begins with Marshall McLuhan. This is because McLuhan is the first theorist to argue that the importance of the media is not located in the contents they circulate but in the form of the media themselves. In fact his somewhat opaque statement that 'the media is the message' (McLuhan, 2001 [1964]: 7) can be interpreted in two ways: first it denotes the ultimate priority of media forms, which indeed impart a crucial message, and second, that the contents of any new medium are the old media. To begin with the latter, McLuhan's argument relies on a somewhat idiosyncratic view of the historical development of the various media. Thus, he considers that speech, orality, was the first 'medium' – he is clearly using a widened understanding of the term. Subsequently, the media that evolved, such as written language, contained speech as its contents; the invention of the medium of print used written language as its contents. Cinema then used print as its contents and so forth. Specific messages and media contents are therefore not as important or relevant as the actual medium itself. On the other hand, this kind of cannibalistic behaviour leads straight back to contents as a means for analyzing media. Following McLuhan's arguments, the contents of the new media incorporate all other previous media (c.f. Levinson, 1999).

But it is the first understanding concerning the primacy of the media that leads to the more radical implications for any media analysis. This is due to the relationship it posits between media, people and societies. McLuhan famously thought that the media are extensions of the human senses. As he put it: 'all media, from the phonetic alphabet to the computer, are extensions of man that cause deep and lasting changes in him and transform his environment' (McLuhan, 1969: 54). More particularly, he viewed the media as either extensions or amputations, but nevertheless as inextricably bound to human beings. For McLuhan, the media can extend our senses, but they can also limit them: a medium can amplify or accelerate existing processes or senses (McLuhan, 2001 [1964]: 7), and this is its 'true' effect or impact. Examples here include the process of mechanization or the replacement of parts of human labour by machines. The fact that human labour is mediated by machines leads to a fragmentation of previously integrated parts of the process. Similarly, the telephone extends human voice, but it also 'amputates' face-to-face interaction – a criticism often faced by the so-called social media in more recent days. In more general terms, the relationship that McLuhan posits between the media and people is one in which the shape or form of the media determines what happens to humans. Humans, or more accurately, the current human condition is seen as the 'effect' of media and technology. It's little wonder that McLuhan faced accusations of media or technological determinism (e.g. Levinson, 1999).

Indeed, it seems that the relationship posited by McLuhan is one in which technology and media cause and determine the changes and directions of human activity, be it social, political or economic. And, moreover, humans are blinded to these effects of the media in the same way that fish are unaware of the water in which they swim: 'As a result, precisely at the point where a new media-induced environment becomes all pervasive and transmogrifies our sensory balance, it also becomes invisible' (McLuhan, 1969: 56). There is a sense in all this that humans themselves are led by the media, not realizing the many and varied effects and consequences. The historical evolution of the media according to McLuhan, who in this seems to follow Harold Innis (1950; 1951), is from orality to literacy, from the spoken word to hand-written manuscripts and from there to print and then electronic media (McLuhan, 2002 [1962]). Each media epoch was characterized by different lifestyles, cultures, trends, economies, and also political systems (Innis; 1951; McLuhan, 2002 [1962]). Oral cultures were linked to tribal forms of socio-political organization and relied on the art of memory. Literate cultures, such as the ones by Greeks and Romans, introduced militarism and the exercise of power from far away (empire). The dawn of the electronic media will for McLuhan inevitably lead to the end of the 'Gutenberg Galaxy', print culture and its main characteristics and organizing principles: nationalism, functional differentiation, rationalization, homogenization and alienation – all these are also clear characteristics of (early) modernity. The uniformity of print is in a sense emblematic of the homogenization effected by this kind of medium – McLuhan further adds that the print age has installed a primacy of the visual over the melange of senses mobilized by the oral and manuscript eras. But what of our era: this, for McLuhan, is in transition from the Gutenberg Galaxy to the electronic era. The electronic media usher in a new culture, in which time and space do not matter as much, due to the immediate and interlinked connections drawn by electronic circuits. The main organizing principles characteristic of the 'mechanical age' of the Gutenberg Galaxy will inevitably become extinct: no more nation-states, no more frag-mented individuals; rather, we will come together as a community in the global village, linked by a series of interdependencies.

It is clear that for McLuhan the motor of human history is not, as Marx would have it, class struggle, but rather media and technological evolution. Technology and media replace Marx's humanism, but also give rise to important questions: what leads to technological change? If humans and their societies are determined by media, then what accounts for shifts in media themselves? Moreover, and following a Marxian theme, are we all equally affected by the dif-ferent media ages? McLuhan would perhaps answer that different media instigate a different division of labour, but the absence of these explicitly political considerations earned him many an intellectual enemy (see for instance, Enzensberger, 1970). Perhaps some answers are found in the work of Friedrich Kittler who relies on, and extends, McLuhan's thought.

Kittler

'The media determine our situation' is the opening line of Friedrich Kittler's *Gramophone, Film, Typewriter* – a statement boldly reiterating McLuhan's 'the medium is the message'. But Kittler's work is much more subtle and nuanced than this statement conveys. His argu-ment fuses Foucauldian archaeological analysis and Lacanian structural psychoanalysis with the media and their technologies in unexpected ways. Foucault famously argued that notions, institutions, disciplines and even selves that appear 'natural' are in fact all constructed, and they form the culmination of years of operation of certain discursive principles and formations, and they reveal the operation of power (see e.g. Foucault's *The Order of Things* (2002 [1966]), *Power/Knowledge* (1980), *The Archaeology of Knowledge* (1989 [1969])). Discourse – or a series of signs, written, spoken or otherwise conveyed – is placed at the centre of such constructions. The job of an 'archaeologist' or later 'genealogist' of the social world is to find the constitutive elements of the issues, subjects, disciplines they are analyzing. Lacan, on the other hand, focused on the way in which subjects or selves become who they are through the operation of linguistic principles (Lacan, 1980 [1966]). Kittler now draws upon these insights arguing that it is well and good to look at languages and their combination into discourses, but we must not overlook the media or the technological networks that made specific kinds of languages and discourses to emerge and assume primacy. Kittler views such languages and discourses more broadly as information and argues that to understand our present condition, we must take into account the ways in which this information is processed and stored. He refers to such configurations as 'discourse networks', which he more specifically defines as networks 'of technologies and institutions that allow a given culture to select, store and produce relevant data' (Kittler, 1992: 369). Kittler then proceeds to a historical periodization resting on the one hand on McLuhan and on the other on Foucault (2002 [1966]).

In his book *Discourse Networks 1800/1900*, Kittler (1992) describes the network of 1800 with the period of alphabetization, which relied on writing as the only means of processing and storing information. All other kinds of signs, sounds, images and so on, had to go through written language in order to be stored. This discourse network was linked to Romanticism as written language was in the first instance a 'technology of symbolic encoding' (Translators' Introduction: xxv), and was primarily associated with literature. Literature, and poetry, was then interpreted as the exteriorization of an inner voice, which sought to capture feelings and ideas in an 'authentic' way. The monopoly of writing was broken by the invention of other media, such as Edison's phonograph and kinetoscope, which allowed the recording and broadcasting of voices, sounds, and images. Remington's typewriter, which was invented at around the same time (1900), constituted the third medium described by Kittler as part of the discourse network 1900. This network revolved around inscription technologies, and was no longer representing the 'inner voice' but rather exteriorized modernity's need to control, rationalize and record data in a standardized manner. Kittler supports his arguments with references to Nietzsche, one of the first authors to use a typewriter, which then made him realize the shift involved: from the expression of 'inner voices', the individuality and idiosyncrasies of writing (by hand) to standardized typography, from an agent of writing to a surface for inscription (Kittler, 1992: 210). The next move, one which Kittler has yet to complete, involves the passage to digitalization, which subverts the serial inscription of data, and leads to new forms of subjects. However, discourse networks can only be methodologically approached retrospectively preventing Kittler from a formal description of a discourse network 2000 (see Kittler and Johnston, 1997: 7)

These links between media technologies and consciousness or subjectivity show the importance of the media, and justify Kittler's statement that the media determine our situation. They do so by virtue of providing us with the material artefacts by which to write, communicate or otherwise understand ourselves and the world around us. There is a clear anti-humanist stance in Kittler, as there is no room for human subjects as the agents of history in his account – rather humans appear as the end result of historically located mediations: romantic, 'authentic', close-to-nature mediated through handwriting, and industrious, rationalized units (individuals) mediated through the technologies of inscription. The same questions as with McLuhan inevitably arise here as well: what about human agency? What may explain media emergence, change and evolution? Kittler's argument, following a Foucauldian understanding of power as enabling (Foucault, 1980), is that technologies make people: that is, media and their technologies make possible the kind of people that we are, and the kind of societies that we have. But then people, enabled by the media, feedback into them thereby leading to shifts and changes, which in turn produce different media technologies, different subjects, different societies and so on. To clarify this point further, in their introduction to Kittler's *Gramophone, Film, Typewriter*, Geoffrey Winthrop-Young and Michael Wutz (1999: xxxv) use the analogy of the Marxian conception of the dialectics of base-superstructure. In Kittler's work, the media-technological 'base' is dialectically related to the discursive 'superstructure'; this dialectical relationship means that there are tensions and conflicts that give rise to new technologies, new media, new discourse networks. The 'motor' of history therefore is technology rather then humanity.

But do humans have any power at all? Where does this leave the politics of technology? In two influential and provocative essays, Kittler declared that 'there is no software' before moving on to discuss the implications of the 'protected mode' of software (Kittler, 1997a; 1997b). He begins by pointing to the explosion of commercial software, which in turn conceals the implosion of hardware. Digitalization means that all underlying operations are reduced to binary code and are hidden from our eyes, which see only the interface of the software we are using. All words that we see appearing in front of us on our word processing program are reduced to 0 and 1, and the voltage difference between them. The use of software and graphic user interfaces ends up obscuring the operations of hardware, which we, as users, never see or understand. This in turn makes us dependent on software companies which seek to acquire a monopoly not only over their own programs-products but also on the knowledge of technical innovations that underlie hardware. From this point of view, software operates as a kind of cryptography, which has strategic functions, mainly to offer a sustained economic advantage to software corporations. For Kittler, because software does not exist independently of hardware or machine, it insists even more vocally that it qualify as property. This has two related results (see also Harris and Taylor, 2005: 85): first, to hide that software is the result of a collective endeavour and not a commodity, and second, to hide the operations by which software giants produce subjects or 'end-users', at the same time obscuring the ways in which they become subjugated. 'End-users' are therefore analogous to the 1800s readers and to the 1900s audiences. They are constrained by the combined operations of both hardware and software, even as they seem to make their life easier. A relevant political response would therefore entail the engagement with all those operations that obscure the actual ways that subjugate us, that make us subjects. The task of critical analysis is precisely to show the ways in which humans and societies are constructed, and that includes not only the logic of software but crucially also the processes and coded routines of hardware. This is Kittler's answer to, and to an extent continuation of, Foucault's genealogical analysis, which he terms information materialism (Kittler, 1997a; 1997b; see also Gane, 2005). Through this method, Kittler seeks to identify the rules or algorithms that guide the transformation of information into material objects (and subjects) and vice versa. Finding the codes, rules and algorithms which govern us as subjects and the material-informational world around us will not offer mastery, but it will at least help us understand that we cannot think of ourselves as masters of the world (Winthrop-Young, 2006).

Kittler's account offers a valuable insight into the role played by technology, by hardware and algorithms in determining life, society and culture. But to accept the primacy of technology appears to reduce the role of human agency: we may not be 'masters and commanders', but we are agents, capable of reflexive and purposeful actions. What appears necessary is therefore an account of technology that does not discount the role of humanity. It is to Bernard Stiegler, the French philosopher of technology, that we turn to find such an account.

Stiegler

The post-humanist strand evident in McLuhan and more clearly in Kittler is also present in the work of Bernard Stiegler. However, while for both McLuhan and Kittler the relationship between technologies-media and humanity-society is one of determination of the latter by the former, Stiegler argues that technology and humanity are coeval or co-originary. Rather than prioritizing technology as McLuhan and Kittler do, Stiegler shows that humans and technology are inextricably bound, they belong together and co-determine each other. This coexistence of humanity and technology is important because it allows us to think of the evolution of both at the same time, without necessarily prioritizing one over the other. It therefore eschews on the one hand the anthropocentric views of technology and media as a tool in the hands of humans, and on the other hand the media-centric views of humans as determined by technology.

The central problem posed by Stiegler in his four-volume work *Technics and Time* concerns the role of 'technics'. The term technics refers to the object of techno-logy, and more specifically to the domain of skills as opposed to episteme, the domain of knowledge. For Stiegler, all human action relates to technics (1998: 94). But what is the relationship between humans and technics, or skills and tools? Stiegler makes use of Derrida's (*Of Grammatology* and *Of Spirit*) insight on prostheses or supplements to humans as ever-present. Derrida showed that the philosophical move to isolate thought (the 'essence' of humanity) from technics or the technological means (supplements) by which it is articulated is in fact impossible: speaking, writing, printing, and crucially, archiving are always there when thought is articulated. Thought, life or even nature cannot be understood without technics: this is what Derrida terms prosthesis of/at the origin or 'originary technicity' (*Of Grammatology*, 1974/1997). Richard Beardsworth (1996: 149) views in this originary technicity Derrida's understanding of human identity: it is locked in the relationship between humans and their supplements so that humans can never be identified with their supplements – they always differ – but also this relationship can never be pin-pointed and captured once and for all (it is always dynamic, deferred). Technicity and technics for Derrida are constitutive of humans, a process which he calls hominization. Derridean deconstruction is therefore the method by which we can find the various processes of hominization.

Stiegler takes over from Derrida expanding but also criticizing his work. He argues that deconstruction needs to become more oriented towards history on the one hand, and towards the materiality of technology on the other. While Derrida theorized abstractly and formally the deferred and different relationship between humans and technics, Stiegler proposes a historically informed account of this relationship, based on the materiality of technology, that is, on the different material forms that technology takes. We can then recognize concretely the various 'hominizations' and we can also articulate a politics of technology.

Following through these arguments, Stiegler begins with an anthropology of technology drawing upon the work of palaeontologist Leroi-Gourhan (1993). Concerned with the problem of human evolution, Leroi-Gourhan argued that humans evolved due to their assumption of the upright position, which then freed their hands for making and using tools. Technology is then seen as a particular kind of memory, a third kind, alongside genetic memory (DNA) and physical memory (nervous system). What characterizes humanity is therefore precisely this third kind of memory, seen as technology, which is also an exteriorized kind of memory as it resides in material objects. For Leroi-Gourhan, anthropogenesis (the 'birth' of the human species) is technogenesis (the 'birth' of technology). But Stiegler criticizes Leroi-Gourhan as not going far enough: in his account, Leroi-Gourhan still gives priority to the human cortex, thereby in effect prioritizing biology over technology. For Stiegler, if we are to speak of originary technicity, the coeval evolution of humanity and technology, then we must understand the cortex and technology, the 'interior' and 'exterior' as mutually and concurrently inventing each other. In this account, the cortex, which refers to reflexivity and ability for symbolic thought, is 'exteriorized' through technology, which then enables and preserves this reflexivity and capacity for symbolism. Stiegler calls this process, the coupling of humanity with technology, epiphylogenesis: 'a recapitulating, dynamic, and morphogenetic (phylogenetic) accumulation of individual experience (epi)' (Stiegler, 1998: 177). While all forms of life are endowed with an individual and a species-specific capacity for memory, humans can conserve and pass on their individual memory even after their death. Epiphylogenesis, the ability to capture and relive human memories and experiences through artificial (technological) means, is not only uniquely human (a condition for hominization in Stiegler's terms), but also the main way in which humans evolve: an evolution that is at once biological and technological. Language is seen as a perfect example of epiphylogenesis: we acquire language as a skill and therefore a technique. Language has its own history and memory that pre-existed us, but which then is taken over by us as individuals, and we carry it into the future (Vaccari and Barnet, 2009). Epiphylogenesis represents the cumulative cultural and historical experiences of humanity, which are preserved and located (and of course also shaped by) technological artefacts. As Vaccari and Barnet put it: 'There is history, there is culture, and there are the artefacts which carry them beyond our death: technics' (2009, unpaginated).

Precisely because the relationship between technology and humanity is one of a dynamic mutual composition (Stielger, 2006), what is at stake is nothing less than the future of humanity.

Stiegler argues that technical objects are the exteriorization of memory-thought, which then condition and circumscribe the 'interior', this very memory and thought. But this dependence on such mnemonic devices, as Stiegler (2006) calls them, entails loss of knowledge, which is then displaced and moved onto these technological objects. Losing our mobile phone, to use Stiegler's (2006) example, means losing all our contact numbers, which are no longer in our memory. Equally, consider the loss of the aptly named 'memory stick', which involves the loss of stored knowledge that we cannot retrieve from our memories. And here we must think, argues Stiegler, what this entails for our future. When in new technologies all the 'know-how' is 'exteriorized' and stored in devices controlled by others (e.g. corporations, governments, armies etc.) then we are faced with two effects. On the one hand, this entails a kind of 'human obsolescence', the deskilling and consequently the 'proletarization' of more and more humans, who after this loss of knowledge become fit only for consumption. On the other hand, we find the assumption of more and more power by the cognitive and cultural industries that run today's societies of control (Stielger, 2006: 18–19). For Stiegler, this leads to a politics of memory, a struggle for control of these technological mnemonic devices. This politics must proceed with an analysis of 'grammatization', the term used by Stiegler (2007) to refer to the ways in which the continuous 'flows' of life are encoded into discrete units: for instance, writing is the grammatization of the continuity of speech, while industrialization entailed the grammatization of the gestures of workers, which from continuous became discrete and from integrated they became fragmented. A relevant politics must therefore look into these processes of grammatization, and how they circumscribe life with a view to found 'a new political economy of memory and desire' (Stiegler, 2006: 41), able to address and expand the limits set by the various 'grammatizations'.

It is clear that Stiegler's work offers a new and fascinating account of the relationship between humanity and technology, between (new) media and society, which accepts the dynamic character of the relationship, while also acknowledging the close and inextricable connections of technology and humanity. However, Stiegler's analytical project (as with Kittler) is primarily a historically oriented one: it is a kind of genealogy of technology-humanity, rather than a sociology. A sociology of new media and technology, on the other hand, can provide detailed and empirically rich information on all areas of life, which can then enable us to better understand the present. Such a sociologically informed account is offered by Manuel Castells.

Castells

While Stiegler proposes a new and radical conception of humanity as always already technological, and McLuhan and Kittler view humanity as determined by the media and technologies, none of these theorists were concerned with a sociology of the new media and technologies, in the sense of looking systematically into the articulations of specific media with specific societies in an empirically informed manner. This is the task undertaken by Manuel Castells in his three-volume work on the network society collectively titled *The Information Age: Economy, Society and Culture* (Castells, 1996; 1997; 1998). In this body of work Castells seeks to empirically apprehend the changes in contemporary societies precipitated by the new media and technologies. Castells is careful to avoid accusations of technological determinism but he is also keen to show the effects that new technologies have in our lives. We can then say that he is assuming a kind of agnostic stance vis-à-vis the relationship between society and technology, while he seeks to empirically apprehend the recent societal shifts associated with new technologies and their media. Since he is still prioritizing the study of technology though, his position can be described as 'soft determinism' (Lister et al., 2009). Castells himself has argued that:

> *Technology does not determine society.* Nor does society script the course of technological change, since many factors, including individual inventiveness and entrepreneurialism, intervene in the process of scientific discovery, technical innovation and social applications, so the final outcome depends on a complex pattern of interaction. Indeed the dilemma of technological determinism is probably a false problem, since technology is society and society cannot be understood without its technological tools. (Castells, 2000 [1996]: 5)

From this point of view, his position stands closer to that of Bernard Stiegler, but without the extensive theorizations to support it.

Castells' main argument is that new technologies are associated with a new form of social organization, which revolves around the idea of the network. Our societies can therefore be understood as network societies, based no longer on the individual, or on the traditional community as in previous societies, but on the network. In his first volume, *The Network Society*, Castells explained that 'as a historical trend, dominant functions and processes are increasingly organized around networks. Networks constitute the new social morphology of our societies, and the diffusion of networking logic substantially modifies the operation and outcomes in processes of production, experience, power and culture' (2000 [1996]: 469). A network is seen as a structure comprised of different, but interconnected points – this structure has come to replace both the individual and the nation-state as the primary form of social organization. And because this 'new morphology' is not limited by geographical conceptions of space and associated limits of time, Castells argues that we have entered a new era, enabled by new electronic technologies, in which space is a space of flows and time is timeless.

Expanding on his arguments, Castells argues that space is the outcome of social construction: understanding the world around us is not so much a matter of perception (as, for instance, McLuhan would have it), but rather the outcome of a social ordering of things. From this point of view, electronic media effectively introduce a new ordering, which has made possible a different conception of space. This new concept of space is then defined not by relations of geographical contiguity but by the exchanges between the different places in which actors are found. Castells suggests that the space of flows has three layers: the first is the layer of electronic circuits which enables materially the space of flows. The second is the layer of nodes or hubs: the disjointed places that set up a network and support exchanges and interactions between actors occupying these places. Finally, the third layer refers to the spatial organization of dominant elites, which directs and articulates the space of flows: for Castells, the space of flows is not the only spatial logic in society; but it is the dominant one because it is used by the global elites. These elites are cosmopolitan, moving across places, but held together through occupying certain spaces: these include secluded residential areas as well as leisure-oriented spaces, which are made to look more or less identical despite their actual physical location.

Time within the space of flows is timeless. The 'linear, measurable, predictable time is shattered in the network society', which is characterized by a compression of time to such an extent that it makes time disappear (Castells, 2000 [1996]: 464). To understand this concept we can refer to the sequence of time that characterized the premodern era: this was determined by the seasons and their influence on agricultural production. Modernity introduced a different time, ordered by divisions between working time and leisure time, while working time was subjected to 'scientific management' (Taylor, 1911) to make it more efficient. The temporal organization of the network society, in contrast, negates time in the sense of eliminating the sequencing of time; for example, the global financial market operates in real time, exchanging massive amounts of capital in mere seconds. Castells argues that timeless time operates only where technology has given rise to 'systemic perturbation in the sequential order of phenomena' (2000 [1996]: 494). Such perturbation may take the form either of near-instantaneity or of random discontinuity. In both cases, time can no longer be ordered sequentially, thereby leading to undifferentiated time. Although Castells accepts that biologically and socially ordered time still apply, timeless time belongs to the space of flows.

These two parameters, the space of flows and timeless time, give rise to the network as the main way by which technologically advanced societies are ordered. Thus, economy becomes increasingly organized through networks and flows between them: networks of finance and companies; and networks of work projects that operate flexibly, on an ad hoc basis, coming together as and when necessary and dissolving or becoming obsolete when they are no longer needed. The politics of the network are increasingly mediated politics, where ideas and ideologies give way to communicative abilities as the main means by which to seek and legitimate power. The society of the network is not characterized by the organic solidarity of modernity, in which people within nation-states depend on each other on the basis of their functional differentiation (Durkheim, 1933 in Giddens, 1972). Rather, the bonds between people in the network society are tenuous and temporary, often based on common views and beliefs, uniting people across borders, but equally fragmenting them within given places.

Apparently unconcerned with abstract theorizing of the nature of the relationship between technology and society, Castells rather assumes that the new media represent a given historical articulation. Insofar as they have enabled the new social configuration of the network, they are linked to shifts in social, cultural, political and economic processes, and from a sociological point of view, it is important to detail these shifts. This view prioritizes empirical over theoretical perspectives, or at least it sees theorizations of new media and society as stemming from empirical investigations of different areas of life. Notwithstanding the insights of theorists such as Kittler and Stiegler, this book will closely follow Castells' more sociologically oriented perspective. On the other hand, empirical investigations already involve some theoretical assumptions that need to be made clear. This book therefore assumes an overall theoretical stance that follows Stiegler's ideas on the mutually determining relationship between humans and technology, while seeking to enrich these insights with discussions of empirical findings and studies.

To acknowledge the dynamism and irreducibility of the couple humanity-technology means that while technology is always there, its new manifestations lead to shifts in existing areas of life, spanning from the economic, to the psychological. These are not determined by technology as such, but by the mutually conditioning relationship between human agents and technological artefacts. Similarly, shifts in the economy, culture and so on bring about changes in technologies as well. More recently, this kind of relationship, or better process, has been termed mediation (Silverstone, 2006; Couldry, 2008; Livingstone, 2009). Mediation can be understood as the dialectical or at least dynamic interaction between media (and the technologies and artefacts that support them) and aspects of life, including self and subjectivity, society and culture, economy and politics. To speak of mediation as a dynamic process requires that no single component assumes priority but that they are all involved albeit often in an asymmetrical or unequal way (see Couldry, 2008). Moreover, to speak of the technological mediation of society requires that we examine a series of fields of life to find out exactly what the results of this process are at this historical juncture. Thus, in this book we will examine the ways in which various areas of life have changed since the spread of the new media. These areas and the rationale behind their choice will be outlined in the next section. This will discuss the structure of the book, the chapters that make it up, as well as the ways in which readers are invited to engage with the contents.

Structure of the Book

The structure of the book is based on the idea that the new media require not only analysis on their main features and characteristics but also an in-depth understanding of their articulations of various areas of life. This does not mean that the new media have unilaterally caused changes and shifts in areas such as the economy, sociality and so on. Rather, by becoming associated with them, an altogether new situation is created. Following Stiegler, the book is not so much looking at the new media themselves, but understands them as 'exteriorizations' of contemporary subjectivity, culture, society, economics and politics. There are bound to be areas that are not covered at all, or covered only very schematically. But the objective of this book is to introduce readers to the various shifts in various areas of life which are associated with the new media, rather than to exhaustively cover everything. Each chapter is meant to be autonomous in relation to others, but all follow along similar theoretical lines, relying heavily on Manuel Castells' ideas of the network society and informational capitalism. The broad outlook of the book is a social scientific one, although some ideas from media and cultural studies are also included. In the end, it is hoped that readers will have acquired a good sense of the direction our societies are taking, of the ways in which the new media have become embedded into various aspects of our lives, and should also become critically aware of some of the not-so-positive developments associated with the new media.

The book begins with a discussion of the broader areas of life, before moving on to the social, cultural and socio-psychological: the logic is that we discuss the various themes beginning from the broader areas, such as globalization and economics, which introduce topics central to the book, such as the network society and informational capitalism, and then move on to a discussion of more specific themes, such as the digital divide, politics, journalism and so on. Thus, Chapter 2 begins with one of the most general themes of the book: the relationship between globalization and the new media. This chapter is concerned with the ways in which theories of globalization understand the role of technologies and new media and, conversely, the ways in which the new media have contributed to the globalization of the economy, society, culture and politics. Chapter 3 follows on some of the points raised in Chapter 2, looking at the economy, and the various ways in which it has become entangled with the new media, leading to the rise of what is known as informational capitalism.

Chapter 4 initiates the discussion of more specific themes, by looking at the divisions created by the new media, as well as the various patterns of consumption that have emerged. This will help us understand the spread of the new media across the world, as well as the various cleavages that structure society and their relationship to the new media. Chapter 5 looks at developments in politics and the way the political process has been mediated by the new media: the changes as well as potential of the new media is discussed alongside the continuities and attempts to co-opt the new media by formal and traditional politics. Chapter 6 acts as a corrective to over-optimistic and near-utopian ideas on the new media, by examining the 'dark side' of the new media, focusing on issues of surveillance, safety and security, looking at conflict, fraud and extreme pornography. Chapter 7 moves on to discuss the shifts in journalism associated with the new media: have the new media caused or precipitated the crisis in journalism, or have they, conversely, led to an altogether new kind of journalism?

Chapter 8 examines mobile media and the shifts that mobility and portability introduce to our everyday lives: the rise and rise of mobile media is linked to profound changes in the ways in which we lead our lives. Chapter 8 further acts as an introduction to the next two themes of the book: identity and sociality. Specifically, Chapter 9 discusses identity, and the ways in which our subjectivity is mediated and constructed through and in the new media. It further examines social identities, such as gender and ethnicity and their articulation with the new media: have the latter ushered in new possibilities for emancipation, or are they merely reproducing stereotypical ideas about gender and ethnicity? Next, Chapter 10 looks at society and community, and examines the new socialities that emerge out of the migration of social life in online, mediated environments. Chapter 10 further looks into the so-called social media: since the vast majority of new media users are also using social media, such as Facebook, Twitter, YouTube and so on, it becomes imperative to study their increasingly important role in social life. Chapter 11 looks at games and gaming, understanding games culture as emblematic of the culture of the new media. Online and computer games are much more than entertainment: they are part of an industry that in many ways reproduces the main principles and values of informational capitalism, thereby deserving special consideration in a discussion on new media. Finally, Chapter 12 rounds up the main arguments and findings of the various chapters, and then looks at the future of the new media, examining some trends and new directions that might shape the future of the things to come.

All in all, this book provides a theoretically and empirically informed introduction to the various socio-cultural, political and economic shifts associated with the new media. Its perspective seeks to be critical but pragmatic: critically understanding and evaluating social changes, while refraining both from any nostalgia for a lost organic world, as well as from utopian, futuristic positions of a 'friction-free' techno-world. But another ambition of this book is to enable readers to engage with the material presented through a series of exercises, called e-tivities. The following section will explain these in more detail.

E-tivities

This book adopts Gilly Salmon's idea of e-tivities as a means by which to enhance learning (see Salmon, 2002). The main idea behind e-tivities, and also behind all kinds of learning, is that we learn more if we are actively engaged in the process. E-tivities offer active online learning experiences to readers of this book in ways that seek to improve and deepen understanding of the main issues involved. They make use of online resources, and also of two key features of Web 2.0: participation and collaboration. Learning is not necessarily a solitary experience: we can learn through reading books, but we can also learn from others and with others, as parts of a group that actively explores ideas and themes, that work with each other to gain a more in-depth understanding through participation and immersion in relevant online environments.

Salmon (2002) identified four main features characterizing e-tivities. First, they begin with a 'spark', a question, a challenge, or a small piece of information. This is followed by, second, online activity by individuals, which then is communicated to others who are expected to respond. This interaction is the third feature, while, finally, the fourth element is the feedback or response by a moderator. A moderator, often a more experienced member or leader of the group, will offer feedback to the learners' comments or posts and will gauge the extent to which the 'spark', the question or challenge has been addressed. As such, e-tivities involve both individual and group activities, while they further entail feedback and critique from a more experienced participant.

The chapters of this book have incorporated such e-tivities but adjusted them to the requirements of the book. Each chapter offers a 'spark' that challenges readers to explore more certain avenues or themes within each chapter. Since this book is primarily addressed to students of new media, the idea is that some of these e-tivities be adopted and developed further in class. But if not, then individual readers can still follow through and extend their learning beyond the written pages in front of them. Thus while the interactive and feedback elements can be easily provided for in class blogs or even in more protected online environments, such as Blackboard, the e-tivities in this book can stand alone, for use by readers in their own time, through exploring areas of interest.

E-tivities (after Salmon, 2002): enhanced learning experiences

Key features:

- A challenge or question (the 'spark')
- Exploration of relevant issues and posting of comments in online environments
- Responses by other group or class members (again through posts in a class blog)
- Feedback by the moderator or class leader

Main benefits:

- Learning through interacting with the material
- Learning through participation and collaboration
- Learning through experiencing issues first hand
- Can be used both as solitary explorations and as group exercises

Conclusions

This chapter was primarily concerned with offering an exposition of the basic tenets of four important thinkers of the new media. Before discussing their positions, the chapter referred to some issues of terminology, and explained the reasoning behind the adoption of the term 'new' media. Even though these 'new' media aren't so new any more, the term was adopted here because it points to the dynamic and evolving features of the media rather than the technologies that enabled them. Sure, they are all digital, but how does this help us understand some of their differences? For example, focusing on the digital or online aspects of the new media does not allow us to understand the subtle ways in which Web 2.0, for instance, has introduced shifts even within these digital media.

Next, this chapter summarized the positions of four main theorists of the new media: Marshall McLuhan, Friedrich Kittler, Bernard Stiegler and Manuel Castells. From McLuhan, we got his insistence on the importance of the media, and their contribution to how we perceive the world. Kittler expanded on these ideas and prioritized technology even further, arguing that human history is the history of technology: the media makes us subjects. Stiegler on the other hand addressed the 'who comes first' conundrum by arguing that humanity and technology are co-originary, they belong together and you cannot have one without the other.

True, therefore, we make technology, but technology also makes us. Castells, finally, inserts a much needed empiricism into the discussion, as he looks at the empirical shifts observed since the advent of new media technologies. These, he argues, can be understood as the rise of the network, itself only made possible through the new media. The boxes below (1.1–1.4) summarize the main points of all these theorists, while the chapters that comprise this book will explore some of these themes in more detail, making use of the insights of all these thinkers.

1.1

McLuhan – Summary of Main Points

Position on Technology:

- Media and technology assume priority
- New media use media as their contents
- The media are the message

Position on Humanity:

- Media as 'extensions of man', causing lasting changes

Position on Society and Politics:

- Media and technologies leading to different forms of socio-political organization

1.2

Kittler – Summary of Main Points

Position on Technology:

- Technological evolution as the motor of history
- Different technologies lead to the constitution of different discourses and power configurations
- Hardware crucial – 'there is no software'
- Emphasis on the materiality of technology

Position on Humanity:

- Different media lead to different subjects:

    discourse network 1800: readers

    discourse network 1900: audiences

    discourse network 2000: end-users

- An anti-humanist perspective

Position on Society and Politics:

- Should focus on the genealogy of discourses to show how we are constituted, but no possibility of mastery over technology
- Should engage with hardware, the algorithms that underlie the user-friendly interfaces

1.3

Stiegler – Summary of Main Points

Position on Technology:

- Technology as an 'exteriorized' memory, a third kind alongside genetic memory (DNA), the nervous system memory (epigenetic), termed 'epiphylogenetic', because it gives rise to new forms and it has a history, it is cumulative and shapes or influences the future

Position on Humanity:

- Technology and humanity belong together, they appear at the same time. Technology is what distinguishes humans from previous kinds
- 'Hominization', the process whereby we are made into humans seen as a result of a dialectic with technology: technology makes us human, and we make technology

Position on Society and Politics:

- Instigates a new politics of technology as a politics of memory
- Looks into the effects of the control of epiphylogenetic devices by corporations, and the loss of skills involved, the proletarization of people
- An explicitly political account

1.4

Castells – Summary of Main Points

Position on Technology:

- Technology viewed from an empirical point of view as enabling certain configurations

Position on Humanity:

- Technologies linked to new kinds of identity

Position on Society and Politics:

- More descriptive than theoretical or political
- Society turned into a network society with new conceptions of space and time

Further Reading

Getting to grips with complex social theory of the new media can be challenging. These three interviews with Kittler, Stiegler and Castells, provide a basic introduction to important concepts, ideas and views that have shaped their theories.

Winthrop-Young, G. and Gane, N., 2006, Friedrich Kittler: An Introduction, *Theory, Culture & Society,* 23(7–8): 5–16.

Venn, C., Boyne, R., Phillips, J. and Bishop, R., 2007, Technics, Media, Teleology: Interview with Bernard Stiegler, *Theory, Culture & Society*, 24(7–8): 334–341.

Rantanen, T., 2005, The message is the medium: An interview with Manuel Castells, *Global Media and Communication*, 1(2): 135–147.

CHAPTER 2

GLOBALIZATION AND NEW MEDIA

Learning Objectives

- To learn about the different approaches to globalization and their position vis-à-vis the new media and technology
- To understand the relationship between globalization and the network society
- To contextualize and learn about informational capitalism and the relationship between capitalism and technology

Introduction

Globalization was one of the most cited concepts in the 1990s social sciences (Waters, 1995) and its prominence continues well into the noughties. *Globalization: Social Theory and Global Culture* (Rolandson, 1992), *Globalization: The Human Consequences* (Bauman, 1998), *Globalization and its Discontents* (Stiglitz, 2003), *Runaway World: How Globalization is Reshaping our World* (Giddens, 2003) are just a handful of titles showing part of the problematique surrounding globalization. The main idea behind globalization is that the world around us is changing in ways that hadn't been foreseen by earlier theories or approaches; this idea is shared by almost all thinkers of globalization, although there is considerable disagreement as to the extent, direction and spread of this change. Given the coincidence of the rise in books and publications on globalization with those on new media, a link is formed between these two. On the one hand, technological developments and media tend to spread across the world, irrespective of borders. On the other hand, different countries often have different priorities or set limits to the spread of technologies and media. Yet the new media are associated with far more cataclysmic changes, in actually enabling the development of a truly global system, or society-culture thereby leading to fundamental changes in the world organization (e.g. Ohmae, 1995). At the very least, new technologies are associated with important challenges to the currently dominant forms of world-organization, such as the nation-state. But the broader question arising here concerns the connection between the new media and globalization. Did they enable globalization? Or was it, conversely, globalization that led to the rise of online, networked communications? Moreover, it is commonplace today to speak of the internet and other new media in global terms, as if they operated in the same way across the world. But is this the case? These are some of the questions and issues that this chapter will address.

We will begin with a discussion of theories of globalization, based on a classification introduced by Leslie Sklair (1999). Here the chapter will also discuss the assumptions and ideas on the new media implicit or explicit in these theories. The final section will seek to formulate some arguments and reach some conclusions regarding the relationship between globalization and the new media.

Theories of Globalization

The abundance of books and publications on globalization complicates any discussion on the subject. There is not only divergence across disciplines, with economists, political scientists and sociologists focusing on different aspects and prioritizing different dimensions, but also divergence within disciplines, with different theorists making different arguments. Given these disagreements, it is especially challenging to define globalization. Although generic definitions do exist – e.g. Rolandson's (1992: 8) globalization as the compression of the world – they tend to reflect the author's differing priorities. This section will therefore avoid defining globalization, preferring instead to expose the various understandings of it as they emerge from the relevant literature. Summarizing and presenting this literature in a concise form is not easy – unavoidably we end up omitting some arguments and emphasizing others. In this section, the theoretical discussion adapts the classification proposed by Sklair (1999). We will therefore discuss three distinct approaches to globalization: (i) world-systems theory; (ii) global culture theory; and (iii) the global society approach, outlining within each framework the role it allocates to new media. In the next section will look at the relationship between global society and Manuel Castells' network society. In Castells' view, globalization is linked not only to changes in the social organization of societies but also in the economic. The rise of global capitalism is something that we should expect under these circumstances. However, the form taken by global capitalism is one, according to Castells, that is, intimately linked to new media technologies. The final section will therefore discuss globalization as the rise of informational capitalism.

World-Systems and Globalization

The world-systems approach with its emphasis on the division of the world, is to an extent reminiscent of a different era, that of the Cold War. Moreover, as Sklair (1999) notes, it does not really deal with 'global' as such, focusing instead on the different national roles of countries within an international system. The main exponent of this approach is Immanuel Wallerstein (2005 [1974]), whose idea is that the world is shaped by capitalism, and to that extent it already operates as a world system, with its own division of labour. This leads us to think that within this system different countries have different roles, and Wallerstein argues that the world had been divided into core, periphery and semi-periphery as early as 1640 (Wallerstein, 2005 [1974]: 65), although there have been historical changes in this international division of labour, with areas previously belonging to the periphery, emerging in more recent years as core.

Implied within this thesis is that the world already operates 'globally' as it were, that there was already a global dimension even as the world was divided into different nation-states. Globalization within this approach existed ever since the world economy became capitalist, and it consisted of the division of labour between countries deemed as core, peripheral or semi-peripheral according to their role in this international division of labour. More specifically, core regions are those that benefit the most from a capitalist economy; they have stable political systems, understood as comprised of strong governments, extensive bureaucracies and armies. Regions in the semi-periphery can be either core regions in decline or peripheral countries seeking to improve their position. Finally, peripheral regions tend to lack strong governments or they may be controlled by other states, and there exist unequal trade relations between periphery and core countries. This system is understood as dynamic, allowing for some mobility between these categories, but on the whole the world-system appears as a relatively stable means of organizing the world. At the same time, it is vulnerable, as a crisis may end up destroying it.

This approach usefully takes into account both historical elements that connected the world long before sociologists had begun discussing globalization, as well as economic elements that both unite and divide the world. In this respect, this approach is very useful in highlighting the ways in which globalization is bound up with inequality and struggles for dominance. But what is the role of technologies and new media in this account? Very limited, it seems. Technologies and media, insofar as they are seen as part of the economy, are analyzed as such: they form part of a capitalist world order, and there is no need to pay any specific mention to them, other than finding their specific role in the current phase of capitalism. Wallerstein and his school do not have much to say about either the media or technologies as bringing about shifts in the world-system, preferring to analyze such shifts in economic or political terms. Thus, changes in the world-system are attributed to the cyclical nature of the economy, which oscillates between periods of growth and periods of recession (see also Schumpeter, 1991). Alternatively, such changes may be the result of political opposition and struggles against the current hegemony. In these terms, world-systems theory appears to overlook the specificity of the new media, and the ways in which they may be associated to shifts in the world-system. It further seems to ignore the cultural dimension of the new media, that is, the ways in which (new) media practices and contents feed into the world-systems.

The latter criticism, that world-systems theory disregards the significance of culture, is one of the main problems associated with this theory (e.g. Boyne, 1990). In focusing only on the economic dimension, it fails to examine the contribution of culture in shaping a world system not only on the basis of economic status but also in terms of the ideological justification of such a system. Culture in Wallerstein is seen as epiphenomenal to the economy, very much along the Marxian base–superstructure division. Within this context, technologies and media can only be understood in terms of their economic, or political economic contribution to the world system, but not in terms of their cultural contribution in mediating the world and its system.

Global Culture

If one of the problems of world-systems theory has been its disregard of culture, then perhaps an approach that focuses on culture might prove more fruitful in understanding the relationship between new media and globalization. Indeed, several authors have argued that globalization is (also) a cultural phenomenon, and that culture needs to be taken seriously when discussing globalization. And in this, the globalization of culture, the (new) media may play a crucial role. In such discussions, globalization tends to be understood as the construction of a unified culture. But more broadly the very existence of such a global culture is questioned by different theorists. Some tend to support the view that the world is moving towards a kind of 'unicity' (Robertson, 1992), while others criticize this movement as Americanization (see Tomlinson, 1999). Against this view, the scholar Arjun Appadurai (1990) understands global culture in terms of flows coming from different directions, holding that global culture is fragmented, diverse and decentred. As Sklair (1999) rightly argues, this approach problematizes culture in globalization as a reality, possibility or fantasy; to this we can add the idea of global culture as a dilemma. In all these, the implicit role of the new media is understood in terms of both their forms and their contents.

Roland Robertson, one of the most influential theorists of globalization, who is often credited with coining the term (Waters, 1995), argues that globalization must be seen as the compression of the world, along with the increased awareness of this. According to Robertson (1992) this process can be seen as comprised of four different dimensions: (i) 'societalization' or the processes by which societies become increasingly organized along similar lines, namely those of the nation-state; (ii) individualization, which refers to the processes by which we acquire a self; (iii) internationalization, which refers to the processes by which the world-system is ordered; and finally, (iv) the processes which give rise to a new kind of global consciousness that concerns humanity as a whole. In this, Robertson argues that he is providing a formal model, which is concerned with the forms which enable the world to move towards unicity (1992: 175). This formulation allows Robertson to include the heterogeneity of the world and its cultures on the one hand, and the existence of global struggles and resistance on the other. These struggles are concerned with the so-called 'problem of globality', which refers to the struggles to define the cultural terms of coexisting in a single world.

While Robertson explicitly spoke of the 'forms' of globalization, such as the nation-state or individualism, others have focused on the 'contents', arguing that globalization represents a kind of cultural imperialism, or the imposition of Western ideas and ideals onto the rest of the world (e.g. Frejes, 1981, cited in Tomlinson 1991). This kind of 'cultural domination' clearly emanates from the West, and most notably from the USA and it is spearheaded by the media.

Jeremy Tunstall has referred to the cultural imperialism thesis as denoting the eventual destruction of local cultures through the 'dumping' of indiscriminate media products mainly from the USA (Tunstall, 1977: 57). Tomlinson (1991) has eloquently criticized this kind of discourse on several grounds, including the difficulty by which we can isolate the cultural, the assumption of cultural passivity by non-Western people, the view that cultures are static and in need of preservation, and so on. Tomlinson concludes that rather than speaking of cultural imperialism as something imposed on passive others, it may be better to reformulate the issue in terms of the resources made available to people in order to 'generate narratives of individual social meaning and purpose' (1991: 173).

In a somewhat more polemical fashion, Arjun Appadurai (1996) argues that globalization must be seen as a decentring and diffused process that emerges both from society's top echelons as well as from the grassroots. The pivotal role in global culture is allocated to the media and migration as they represent the movement of images and the movement of people. Appadurai further includes the flow of ideas, technologies and finances and argues that together they form the new landscape of globalization: ethnoscapes, mediascapes, ideoscapes, technoscapes and financescapes referring to the movement of people, media images, ideas, technologies and money respectively, all create a new kind of global world. This world though is primarily constituted by imagination, and especially through the 'disjunctures' generated when one of these scapes confronts another: when, for instance, Turkish immigrants in Germany watch Turkish films via satellite (Appadurai, 1996: 4) or, we could add, when mobile phones are used in an African village that lacks basic amenities, different possibilities for imagining one's self and the world are generated. This is a productive relationship that gives to global culture a positive spin, and from our point of view, prioritizes the role of the media and technologies.

In more general terms, though, what precisely is the role of the new media within this paradigm? Insisting on the role of culture in globalization certainly elevates the importance of the media in general: these are seen as providing cultural contents, the raw materials as it were for the creation of this global culture. This view makes no distinction between 'mature' and new media – this is understandably so, since most of the relevant works were written in the early 1990s, before the new media explosion. On the other hand, there is no reason to assume that the new media significantly change the argument: they too have 'contents' or contain representations that could be seen as a continuation of the same role: to provide the building blocks for imagining a global world. There is, however, another role for the new media implicit in this account, and this concerns the new media forms and artefacts, whose use has certainly spread across the world and can be seen as a contributory factor in the creation of a global culture: this cannot be imagined separately from using not only the internet, and its various applications, but also a mobile phone, an MP3 player, a digital camera and so on. This approach therefore allocates an important role to the new media, that of providing the contents and forms of global culture.

The contribution of culture to globalization is undoubtedly crucial. However, a question here concerns the very dynamic of globalization in terms not only of contents, images or representations, but of structures and institutions. Thus, in emphasizing culture as contents and representations, we may end up overlooking the structural dimensions of globalization, which may be of equal, if not more, importance. These may be subsumed under the label global society.

Global Society

To an extent, conceptions of global society are a continuation of understandings of global culture. Global society concepts however go much further and perhaps also deeper into understanding globalization. They focus on the structural dimensions of the world, and examine the shifts associated with the turn to globalization. Such shifts are mainly understood through the concept of modernity, which is seen as having spread across the world (e.g. Giddens, 1991; Appadurai, 1996). Two important questions arise here: the first question concerns the extent to which this global society refers to a single, interconnected social entity, albeit one characterized by internal diversity. The starting point of this question is found in arguments by Giddens (1991) and Robertson (1992) on the rise of a kind of global consciousness or awareness. They are further supported by normative models such as David Held's cosmopolitanism (Held, 2003). Secondly, theories are called to address the extent to which globalization actually describes a new phenomenon. For instance, references to globalization under a different name are found in Marx, and even earlier, leading some to argue that there is nothing new in globalization (e.g. Hirst and Thompson, 1999). Sklair (1999) however disagrees, arguing that the current form of globalization is unique. These different arguments have important implications on the position and role of the new media.

How might we understand global society? A potential answer is found in the works of Anthony Giddens (1990), who theorized modernity in terms of three defining dimensions. The first of these concerns the separation of time and space. In pre-modern, traditional societies space could only be experienced directly through moving, and time was linked to this movement across spaces. Modernity on the other hand, is characterized by an increased distance between these two, as space can be imagined rather than experienced, and time is therefore no longer bound to space. A second dimension of modernity concerns the development of disembedding mechanisms, such as symbolic tokens and systems (for instance the system of credit), trust and so on. These, as Giddens (1990: 53) put it, 'lift out' life and experience from their localized contexts, reorganizing them on the basis of new time–space divisions. Finally, modernity is characterized by the reflexive appropriation of knowledge, which refers to the ways in which the production of knowledge feeds back into the (re)production of social institutions. These characteristics of modernity, and specifically late modernity, along with the institutions of modernity are now found in almost all areas of the globe. The institutions of modernity include industrialism and capitalism, as well as surveillance and military power (see Giddens, 1990: 59). Globalization is therefore the spread of modernity across the world, which ends up first relativizing the 'West', which is seen as the birth-place of modernity, and second introducing changes in these institutions. Thus, capitalism becomes global capitalism, industrialism has led to an international division of labour (c.f. Wallerstein, 2005 [1974]), while the mechanisms of surveillance have been undertaken by the nation-state as a form of political organization that rules over specific territories and regions. Finally, military power has led to global military order – we only need to look at recent wars in Iraq and Afghanistan for concrete examples of this order.

Giddens does not offer a clear causal explanation for the shift towards globalization, or in other words for the reasons underlying the spread of modernity. Rather, his account rests on the argument that the constitutive dimensions of modernity make it an inherently dynamic and unstable form; in these terms, it is not surprising that modernity overtook other, more static systems, resting on traditional mechanisms and institutions. This view, however, implies that globalization is, if not coterminous with modernity, then certainly its consequence. If this is the case, then the current phase is not something new or unexpected, but rather the result or culmination of a range of factors, the grains of which were already present in modernity. Technology and media are therefore not the pivots of such developments, but rather they are themselves the complex result of an interaction between the existing dimensions, structures and institutions of modernity. We cannot, in these terms, theorize technologies and media separately from the dimensions and institutions of modernity. Insofar as they are technologies, they can be located within the dimension of industrialism, and insofar as they are media and trade in contents, they can be located within the dimension of capitalism. In a broader sense therefore for Giddens, globalization as well as new media and technologies must be seen as some of the 'consequences of modernity'.

Giddens' account raises the question of whether indeed there is anything radically new about this specific phase of modernity, referred to as globalization. Simply put, the question here is, are we dealing with a new historical phenomenon, or is it merely the current phase of modernity or advanced capitalism? David Held and his colleagues (1999) have classified the answers to this question in three categories: the hyperglobalizers, the sceptics and the transformationalists. Although all three positions acknowledge the recent trends associated with globalization, they formulate different proposals regarding their origin and novelty. The hyperglobalizers (e.g. Ohmae, 1995) hail the dawn of a new era, arguing that we have entered a new phase, characterized by an unprecedented interconnectedness among all regions of the world. To this, the sceptics posit that in actual fact the world economy is less interconnected than in the nineteenth century (e.g. Hirst and Thompson, 1999), and that rumours of the death of the nation-state are exaggerated, as national governments are still the main political actors on the world stage. The transformationalists, finally, assume a more moderate position, arguing that while globalization has brought about many changes, it is also characterized by a lot of continuities as well. More importantly, they argue that globalization is a dynamic process which can be steered or driven towards different ends – to this effect theorists such as Held propose a new cosmopolitan political order that will seek to address political problems from a global, or cosmopolitan, point of view. When it comes to the new media, it is not unexpected to see that hyperglobalizers consider them as one of the driving forces of globalization (see Giddens, 2006: 60). In this respect, the position of hyperglobalizers appears very close to that of media theory, that is of Innis and McLuhan, for whom new media always ushered in a new era. As always with this position, however, there are important problems regarding this kind of technological determinism. On the other hand, sceptics and transformationalists see new media and technologies more broadly as part of the forces of capitalism and modernity respectively. As we argued in Chapter 1, we need to consider the new media as involved in a dynamic relationship with other institutions or areas of social life – they are both determined by and determining such institutions. Since this historical juncture is understood as (late or for some post) modernity, then we must agree with the transformationalists and view the new media not as determining globalization or global society, but as an inextricable part of late modernity. As such, they are inevitably involved in globalization but not necessarily in a uni-directional causal way. But if we want to be more precise about the relationship between globalization and the new media, we need to refer to Castells and his concept of the network society.

Globalization and the Network Society

An important question that springs to the mind of readers of Castells concerns the relationship between the network society and globalization. Are these synonymous? Is the network society a global society in the terms discussed above? If this is the case then what does the term add to the above discussion? In his work Manuel Castells painstakingly maps out the empirical changes in society, economy and politics introduced in the past decades, concluding that we can now talk of a new kind of society, which he terms the network society. We discussed some of its characteristics in Chapter 1, in which we saw that Castells assumes a kind of soft determinism vis-à-vis the new media (Lister et al., 2009). Yet the question of the relationship between new media, globalization and the network society is still not very clear. We shall argue here that globalization is a dynamic process which introduces changes in social organization, and that the outcome of this process is a new kind of society which can be understood as a network society. The process of globalization is not determined but *enabled* by the new media and technologies.

Specifically, Castells views globalization as involving not only the increase of interconnectedness in the world, but also as leading to a series of transformations in the sphere of the economy and work, as well as in the redistribution of power in society, the reorganization of the nation-state and the rise of cultural identities. In an important article, Carnoy and Castells (2001) argue that globalization would not be possible without the rise of a technological paradigm, which was itself based on the 'revolution in information and communication technologies' (p. 5). But, they argue, new technologies were only the medium of globalization – and here we see echoes of arguments on mediation. The actual source of globalization for Carnoy and Castells is the process of capitalist restructuring that begun as a response to the crisis of the 1970s. The new regulatory regimes that emerged, including the doctrines of deregulation, liberalization and privatization, were not due to technologies but to decisive action by states and corporations, which incidentally are the main actors within the political organization of modernity. These arguments place Carnoy and Castells in-between the categories of sceptics and transformationalists, as they prioritize both forces of capitalism and those of modernity as the causes of globalization. But importantly, they consider the new media as mediating between globalization and the previous social order (nation-state based capitalism). A similar argument is found in Held et al. (1999), who propose a framework for globalization, according to which globalization is seen as referring to the transformations brought about 'by linking together and expanding human activity across regions and continents' (p. 15). Underlying Held's views is the idea that globalization as a process is made possible by new technologies and media: otherwise, how could human activity (economic, social or political) be linked and expanded across geographical and time limits?

If therefore we see globalization as a process enabled or mediated by new media, then what of the network society? This, it follows, must be seen as the outcome of this process of globalization. In other words, if globalization introduces a series of transformations in social, economic and political organization, then the collective outcome of such shifts is a new kind of society, which Castells describes as the network society. The characteristics of this society are not determined by either technology or other actors (e.g. states or corporations), but rather they are all mutually shaping each other, resulting in the formation of networks that operate across geographical borders, thereby undermining the previous form of social organization that was based on geography, territory and its associated time. Although there is no doubt that Castells, Held and many other theorists have captured important dimensions of globalization and the emergent new kind of society, many questions remain. For example, is this process (globalization leading to the network society via new media) the same across the globe? One would expect this to be the case as otherwise we cannot speak of a globalized society. However, developments may be a bit more complex: after all, a globalized society does not necessarily mean that all follow the same rate of development. But an important dimension of Castells' argument is that we cannot speak of a globalized society without mapping the changes brought about by such a process in all areas of life. While changes were admitted by the previous perspectives as well, Castells' arguments highlight, if not prioritize, the role of the economy and specifically of capitalism. But globalized capitalism is no longer the industrial capitalism of the nineteenth and mid-twentieth centuries. It is a different kind of capitalism that requires detailed analysis and discussion. This is the task of the next section.

Capitalism and Globalization: Informational Capitalism

That capitalism contains within it the seeds of globalization was already known and discussed by Karl Marx, the first theoretician of capitalism. For Marx, capitalism could only survive through expansion; this is what led to colonialism and eventually to the process of globalization as we observe it today. In *The Communist Manifesto*, Marx and Engels (1969 [1848]: 108) commented: 'the need of a constantly expanding market for its products chases the bourgeoisie over the whole surface of the globe. It must nestle everywhere, settle everywhere, establish connections everywhere'. But in so doing, capitalism evolves and mutates into a different form.

The form of globalized capitalism is, according to Castells, informational capitalism, and this kind of capitalism relies on new media and new technologies just as much as industrial capitalism relied on the know-how of the industrial and scientific revolution of previous centuries. To understand and contextualize these changes, we are going to take a brief detour in the history of capitalism.

The political theorist David Held (2006: 98) holds that two concepts can be used to unlock the historical development of capitalism: social formation and mode of production. Social formation refers to the specific institutions, relations and cultural practices that constitute given societies. The formal definition of a social formation is that it refers to a 'totality of instances articulated on the basis of a determinate mode of production' (Althusser and Balibar, 1970: 207). In accordance with Marxian theory, these social formations derive from specific modes of production: by mode of production we mean the ways in which surplus production is generated and used. In other words, how we make and use excess produce determines the 'mode of production' which in turn determines the kind of society we find ourselves in. For Marx, because surplus production is generated through 'surplus value', that is, through the value that workers generate over and above their wages, and which is appropriated by the owners of capital, our social formation can be characterized as a capitalist one (Marx, 1969; Held, 2006). Preceding the capitalist mode of production was the feudal mode, in which the ruling class of land-owners owned not only the land but also the workers who lived and worked in the land.

Although capitalism was first manifested as agrarian capitalism, it is in its industrial phase that it reached its first peak. In her analysis, Ellen Meiksins Wood (2002) argues that industrial capitalism presupposed agrarian capitalism, as it created a class of non-agrarian labour force, who on the one hand sold their labour for wages and on the other drove the process of consumption of food and textiles, which fed into the early process of industrialized mass production. Additionally, merchant capitalism eventually led to industrial capitalism, through its provision of the necessary raw materials. For Marx (1959 [1844]), industrial capitalism begins in the late eighteenth century and is characterized by the introduction of machinery in the workplace, and the associated complex division of labour and routinization of tasks, which eventually lead to the alienation of the workers both from the process of production as well as from the things they produce. In classic Marxian theory therefore, the main characteristics of industrial capitalism include a sharp class division, in which people are divided between those who own capital and the means of production, and those who sell their labour. Capitalists use their money to buy the raw materials, equipment and labour necessary to produce certain goods, which they then sell for profit. The paradigmatic case of industrial capitalism is that of manufacturing goods, which are then marketed and sold in ever expanding markets. But Marx further thought that the system of capitalism was dynamic, driven by the dialectical relationship between four distinct spheres: technology, production, finance and products (von Tunzelmann, 1995). Changes in one would inevitably lead to changes in another. Technological innovation is therefore expected to trigger shifts in the production process, finance systems and the actual products themselves.

Based on this, in the 1970s theorists such as Daniel Bell and Alvin Toffler spoke of the coming of the Post-Industrial Society (Bell, 1973) and the Third Wave (Toffler, 1970), which would follow and supplant industrial capitalism. For Daniel Bell, there is a clear histori-cal progression from agrarian to industrial societies, and from industrial to post-industrial, information societies, which prioritize the provision of services rather than the production of goods. This shift is explained by technological innovation, which brought about increases in productivity on the one hand and in efficiency on the other. These allow or 'free' a part of the labour force from having to work the land or in the factory. This freed up labour force is then able to create-find employment in the provision of services rendered possible through the increased efficiency and productivity in the processes of production. These services include education, health care, entertainment, tourism, communication and so on. As productivity and wealth further increase, more and more people will become part of the service economy, thereby eventually replacing industrial with post-industrial society. Indeed, Bell cites data from the US showing a decline in industrial manufacturing jobs and a rise in services. In assessing this new kind of society, Bell is very optimistic: the profit maximization and alien-ation that characterized industrial capitalism will be replaced by a caring society, providing person-to-person services. But is this enough to support his contention of a shift towards a new kind of society?

Not really, argues Frank Webster (2002), for whom Bell's account is flawed on several grounds. Firstly, Bell argues that the wealth producing sectors of agriculture and manufacturing subsidize the service sector. However, detailed empirical evidence shows that in fact the service sector is directly involved in wealth generation, as it is primarily aimed towards supporting industry and manufacturing and not people or consumers themselves. In this sense, services support, maintain and even increase the wealth of other sectors. From this point of view, it is not services such as health care that are placed at the centre of the service economy, but rather banking, advertising/marketing services, accounting and financial services etc. Secondly, Bell's argument rests on a sharp division between service and manufacturing jobs, but in reality these are more interconnected than he supposed. For example, when an accountant is working in a bank, the job is classified as a service one, while when they work in a manufacturing unit, the same job is seen as part of the manufacturing sector (Webster, 2002: 47). But even the decline in industrial-manufacturing jobs is questionable, argues Webster, since losses in manufacturing jobs might be the result of economic recession and the rise of neoliberal policies in the 1980s. Following Webster, we cannot claim that the rise in service jobs can lead to an altogether new kind of social formation.

It seems that in many ways, Daniel Bell has overstated his case. It may be that we must look both for change as well as for important continuities in the economy and society more broadly. This is exactly what Manuel Castells has sought to do by coining the term informational capitalism. In Castells' analysis, technological innovation is associated with a rise in informa-tionalism, in which the main 'source of productivity lies in the technology of knowledge genera-tion, information processing, and symbol communication' (Castells, 2000 [1996]: 17). In these terms, technological innovation is driven by informationalism, and it is oriented not so much towards maximizing output (as in industrialism) but 'towards the accumulation of knowledge and towards higher levels of complexity in information processing' (ibid.: 17). Following the

Marxian formulation of the dialectical relationship between technology, production, finance and products, Castells' argument implies that informationalism has had an impact on all. But he takes it further than this, because he introduces on the one hand political factors, and on the other cultural factors that have been omitted in other analyses. Thus, for Castells, informationalism emerged as the answer to the need for capitalism to restructure following the recession and oil crises in the 1970s and 1980s. These crises that signalled the end of the post-war period of growth led to a structuring that revolved around four main goals: to deepen and expand the capitalist logic of profit seeking; to enhance the productivity of both labour and capital; to globalize production, circulation and markets, unleashing possibilities for profit seeking beyond national-regional confines; and ensuring the support of the state through policies in favour of deregulation and 'competitiveness'. Technological innovation and associated organizational change was put to the service of these political and policy goals, leading to a technologically supported kind of capitalism. This led Castells to argue that informationalism, rather than leading to a new kind of social formation, has, in fact, led to the expansion and rejuvenation of capitalism. At the same time, the mode or production still remains capitalist, since it still revolves around profit, and relies on surplus value and capital gains as ways for increasing profit. While this restructuring of capitalism and the turn towards informationalism have been global, different societies have responded in different ways, reflecting cultural, political, and historical differences.

In informational capitalism we have therefore on the one hand the ever present quest for profit, but informationalism has given rise to new possibilities for profit, found not in the number of units produced and sold, but in the ways in which knowledge and information can generate new opportunities for profit. But what are the main characteristics of this kind of informational economy? To begin with, it is clear that informational capitalism operates within a neoliberal economic policy regime, which has led away from regulation protective of workers and public goods and in favour of an expansion of investment, enterprise and eventually profitability. Secondly, it should be pointed out that informational capitalism relies on its global spread, although this does not necessarily lead to similar levels of informational development across the globe. Within this broader climate of deregulation but also of globalization, we can discuss the rise of global finance as an example par excellence of the dynamic of global informational capitalism.

Finance, or the driving force of capitalism, has changed significantly in the last few years. To begin with, informational capitalism is characterized by an increased importance of finance systems, which quite literally capitalize on information and knowledge, as well as on the new, networked, information technologies. The most important development regarding finance is that capital is never allowed to sleep: it performs 24/7 across the globalized financial markets. Restrictions on the movement of money have been lifted and transnational transactions account for more and more of the gross domestic product of both advanced and developing countries. Capital that may come in the form of pension funds, mutual funds, independent and institutional investors is continually re-invested in areas that may yield higher profit. Information and knowledge about new opportunities, developments and calculated risks allow capital to yield increasingly higher returns without actually anything being produced and sold. The global flow of capital has led to the global interdependency of financial markets, which is aided and abetted by new technologies that allow high speed processing of transactions. On the other hand, such global flows of capital are increasingly disconnected from the actual performance of localized economies, in an almost paradoxical reversal, in which the actual performance of localized economies depends on the performance of globalized financial markets (Castells, 2000 [1996]). The outcome of this has been felt by most of us after the collapse of financial giants such as Lehman Brothers in 2008 which led to a crisis in the so-called 'real economy' on a global scale. In short, deregulated and globalized finance operates in ways determined by information and knowledge, enabled by information technologies.

Conclusions

This chapter was concerned with the relationship between the new media, and more specifically the internet and globalization. In addressing this relationship we began with globalization. This is essentially a contested term, as different theorists describe it in different ways and offer different explanations regarding its origins. Box 2.1 summarizes the main points of each position.

To conclude, globalization and the associated developments in new media and technologies spread and affect the whole world in ways that are not yet clearly discernible. Nevertheless, some patterns have already emerged, and part of this book's remit is to examine these in more detail, especially as they affect the economy and work, the self and identity, the political system and so on. The next chapter will look at the economy and the new media, seeking to outline not only some of the major shifts, but also their implications for society.

2.1

Summary of Main Positions

World System Theory – Wallerstein

Main Points:

- Division between core, periphery and semi-periphery, based on contribution to world economy

- Main criticism: disregard of the role of culture

Position on New Media:

- Marginal. They are significant only insofar as they are seen as businesses or components of a capitalist economy

Global Culture – Rolandson, Appadurai

Main Points:

- Rolandson: the world is characterized by a kind of unicity brought about by processes of societization, individualization, internationalization and the rise in global consciousness
- Appadurai: World is characterized by a series of flows with no set direction – mediascapes, ethnoscapes, ideoscapes, financescapes, technoscapes
- Main criticism: focus mostly on culture often overlooking structures and institutions

Position on New Media:

- (New) media provide the contents and forms of global culture
- Global culture is due to the ideas and images spread by the (new) media across the world, but also by the consumption and use of media forms and artefacts

Global Society – Giddens, Held et al.

Main Points:

- Gidens: globalization refers to the global spread of modernity, and its processes of time-space separation, disembedding mechanisms and reflexivity
- Dynamic, unavoidable but also unpredictable spread

Position on New Media:

- Varies: insofar as new media are seen as part of the institutions of modernity they must be analyzed as such
- Hyperglobalizers (e.g. Ohmae, 1995) but also Sklair (1999) hold the new media as pivotal

Network Society – Castells

Main Points:

- Relationship between globalization and network society: globalization referring to the process by which societies are transformed, while the network society can be seen as the outcome of these transformations
- Networks operate beyond borders and across time – they are truly global

Position on New Media:

- New media technologies as the medium of globalization
- Without the new media we couldn't have globalization

E-tivity: Identifying Globalization

This e-tivity seeks to engage readers with the meanings of globalization and their links to the new media. The goal of this exercise is to enable readers to grasp the significance and implications of globalization, and also to see how closely it is linked to the new media. At the same time, we have insisted throughout that globalization is linked to new cleavages and inequalities or also the persistence of some old patterns of inequality. This exercise will help us identify some of these.

Objective: To understand the forms of globalization in the new media, and to identify some old and new forms of inequality.

Task 1: Go to a site such as Yahoo! or Google.

- What language is it in? If it is in English, try to find it in other languages, e.g. in Portuguese, Greek or Dutch but also in Arabic (go to www.mak-toob.com, which belongs to yahoo and http://www.google.com/intl/ar/), and in other languages of your choice).

- Compare the various interfaces in terms of design similarity and report your findings. What are some of the most important differences and to what can we attribute these?

- On the basis of your findings, how do these sites contribute to globalization?

- Do they help counter existing inequalities or do they repeat and perpetuate them? Or do they, alternatively contribute to the formation of new inequalities?

- Are all languages represented equally in these sites? Which are missing? What does this tell us of the significance and global role of the countries whose languages are not represented? On this basis, can we construct a new world-system a la Wallerstein? Which countries would be in the core, periphery and semi-periphery? Which criteria would you use?

Task 2: Go to a social networking site, such as Facebook.

- If you have an account log in, and go through your network of friends. Where are they located and where do they originally come from? How significant is sharing the same territory for inclusion in your network of friends?

- Are you a member of any groups? Where are these based? To what extent are their goals based on territories?

- What is the significance of space or territory for your networks?

Task 3: Go to an online mapping tool, such as www.mapme.com (you need to open an account), and construct a map of all your contacts. Where are they spread? Would you say that territory is still significant? To what extent? Consider also the new space that is formed through connecting all your friends – this is an example of Castells' 'space of flows'.

Further Reading

Globalization creates a series of challenges to existing forms of political and cultural organization. The following articles are giving us an idea of some of the changes and their wider significance as well as emphasizing the many continuities that shape our world. Sangeet Kumar's article looks at the ways in which Google, acting as a distributed network, undermines national sovereignty and creates a new kind of de-centered, globalized superpower, which may, paradoxically, reinforce existing power hierarchies. Graham Murdock's article looks at the ways in which globalization and digital network literature ignores continuities as well as the role of structural factors in determining the shape of things to come. It is crucial, argues Murdock, that we retrieve the possibility of critique. Alberto Martinelli's introduction to *Current Sociology*'s Special Issue on Globalization discusses the various approaches to globalization, including hyperglobalizers, neo-marxists, hybridization theories and so on, with a view to acquiring a deeper understanding of processes of globalization. The final article, by Kwang-Suk Lee, is an applied case study, which looks at how South Korea became part of what Hardt and Negri have called Empire.

Kumar, S., 2010, Google Earth and the nation state: Sovereignty in the age of new media, *Global Media and Communication*, 6(2): 154–176.

Murdock, G., 2004, Past the Posts: Rethinking Change, Retrieving Critique, *European Journal of Communication*, 19(1): pp. 19–38.

Martinelli, A., 2003, Global Order or Divided World? Introduction, *Current Sociology*, 51(2): 95–100.

Lee, K-S., 2008, Globalization, Electronic Empire and the Virtual Geography of Korea's information and Telecommunication Infrastructure, *International Communication Gazette,* 70(1): 3–20.

CHAPTER 3

(POLITICAL) ECONOMY AND NEW MEDIA

Learning Objectives

- To understand the new economy and the rise of informational capitalism
- To learn about shifts in the production, circulation and consumption of goods
- To critically apprehend changes in employment and labour
- To learn about the new media industry

Introduction

Accepting Castells' argument that the network society constitutes a new social formation in which the network organization takes precedence, implies that this new formation must include shifts in the economy precisely as an outcome of this network organization. We should therefore expect the economy to change as a result of the network and its associated technologies. But why are such changes important? What is the role of the economy and what is its relationship to the new media and society? More broadly, therefore, the question here concerns the relationship between the economy, society and the new media. All too often we come across rather polarized views on the role of the economy. Some theorists view the economy as the determining factor not only of the media, but also of society itself – this is found in the classic Marxian approaches to the (new) media; conversely, emphasis on the symbolic aspects of the (new) media, their uses and users and their differential appropriation and interpretation assumes that the economy has only a marginal role to play. It is crucial therefore to bridge the two positions, and to view the role of the economy not as determining but as one of the co-determinants of society, along with politics, culture and human agency. In doing this, we follow Robin Mansell's (2004) call for a revitalized political economy of the internet and the new media more broadly.

Mansell (2004) argues that if we are to understand the new media, in terms of contents, communications and services, we need to understand the processes that produce them, and more generally the ways in which they are located in capitalism, as well as the ways in which these influence and shape new media use and consumption patterns. Typically, the political economy of communication examines the conditions of media production, distribution, and consumption, and the ways in which they are structured by power (Mosco, 1996). A political economic approach would include examinations of the overall position of new media businesses in the global economy, investigations of patterns of ownership, distribution of products and services, as well as studies of use and consumption practices. The political economy view, although it privileges the economic as an entry point into the study of communicative and more broadly social practices, is not necessarily reductionist: it does not assume that all kinds of social relations are reduced to economic relations. Rather, the most recent approaches are fully aware of the contribution of other factors, symbolic, historical, political, as well as reflexive, coming from citizens, from people and their actions, that all interact in an asymmetrical way leading to a fluid, indeterminate and dynamic set of relations of production, distribution and consumption of new media artefacts, technologies, services and contents. Following this logic, this chapter will examine first the relations of production of the new media: who owns the means of new media production, to use the well-known Marxian formation? Under what circumstances are new media (as artefacts, technologies, contents, services etc.) produced and by whom? Subsequently, we need to look at the distribution and consumption patterns to complete the circuit of the political economy of the new media.

However, this understanding of the political economy of the new media, assumes that they are just another kind of product or service. But if we are to take Castells' view seriously, then we must also consider the ways that the new media are changing the very operation of the economy. Indeed, Vincent Mosco's renewal of the political economy approach explicitly holds that communication processes and late capitalist societies are mutually constituted (1996: 71). Coupled with Castells' approach to new technologies and the rise of the network, it follows that the new media are fundamentally transforming capitalism. From this point of view, the discussion of the political economy of the media must be preceded by a broader discussion of the ways in which the economy is organized under the new media. Is this economic organization still capitalist in the same way as it was in the industrial paradigm of mass production?

Before embarking in a discussion of all these issues, however, we need to highlight that the perspective assumed here is a critical one. In general, political economic approaches seek to find and outline power differentials and asymmetries with a view to correcting them, thereby contributing to the creation of more equitable and just societies. This is the position that this chapter adopts in its examination of the economy. On the one hand, we are concerned with showing the changes that have occurred since the advent of the new media, while on the other, we aim to show the continued or new kinds of inequalities that have been created. Equally, this chapter is concerned to show the contributions of a dynamic economy to society, the new and innovative possibilities it creates. But so long as the overall context is one of profit-driven capitalism, inequalities inevitably prevail and commercial considerations win over considerations of the public good.

This chapter will therefore begin with a discussion of the production and consumption processes under informational capitalism and their relationship to new media technologies, followed by an examination of the political economy of the new media. The chapter will finally conclude with an e-tivity, drawing upon aspects of the preceding discussion.

Production and Consumption in Informational Capitalism

We argued in the previous chapter that the globalization of capitalism is associated with a new kind of capitalism, which Castells has termed informational capitalism. Informational capitalism refers to the new kind of economic organization that on the one hand relies on the new media and technologies, and on the other it imposes their logic on all areas of production and consumption. To understand how this dynamic operates we need to consider the new media as agents of this kind of change in themselves. Such changes include the so-called informationalization of production (i.e. the ways in which the process of production depends on information) and the associated shift towards the production of information and knowledge. In addition, we must examine the implications that these changes have for employment and workers, and the kinds of resistance and critique that have emerged vis-à-vis this kind of capitalism.

Production and Employment in Informational Capitalism

The globalized and deregulated processes of informational production can, in Castells' thought, be understood through the main concept of the network. Production, rather than mass and 'routinized', relies instead in the formation of informational networks, which generate the information, knowledge and techniques that lead to a more rationalized or efficient production. These informational networks operate as add-ons to industrial production rather than replacing it. From this point of view, industrial and agricultural production processes are all encompassed in new economic networks, which are enabled and mediated by new technologies (Castells, 2000 [1996]; Barney, 2004). While informationalism informs industrial and agricultural production, it has also given rise to a new kind of production model. If we accept that the car manufacturer Ford was the paradigmatic model of industrial capitalism, Castells holds that Cisco, a US-based company that makes switchers and routers, can be considered paradigmatic of informational capitalism. Castells reports that Cisco actually only owns 2 of the 30 plants that produce its switches and routers, sells its products almost exclusively online, and employs mainly engineers, researchers, managers and salespersons. By contracting out the production, through operating mostly online, and through building strategic alliances with other players in the field, Cisco has managed to drastically cut costs and maximize profit. It is essentially a manufacturing company that does no manufacturing itself, but rather produces and markets the know-how, design, and relevant information on the kinds of products it sells. More broadly, informational production is characterized by a network organization, whereby different aspects of the production process become autonomous and operate as separate nodes connected to a larger network. This model of the network enterprise is, for Castells, characteristic of the new kind of production process within informational capitalism. The network enterprise is deterritorialized, internally decentralized, segmented across various chains of production and distribution, it relies on ad hoc joint ventures and strategic alliances with other networks-firms, and it has built within it the potential for synchronous interaction with customers, which gives rise to a process of mass customization and personalization typical of the new kind of consumption model within informational capitalism (Castells, 2000 [1996]; 2001; Barney, 2004).

These shifts within the capitalist mode of production have led to associated changes in employment or labour. Shifts in these were already noted by Bell and others, who assumed that the decline of manual labour and the rise of the service sector will lead to new, kinder, economic and social arrangements. But it turns out that these shifts in employment are more complex and leave considerably less room for optimism. To begin with, Castells' (2000 [1996]) analyses of employment trends in the G7 countries confirmed the trends observed by Bell (1973) and other theorists such as Alain Touraine (1971). Thus, in the G7 countries (USA, UK, Japan, Germany, Italy, France and Canada), in the years 1970–1990 there was an average of 4.72% increase of service jobs, including both producer services and social services. But this is not the only change. Based on his analyses of the data on the G7 countries, Castells highlights several trends in employment in informational capitalism: the informationalization of employment has led to a steady decline of agricultural and manufacturing jobs; the rise of both producer and social services; the increasing diversification of service activities as sources of employment; and the expansion of both upper (e.g. managerial) and lower (e.g. clerical and retail) levels on the occupational structure; this in turn reflects 'a relative upgrading of the occupational structure over time' (2000 [1996]: 244). To some extent, these broad trends might be taken to imply a general improvement of working conditions, since, after all, a service worker may be seen as enjoying higher levels of job satisfaction and status than a manual worker – indeed this is partly Daniel Bell's argument. But a proper evaluation of the conditions of working life under informational capitalism must take into account changes not only in the occupational structure but also in the working conditions and generally the working lives of people.

The most prevalent trend in the working conditions under informational capitalism is the increased importance of flexibility in work (Castells, 2000 [1996]; Barney, 2004). To understand the changes introduced by flexibility in employment, Darin Barney (2004) looks at the typical form of employment under industrial capitalism. A typical worker was employed full time, in a well defined job, in which *he* (typically workers were men) knew exactly not only the tasks but also the routinized ways in which he should carry them out. The job was permanent, and carried out at a fixed place of employment provided by the employers. Workers typically remained in the same job throughout their working lives, or otherwise sought promotion within the same firm: in short they followed a set career pattern over their lifecycle (Castells, 2000 [1996]). Employment in industrial capitalism was *institutionalized* (Barney, 2004: 95, my italics) and as such it was much too inflexible to respond to the needs of a capitalist system that requires constant innovation and growth. Under the pressure of the requirements of the new kind of production, such as globalization and deregulation, and a decentralized, network organization, labour had to be made *flexible*.

In practice, rendering labour flexible has led to the creation of non-standard forms of employment. These are non-standard in several ways: in terms of time, with work being part-time, or flex-time; in terms of distance, with tele-work, based at home or even in a different country; in terms of relationship to employers, with work increasingly undertaken as an external contract, ad hoc or freelance work. The results of these new forms of work and more generally of the 'flexibilization' of labour include: the feminization of labour, with more and more women participating in the workforce in non-standard ways; and the loss of a clear career path, with more and more people changing jobs, functions and employers. The increasing precariousness of flexible labour has led to an emphasis on continuous training and lifelong learning, pointing to an increasing gap between the educated and skilled workers and the low or unskilled ones. These developments in the field of employment are generally linked to the demands of production under informational capitalism, and can be more specifically associated to the increased importance of information and communication in the production process. But we must also note here that most of these developments were brought about by new technologies. Thus, tele-work is made possible because of technologies of instant and reliable communication and data transfer. Further, the increased productivity associated with technological innovation has given rise on the one hand to the need for a more educated and technologically literate labour force, and to flexible, ad hoc or part-time work.

How might we assess these new forms of employment? If we look at tele-work as a case study, we can see that it entails important benefits both for employers and employees. In a cost-benefit analysis, Gareis (2003) reports that tele-work and freelancing has important advantages for employers because new forms of work allow them to adapt to changing market conditions. This includes the ability to deploy workers exactly *when and where* they are needed. At the same time, they can decentralize responsibilities and delegate decision-taking to workers, thereby removing a layer of management, allowing them to cut costs. From the point of view of employees, tele-working may allow them to better match private requirements and preferences with work demands. This is especially the case with working mothers, for whom tele-working allows them to arrange working times to match child care requirements and to be closer to their children. Tele-workers can also choose to work where it is most convenient or pleasurable, avoiding the costs of commuting. In terms of work organization, they are able to take more control of their own tasks and to organize their work according to their preferences and priorities. But tele-work is not always or necessarily positive. Based on a study of tele-work in six countries (Bulgaria, Germany, Israel, Italy, Norway and UK), Brynin and Haddon (2007) argue that spread and effects of teleworking depends on the definition of what constitutes telework. They propose a classification scheme that includes: any work at home entailing use of the internet; any work at home entailing use of a PC but not the internet (net-based home-working); work where use of a mobile phone is important, but not the internet or a PC; home-workers: people who do any work at home, but without the internet, a PC or mobile phone; and workers at one or more workplaces, excluding the home (multi-locational work). Anderson and Yitri (2007), based on the same classification scheme, report overall higher levels of satisfaction for home-workers, while the highest levels of satisfaction are reported by internet-workers. However, their results showed no statistically significant difference between new forms of work and life satisfaction. Anderson and Yitri conclude that tele-work is mostly based on pragmatic choices, and is often a temporary solution. They propose to view it as a style of work rather than a mode, as most tele-workers appear to slip in and out of tele-work.

Critical Approaches: Virtual Class and Immaterial Labour

The broader question arising in connection with these developments concerns the fate of the working class or Marx's proletariat. Has the proletariat become extinct? Does it fare worse or better under conditions of flexibilization? Despite the optimistic tone of most relevant literature, significant benefits for workers failed to materialize. Although certain people benefited and prospered in the new work order, others lost out massively, and whole communities and ways of life were destroyed. De-industrialization and the loss of manufacturing jobs without any provision for the unemployed left thousands in misery and perpetual unemployment. A case in point is the US city of Detroit, the famous Motor City, which was the paradigmatic city at the peak of industrial capitalism, with Ford, General Motors and Chrysler all based there. Detroit acutely felt the crisis in the automobile industry, once the pivot and driving force of industrial capitalism: in July 2009, the Michigan Department of Energy, Labor and Economic Growth reported a unemployment rate of 17.8% in the Detroit Metropolitan Area. The city has lost more than 30% of its population in the last 30 years, and recent foreclosures have made houses cheaper than cars in some areas.

In general, several critics note that within the new forms of work, and the spreading ICT sector, instead of the decentralized and more equitable distribution of wealth and status, we encounter a new hierarchy. Arthur Kroker (Kroker and Weinstein, 1994) calls this the virtual class, with little or no ethics, no understanding of justice, and cynical calls such as 'Adapt or you're Toast'.

> Against economic justice, the virtual class practices a mixture of predatory capitalism and gung-ho technocratic rationalizations for laying waste to social concerns for employment, with insistent demands for 'restructuring economies, public policies of labor adjustment,' and 'deficit cutting,' all aimed at maximal profitability. (Kroker and Weinstein, 1994: 1)

Kroker's point is that the virtual class is the next generation of the bourgeois/dominant class – it is invisible, dispersed, and without any class consciousness, and everywhere characterized by 'predatory capitalism and computer visionarism' – see Kroker's discussion with Geert Lovink (undated). The virtual class is authoritarian, socially disinterested and even contemptuous of these working class people who failed to adapt – they are the primary advocates of TINA (There Is No Alternative), foreclosing any possibilities to look for other ways of living/working with technology.

While the concept of the virtual class was an early attempt to resist the neo-liberal techno-capitalism, in more recent years, the spread of information sector workers leads to a rethinking of the working class. Maurizio Lazzarato (1996) attempted to trace the changes in production and labour relations and processes effected through the informationalization and intellectual-ization of work through a critical prism. For Lazzarato the new kind of labour can be character-ized as immaterial labour. Immaterial labour refers both to the changes in work whereby most jobs require information processing and computer skills, and to the activities that produce the cultural contents of commodities: 'the kinds of activities involved in defining and fixing cul-tural and artistic standards, fashions, tastes, consumer norms, and, more strategically, public opinion' (Lazzarato, 1996: 113). In immaterial labour, the cycle of production only comes into operation as and when required by the 'capitalist'; once the job is done, the cycle dissolves. Thus, precariousness, hyperexploitation, mobility, and hierarchy are the typical characteristics of immaterial labour. Moreover, immaterial labour blurs the boundaries between work and leisure: work is life and life is work. In addition, immaterial labourers have to have managerial skills as well, to coordinate with both those above them, others within immaterial labour, and the ultimate consumers of the commodities they will produce.

In addition, the involvement of intellectual labour in all forms of work today implies for Lazzarato the engagement of processes of subjectivity and affect: the worker is not merely per-forming a task, they are thoroughly invested in the work they are doing: they also end up (re) producing themselves. Immaterial labour 'gives form to and materializes needs, the imaginary, consumer tastes, and so forth, and these products in turn become powerful producers of needs, images, and tastes' (Lazzarato, 1996: 136). Immaterial labour therefore has the capacity to trans-form the person who produces/consumes commodities, and for this reason Lazzarato argues that it must be seen as producing a social relationship – immaterial commodities are successful only insofar as they produce such a relationship of innovation, production and consumption.

If Fordism and the industrial mode of production introduced consumption into the produc-tion cycle, then the informational mode of production must be seen as introducing *communica-tion* (Lazzarato, 1996 but c.f. Castells, 2000 [1996]) thereby transforming both industry (now focused on sales and consumer relations) and services (now focused on relationships with cli-ents). From the point of view of workers or the immaterial labour force, Lazzarato observes that they produce both subjectivity (the principle content of social communication) and economic value. The new model is therefore putting subjectivity to work in generating cooperation with other workers as well as in the production of the cultural contents of commodities. The points raised by Lazzarato imply that the new labour force and kinds of work that have evolved in infor-mational capitalism represent a distinct phase of labour-capital developments, in which labour is at once more autonomous and more creative than under conditions of industrial capitalism.

The autonomy of the new labour force resides in its independence from wage labour, and its creativity is found in building new relationships between producers/consumers, authors/audiences. Their economic valorization, i.e. that they circulate as commodities in a capitalist organization, should not obscure either autonomy or creativity. To an extent, therefore, the new conditions of labour involve a new degree of autonomy and creativity of workers that effectively counters the kind of alienation identified by Marx. The next step is to attempt to reach new, alternative, more equitable and just modes of economic organisation.

Informational Products and Consumption

One of the key contributions of Lazzarato's immaterial labour is his observation of the ways in which production and consumption of informational/communicational products are inextricably bound together. Because of the focus of labour on communication, and because of the increased creativity and autonomy of labour, the role of labour is no longer limited to production of commodities, but to the creation and management of a social relationship with consumers. For Lazzarato, immaterial labour gives form and materializes parts of our imaginary, our needs, tastes and so on: in other words, immaterial labour seeks to both satisfy consumer demands and needs and to establish these. This is why Lazzarato argues that the 'raw material' of immaterial labour is subjectivity and the ideological-cultural environment within which this subjectivity lives. This is done on the basis of the social relationship built by the new production and consumption processes under informational capitalism: this social relationship is first and foremost a communicative relationship that requires the constant exchange of information between producers and consumers. Because essentially the products of immaterial labour are based on processes of communication, each commodity acquires its 'use value' on the basis of the value of its cultural and informational contents. Moreover, the particularity of these commodities lies on the fact that not only are they not destroyed in their consumption, but their circulation and consumption creates, transforms and enlarges the cultural environment of consumers.

More specifically, immaterial commodities, or commodities produced by immaterial labour, argues Lazzarato (1996), transform the persons who use them and to that extent the process of production involves the (re)production of a social relationship with consumers: this is understood as communication. And this kind of social relationship, as all relationships, is based on reciprocity. Consumers can no longer be expected to passively consume products that are mass produced, as it was under conditions of industrial capitalism. Rather, they intervene on the process of production in two ways: they integrate production and consumption, and they give meaning to the consumption of specific commodities. Integrating production with consumption effectively means that consumers have a direct input in the kinds of products to be produced. Techniques developed in marketing and sales which offer information on consumer habits and preferences, are as integral a part of production as technical innovation and design. No product or commodity is ever produced without a thorough research of its reception by the public: often, consumer research leads to changes in design and marketing, thereby leading to a production process that is effectively integrated with consumption. At the same time, consumption of cultural commodities attaches meaning to them, and places them onto a specific cultural hierarchy. Consider for example the consumption of exclusive products, such as champagne and brandy by famous rappers, or Burberry scarves by less affluent parts of the population. This very act of consumption produces a new meaning for these commodities. In this sense, consumption is at the same time the production of meaning which attaches itself to commodities. Consumption can also be seen as a communicative act, in the sense that it immediately communicates something both for the consumer and for the products they consume. What does informational capitalism imply for the new media? This will be addressed next.

The Political Economy of New Media

Classical political economy of the media emphasizes the ways in which processes of media production and consumption reproduce dominant relationships (Golding and Murdock, 1979; Mosco, 1996). Because it relies on Marxian theory, it prioritizes the role played by capital in shaping these processes. It comes as no surprise therefore that most such analyses have focused on media ownership and the ways in which it has influenced the production and contents of the media. Consumption, in these terms, was seen as secondary in that it was seen as determined by production and contents: after all, audiences can only read or watch what production makes available to them. Studies such as Herman and Chomsky's (1989) *Manufacturing Consent* outlined the role played by concentration of media ownership in the hands of a few powerful corporations, as well as the role played by advertising as one of the most important sources of media income. These, argue Herman and Chomsky, act as 'filters' allowing only certain contents, news stories and frames passing through and receiving media attention. But this emphasis on the production side and ownership has tended to overlook both the polysemy of media texts as well as the act of consumption itself. A proper critical political economy, argues Mosco (1996), should examine all these aspects, with a view to outlining the contribution of the media to democratic politics and the barriers to this. Following Mosco, and Robin Mansell's injunction, we will look at all these processes and their interaction.

New Media Production

If we accept that new media not only operate under conditions of informational capitalism, but also dictate developments therein, then the issue of ownership of new media acquires a new significance. One of the most important aspects in ownership and more broadly in new media production concerns the issue of convergence. Convergence can be taken to mean at least five distinct meanings, including technological, economic, social, cultural and global convergence (Jenkins, 2001). Technological convergence effectively refers to the digitalization of all media contents, which in turn implies that once produced, media content can circulate freely in all kinds of media, having no need for conversion of any sort. Technological convergence can also refer to the meeting between telecommunications and media companies: the economist Jonas Lind (2005) argues that the convergence between telecommunications, media, consumer electronics and ICTs was envisaged in the 1970s, but could only take off in the 1990s, on the basis of digitalization of contents. Although full convergence has not yet been achieved, the partial convergence made possible through digitalization has given rise to new opportunities for alliances and mergers in the industries involved. While a tendency towards economic convergence or concentration, vertical and horizontal, was already there in the media industry, this convergence opened up the way for further integration between the various aspects of media production and distribution.

Specifically, horizontal concentration refers to cases when a firm in one line of the media owns or buys an interest in another media firm, not directly related to the original one. For instance, News International is a good example of a horizontally concentrated company, as it owns newspapers (e.g. *The* (London) *Times, Wall Street Journal* etc.) as well as broadcasting channels (e.g. Fox News, BSkyB), while notwithstanding its recent sale, the initial acquisition of MySpace introduced News Corporation in the world of user generated online content. Vertical concentration refers to instances when a media form owns or buys an interest in a company further down the media production chain, thereby increasing its control over the process of production and distribution. For example, the famous and ill-fated merger between AOL and Time Warner was thought to be a perfect opportunity to integrate media content (Time Warner) with an online distribution platform (AOL). Although this merger failed, with the two firms eventually parting company, it has not put off other mergers, such as the Comcast and NBC merger in December 2009. NBC, previously owned by General Electric, was bought up by Comcast, officially classed as a telecommunications company, and one of the bigger cable and DSL providers in the USA. The deal has been controversial: Congressman Henry Waxman criticized the move, because it 'raises questions regarding diversity, competition, and the future of the production and distribution of video content across broadcasting, cable, online and mobile platforms' (Szendro Bok, 2009: unpaginated). In the world of new media firms, the acquisition of YouTube by Google for $1.54 billion strengthened even further the power that Google holds over information on the internet. In addition, there are strategic alliances, with media content providers teaming up with distributors and service providers in deals that while ostensibly serving customers ultimately end up creating large monopolies and damaging diversity. For example, there are alliances that offer packages of telephone services, cable TV and broadband internet, or similarly between mobile phone companies and content providers. In the first instance we can therefore conclude that the tendencies towards concentration and integration are amplified in the era of technological and economic convergence. These tendencies are ultimately putting consumers at a disadvantage because they seek to acquire more and more control over processes of media production and distribution, while at the same time cutting costs and maximizing profits, eventually damaging diversity of contents and a healthy competition between different firms. More control of the processes of production and distribution effectively acts, as Herman and Chomsky (1989) argued, as a means by which to limit free speech.

Who are the main players in the field of new media production? Technological and economic convergence implies that we need to take into account the involvement of more than one type of industry. In its report on the Global 500 top corporations, *Fortune* lists the 34 top industries in terms of growth in revenues in 2009. Of these, we can identify as relevant to the new media field: telecommunications (no. 16), network and communications equipment (no. 23), entertainment (no. 26), and computer/office equipment (no. 29). To these we may add internet services and retailing, which although not in the top 34 fast growth companies, are still important for our analysis. Another relevant industry is the software production industry that is equally important for understanding the political economy of the new media. Tables 3.1 and 3.2 overleaf present the top five companies in each industry as reported by the Global Fortune 500 in 2009.

Both tables give a clear idea of the huge amounts of money involved in the new media business. They are also revealing of the dominance of US-based companies, such as AT&T, Microsoft, HP, Google etc. In addition, these are industries and firms that sell specific products and services to global markets: they offer equipment, telecommunications connections and software in ways that enable the new media to operate. From this point of view, these industries and firms operate in ways commensurable with industrial capitalism, based on mass production and control of distribution. But in some ways these tables are mystifying: where are all the famous internet-based companies that have promised to generate new sources of revenue and new modes of capitalist operation? Where are Facebook, Twitter, MySpace, YouTube et al.?

To begin with, MySpace was until recently owned by News Corp, while YouTube is owned by Google. While neither News Corp nor Google post detailed financial statements by company, both MySpace and YouTube are said to have lost advertising income in recent years. According to research by eMarketer, MySpace is said to face a drop of 21% in its advertising income in 2010, dropping from $490 million in 2009 to $385 million in 2010 (Emarketer, 2009). Projections in mid-2009 about YouTube reported that it was due to earn about $240 million, but would still end up in the red, as it would have to pay for overheads, content licensing and bandwidth costs amounting to almost $711 million (Spangler, 2009). While other reports estimated YouTube's losses to be much less (Paczkowski, 2009), its revenues are still far behind those of the more established companies listed in the above tables. Since YouTube is not a publicly listed company, its owners, Google, are not under obligation to publish yearly accounts, thereby confounding the mystery surrounding its profitability. By mid 2010, however, a Citigroup report projected revenues of $945 million for 2010 – but did not offer any calculations of expenditure and costs (Ostrow, 2010).

Facebook, on the other hand, can be described as a success story: its projected revenues for 2009 were put at $550 million, of which $125 million were expected to come from brand ads, $150 million from Facebook's ad deal with Microsoft, $75 million from virtual goods and $200 million from self-service ads (Carlson, 2009). It should be noted here that all revenue for Facebook is based on the classic media business model of selling advertisements, or users to advertisers (c.f. Smythe, 1981). From this point of view, the internet is more or less subject to the same pressures as other, offline media. Twitter, another much discussed social networking site, does not have a clear revenue model: its CEO, Evan Williams, was directly asked

Table 3.1 Top Five companies per industry

Telecommunications			Network Equipment			Entertainment		
Name	Rank	Revenue ($ million)	Name	Rank	Revenue ($ million)	Name	Rank	Revenue ($ million)
AT & T	29	124,028	Nokia	85	74,224	Time Warner	159	46,984
Nippon	44	103,684	Cisco	191	39,540	Disney	201	37,843
Verizon	55	97,354	Ericsson	265	31,688	News Corp	250	32,996
Deutsche Telekom	61	90,260	Motorola	282	30,146	Bertelsmann	347	25,647
Telefonica	66	84,815	Alcatel-Lucent	360	24,859	Maruhan	452	20,465
TOTALS		500,141			200,457			163,935

Source: Global Fortune 500, 2009

Table 3.2 Top Five companies per industry

Computer & Office Equipment			Computer Software			Internet Services & Retailing		
Name	Rank	Revenue ($ million)	Name	Rank	Revenue ($ million)	Name	Rank	Revenue ($ million)
Hewlett-Packard	32	118,364	Microsoft	117	60,420	Google	423	21,796
Dell	115	61,101	Oracle	408	22,430	Amazon	485	19,166
Fujitsu	161	46,714	Symantec	n/a	5,874	Liberty Media (online retailers)	n/a	10,084
NEC	182	41,962	CA (IT management software)	n/a	4,277	ebay	n/a	8,541
Canon	190	39,611	Electronic Arts (digital games)	n/a	3,665	Yahoo	n/a	7,208
TOTALS		307,752			96,666			66,795

Source: Global Fortune 500, 2009

about Twitter's revenue models and prospects in the Web 2.0 summit in 2009, but failed to offer a definitive response. On the other hand, Twitter managed to attract considerable investment, which implies that they have some idea of how to provide a return for this investment. According to Nasdaq.com, Twitter, whose strategy has been to attract users by offering free microblogging accounts, has brokered deals with Google and Microsoft's search engine, Bing, which are thought to be worth about $25 million, helping Twitter generate profits for the first time (Monfort, 2009). Other means by which Twitter can generate income is by selling analytics and user statistics to interested parties. But both options, advertising and selling analytics, are typical (offline) media revenue models.

The conclusion we can draw so far is that although there are considerable amounts of money involved in new media businesses, there are no clear solutions to income problems. In addition, notoriety and popularity with users is not always translatable to economic viability. On the other hand, success stories seem to have made use of strategic alliances, and to combine older media revenue models with new media user dynamics. Attracting regular users in sites such as Facebook and Twitter has the potential to attract advertisers, who can see a new means of reaching these audiences/users. In his original formulation on the audience commodity, Dallas Smythe (1981) argued that the main media product is in fact the audience, which is sold to advertisers: this is very clearly the case for new media companies. Given that most online content is produced by users themselves, new media companies need to find new ways for attracting audiences, and this is primarily done through delivering new and innovative platforms for users to post their contents; these may include blogs and microblogs such as Twitter, video streaming sites such as YouTube, picture sites such as Flickr, and social networking sites such as Facebook. In all these, the users are commodified in the sense of being sold to advertisers in more than one way: first through advertisers using (or colonizing some would say) the same platforms/space as users, and second, through selling analytics, that is, information concerning users, including demographics or preferences, to advertisers and other interested parties. From this point of view, the production of new media relies almost exclusively on the commodification of audiences. But what appears to be missing is a strategy for selling content: and this will be unlikely to come any time soon, as the major content providers on the internet are the users themselves. From this point of view, although the new media are subjected to the same kind of market and advertising pressures as the older media, they lack the kind of content monopoly enjoyed by the latter. Clearly, this limits considerably their abilities to generate profit. But what does this mean in terms of the diversity and availability of free content online? This will be examined in the next section.

New Media Contents

In classic media political economy the main argument is that the economics of media production influence and shape the contents in ways that ultimately limit the diversity of media contents. The tendency towards monopolies or oligopolies, clear in vertical and horizontal integration, results in limited diversity, since most corporations are reluctant to risk with unknown, alternative and even controversial contents, while seeking to make the most of existing products. Typical of this is the tendency to have sequels, such as *Harry Potter*, *Lord of the Rings*, *Pirates of the Caribbean*, *Twilight* and so on, whose contents are distributed as books, films, magazine contents, and digital games, and which are co-promoted across all the media platforms owned by corporations such as Time Warner, Disney etc. The result is that cultural works and more generally content that may not guarantee such massive returns ends up ignored, and that most mainstream (offline) media push very similar kinds of contents.

But now, the new media is said to change all that: first, as evidenced in the famous *Time* cover of 2006, users are the main players in the new media. Their contributions, collaborations, creative exchanges, pictures, video sharing and mashups provide the contents for the new media, and given the vast diversity of users online, we can expect a similar diversity of contents. Crucially, these contents, precisely because of the prioritization of users, are not subject to the controls and limits imposed by mainstream media. Anyone can publish anything online. But how does this work in a political economic way? What is the relationship between user generated contents and the economy of the new media? This can be summarized in terms of a tension: a tension between the tendency of user contents towards diversity, and the tendency of 'monetization' or capitalization over such contents to impose certain limits and controls to this kind of diversity and online exchanges. Economics operates through managing and regulating supply and demand: when supply of contents is unlimited, then it is difficult to generate any income by convincing people to pay for contents. This puts a tremendous amount of pressure on older media, which need to come up with new strategies, and second on new media companies which need to create new ways of generating sustainable income and securing growth. To this we must add the rise of file sharing systems online, which has created new challenges for media companies. Filesharing software such as BitTorrent allows users to download films and other contents, breaking the monopoly over contents enjoyed by media companies through the copyright system. Music production has also been subjected to these kinds of pressures, and has been forced to rethink its relationship with audiences. All these create an explosive mix that at the very least will lead to considerable changes and restructuring in the years to come.

The explosion of user generated content over the internet in the last decade should not come as a surprise: the rising levels of education enjoyed by more and more people as well as dissatisfaction with the limits of mainstream media, have meant that the creation of user-friendly platforms met a rising need for self-expression, individual creativity and connection between like-minded people. This started with the creation of World Wide Web, but did not really take off until the rise of blogging applications such as blogger and wordpress. With blogs numbering almost 185 million in 2008 (Universal McCann, 2008), not including the 500 million or so Facebook, MySpace, and other social network users, as well as those microblogging in Twitter, it is clear that this kind of online self-publishing has become mainstream, and engages people from all walks of life and from almost all places on earth. In its 2009 State of the Blogosphere survey, Technorati reports that about 72% of all bloggers it surveyed are 'hobbyists', that is, they are amateur bloggers, blogging mainly for fun, although there is a rise in professional blogging, which is mainly seeking to advertise brands (Technorati, 2009). The contents of blogs are extremely varied, but Technorati lists self-expression and sharing expertise as the top motivations for blogging. This implies that contrary to the mainstream offline media control over content production, online platforms are run by users, who can more or less blog about anything they want. From this point of view, the relationship between content production and use is disrupted, as new media seek to make platforms available to more and more users, offering more and more new features to attract them. In addition, in many ways the key is to link, tag, arrange, classify and search these contents, hence the rising importance and power of search engines.

This wide availability of varied and free content puts pressure on the typical media business model, according to which revenue is secured through selling contents to audiences, and audiences to advertisers. In addition, media companies have found their once tightly controlled content freely distributed across the web. Their response to this changing relationship with contents has been three-fold: they sought to control access to content, monetize contents and introduce legislation penalizing filesharing. It comes as no surprise that upon finding their contents distributed online for free, media entertainment companies sought to control access to them and demand compensation for their use. Applications such as Gnutella, BitTorrent and Kazaa, introduced new modes of file distribution, difficult to control and regulate, as they operate globally on a peer-to-peer basis. Such applications allow users to upload and download films and other copyright restricted content, and operate on the ideological premise that information is and should remain free (see Poster, 2007). Of course, media corporations could not remain idle. In order to control access to contents, they sought to develop encryption mechanisms. Recently, Adobe Systems has entered into a strategic alliance with Time Warner in order to collaborate in 'discovering and monetizing content' (Adobe, 2009). Partly, this monetization of content is to be achieved through the development of what is known as 'digital rights management'. This refers to any kind of restrictive technology used in order to control usage of digital media or other devices. By controlling access to contents, media firms can charge users for downloading or using their contents, returning to an older business model. Monetization of content, in these terms, is little more than a euphemism for selling content. Given that advertising revenue is not enough to cover costs and raise profits, media companies feel under pressure to devise ways for charging for contents. This can be achieved through the institution of 'pay walls', already operating in some newspaper sites, and/or through the more precise targeting of audiences and readers. The operating premise for pay walls is simple enough: typically, they offer some free content, usually a headline or a first paragraph, asking the reader to pay in order to read the rest. The extent to which such pay walls can be successful is still under question, given the vast availability of online contents for free: why would a reader pay for content that may be found elsewhere for free? From this point of view, 'monetizing contents' also includes strategies for making content more attractive to readers. Such strategies may include targeting specific informational needs, or more innovatively, to integrate users in the process of value creation (Mabillot, 2007). Mabillot's argument is that integrating users in the creative process through, for example, letting them contribute to the discovery of new talent or new contents, enhances the product for them, because it leads to new experiences and a deeper level of engagement. From this point of view, content providers must not only come up with the contents alone, but with new ways of engaging users.

Finally, media firms, but also more generally the impact that filesharing and free content downloading has had on the economy, have put governments under pressure to pass legislation that penalizes users for downloading protected contents. The Digital Economy Bill, under discussion in the UK in 2009–2010, places the burden for monitoring users for copyright infringement on internet service providers, and proposes a three-strikes system, in which users who are caught downloading protected content illegally will have their internet cut off. In France, a similar law is known as *Hadopi*, after the agency it creates for the monitoring of illegal downloading, the Haute Autorité pour la Diffusion des Œuvres et la Protection des Droits sur Internet (Hadopi), or High Authority on Diffusion of Works of Art and the Protection of the Rights on the Internet. According to this law, which is enforced from 2010 onwards, users will be disconnected if they are repeatedly caught downloading illegal contents, or if they allow others to use their connection for illegal downloading. We have yet to see how such laws will work in practice, but already there is mounting opposition against them, both from consumer groups protecting privacy and consumer rights, as well as from internet activists who hold that restriction of information amounts to loss of free speech. Indeed, the European elections of 2009 saw the Swedish Pirate Party gain one MEP, and another one when the Lisbon Treaty was ratified in December 2009. The success of the Swedish Pirate Party, which essentially seeks reform of copyright laws, has led to the development of Pirate Party International, an umbrella organization for all pirate parties operating in several countries around the world. Notwithstanding such strong opposition against this kind of restrictive legislation, the current trend globally is to introduce legal limits and controls to filesharing and downloading content protected by copyright laws. The extent to which such efforts will be successful in turning the tide against internet downloading remains to be seen.

We have seen in our discussion of contents that the new priority acquired by use in the media triptych production-contents-use (or reception) has led to significant shifts in content production and distribution. The responses of media firms – content control, monetization and anti-piracy legislation – can only prove effective insofar as they are accepted by users. We can now move on to discuss the use of new media from a political economic perspective.

Using New Media

The rise and rise of users as the most important parameter in the new media equation has led to a renewal of the democratic appeal of the media. The wider participation in the media entailed in the technologies of new media, as well as the more active part played by users in choosing, publishing, commenting, linking to, and reading online contents, are, for some, signalling a major shift from a kind of passive media consumption to active use and participation. These, in turn, may contribute to the democratization of the media, as well as to the proper functioning of the public sphere as a space where people can contribute their arguments and opinions free of vested interests and coercion (e.g. Kahn and Kellner, 2004). At the same time, this emphasis on the user dimension unleashes the creativity of 'crowds', leading to the rise of a media culture that is at once a participatory culture (Jenkins, 2006a). There is little doubt that this is a positive development, in that it reverses the traditional linear logic of a media source communicating contents to audiences. There are now multiple sources of contents, communicating with each other, and engaged in what appears to be a dialogue rather than the one-sided monologue that was typical of the mass media era.

The neologism 'crowdsourcing' is often used to point to this kind of new collaborative culture of the users. Jeff Howe (2006), the *Wired Magazine* editor who is credited with coining the term, defines crowdsourcing as 'the operation of open source principles to fields outside of software' (Howe, undated). People contribute, share information, and collaboratively improve ideas, projects and products. Just as open source is meant to improve software and return it to the community of users, crowdsourcing is meant to improve concepts, through a kind of collective brainstorming. There is little doubt that this is one of the most unique and attractive aspects of new media use. This collaboration between users entails a significant promise for improvements in all spheres of life (Brabham, 2008). However, most of its current applications are in the field of business. As Brabham points out, this kind of distributed problem solving and production technique 'is a killer business model, effectively stitching the market research process into the very design of products, minimizing overhead costs, and speeding up the creative phase of problem solving and design' (Brabham, 2009: np). For many, the issue is not how to put this collective intelligence to use for the general public good, but how to harness it for profit (O'Reilly, 2005). From this point of view, the broader question here is that although use of the new media relies on new, wider participatory practices, the extent to which these may be linked to socio-cultural and political improvements is questionable. To what extent is this new collaborative model of media use linked to the democratization of the new media and more broadly of the public sphere? This is the question that we will try to address next.

Interrogating the concept of convergence, Henry Jenkins argues that rather than viewing it primarily as the result of technological developments, we should understand convergence as the result of changing consumption practices by audiences or media users. For Jenkins (2006b), convergence represents a cultural shift, in which consumers actively produce contents, seek new information and make connections between disparate media contents, and they do so using a variety of media platforms. From this point of view, such consumption of new media contents is at the same time production of new content. Moreover, Jenkins argues that more and more consumption or use is collective, that is more and more media users seek information, speak to and interact with other media users in ways that enable them to get the most out of the (new) media. In these terms, this active and creative use of new media contents significantly alters the logic by which media audiences operate and this in turn triggers changes in the media industries. Thus, to use Jenkins' example (2006b: 16) a teenager doing homework may juggle four or five windows at the same time, searching the internet, chatting with friends, downloading music, word-processing an essay, responding to emails and so on. Similarly, fans of a popular TV series may operate their own fan club, write new dialogues and story lines, make their movies and post them on YouTube, debate with others to find subtexts and explanations, exchange trivia, buy or sell autographs and so on. This often unpredictable audience behaviour is ambiguously received by media producers, who on the one hand may want to encourage active consumption as it offers more satisfaction and a wider range of experiences, while on the other seek to capitalize on it and retain control over their products. In his book, Jenkins discusses the example of young *Harry Potter* fans, who write their own Hogwarts stories, but end up facing the wrath of media industries who do not want to relinquish control over their intellectual property. For Jenkins, it is crucial to examine these conflicts and compromises between different media users and between users and industries, because 'they will define the public culture of the future' (2006b: 24). This is due to the fact that the ways in which we participate in popular culture provide blueprints and protocols for our wider public and political behaviour. Thus, through media consumption and use, we learn ways of public participation that in turn may influence political participation and outcomes.

This is precisely why the question of the extent to which this kind of media use is linked to democratization is so pertinent here. This involves examining a series of questions of which the most obvious one concerns the question of equality of the participants or media users. But perhaps preceding this, we should first examine what is meant by the term 'democratization'. Jenkins (2006b: 241) quotes Cara Mertes, a producer for the US Public Broadcasting Service, who posed several questions regarding the links between Current TV – an online digital television channel supported by former US Vice President Al Gore. Paraphrasing Mertes (and Jenkins, 2006b), we can pose the following questions regarding democratization and media use/consumption: is user content more democratic because it provides the kind of information necessary for a democracy to function? Is media consumption more democratic in its effects (i.e. mobilizing more people to participate in the political process)? Is it more democratic in its values (i.e. fostering rational-critical debate) or its process (in widening access and expanding participation)? Reaching a clear cut answer is difficult, given the vast diversity of online contents. However, as Jenkins suggests, we may focus on the potential of user participation to achieve these ends. That said, there are obstacles standing in the way: not all participants are equal – in Jenkins's analyses, the demographics of new media users show that they are typically middle class, white, college educated men; but what about women, people from ethnic and cultural minorities, older people, those who don't have internet access, those who lack computer and language skills? These digital divides present clear hurdles that need to be overcome (see Chapter 4). In addition, we have the responses of media conglomerates who seek to retain power and more broadly the responses of the system of commodity and informational capitalism, which operate on the premise of profit maximization thereby marginalizing and effectively destroying anything else.

In an important article, Lincoln Dahlberg (2005) notes that attention is one of the most valuable resources online, and media corporations are in a privileged position for attracting and keeping attention. Large and well known corporations vie to keep users engaged within their own online environments, and for the most part they succeed. Dahlberg refers to the kind of online environment offered by portals such as Yahoo! and AOL, but his observation is valid more broadly. In Table 3.3, we can see the top ten web companies, the kind of audiences they attract, their reach and the amount of time spent per person. To find that Google, Microsoft and Yahoo! are the top three is not really surprising. The point here is that notwithstanding users' active content production and exchanges over the Web, corporations are not far behind them in seeking to exploit such use for profits. And in doing so, the possibility for circulation and exchange of information vital for democracy, as well as rational-critical engagement with arguments, is notably diminished: online corporations prioritize the mainstream, offer easy-to-digest pseudo-information on celebrities and lifestyles, and discourage alternative and contentious uses and arguments. In opting for traffic maximization they steer clear of any substantial controversy, although they may cultivate some kind of minor controversy and scandal, usually involving private lives, to attract notoriety and more traffic. In addition, when users are searching for alternative viewpoints, algorithms and search optimization methods used by engines such as Google ensure that such alternatives will end up beyond the second or third results page. Although Google's algorithm is a corporate secret, it is clear that the more linked a site is the more likely it is to appear in the first few pages of the search results: and here is where corporate sites have an advantage as they represent powerful and well-known brands and are therefore more likely to be linked to by other sites in the web, improving their overall visibility. In these terms, users are being controlled and manipulated by online corporations which seek to control and circumscribe use in order to capitalize and 'monetize' it. Perhaps the best example of such practices could be the way in which Facebook operates: relying on users hooking up with other users, it has created a huge community of global users, who are then sold to advertisers. As Dahlberg suggests, online corporations constitute users primarily as consumers, or at least as private individuals and strategic actors (see also Patelis, 2000).

But do they succeed in controlling online use and traffic? The jury is still out. Dahlberg himself discusses alternative efforts as well as possible practices by which the internet's public character may be safeguarded. There is no doubt that controlling web contents is a near-impossible task, although there are numerous motives, both political and corporate, to do so. In these terms, it is perhaps better to see this, along with Jenkins, as a kind of struggle between users, within different communities of users, as well as between users and corporations. The struggle is ongoing and has no clear winners, but this does not mean that we can sit back and watch. We must remain vigilant, ensuring that the already unequal terms of this struggle do not become any worse, and perhaps help level the field, through insisting on a plurality of engines, a diversity of portals and providers, and clear criteria for inclusion/exclusion of different points of view. It is also clear that notwithstanding the corporate efforts to

Table 3.3 Top 10 Global Web Parent Companies, Home & Work, October 2009

	Parent	Unique Audience (000)	Active Reach %	Time Per Person (HH:MM:SS)
1	Google	353,880	83.75	2:52:53
2	Microsoft	317,671	75.18	3:13:13
3	Yahoo!	237,342	56.17	2:20:27
4	Facebook	199,961	47.33	5:47:04
5	eBay	159,424	37.73	1:51:02
6	Wikimedia Foundation	147,584	34.93	0:15:36
7	AOL LLC	134,635	31.86	2:22:51
8	News Corp. Online	120,681	28.56	1:07:49
9	Amazon	117,255	27.75	0:24:16
10	InterActiveCorp	114,749	27.16	0:12:48

Source: Nielsen NetView - http://en-us.nielsen.com/rankings/insights/rankings/internet

control and circumscribe online use, the proliferation of collaborative networks, and more broadly the increased significance of collaboration and rise of collective intelligence – evidenced in projects such as Wikipedia – signals a paradigm shift towards new patterns of use that are not as easily tamed, especially by old-fashioned corporate practices. On the other hand, such corporate players continuously develop new ways for controlling and harnessing collective intelligence. Again, Facebook, YouTube, and other social networking sites provide an example of this, as they rely precisely on collective use. For some thinkers, such as Jenkins, the very term of Web 2.0 is thought to represent a business model that puts to (commercial) use grassroots participatory practices associated with collective use and linking up/networking with others. All in all, we may conclude that there is an ongoing, constant struggle between users and those seeking to commercially exploit or politically control such users.

Conclusions

This chapter examined the shifts in the economic organization of society that are linked to the rise of the new media. We argued, along with Manuel Castells, that these changes still take place within the dominant social formation of capitalism, and hence share important similarities with institutions and practices of industrial capitalism. Following Castells, we termed the new social formation 'informational capitalism', to denote that, to the extent that it is capitalist, it revolves around the same quest of profit and entails the same dynamic between labour and capital as with the previous paradigm, that of industrial capitalism. But to the extent that it is characterized as *informational*, this kind of capitalism is substantially different to the industrial one, and we must study its differences in order to understand how the economy and society are changing. Box 3.1 overleaf summarizes the main changes.

This chapter further examined the political economy of the new media industry in which we saw that the process of new media production is dominated by some major corporations, but that it also expands across several industries, including entertainment, computer equipment, network equipment, online retailing, computer software producers and telecommunication. Following along the trend on media concentration firms build strategic alliances, enabling them to optimize production and build upon their strengths. But traditional mainstream media companies have seen their monopoly over contents under attack by the rise of user-generated contents. The free availability and vast diversity of online contents have created important problems for the traditional media business model that relied both on advertising and on selling contents. Faced with these problems, media corporations seek to introduce legislation regarding copyright-protected content; try to identify new ways to 'monetize' contents; and create new ways for controlling access to contents. All of these are resisted, leading to a new cycle of control and resistance. A similar struggle is taking place with respect to user behaviour more broadly, as on the one hand we have almost unprecedented numbers of people participating online in new collaborative ways, while on the other we have major media corporations seeking to 'streamline' such use; to commercially exploit it in order to maximize profit. Box 3.2 summarizes the main issues associated with new media production, contents and consumption/use.

In many ways, the new social formation ushered in by the new media has provided us with marked improvements in the processes of production and consumption. But equally, it may be thought of as perpetuating inequalities while also creating some more. Powerful corporations still control or seek to control and harness the labour of the many, and in some cases they do this without providing any kind of compensation or payment for services they use. The exploitative nature of capitalism reducing everything to profit and loss is still the dominant logic within informational capitalism. Yet there are glimpses of a new dynamic, one that speaks of user empowerment, of widened and more distributed (networked) participation in common, public cultures, and in Lazzarato's terms, of immaterial labour force's increased autonomy and skills. And it is here, perhaps, that we may locate the potential for change, for a struggle towards a more equitable distribution of wealth and power in society. But this is, first and foremost, a political question. To this we shall turn in the next chapter.

3.1 Comparison between Industrial and Informational Capitalism

Industrial Capitalism

Production:

- Mass, relying on capital, raw materials and machines
- Paradigmatic industry: car manufacturer Ford

Labour:

- 'Rationalized', alienated, based on 'scientific management'

Consumption:

- Passive: consume mass products as offered

Informational Capitalism

Production:

- Networked (distributed) and informationalized, relying more and more on information
- Relying on global finance: money generating more money
- Paradigmatic industry: network equipment firm Cisco Systems

Labour:

- Immaterial, producing both subjectivity and commodities, more autonomous but also more precarious

Consumption:

- Active, customized and involving subjectivity

3.2

The Political Economy of the New Media

Production:

- Who 'rules' the new media? Main industries: telecoms, network equipment, entertainment, computer and office equipment, computer software, and internet services and retailing. Strategic alliances between firms seek to optimize production, but a general successful new business model lacking. Advertising and charging for contents still the dominant revenue models

Contents:

- The rise of user-generated contents has given rise to a tension between corporations seeking to control contents (digital rights management) and the diversity, multiplicity and free availability of online contents

Use:

- Relying on participation, collaboration, collective intelligence (crowdsourcing). In some ways more democratic, but also a tension between corporate attempts to circumscribe and capitalize on use and user struggle to remain independent of any patrons.

E-tivity: Online Users: Consumers, Workers or Citizens?

The role of online use or consumption of new media is by no means as clear cut as consumption of older media was. The lines between media use and production are blurred, and a significant part of the argument in this chapter is that there is an ongoing struggle between new media corporations that seek to control and capitalize on user participation and users themselves that seek to remain free and independent. This e-tivity is designed to show the tensions between use as consumption, production and participation.

Objective: to identify the various ways in which users are constituted online as well as some of the stakes involved.

Task 1: Go to an internet retailer, such as Amazon, or Ebay.

- What kinds of experience do these sites offer?
- What kinds of actions-options are available to users?
- What type of participation is required in these sites?

Task 2: Go to a social networking site, such as Facebook or YouTube.

- How are you addressed in these sites?
- What kinds of actions-options are available to users?
- What kind of participation is required or expected in these sites?
- How does it differ to the one above? What are the similarities shared between these sites and the internet retailers?

Task 3: Go to a news blog, such as The Huffington Post or Daily Kos, or any other collaborative news or political blog.

- How are you addressed in these sites?
- What kinds of options do you have as a user of these sites?
- What kind of participation is expected in these sites?
- How does it differ to the ones offered by the previous types of sites?

In which sites is the user more independent? How does each type of site seek to control and circumscribe use? Which type of site (if any) affords more user participation? Which is more democratic and in what ways? (Think of Cara Mertes' questions on democracy and Current TV, in Jenkins, 2006b). What are some of the ways in which users may resist or undermine attempts to limit and control their use?

Further Reading

The following articles highlight the importance of the economy and specifically of the political economy of the new media. Robin Mansell calls for a revitalization of the political economy of the new media, through studies of production and consumption of new media as commodity forms. Rosalind Gill and Andy Pratt explore cultural work from the point of view of the Italian autonomist tradition, and explore the ways in which informational capitalism has given rise to the *precariat*. Christian Fuchs focuses on another dimension of the new media economy, that of the 'gift', or the unpaid labour of new media consumers. He argues that this free labour ends up commodifying the users themselves, leading to the need to develop a new critique and a new approach to the political economy of the new media.

Mansell, R., 2004, Political Economy, Power and New Media, *New Media & Society,* 6(1): 96–105.

Gill, R. and Pratt, A., 2008, In the Social Factory?: Immaterial Labour, Precariousness and Cultural Work, *Theory, Culture & Society*, 25(7–8): 1–30.

Fuchs, C., 2009, Information and Communication Technologies and Society: A Contribution to the Critique of the Political Economy of the Internet, *European Journal of Communication,* 24(1): 69–87.

CHAPTER 4

CONSUMPTION AND DIGITAL DIVIDES

Learning Objectives

- To learn about the unequal patterns of new media diffusion
- To understand the concept of digital divide
- To develop an understanding of the role played by age, gender and race/ethnicity in the diffusion of the new media
- To understand the implications of the global spread of the internet and the new patterns of inequality

Introduction

For many years, quite understandably, the main question concerning the new media was that of access. One of the primary concerns not only of theorists but also of states was the extent to which people have access to new media, and also how to overcome the digital divides that will emerge. However, following some 20 years of the commercialization of the internet, mobile phones and other new media, the rate of the spread of the new media indicates a diffusion that seems to be first irreversible and second almost catholic. But does this mean that there are no divisions between users? Part of this chapter's remit, then, is to look for any differentiations between users and types of uses. Just as students of the mass media were concerned with audiences, their likes and dislikes, as well as any media effects on audiences, students of the new media must move beyond the spread of the new media, and to examine any new cleavages that form between users, in terms of preferences, but also in terms of other demographic factors, such as age, class, ethnicity and so on. At the same time, inequalities do not only exist within countries but also between countries and regions. In our discussion of globalization, we discussed the unequal patterns of global development, and the pressures of processes of globalization on developing countries. It remains to map and understand the global internet, the patterns of diffusion of the new media across the globe, and to identify the new developments as the spread of new technologies takes hold globally.

This chapter begins such a discussion by examining, firstly, the global internet, its spread and the emerging patterns of inequality. Secondly, it will look more closely into the issue of digital divides, its underlying assumptions, and logic. It will be seen that while the digital divide began life as a simple case of the information haves and have-nots, it is now considered a much more complex case of how people use the new media and more broadly a case of new media literacy.

The Global Internet

The question regarding the global spread of the internet concerns the pattern of its distribution across the globe. In other words, do all countries in the world have equal access to the internet? Of course, most of us suspect that this is unlikely to be the case. Most of us are aware of the general pattern of wealth distribution across the world, with the north-western world possessing most of it, and the east and southern regions being worse off. It is likely therefore that the diffusion of the internet will follow a similar pattern. On the other hand however, the pattern of growth of internet usage reveals a somewhat different picture. This section will discuss the emerging patterns and overall picture.

The internet, as its name reveals, is the network of networks: the overall arch-network that consists of all the smaller online networks found in the world. The main idea regarding networks, as we saw in Chapter 1, is that they are not hierarchical but widely diffused. Indeed, Figure 4.1 shows the distribution of IP addresses in the world in 2007: the bigger the dots, the more the IP addresses – the large dots contain more than 1,000 IP addresses, while the small

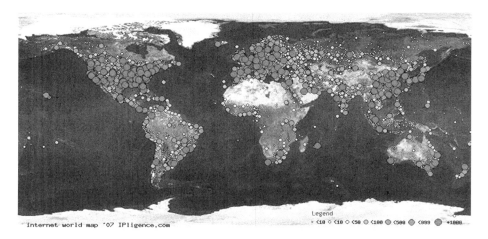

Figure 4.1   Internet world map, 2007

Source: www.ipligence.com. Offered as a free tool.

ones ten or less. We can see immediately that the pattern reflects the actual general global wealth distribution: most dots are found in North America (about 56%) and Europe (22.5%), less in Asia (14%) and much less in South America (about 3%) and Africa (about 1.5%).

More recent data from 2009 reflect a similar pattern. Table 4.1 summarizes the information. This table shows again that the pattern of internet diffusion follows the global distribution of wealth or development. The more developed a region the more likely it is to have a high degree of internet penetration: thus, in Africa only 6.7% of its population has access to the internet as opposed to North America's 73.9%. Pooling these data together we can see that on average only about 24.7% of the world's population use the internet. In these terms, it is difficult to support the claim that the internet, or more broadly the new media, has brought about globalization. It is much more likely that, as Carnoy and Castells (2001) argued, governments and corporations have used the new media to further objectives such as deregulation and free movement of capital.

There is, however, one aspect in this table that requires further analysis. This concerns the percentage of growth in internet usage in the last decade or so. While this is very high across the world, it also appears to have an inverse relationship with the pattern of use, such that the less the internet usage the higher its growth across time. Thus, in North America, for example, we see growth of 132.9% and in Africa and the Middle East we see a staggering 1,360%! To some extent, this is not entirely unexpected, since the lower the usage the more the margin for it to grow. On the other hand, the almost exponential growth of the internet in the world's developing regions in a relatively small period of time shows the speed by which the internet is spreading. This, in turn, reveals the necessity for the world to catch up – and this necessity is not only the result of a quest for development on behalf of less developed regions. It is also a requirement by global corporations in the framework of globalized capitalism. Indeed, if the North American and European markets are close to saturation, what is left other than to seek expansion in Africa and Asia?

Table 4.1 Global Internet Use

World region	Population (est. 2009)	Internet users	Perecentage of population	Growth 2000–2009
Africa	991,002,342	65,903,900	6.7 %	1,359.9 %
Asia	3,808,070,503	704,213,930	18.5 %	516.1 %
Europe	803,850,858	402,380,474	50.1 %	282.9 %
Middle East	202,687,005	47,964,146	23.7 %	1,360.2 %
North America	340,831,831	251,735,500	73.9 %	132.9 %
Latin America/ Caribbean	586,662,468	175,834,439	30.0 %	873.1 %
Oceania/ Australia	34,700,201	20,838,019	60.1 %	173.4 %
TOTAL	6,767,805,208	1,668,870,408	24.7 %	362.3 %

Source: Internet World Stats – www.internetworldstats.com/stats.htm

Indeed, Figure 4.2 illustrates the point nicely. Although Asian internet users represent only about 18.5% of the total Asian population, in absolute numbers this translates to 704.2 million users, that is, almost twice as many as in Europe and almost three times as many as in North America! While the overall proportion of users per population is higher in the developed regions, the striking difference in terms of numbers shows that we must not rush to conclusions. To insert some historical perspective in this, we may refer to industrialization and its spread across the world. To begin with, industrialization did not spread in an equal manner across the world. While some nations, such as the UK, Germany, France and the USA, industrialized early, other nations remained largely agricultural, often relying on exporting raw materials to the industrialized nations. These patterns led to a long-standing dependency of agricultural and less industrialized nations on the more developed, industrialized ones (see Wallerstein, 2005 [1974]). Although this led to a quest to industrialize in less developed nations, the actual spread of industrialization was nowhere near as fast as that of the internet, and in fact many regions of the world never industrialized at all. While it is conceivable that some regions of the world may remain offline, given these rates of growth, as well as the relatively low costs of going online, this is unlikely. The broader point here is that although the existing patterns of internet use show the usual more developed countries as having more users than the less developed countries, the rates of growth show that a different dynamic may be in place.

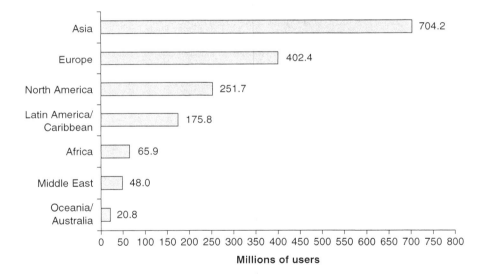

Figure 4.2   Global internet users in absolute numbers

Source: Internet World Stats – www.internetworldstats.com/stats.htm
Estimated internet users are 1,668,870,408 for 30 June 2009
Copyright © 2009, Miniwatts Marketting Group

Perhaps this comparison with industrialization is not a fair one. After all, industrialization relied on a different kind of technology. Yet, following Castells, but also Lazzarato, as we have seen in the previous chapter, we may argue that the internet and the new media introduce changes to the world economy, to processes of production, labour and consumption in ways that parallel those of industrialization and the shift towards mass production. This introduces profound changes, and it may affect existing patterns of inequality. The rate of diffusion of the internet, along with the actual numbers of users, point to the need to revise original ideas on inequality and the domination of the internet by the usual suspects. Figure 4.3 shows the top 10 languages of the internet. While English is, not surprisingly, number one, it is closely followed by Chinese, and given the patterns of growth we observed above, it is more than likely that Chinese will overtake English in the next few years. While it may be too soon to reach any

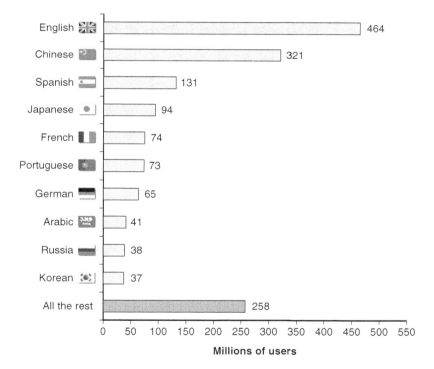

Figure 4.3 Top ten languages of the internet

Source: Internet World Stats – www.internetworldstats.com/stats7.htm
Estimated internet users are 1,596,270,108 for 2009Q1
Copyright © 2009, Miniwatts Marketing Group

definite conclusions, it is likely that new cleavages will develop that will not necessarily follow the patterns of global inequality we are familiar with.

The rise of the Chinese internet, but also the prominence of Spanish, Japanese and Arabic, is a clear indication of the workings of a society that must indeed be thought of in global rather than national terms. If we follow the arguments in earlier chapters, especially those of Giddens and Castells, then we can see that the dominant characteristics of the global internet repeat and amplify those of late modernity and its global spread. Firstly, although the internet is not diffused in an equal manner across the world, it is nevertheless found in all countries of the world. This global spread of the internet along with its rate of growth, point to increased interlinking of areas and parts of the world, but also to significant changes, which we may associate with globalization and the network society. Thus, the internet's time – which is timeless, always-on – increasingly becomes the global time. The internet's space, which is a space of flows rather than of territories, increasingly becomes the dominant form of spatial organization. In addition, the use of the internet by all those millions of people has the effect of what Giddens (1990) has called a disembedding mechanism: it lifts life experiences from their localized contexts and reorganizes them in different ways, commensurable with timeless time and the space of flows, characteristic of the network society. Finally, insofar as the spread of the internet is indeed global, the role and significance of the 'West' is diminished. All these point to the ways in which the global internet is linked to and amplifies the characteristics of the global network society.

Users and Divides

The section above looked at the spread of the internet and mobile media in the world. We saw that the spread of the internet still continues with the numbers subscribing to broadband internet being on the increase. Mobile media are also spreading, although in some countries subscriptions have exceeded 100%. In general it seems that, on a global scale, new media diffusion has not yet reached saturation point or any kind of plateau. Yet while things are moving towards some sort of equilibrium, with astonishing new media growth rates in developing nations and much smaller rates in developed nations, we also need to understand what is going on among users within nations. The main assumption so far has been that it is sufficient for people to have access to the internet and other new media, in order to benefit from them. But do all users make the same use of the new media? Are there any differentiations, and if so along which lines? What are the new cleavages effected by the new media? Are race/ethnicity, class and gender still relevant as dimensions for differentiation? This section will examine these questions, beginning with a theoretical discussion of the digital divide. Next, it will move on to discuss the new cleavages that develop and the differences in the ways that the new media are used. Through these, it will sketch the new picture of digital divide emerging and will discuss some of its consequences.

What is the Digital Divide?

Belying its apparent simplicity, the notion of digital divide is in fact quite complex and multi-level. Typically, the divide is seen as a case of information haves and have-nots, of people who are either connected to the internet and have access to other new media or not. It is this kind of thinking that underpinned relevant policy, which sought to remove barriers to access and to encourage new media use by as many people as possible. However, this ideal of universal access is seen as relying primarily on an economic logic, which lacks, as Webster put it, 'sufficient sociological sophistication' (1995: 97). Echoing such arguments, DiMaggio and Hargittai (2001) suggest a conceptual shift from talking about digital divide towards digital inequality. This, they argue, provides a better picture of the kinds of inequalities that exist vis-à-vis the new media. Their work suggests that digital inequality may be located across five dimensions. These include (see also Hargittai, 2002):

- technical means (the actual artefacts but also level of connectivity and so on)
- autonomy of use (do people actually own these artefacts and access to them or do they have access at work, school, public library etc.?)
- use patterns (how do people actually use the new media)
- social support networks (the extent to which other people around us use the new media and are able to help us)
- skill (the extent to which we are able to use the new media)

The main point here is that the differences and inequalities between people are more complex than just access as implied by the digital divide rhetoric, and must be addressed as such.

It is worth noting that many of these mediating factors are present in the diffusion of technology more broadly. Specifically, in his work of technology diffusion and adoption, E.M. Rogers (2003) developed a model which describes the ways in which people decide on adoption of a particular technological innovation or artefact. Rogers understood this diffusion as primarily a process of communication, concerning the ways in which technological innovation is communicated through certain channels, over time, among people within given social systems. However, he recognized that this process was affected by a number of factors. His complex model attempts to integrate factors concerning, firstly, the users: such factors include personal characteristics, such as general attitudes towards change and so on; secondly, the broader socio-political context, and the extent to which it supports the technology in question and its adoption, as well as the more micro-environment, in which opinion leaders and other change agents, such as the mass media, encourage and support the adoption; thirdly, the (perceived) characteristics of the artefact or medium itself, for example the perceived benefits of its use, the extent to which it can be tried and tested and so on. Rogers further proposed that there are certain adoption types, characterized by the speed by which they adopt innovations. These are:

- Innovators: venturesome, educated, multiple info sources
- Early adopters: respectable social leaders, popular, educated

- Early majority: deliberate, many informal social contacts
- Late majority: sceptical, lower socio-economic status
- Laggards: traditional, fewer info sources, fear of debt

Although this model is characterized by a certain linearity, beginning with the innovation and ending with its adoption, it is suggestive of some of the complexities involved, as access to the innovation itself is but one of the relevant factors. At the same time, we can see that the typical inequalities of socio-economic status are evident in the ways in which people decide whether to adopt or not. On the other hand, Rogers' model assumes an individualistic point of view, in which ultimately the decision rests with the individual – this tends to overlook the more subtle ways in which inequalities get grafted into decisions to adopt and use technologies and new media.

In a thoughtful article, Neil Selwyn (2004) raised several objections to the kind of dichotomous thinking surrounding the digital divide, and attempted to distinguish between the different elements involved in digital inequality. Selwyn begins his own formulation of a more sophisticated understanding by questioning the understandings of information and communication technologies (ICTs) and the concept of access. He argues that notions of digital divide rely on a broad umbrella term, such as ICTs, which includes a variety of new technological applications. To understand more precisely the relevant divisions we must specify the kinds of new media in question. Different kinds of new media correspond to different kinds of resources (or lack of them), and as such, they are not analogous to each other. Secondly, the notion of 'access' points to the primacy of hardware, or the physical media artefacts; it assumes that as soon as people have access to these, equality will ensue. Selwyn (2004) argues that we must understand access not in dichotomous but in hierarchical terms: it is not only a matter of having access to a new medium, but also what kind of access one has. Such access may be limited in terms of devices, software tools, or services, and even if one has physical access their use of new media may be limited. This is why, as Selwyn argues, we must not conflate access to new media with use of new media. While clearly access is a necessary condition for use, this use is variable and complex. The different levels of use point to the need to examine more precisely what users do with the new media. Selwyn speaks of 'engagement' of users with the new media, to denote the different relationships they build with them. Finally, Selwyn holds that to understand the importance of engagement – or even access and use – of the new media, we must seek to understand the kinds of outcomes this may have in terms of productivity and consumption, as well as in terms of socio-political activities.

Based on this kind of critique, Selwyn formulates a concept of digital divide which sees it in terms of stages which are mediated by certain resources available to individuals. The four stages he identifies begin with formal access to new media as artefacts and contents. Here people need to have access, at least in theory, to new media in contexts such as work, home and the community. The second stage concerns effective access to the new media, which refers to the actual contact and use of new media. The third stage is that of engagement with the new media, which is the stage of meaningful use, with users exercising control and choice over the media and contents they are using. The fourth and final stage is that of the outcomes of new media use, in terms of participating in society – this participation is seen in both economic-instrumental terms and in socio-political and cultural terms. But how do people move from one stage to the next? Selwyn's (2004) argument, based on the sociologist Pierre Bourdieu's (1997) argument on the different forms of capital, is that people can move stages through their possession of one or more kinds of capital. These kinds are economic, social and cultural capital. Economic capital in this context refers to the actual material resources, and the capacity to buy different kinds of new media. Social capital refers to the kind of networks in which people find themselves, and the extent to which these offer technological support, help and know-how in the use of new media. Cultural capital can be distinguished between embodied and objectified cultural capital. The embodied kind refers to the actual internalization of knowledge concerning the new media, the kind of education, instruction and training people receive in this field. Objectified cultural capital refers to the socialization into technology use and the kind of exposure one has to the new media through friends, family and other agents. One of the most important contributions of Selwyn's article is that we must stop considering the digital divide in terms of mere access to the new media and that we should go into the nuances and shades of new media use and non-use.

Indeed, while universal access – in terms of the first stage to which Selwyn referred – may not yet be a reality, the growth rates suggest that it is likely that most people in most nations will have access to the physical media artefacts and their contents in the next few years. However, the differences and nuances involved in how people actually use and engage with the new media, suggest that there are other inequalities at work. Some of these are those we are most likely to encounter in the offline world. Such inequalities run across, as Peter Golding has put it, 'the abiding fault lines of modernity' (2000: 179, in Selwyn, 2004: 358). They include income inequalities, but also age, gender and ethnicity/race. To reiterate: the dividing lines are not only or primarily between groups who have access to the new media, but also between the various uses and engagement with the new media by such groups. To better understand the kinds of divisions involved, we will in turn examine age, gender and ethnicity.

Age and New Media Use

One of the most robust and persistent findings regarding internet use concerns the relationship between age and use. Findings from countries as different as the United States and Cyprus reveal that the older you are the less likely you are to make use of the internet and other new media. As early as 2000, Papacharissi and Rubin suggested that age may be a relevant parameter predicting internet use. Since then, more and more surveys have found that age is inversely related to internet and other new media use, and moreover, these findings persist even in recent years. Thus, the Oxford Internet Institute Survey administered in 2005, 2007 and 2009 reports that while almost 92% of under 18 year-olds are using the internet, less than 20% of those aged 75 years and above are online (see Figure 4.4).

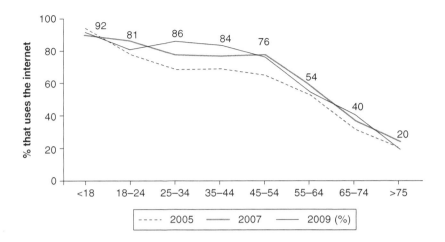

Figure 4.4 UK internet use by age
Source: OxIS (Dutton, Helsper and Gerber, 2009: 17)

In the USA, the Pew American Life and the Internet 2009 survey reports that while 93% of all teenagers are online, this is the case with only 38% of those aged 65 and over (see Figure 4.5).

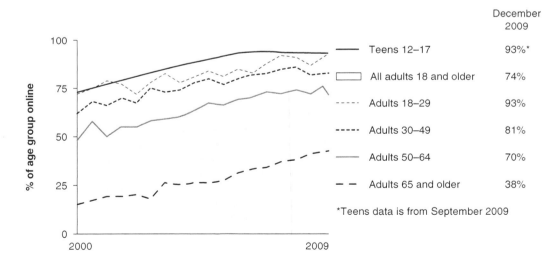

Figure 4.5 Internet use by age in the USA
Source: Pew Internet and American Life Project, http://www.pewinternet.org/ Infographics/2010/Internet-acess-by-age-group-over-time.aspx

Similar findings are reported in other countries as well. For instance, all the World Internet Project (WIP) countries found that online use is inversely related to age. The World Internet Project countries include some 32 countries and regions across the world, ranging from Argentina to the USA, and including China, Japan and Russia among others (see http://www.worldinternetproject.net/ for more information). In the latest WIP report (2010), all of the reporting countries except Mexico found that 79% or more of adults between 18 and 24 years old go online. However, the report also found continued low percentages of use among older respondents. In addition, even when they went online, the range of uses was small in the older age cohorts. Only two countries differed: in the USA and Sweden, 40% of users over 65 years old went online. Six countries report that 10% or less of those 65 or older use the internet (Cyprus, Czech Republic, Italy, Macao, Mexico and Portugal).

While age may be a predictor of new media, and especially internet use, there is some evidence that the concept is not differentiated enough. There are two problems potentially involved here. Firstly, even if we know someone's age, there is still enough variation among age cohorts that need to be accounted for. Secondly, the closing age gap found in high diffusion countries suggests that it may not be age as such but rather generation that is the main explanatory factor of such findings. In the case of the former, Helsper (2010; see also Dutton, Helsper and Gerber, 2009) explored the concept of life-stage to denote the different social roles occupied by people. Specifically, she defines life-stage as the 'points in a person's life where daily rhythm and routine alter drastically due to a change in a person's role in society' (Helsper, 2010: 355). She identifies occupational shifts and relationship developments as two major life-stage shifts. The logic behind the life-stage approach is that occupational changes may be a more accurate predictor of new media use, and that they may further account for any variation observed within age cohorts. Indeed, the Oxford Internet Institute survey found significant differences between students, those in employment, those who are unemployed and the retired. Students and employed persons reported the higher levels of use while the unemployed and retired gave the lowest.

While these findings are suggestive of the kind of dynamic at play here, they do not tell the whole story. Although age and life-stage are related to new media use, the findings from high diffusion countries such as the USA suggest that more and more older – and presumably retired – people go online. If this is the case then it seems that age and life-stage may not always predict new media use. This has led researchers to suggest that it may not be age as such, even when combined to life-stage, but the generation to which one belongs that is a more accurate predictor of new media use. In other words, it is not the case that all over-65s fail to use the internet/new media but that their generation is not familiar with this technology and they lack the social and cultural capital that would allow them to go online. Indeed, research on generations and the internet seems to support such an argument. The findings of the 2009 Pew Internet and American Life report on Generations seem to confirm this relationship between generation and new media use. Figure 4.6 summarizes this relationship.

It is clear from this chart that different generations have a somewhat different relationship to the new media, but objections may be raised regarding the wider applicability of these findings outside the USA. Perhaps it is better in broad terms to distinguish these different generations between those who grew up with the internet and those who didn't. The media

Generation name	Birth years, ages in 2009	% of total adult population	% of internet-using population
Gen Y (Millennials)	Born 1977–1990, ages 18-32	26%	30%
Gen X	Born 1965–1976, ages 33-44	20%	23%
Younger Boomers	Born 1955–1964, ages 45-54	20%	22%
Older Boomers	Born 1946–1954, ages 55-63	13%	13%
Silent Generation	Born 1937–1945, ages 64-72	9%	7%
G.I. Generation	Born -1936, age 73+	9%	4%

Source: Pew Internet & American Life Project December 2008 survey. N=2,253 total adults, and margin of error is ±2%. N=1,650 total internet users, and margin of error is ±3%.

*All generation labels used in this report, with the exception of Younger - and Older - Boomers, are the names conventionalized by Howe and Strausss book, Generations: Strauss, William & Howe, Neil. Generations: The History of America's Future, 1584 to 2069 (Perennial, 1992). As for Younger Boomers and Older Boomers, enough research has been done to suggest that the two decades of Baby Boomers are different enough to merit being divided into distinct generational groups.

Figure 4.6   *Generations explained*

Source: Reproduced from the Generations Online 2009 Report by the Pew Internet and American Life Project – http://www.pewinternet.org/Reports/2009/Generations-Online-in-2009/Generational-Differences-in-Online-Activities/Generations-Explained.aspx?r=1

mogul Rupert Murdoch famously referred to the former as 'net natives', and indeed research suggests significant differences between net natives and those who were introduced to the new media at a later stage in their lives. In brief, in the Pew study of 2009, younger users were more attuned to instant messaging and social networking sites than email to keep in touch with contacts. Older generations were more inclined to use the internet in an instrumental way, as a tool for shopping, banking, getting information and so on, while younger generations use it more for entertainment purposes, downloading music, sharing videos, gaming etc. While to some extent this may be the result of different needs at different stages, it also shows the degree of familiarity of different generations with new technologies and the latest online applications.

But differentiation exists within generations as well. Livingstone and Helsper (2007) argue that research into digital inclusion should move beyond who is and who isn't accessing the internet, and concern itself with finding the range and quality of use among different groups. In their study of young people (ages 9–19) and their parents, they found firstly that access varied not only with age but also with socio-economic status (SES): thus, the older and the lower SES people were less likely to use the new media. The more middle-class children had more access points than their working-class counterparts, while also this access was more likely to be in their bedroom. These results are certainly not unexpected: while innovations become more and more diffused across the socio-economic spectrum, higher SES people still retain their advantage through having more points of access. On the other hand, when Livingstone and Helsper (2007) took out the issue of access, they found no significant differences in the extent of use among lower and higher SES children. At the same time, age and gender differences persisted: girls and younger (9–11 years old) users reported less usage. This shows that when access is provided young people spend more time online, using the internet more often and as a result have higher levels of new media literacy (Livingstone and Helsper, 2007).

What kinds of conclusions can we reach regarding the relationship between age and the new media? There is clearly an inverse relationship such that the older a person is the less likely they are to be found online. This has raised some policy concerns: Jeffrey Cole, of the World Internet Project (2010), remarked that getting older generations online is a global concern, as the world's most important information is now online. In terms of the issue of digital inequality the policy implications are evident: we must devise ways in which older generations are encouraged to use the new media and are taught the relevant skills. As more and more services migrate online it is important for people of all ages to have access and know how to use the new media. At the same time, the very young are discouraged from spending too much time online because of parental control of the points of access, but also because – as with the older adults – they may have limited skills and know-how. The policy implications here are not so clear: it is more than likely that, with time, these young users will become skilful users while as we shall see later there may be good reasons to limit their time online or using other new media. But while age was found to be an important predictor of new media use, another kind of differentiation also persists: that of gender. To this we turn next.

Gender and New Media Use

Given that gender still remains a predictor of many inequalities, such as those of income and opportunity, it is expected that new media use will vary as a function of gender. Studies, however, reveal a mixed picture: while some inequalities in terms of use/non-use tend to diminish at least in high diffusion countries, inequalities in extent and kind of use persist. Does this mean that gender remains a factor in determining new media use? Do women suffer new media exclusion, which deprives them of even more opportunities? What may be the policy implications of gender differences in new media use? A long-standing demand of the feminist movement has been to fight material and symbolic discrimination: access to the new media and high levels of new media literacy may enable women to attain a higher level of equality. But while research suggests a closing gap when it comes to access, the persisting gender differences in degree of use may undermine the quest for (digital) equality.

Indeed, the World Internet Project reports clear differences in the use of technology between men and women. As Figure 4.7 shows, in six countries (Chile, Colombia, Cyprus, Italy, Macao and Mexico) the difference between men and women who use the internet is 8% or more. In other countries, however, the gap is considerably smaller: for instance, in Czech Republic, Sweden and the USA the gap is less than 4%.

In their study of the internet in the UK, the Oxford Internet Institute Survey (OxIS) reports that while there is a gender gap in the use of the internet among UK men and women it is steadily diminishing. While in 2003 the gap stood at 9% (64% of men and 55% women used the internet), it had fallen to just 3% in 2009 (71% and 68% of men and women respectively used the internet). Although the gender gap may be closing in terms of access, there are still significant differences in the extent and kind of use of the internet. Thus, the OxIS (Dutton et al., 2009) reports that while 65% of men feel confident about their technical skills, only about 36% of women feel the same. Moreover, while men look for information on news and sports, women look for health information. However, while men undertook almost all communicative activities more often than women, the differences were not large. The area where gaps were larger is leisure and entertainment: men are more likely than women to listen to and download music and videos, to play games, look at sites with sexual contents and gamble (Dutton et al., 2009). In other studies, Fallows (2005) (reporting for the Pew American Life and the Internet Project) reports

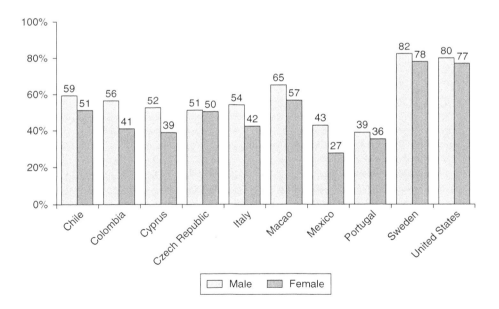

Figure 4.7   The gender gap of internet use
Source: http://www.worldinternetproject.net/

similar findings: in general, men use the internet for recreation more than women, they look for more kinds of information compared to women, they are more likely to use it for banking, and are more interested in technology. Women, on the other hand, are more likely to use email to communicate with friends and family and in general to pursue personal relationships in online contexts. More broadly, however, the Pew study reports that men and women are more similar than different, and even in areas where they differ, the gap is closing (Fallows, 2005). Similarly, other studies in online habits report some differences that may be taken more broadly to reflect the differing social roles of men and women. For instance, Gustavo Mesch (2010) conducted a study on Israeli users of social networking sites (SNS), and found that their use corresponds to traditional gender roles: men have a higher preference for business-like social media, such as LinkedIn, while women prefer MySpace, which holds more appeal for artists and music fans.

It is tempting to conclude that matters tend towards an equilibrium that approaches gender equality, and that therefore there is no need for any kind of policy intervention, as, in time, gender inequalities online will disappear. However, research shows that time alone cannot produce digital equality. In her study on gender, life-stage and generation, Helsper (2010) found that gender interacted with generation and life-stage in the following manner: while generation predicts levels of new media use, gender differences are predicted more accurately by life-stage. In other words, women belonging to younger generations will tend to change their online habits depending on the life-stage they find themselves. This life-stage, understood in terms of employment and marital status, appears to be more a determinant of gender differences in online use than generation alone. Helsper (2010) found that activities such as online shopping and sexual information-seeking vary as a result not only of gender but also of life-stage – this, she argues, is the result of the complex interplay between generation, life-stage and gender. More broadly, these findings show that internet use reflects offline roles and needs. To the extent, therefore, that gender inequality exists in our society, it is expected to be reflected in the new media. As far as policy is concerned, the requirement here is that we remain vigilant: gender inequalities will not go away on their own, but only as a result of sustained action, and pressure on policy makers to take gender issues into consideration.

Race/Ethnicity and New Media Use

The patterns observed so far in connection with new media use show that differences reflect differences in cognitive ability and new media skills because of lack of relevant training as well as because of lack of opportunity. Thus, we saw that the older and younger people have less access to the new media, and while the former have fewer opportunities for acquiring relevant skills, the latter may lack the relevant cognitive abilities – this is true for the very young. In addition, gender differences may reflect both the unequal structures of opportunity offered to men and women as well as the ongoing differences in gender roles into which they are socialized. It is therefore expected that similar conditions will apply to the relationship between ethnicity and new media use: given that, broadly speaking, those belonging to ethnic minorities are disadvantaged when it comes to opportunities, access and training, their new media use is expected to be different to that of ethnic majorities.

Indeed, in the 2002 survey by Pew American Life and the Internet, 55% of African Americans and 46% of Hispanics were not using the internet, compared with 40% of whites. Moreover, the survey reported that for African Americans the difference persisted even at equivalent incomes: the percentages of low earners (under $20,000) using the internet was 32%, 25% and 28% for whites, African Americans and Hispanics respectively. Notably, the difference remained even when educational level was included: users with low educational levels (less than high school) were at 24%, 15% and 26% respectively for the three ethnic groups. The study concluded that race/ethnicity was a strong predictor of internet use on its own. Interestingly, though, when a later survey examined Latinos and their internet use in 2006–2008, it was found that internet use among them grew by 10 percentage points from 54% to 64% when the corresponding rates for whites and African Americans were 4% and 2% respectively. The rise was higher for foreign born Latinos, whose use grew by 12% from 40% to 52%, and for low earners whose use rose by 17% from 39% in 2006 to 56% in 2008 (Pew Hispanic Center, 2009).

As with age and gender, the rates reveal a closing gap, but the issue of inequality still remains if we look at intensity and kinds of use. Thus, a US-based study by Jackson, Zhao, Kolenic, Fitzgerald, Harold and von Eye (2008), found that in general white children were using computers longer than black children, and black boys used both computers and the internet less than other groups. Interestingly, though, black girls used the internet more often than any other group. Their use was of such intensity that it often surpassed that of the stereotypical technophiles, that is, white boys. Of all the groups studied, black boys were found to use all kinds of new media the least, with one exception: they played video games more than black girls and as much as their white counterparts. In general, these findings show that while race can lead to some differences in use and intensity of use, we need to combine it with other demographic characteristics to get the full picture. In these terms, the statistics on use that show a tendency towards equal use of the new media among black and white groups in the USA, mask the differences within these groups. In the Jackson et al. (2008) study, one of the most important findings was that all differences in race were qualified by gender; the study reports that the only effect of race in which gender did not play a part was that African Americans were more likely than Caucasian Americans to search for religious and spiritual information and to use the internet to search for jobs.

Other interesting findings concerned first the role played by the parent's socio-economic status and second the relationship between new media use and academic performance. Specifically, Jackson et al. report that the more education the parents had received, the longer the children's use of IT. Similarly, children of those with higher income were using new media for longer. In addition, children whose parents had more education used the new media more often. Children of cohabiting couples played less video games, and those of employed parents used mobile telephones more frequently. In terms of academic performance, the children who used computers for longer had higher grades than those who had used them for a shorter period. On the other hand, children who played more video games had lower grades than those who played less. Mobile telephones did not seem to affect academic performance. All these findings show that race alone cannot act as a predictor of new media use and that it interacts with other factors, such as socio-economic status and gender.

Similarly, a recent study by Eszter Hargittai (2010) tested several demographic factors among US college students, such as educational background, gender and race/ethnicity in terms of their relationship to online skills and autonomy of use. All of these, educational background, gender and race/ethnicity were found to operate independently and to lead to variation in online skills. Specifically, Hargittai found that African American and Hispanic users were more likely to report lower levels of Web know-how – and this was found to be the case for women, and those of lower educational backgrounds. However, a note of caution should be inserted here: the variable of online skill was self-assessed, and it has been found that women underestimate their online skills (Hargittai and Shafer, 2006). Nevertheless, Hargittai argues that perceived online skills can have real consequences on online uses and behaviours, such as content sharing and so on. But the point made in this study is that even within the so-called digital generation, there is considerable variation in the distribution of online skills, and, moreover, that this variation is due to race/ethnicity, as well as socio-economic background and gender. Hargittai holds that these factors lead to differentiated contexts of use and experiences which in turn affect new media skill acquisition and use in later years. In simple terms, since users from poorer backgrounds are less likely to have early access to new media, and autonomy (i.e. to own their own computers), it is likely that this will affect future new media use and skills.

The policy requirements here are evident: if length and autonomy of new media use is positively correlated with academic performance, especially in children and young people, then we ought to ensure that measures be taken to address this. Similarly, paying attention to nuances and diversity among groups will ensure that measures are taken where required. In short, the discussion of age, gender and race/ethnicity shows a clear link between demographic factors and new media use. There is little doubt that offline differences and inequalities affect and influence online and other new media use. In societies that understand themselves as democratic, policy should address such inequalities in use, as they are likely to feed into and perpetuate other inequalities.

Conclusions

This chapter examined the various issues surrounding new media use. The most discussed issue here has been the divides or differences in new media access and use by different groups of people. Box 4.1 overleaf summarizes the main points.

In conclusion, most of the literature seeks to find ways that ensure widened access to the new media, on the assumption that the use of the new media and especially the internet is a good thing and that there shouldn't be any exclusions. While this is indeed a normative obligation for social scientists, there are issues involved here that need to be spelled out more clearly. We need to problematize this use, and to begin questioning some of the assumptions involved. For instance, there is no question of seeking to widen access to the mass media, to television for example, as this is considered a matter of personal choice. This implies that the new media are considered to offer something more, over and above what the mass media have to offer. Indeed, as more and more information moves online, and as more and more services use the new media, access and know-how are necessary for all. At the same time, the patterns of diffusion of the global internet reflect not only the changing patterns of development but also the pressures of globalized informational capitalism, which is predicated on expansion and the spread of new, informationalized modes of production and consumption.

4.1

Summary of Main Points

The Global Internet

Divides reflect development divides:

- The more developed a country the more likely it is to have a high percentage of internet users
- But in absolute numbers of users, developing countries and regions prevail over developed ones
- Equally, the rates of growth of internet/new media use in developing nations show a very rapid expansion of new media consumption

Such patterns reveal the underlying dynamic of global informationalized capitalism and the shifting configurations of inequality.

User Divides

Divides in terms of access and kinds of uses:

- Age: the older you are the less likely you are to use the internet/new media
- Life-stage (in employment, married etc.) and generation may be relevant variables
- Gender: in general, more men than women use the internet/new media, but rates tend towards equalization
- But differences remain in kinds of uses: men are more confident in their technical skills and use the internet for instrumental purposes (e.g. banking) and for entertainment, while women use it more for communication
- Ethnicity: some inequalities persist; in the USA, less African Americans and Hispanics are using the internet

Gap is closing but ethnic differences are mediated by other demographics, such as gender and age.

E-tivity: Understanding New Media Use

The task here is to assume the role of a social scientist and research the issue of new media use. Begin by monitoring your own new media for a few days: how many kinds of new media do you own? How many minutes do you use each per day?

Based on these notes, you will then devise a questionnaire regarding new media use. This should have three sections.

- First, demographics, such as age, gender, ethnicity/nationality, occupation, educational level.
- Second, new media ownership: which and how many new media (mobile phone, internet-enabled mobile phone, netbook/laptop, MP3 player, games consoles and so on).
- Third, how much time spent on each medium, including on social networking sites, emailing (personal, school or work-related), texting, gaming, etc., for example: no time; less than an hour; 1–2 hours; 2 hours and above.

Then distribute the questionnaire among your friends and contacts, trying to get at least 50–100 responses. What do your findings indicate? Who uses more new media and which kinds are the most popular? What is the average time spent, for instance, texting or on a social networking site? What are some differences and some similarities? What are the broader conclusions that can be reached?

Further Reading

The purpose of the articles here is to describe and explain the various aspects of the digital divide. The first article, by Drori and Jang, describes the global digital divide, by looking at the ways in which different countries differ in their adoption and use of the new media. They conclude that rather than reflecting income inequalities between different countries, a more likely determinant is what they describe as cultural features, i.e. the ways in which countries have managed to network into the global network society. Neil Selwyn's article represents an attempt to clarify the very concept of digital divide, through looking at the ways in which it is articulated in political and popular terms. Following up on the theme of culture and its articulation with technology, Joanna Goode's article develops the idea of a technology identity, which is adopted by people vis-à-vis their relationship with technological artefacts and new media, and which appears to account for the variance in technology adoption by different people. The final article, by the late Everett Rogers, the theorist of diffusion of innovation, represents an early attempt to conceptualize the digital divide, which is rendered more complex by the introduction of categories such as learning divide, content divide and so on.

Drori, G.S. and Jang, Y.S., 2003, The Global Digital Divide: A Sociological Assessment of Trends and Causes, *Social Science Computer Review*, 21(2): 144–161.

Selwyn, N., 2004, Reconsidering Political and Popular Understandings of the Digital Divide, *New Media & Society,* 6(3): 341–362.

Goode, J., 2010, The Digital Identity Divide: How Technology Knowledge Impacts College Students, *New Media & Society*, 12(3): 497–513.

Rogers, E.M., 2001, The Digital Divide, *Convergence: The International Journal of Research into New Media Technologies*, 7(4): 96–111.

CHAPTER 5

POLITICS AND CITIZENSHIP

Learning Objectives

- To understand the relationship between politics and the new media
- To critically apprehend continuities and changes in politics as a result of the new media
- To learn about various instances in which the new media have been credited with positive effects on the political process
- To develop a critical understanding of the role of Web 2.0 in the political process

Introduction

The openness and directness of the internet and the new media as means of communication have given rise to hopes regarding the political system and its further democratization. While the mass media model of communication has been hierarchical, closed to the majority of the citizens and operating in a uni-directional mode, the new media seem to entail a promise for something more. Their open and informal character, their interactive attributes, as well their wide reach provide new opportunities for politicians to communicate with citizens, for citizens to communicate with each other, and for people to mobilize in order to achieve certain political goals. More fundamentally the new media entail the possibility for a more radical renewal of political life, which will be at once more democratic and more encompassing than ever before. These high expectations are attributed to three main factors: firstly, because the new media 'democratize' information both in its production and in its dissemination aspects. Secondly, because of the possibilities offered by the new media for active participation, for forming interest groups and coalitions, and for mobilizing people. Thirdly, because of the possibilities for online discussions and deliberations on issues of importance that breathe new life into the public sphere (Dahlberg, 2001).

But are the new media really capable of delivering on these promises? In his work, Castells (2004 [1997]) has detailed some of the changes that take place due to the new media. Network politics, for Castells, revolves around the ability to use media and information – this is why he refers to it as informational politics. This new kind of politics, linked to new media and technologies, is decentralized and de-linked from territories and national politics. It is, in many ways, a globalized politics. Finally, it is driven more by citizens than by politicians, giving new momentum to activist politics as, for example, we have seen in the environmental politics of the past few years. Notwithstanding these changes, questions regarding first the democratic aspects of this politics and second its overall quality still remain. Cynics might note that some 25 years since the expansion of the internet, and its popularization through the World Wide Web, nothing much has changed in the world of politics. Serious questions have arisen, concerning issues of access to the new media, since the various digital divides means that not everyone has equal access and can use new media in an equal manner. In addition, the quality of the debate or discussion taking place in online environments is subject to a lot of criticism: does it really qualify as deliberation (Dahlberg, 2001; Papacharissi, 2002)? Moreover, Cass Sunstein (2001) argues that the internet is in fact linked to a fragmentation rather than a renewal of the public sphere, in which people typically only visit sites concerning their own interests and rarely come across other viewpoints and ideas. Finally, there are justified concerns regarding the quality of information on the internet, as often there is no way in which we can check the credibility of the source and the accuracy of the information we are reading. All this implies that the relationship between the political process and the new media is far from straightforward.

This chapter will review the relationship between the new media and political life, arguing that in this field, developments are led not by politicians or other big players, but by people themselves. In fact, as we shall see, while citizen-related political practices may be changing through the new media, governments, politicians and political institutions more broadly have been slow on the uptake, and tend to follow rather than lead developments. On the other hand, we shall also see that the development of new online political practices does not always guarantee either political success or improved democracy. In other words, they are not always linked to more transparency, accountability and legitimacy. However, there is still a lot to be gained from the use of the new media in politics, not least the increased role allocated to everyday citizens, who are no longer only required to cast their vote every four years or so, but they can and often they do comment, discuss and criticize political developments on an everyday basis. Will that trigger changes linked to fundamental shifts in the polity? We will have to wait and see.

In pursuing these arguments, the chapter divides political life into three areas: first, formal political life, from the point of view of organized political parties, governments and other political institutions. What have they made of the new media? In which ways have they improved their practices? To what extent have they been successful in their use of the new media? Secondly, this chapter will examine the alternative forms of politics, as seen in political activist organizations, which have profited considerably from the opportunities offered by the new media. When and under what circumstances has new media activism proved successful? Examples will be drawn from the anti-globalization movement, environmental movements and anti-war activism. Third, this chapter will look at citizen-based political initiatives and practices, in order to find out if there have been any changes in everyday citizenship. This will entail a discussion of the Web 2.0 and the related development of new forms of political participation and engagement. This section will review the political role of Web 2.0 applications, such as blogs, Facebook, YouTube, and other social networking sites to see if Web 2.0 has ushered in a new kind of politics.

Politicians and New Media: Politics as Usual?

For a long time the discussion on the relationship between (formal) politics and the new media was polarized between those who hoped the new media would revolutionize traditional politics and those who thought that the internet would destroy the political process. In characteristically upbeat prose, Howard Rheingold (1993: 14) argued that '[t]he political significance of CMC lies in its capacity to challenge the existing political hierarchy's monopoly on powerful communications media, and perhaps thus revitalize citizen-based democracy'. The early 1990s were in many ways characterized by an unbridled optimism regarding the abilities of the new media to radically transform our lives. Along with Rheingold, other authors, including Nicholas Negroponte (1995), and the then US Vice-President Al Gore, envisaged a new kind of online politics in which citizens would directly participate and the internet would be a modern version of the Athenian Agora (Gore, 1994). A series of relevant publications explored this relationship primarily from an optimistic, hopeful point of view. Books and articles such as, among others, Lawrence Grossman's *The Electronic Republic* (1995); Graeme Browning's *Electronic Democracy* (1996); Wayne Rash's *Politics on the Net* (1997); and Rosa Tsagarousianou et al.'s *Cyberdemocracy* (1998) are indicative of the explosion in the field of new media and politics in the 1990s. In short, the main arguments here were mostly based on analyses of the technological possibilities offered by the internet and held that because of the speed and directness that it introduces in communication, because of the sheer volume of information that it can process and because of its interactive features, political life was likely to change from a hierarchical, top-down model, in which citizens are required to merely cast their vote every four years or so, to a much more decentralized process, in which citizens can have more control and in which politicians can 'narrowcast' their messages, targeting specific citizens (see Abramson, Arterton and Orren, 1988).

Conversely, a more dystopian vision of the relationship between the new media and politics was highlighting other, much more negative, outcomes for the political process. Sunstein's (2001) cyber-balkanization arguments on fragmentation and polarization of the public sphere had a sobering effect on the hyper optimism of other authors. Similarly, long-term engagement with the new media was accused of contributing to a loss of social capital, that is, of the social relationships and supporting networks that people build in their face-to-face encounters with others (Etzioni and Etzioni, 1999; c.f. Putnam, 2000). Others accused the new media of promoting a kind of techno-elitism in which it is mostly those who are technologically savvy or computer-literate that profit from the new media (see Warnick, 2002). Yet another dystopic strand concerns the ability of the new media to cast a very wide net of surveillance that follows every key stroke and every digital track we leave behind (Poster, 1995; Lessig, 1999). These critical points polarized the debate between a cyber-utopian and a cyber-dystopian version of the relationship between the new media and politics.

The Normalization Thesis

However, by the late 1990s–early 2000s, several studies came up with actual empirical findings which could allow for a more realistic assessment of the impact of the internet on formal politics. Based on such empirical findings, Resnick (1998) suggested his 'normalization thesis'. Specifically, in an important chapter, David Resnick (1998) argued that while the early internet may have provided a fluid and unstructured space for debates and polemics, its spread across the board meant that offline players have moved online, thereby influencing more or less the whole of the internet. The egalitarian and participatory character of the early internet has given rise to the sleek work of digital consultants and political marketing executives, who design, research and promote political websites belonging to politicians and political parties. And they, argues Resnick (1998; Margolis and Resnick, 2000) don't have in mind deliberation and discussion, but rather persuasion and promotion: they want to use the internet much in the same way they used the mass media. And this, for Resnick, leads to a normalization of the internet: as more and more traditional political players move online, the internet loses its 'natural state' of political innocence and becomes dominated by the usual offline interests. In these terms, it's neither cyber-utopia nor dystopia but rather politics as usual on cyberspace. But is Resnick's assessment really right?

Well, Resnick was writing in the late 1990s, but by now, a decade into the twenty-first century, things have moved on. While there is no global directory of online political parties, it is safe to assume that by 2010, most political parties in the developed world have an online presence. This presence is important for them as it allows them to accomplish several goals. Gibson and Ward (2003) argue that political parties use the internet in at least three ways. First, for administration: political parties go online to provide and manage information about themselves, their positions, goals, manifestos, policy proposals and so on. Second, they use the internet for campaigning: to recruit new members and potential voters, to target specific groups, for example young people, who are most likely to go online for information, to try to set the agenda for the election, bypassing the mass media, but also to retrieve information about visitors to the site, getting an indication of the kind of demographic that is interested in them. Third, political parties use the internet for internal organization: they can canvass their members' views on certain topics, they can discuss policies, encourage donations, but also conduct e-ballots or referenda with users and/or members.

While Gibson and Ward focused on the instrumental uses of the internet by political parties, Pippa Norris (2003) examined the wider effects that going online has for the political process. She found that political party websites can function first as a *pluralistic civic forum* by facilitating the voice of oppositional challengers and increasing the visibility of minor and fringe parties, so that attentive citizens can learn more about the range of electoral choices. Thus, while in the mass-media dominated era it was only the top parties that received attention by the press and television, the internet makes sure that all of them can be represented online, offering a platform for them to present their ideas, policies and manifestos. Second, party websites can function as a *channel for political participation* by facilitating interactive linkages between citizens and parties. This allows a kind of direct communication that was almost impossible in the mass media era, and which certainly has important advantages for citizens who can directly question politicians on matters of interest.

Although certainly bringing advantages to the political process, it is highly questionable to argue that formal politics have been radically altered due to the new media. More empirical research in the areas of e-government, e-parliament and e-parties shows clearly that formal politics is only slowly embracing the new media and that in doing so they tend to impose the offline, traditional political logic rather than the new media logic of bottom-up interactivity, cooperation and participation. Specifically, in e-government the focus has been on managing the process of government more efficiently rather than encouraging citizen participation. In their article on e-government, Chadwick and May (2003) identified three models of e-government, the managerial, consultive and participatory, and found that the managerial model was the more likely to dominate. The managerial model is characterized by:

> a concern with the 'efficient' delivery of government/state information *to* citizens and other groups of 'users'; the use of ICTs to improve flows of information within and around the organs of government; a recognition of the importance of 'service delivery' to 'customers'; the view that speeding up of information provision *is by itself* 'opening up' government; a general absence of user resource issues such as ability to receive and interpret information; and 'control' as the defining logic. (Chadwick and May, 2003: 272, italics in the original)

This focus on efficiency and the management of online presence is also characterizing e-parliaments. Stephen Coleman (2009) argues that through their online presence, e-parliaments seek to manage their visibility, how they come across, their role and contribution to the political process, but they largely fail. This is because of the 'hypermediated' environment of the twenty-first century, in which politicians, MPs and government members cannot altogether control how they come across to the citizens (Coleman, 2009; c.f. Thompson, 2005: 42). Parliaments have attempted to use the internet in ways that make the legislative process more transparent and open, and to provide citizens with the opportunity to comment on aspects of the process. But this does not necessarily translate to more power to the citizenry, since their consultations are 'managed' and mediated by the parliament, rather than allowing for designated civic space to emerge (Coleman, 2009). As for the e-parties, although as Norris noted the internet provides room for minor and alternative parties to voice their ideas and manifestos, the increasing employment of digital consultants means that the bigger and more powerful parties are likely to have a more visible online presence. The increasing profession-alization of online presence, combined with the established 'brand-name' of large political parties, means that it is unlikely that the new media will contribute to any radical redistribu-tions of power in the party system.

So far therefore, evidence supports Resnick's (1998; Margolis and Resnick, 2000) 'normal-ization thesis'. Internet formal politics appears to be 'politics as usual': the internet seems to be dominated by the same interests as the offline world. Political institutions, parties and governments use the internet for their own purposes, such as promotion, persuasion, campaigning, administration and so on, rather than to allow citizens to communicate and participate directly in the political process. In this sense, the internet becomes a facilitator of existing, formal politics rather than offering new opportunities. It is mainly used for effi-ciency rather than to add to accountability, transparency and participation, or in other words to broaden democracy. An explanation for this may be found in the paradigm of 'new insti-tutionalism'. This theoretical perspective comes from political science and it is based on the idea that institutions matter: in other words, institutions often operate on the basis of their own interests, values and norms, with the result of shaping other organizations in society, as well as individuals working in these institutions and organizations (see Jepperson, 1991). If we accept that the new media are shaped not only by technology, but also by people, social structures and institutions, then it follows that political institutions seek to re-create the internet in their own image.

But accepting wholesale the normalization thesis disregards some of the broader 'effects' or outcomes of the use of new media in politics. To begin with, there is no doubt that the new media have allowed politicians to directly address citizens and voters, without the need for the media to mediate. This has contributed to the disintermediation (Hall, 2001) of politics, as politicians no longer need to rely on the media to convey their messages and communicate with voters. Through websites, emails, mobile phone text messages and other applications they can form a direct relationship with their potential voters and respond directly to their concerns. From the citizens' point of view, the use of new media facilitates decision-making during elections, as they have access to all the necessary information, often directly from political parties themselves. They can engage in policy and other debates, which may ulti-mately have some influence in policy making. Finally, they are able to communicate directly with politicians and inform them of pressing issues and problems that need to be addressed. Additionally, Pippa Norris (2003) cites evidence that shows that use of the internet is linked to increased levels of civic engagement. Notwithstanding these important contributions, the new media in general have failed to reverse the trend for political apathy and cynicism. Moreover, online civic engagement is highly stratified, revealing that offline cleavages apply online as well. In their 2009 study on the Internet and Civic Engagement, Jones and Fox for the Pew

Internet & American Life Project, report that the well-off and well educated are more likely to participate in online political activities. Similarly, previous studies report that those who use political party sites are already more interested in politics, have more resources and are already involved in politics (Cornfield et al., 2003). Finally, it may be argued that the promotional politics in which most political parties and institutions are engaged in, discourage actual deliberation and push towards conformity and agreement with given policies. The broader conclusion that we can draw here is that, at best, the relationship between formal politics and the internet is an equivocal one, mostly because of the spillover of offline divisions and interests in online environments. But is this the case across the broader political spectrum? The next section will discuss activist politics and new media and the changes these have ushered in the field of politics.

Political Activism and New Media

Bypassing formal politics, citizens organize on the basis of common interests and goals. Political activism, from this point of view, is part of the broader civil society, that is, the part of society that 'refers to the arena of un-coerced collective action around shared interests, purposes and values' (LSE Centre for Civil Society, 2004: np). Civil society is therefore separate from both formal political institutions and business interests, and operates on the basis both of collectively shared interests as well as more sectarian interests. Pursuing such interests and goals through political means may be understood as political activism. Although necessary for the proper functioning of democracy, political activism is not always or necessarily progressive. It can be both 'progressive', that is, supporting reform towards equality and justice, and 'conservative', in favour of conserving the status-quo or even 'reactionary', that is, reacting mainly against progressive goals. The focus in this chapter will be on progressive politics, and the democratic gains involved in engaging with the internet. The discussion will begin with a review of internet-native practices, such as hacktivism, and then move on to discuss the ways in which the new media have changed the political activism of social movements.

Net Native Activism

'Hacktivism', with its roots in the cyber-libertarian aspects of the internet, began as a movement for the freedom of information. The first and most well known hacktivist group was the Cult of the Dead Cow (see Box 5.1 overleaf). Based in Lubbock, Texas, and founded in 1984, the Cult has been one of the most influential online activist groups. Having coined the term 'hacktivism' in 1996, the Cult embarked on a series of actions aimed first to promote the freedom of information online, but also to protect users from surveillance and invasion of their privacy.

5.1

Excerpt from the 'About' Section of the cDc site

For over twenty years, the cDc has proven itself as an innovative force in the computer underground. In 1984, the cDc invented the electronic publication. In 1990, the cDc's HoHoCon defined the modern computer underground convention. In every U.S. Presidential Election since 1992, the cDc has run a candidate. In 1994, the cDc became the first computer undergound group to have its own Usenet newsgroup. In 1996, the cDc coined the term 'hacktivism'. Also in 1996, the Ninja Strike Force (cDc's elite cadre of cheerleader-assassins) was founded. In 1997, years before everyone and their dog had jumped on the file sharing bandwagon, it was distributing original mp3-format music on its website. In 1998 and 1999, the cDc's 'Back Orifice' series was launched to open the eyes of consumers regarding the security of their computer operating systems. To this day, Back Orifice and BO2k are among the most popular remote system administration tools among both hackers and IT professionals. Since 1999, Hacktivismo (a special projects group within the cDc) has been at the forefront of the ongoing struggle for human rights in and out of cyberspace. In 2002, the cDc and Hacktivismo drafted their own human rights-friendly software license and earned further distinction as the only underground computer group to ever receive U.S. Department of Commerce approval to export strong encryption in software. In 2004, the cDc and the NSF launched the Bovine Dawn Dojo Forum, the greatest on-line community of all time. Nothing can compare to the money-throwing, stage-diving, crotch-grabbing, guitar-wailing, inter-species sex-depicting, computer-smashing & panty-wetting experience that is a live cDc performance.

And that's just the beginning...
(http://w3.cultdeadcow.com/cms/about.html)

Although undoubtedly the first of its kind, this strand of hacktivism is in fact one of two approaches to online activism, as distinguished by Tim Jordan (2007). Jordan refers to the kind of hacktivism practised by the Cult of the Dead Cow, as 'digital correctness' (Jordan, 2007). Digital correctness is linked to freedom of information on the web, and to the open source movement. This rests on the premise that access to information is a human right, and its deprivation is a human rights violation. Their goal is to write code that resists attempts to censor the internet but which also protects users from surveillance from authorities. cDc have written and disseminated code such as CameraShy and Six/Four both aimed to enable users to bypass censorship systems and Torpak, a portable browser that leaves no traces. Downloading and using some of these programmes allows users to visit prohibited sties without any fear of being traced.

In general, the main adversaries of digitally correct hacktivists are national governments and corporations that seek to control information for political and business purposes respectively.

Figure 5.1 cDc's Goolag campaign.

Source: www.cultdeadcow.com

Are they successful? To some extent, they are. The 'goolag' campaign, launched in 2006, was cDc's response to Google's acceptance of Chinese censorship of the internet, and consisted mainly of a series of logos (see Figure 5.1) which were then downloaded, printed on t-shirts and so on, with the proceeds going to the NGO Human Rights in China (www.hrichina.org). Goolag is a word play – or mash – between the words Google and gulag, the latter referring to the notorious Soviet concentration camps which held scores of political prisoners. In February 2006, the cDc also issued a press release about the campaign, in which Microsoft, Yahoo!, Google, and Cisco were described as the 'Gang of Four' due to their appeasement of Chinese restrictive internet policies. The press release essentially criticized the US government for failing to support human rights and free speech in China (cDc, 2006). In February 2008, cDc released the 'goolag scanner', which essentially identified vulnerabilities in websites, which can then be used to circumvent governmental restrictions on internet use (Mashable, 2008). Although it is difficult to credit the 'goolag' campaign with the u-turn in Google's policy, the campaign has certainly raised awareness on this issue. Figure 5.2 shows the kind of censorship at the centre of cDc's activism.

This is what they are against: the control and censorship of information and its malicious and exploitative use by governments and corporations. From this point of view, hacktivism is oriented towards the infrastructure of information (Jordan, 2007). When, in the summer of 2009, Iran was rocked by protests over the election result, hacktivists helped the flow of information

Figure 5.2 Access denied

Source: www.cultdeadcow.com

through applications such as TOR (The Onion Router), an open source software that allows users to remain anonymous, through routing requests for information through other users. Additionally, initiatives such as Psiphon (www.psiphon.ca), that produce code which bypass filtering of access, have helped people in various countries, including Iran and Kyrgystan (Deibert and Rohozinski, 2009). In the meantime, hacktivists such as Oxblood Ruffin, the spokesman of cDc, raise awareness over censorship practices (Ruffin, 2009). These kinds of hacktivist initiatives have proved helpful in empowering people, but have never really managed to galvanize widespread resistance to controlling and censoring information. On this matter, 'mass action hacktivism' may prove more effective.

Mass action hacktivism is more directly concerned with intervention in cases where they consider democracy and social justice are under attack. Through promotion of disobedience actions, such as 'virtual sit-ins', 'distributed denials of service attacks (Ddos) and other ways of interrupting the 'electronic veins of society' (Jordan, 2007: 77), they seek to raise awareness, protest and eventually change the world. They therefore depend on others to agree and act in the same manner.

Movements such as the Electronic Disturbance Theatre (www.thing.net) and the Free Range Activists (http://www.fraw.org.uk/index.shtml), have attacked corporation sites and paralysed e-services, through mobilizing a large number of people to act in the same manner. Ideologically, mass action hacktivism is allied to the anti (capitalist) globalization movement, and is anti-neoliberal. Examples of their activism include the No Bill Inside initiative, a campaign against Microsoft and other paid-for e-tools (see Figure 5.3 for an illustration of mass action hacktivism). The main means of this campaign is a 'browser alert' tool which pops up every time a site is opened through Internet Explorer, Microsoft's browser. The pop up window alerts users

Figure 5.3   Mass action hacktivism

to the costs involved in the use of this browser and the fact that it does not operate on the basis of public good, but in order to enrich some corporation. Another campaign, Keep it Simple, alerts users to the environmental cost of graphic heavy interfaces. The Electronic Disturbance Theatre, on the other hand, have led 'denial of service' attacks against the Minutemen – a militia style organization opposing Mexican immigration to the USA – as well as against Mexican neo-liberal authorities and corporations. These denial of service attacks were accomplished through 'floodnet', a tool that automates such attacks, making it possible to paralyze entire sites. In other actions, in April 2009, the Electrohippy collective called on people to resist intellectual property laws, through celebrating the World Intellectual Privateers Day. In a concerted action across the internet, they called on people to select a piece of information or any kind of creative work that should be in the public domain, but is controlled by intellectual privateering rights, and to share it as widely as possible. This is an act of civil disobedience since it involves break-ing the law, albeit in the name of the public interest. Both digitally correct and mass action hacktivism rely exclusively on net-native practices and although they engage with wider politi-cal issues, such as free speech, human rights and so on, they remain focused on the internet. This is not necessarily the case when existing social movements migrate online.

Social Movements and the Internet

Social movements form part of civil society, that is, they are formed by citizens, for the purpose of promoting some political or social issue. In general, social movements have sought to bring around changes in socio-political organization mainly through collective action, protests and mobilizations, with some notable successes. The labour movement of the early twentieth cen-tury has managed to secure workers' rights and to contribute to the formation of welfare states (Tilly, 2004). Similarly, the feminist movement has achieved many gains for women, including the right to vote. While traditionally social movements have involved street protests and other means of collective action, they have been quick in exploiting the possibilities offered by the internet. They have used it for, among other functions, the circulation of information on their cause; the organization of protests and demonstrations; the promotion of specific viewpoints and ideas; the encouragement of debate and deliberation across a range of issues. But the focus on these functionalities of the internet may obscure the actual shifts that take place in the ways in which social movements operate. W. Lance Bennett (2003) argued that the new media have transformed the very nature of protest movements. Bennett was primarily talking about global social movements, and to a large extent this globalization of movements may be seen as an outcome of new technologies (see also Chapter 2). On the other hand, local movements still exist, and most of Bennett's observations may be applicable to them as well. Because of the new media, protest movements have become 'polycentric': they have multiple hubs and oper-ate from all of them. Similarly, they have become 'polycephalous', that is, they are no longer represented by a central leading figure, but have many local representatives. Finally, protest movements are no longer about ideology and ideological differences, but are 'more about personal and fluid forms of association' (Bennett, 2003: 147).

Bennett further identified the main characteristics of online social movements. The continuous nature of the internet allows social movements to be involved in permanent campaigns. Partly, this is also due to the fact that online movements have no central leadership, making it difficult to switch campaigns on and off at will. In addition, communication found in movement sites is more about personal experiences and narratives and less about ideology. This potentially allows people to relate more to the movement's goals rather than the mere provision of information. Again, this not totally due to new technologies: it reflects broader historical political shifts that have seen the demise of the large ideological blocs of the twentieth century, and the rise in 'soft', identity-politics. In addition, because of a lack of a central binding ideology, the ties between supporters are not strong, and the overall internal organization of the movement is that of a fluid network rather than a solidary community. Although on the one hand this may be seen as weakening the movement, on the other it offers it a tactical advantage as movements can regroup and reconfigure themselves with relative ease. Finally, online movements are not as dependent on the mass media for communication, as they form part of smaller public spheres, with relatively autonomous communicative networks. This, in turn, enables them to reverse information flows, and feed or influence the agenda of the mass media. Nevertheless as Bennett points out, the strengths of the online movements are inseparable from their weaknesses. Some of these vulnerabilities include the weak ties between members of movements as well as between movements themselves; these lead to unstable coalitions that may undermine sustained efforts to bring about change. At the same time, the widespread lack of a clear ideological stance leads to lack of clarity about goals, and weak idea-framing. These, in turn, may confuse publics and ultimately sabotage efforts for change.

To what extent have online social movements been effective? They appear to be more successful in short-term campaigns rather than in bringing about lasting change. For example, online campaigns against sweatshops run by Nike, GAP and others have been relatively successful, but broader neo-liberal policies still remain widespread. Similarly, environmental online activism may be able to claim some local successes, but as we have seen in Kyoto and Copenhagen in 2009, pressure from the environmental movements has failed to influence the relevant political agenda. Moreover, notwithstanding W. Lance Bennett's arguments on shifts in movement organization, many movements still operate with an old-fashioned model based on leadership and national politics. For instance, Gillan and Pickerill (2008) report that the anti-war movement in the UK, USA and Australia in fact made little use of the network-style possibilities and was primarily used as a tool for efficiency. In the end, however, this may not be the fault of either the movements or the technologies that support them: global geo-politics is not democratic and hence it is unlikely to respond to bottom up pressures for change.

In an overall assessment of activism and the internet it can be argued that as initiatives, hacktivism projects show the wealth of imagination and depth of political feeling and engagement in citizens. The internet provides yet another terrain for struggle – where one can argue that the grounds are a bit more equal, although it is not by any means a 'level playing field'. In conclusion, however, there are considerable grounds for an overall pessimistic assessment given the relative lack of success for online social movements. This may well be due to a kind of spillover of offline politics online – as long as political institutions seek to shape the internet after their own image, and as long as political practices remain rooted to an offline model, things are unlikely to change. But recently, the rise of Web 2.0 has given grounds for optimism. Why? This is what we will examine next.

Web 2.0 and Politics

The rise of Web 2.0 has signalled a turn in thinking about new media and politics. This turn is mostly attributed to what Tim O'Reilly (2005) has called 'the architecture of participation'. In other words, Web 2.0 is linked to the development of a new technical infrastructure that further democratizes publishing and participation. Users are both producers and consumers of online content, and both big players and individual users have the opportunity to participate on a more equal footing. Applications such as blogs, wikis and more broadly the so-called social media, led to the hope for a more participatory, and hence more democratic, model of politics. And this time, this model will emerge from the new media, democratizing first the internet, and then possibly spreading outwards, spilling over to the rest of society. This kind of democratization, revolving around ideas of freedom of choice and the empowerment of individuals, refers to a particular model of democracy, the liberal-consumerist model.

More broadly however, how can Web 2.0 contribute to democratic politics? We can identify three possible scenarios (Siapera, 2008). Firstly, Web 2.0 applications such as blogs and Twitter may replace mainstream media. Journalism's main political functions have been to provide information for people to be able to form a public opinion, to express this public opinion, and finally, to hold governments, politicians and other powerful socio-political actors accountable for their actions (Habermas, 1996). However, journalism has been under attack for failing to fulfil its political functions, because it prioritizes the business side of making money at the expense of serving politics. Now that Web 2.0 is democratized publishing, these political functions may be taken over by people themselves, who can undertake the provision of information, the expression of public opinion and the watching of political actors. Second, Web 2.0 may contribute to democratic politics because it encourages direct communication between political actors at all levels, and because it allows for deliberation and actual communal thinking about issues. In this manner, Web 2.0 takes over the role of the public sphere as a space for communication, deliberation and communal thinking, and in this manner democratizing politics; here we should also place the role of Web 2.0 in enabling direct political action, bypassing traditional political institutions and changing the face of protest and activism. Third, Web 2.0 may provide a kind of training ground for the formation of new kinds of subjectivity, which may in the long run prove beneficial to democratic politics. In this way, Web 2.0 introduces shifts within people themselves rather than to the broader system. It is likely that all these scenarios operate at the same time. But does this mean that politics has become more democratic?

Blogs as Political Journalism

Looking into blogs-as-political journalism in some more detail, it seems that research is divided. Technorati.com, the site that provides daily analytics on the blogosphere, has developed a measure for ranking blogs, based on the number of links they receive from other blogs. This measure of authority is subsequently used to decide which blogs are at the top, that is, they are more linked by others in the blogosphere. While these rankings change, they allow us to get a snapshot of the blogosphere and its main players, the most visible and quoted blogs. Figure 5.4 presents a list of the top 30 blogs in February 2010.

The blogs with a star next to them are political blogs, as identified by Technorati. This includes blogs commenting on aspects of the political world. The rest are an assortment of technological, business and entertainment blogs. The top blog, The Huffington Post, as well as other blogs, such as The Daily Beast, post journalistic articles, often written by professional journalists or authors, with comments and analysis on politics and other aspects of socio-cultural life. In addition, there are several blogs that belong to well known journalistic brands, such as the *New York Times* and CNN. In many ways, it seems that blogs complement or even in some cases replace traditional, offline journalism. While we will examine the implications that this has for journalism in a later chapter, the political ramifications are many. First, blogs may replace offline journalism, but they are not necessarily any different to it. Although there are clearly some differences, it is clear that many bloggers are in fact journalists – this is certainly the case for The Huffington Post, which recruits professional writers. From this point of view, blog posts often take the form of traditional newspaper articles. At the same time, it is not clear how such blogs are financed. Although they generate some money through advertising,

---

Top 30 blogs

1. Huffington Post*	11. TMZ	21. Lifehacker
2. Endgadget	12. Media Decoder	22. Political Punch*
3. Gizmodo	(*NY Times*)	23. Business Insider
4. Mashable	13. Hot Air*	24. Hotline on Call*
5. Techcrunch	14. The Daily Dish*	25. Newsbusters.org*
6. Boing Boing	15. ReadWriteWeb*	26. Breitbart TV
7. Gawker*	16. CNN Political	27. Physorg.com
8. The Corner*	Ticker*	28. The Caucus
9. The Daily	17. Think Progress*	(*NY Times*)
Beast*	18. Bits (*NY Times*)	29. Paul Crugman
10. Ben Smith's	19. Jezebel	(*NY Times*)
Blog*	20. Big Government*	30. Daily Kos*

Figure 5.4 Top 30 blogs, 2010; * political blogs as identified by Technorati

Source: www.technorati.com

is it enough to guarantee journalistic autonomy? The \$315 million sale of The Huffington Post shows the increasing extent to which the market gets involved in blogging. This is an important issue, as on the one hand professional writers are subject to the pressures of the market while on the other hand, amateur writers are not as well equipped to search, report and provide authoritative comment on important political issues.

Nevertheless, there are several reports regarding the muckraking role of blogs, which seem to have broken quite a few scandals. For many, blogs are seen as the new investigative journalism. For instance, the resignation of Trent Lott, a USA senator accused of making racist remarks was so extensively reported and commented upon in the blogosphere, eventually making his resignation inevitable (Drezner and Farrell, 2004). However, Lott's remarks were originally broadcast on the US public broadcasting service and while ignored by the mainstream media, they were picked up on, repeated and amplified in the blogosphere. From this point of view, this wasn't a scandal that was 'broken' by the blogosphere but a case in which it reframed this particular event resulting in a resignation. In the case of Dan Rather, the respected CBS anchorman, on the other hand, it was right-wing bloggers that 'broke' the 'scandal'. When Dan Rather broadcast an item on a memo regarding the military records of George W. Bush during the election campaign of 2004, the right-wing blogosphere found out they were fake, and forced Dan Rather to resign (Cornfield, Carson, Kalis and Simon, 2005). An equivalent case, perhaps more serious and more notorious, was the case of Jeff Gannon, who ensured access to the White House press corps. Gannon worked for Talon News agency, a conservative news outlet, and systematically posed 'soft' questions to the President. Bloggers found that in fact he was a male escort with no journalistic background, obtaining daily passes to the White House although apparently he did not qualify as a journalist (Kahn and Kellner, 2007). These are just some of the scandals that were discussed by the blogosphere, but such cases are far from typical, while they also seem to be heavily concentrated in the USA. Although there may be other instances elsewhere where the blogosphere shed light on curious political incidents, it can hardly be claimed that it has taken over the function of investigative or watchdog journalism. Thus, on this evidence, it is difficult to conclude that blogs, as an example of Web 2.0 media, introduce radical shifts in politics because they replace journalism.

Blogs, Public Opinion and Political Action

On the other hand, it may be that blogs contribute to the formation of public opinion, as they allow direct communication between citizens as well as between citizens and politicians. From this point of view, blogs, as well as other applications such as social networking sites and microblogging, might contribute to the political process because they provide another platform for the public sphere and because they allow for direct communication (and even deliberation) on issues of common interest. To examine these contributions, researchers have sought to identify the quality of the discussions on blogs and social networking sites. A well researched case was 'Blog for America', the blog of Howard Dean – one of the politicians who in 2004 entered the race for the nomination for presidential candidate in the Democratic Party. He was eventually beaten by Senator John Kerry, but his blog was one of the first instances that a politician used Web 2.0 applications to address citizens directly. Kerbel and Bloom (2005) found some evidence of in-depth discussion of policies and policy proposals in the site, but mostly these took place among supporters of the same cause. This did not qualify as debate or deliberation, but rather 'Blog for America' allowed some discussion, and favoured a lot of celebratory language. In another study of the same blog, Janack (2006) found evidence for policing and disciplining of any dissenting voices: posters that questioned or criticized Dean, the Democrats or their policies, were either silenced or ostracized as 'trolls'. In general, there is some evidence for uncivil and spam posts found in the political blogosphere at large – the 2007 debates on blogging ethics are a testament to the concerns raised regarding the quality of the blogosphere. Two notable personalities of Web 2.0, Tim O'Reilly and James Wales – the founder of Wikipedia – proposed a series of ethical rules for blogging (O'Reilly and Wales, 2007). While these never really caught on, it is difficult to argue that blogs create or sustain discussion or deliberation on political issues. But few can dispute the power of blogs and other networking applications in enabling direct communication and even sustaining publicity.

A well known example of the contribution of Web 2.0 applications is the role of Twitter, the microblogging application, in the aftermath of the Iranian election in June 2009. When the results which favoured the incumbent President Ahmedinejad were disputed by protesters in Iran, a number took to Twitter to protest and declare their support for the other presidential candidate, Mir-Hossein Mousavi. Accessible through mobile phones, Twitter further allows the grouping of posts on the same topic – known as a 'trending topic' – while it also offers the possibility to 'retweet', that is to repeat and spread someone else's tweet. Finally, unlike email and social networking sites such as Facebook, Twitter makes its contents publicly available. As protests in Iran escalated, Iranians began to tweet events in real time. Tweets were written in both Farsi and English and gave information about what was going on in Iran:

> Woman says ppl knocking on her door 2 AM saying they were intelligence agents, took her daughter

> Ashora platoons now moving from valiasr toward National Tv staion. mousavi's supporters are already there. my father is out there!

> we hear 1dead in shiraz, livefire used in other cities RT (quoted in Grossman, 2009: np)

Such was the power of Twitter that the US State Department asked them to postpone scheduled network upgrades to allow for the uninhibited communication by Iranian protesters (Grossman, 2009). There is no doubt that Twitter emboldened protesters, gave the impression that they were not alone, and held Iranian leaders and officials accountable to the rest of the world. On the other hand, while Twitter allows people to communicate, there are no guarantees regarding the authenticity and credibility of the tweets. Grossman reports that it is likely that Iranian intelligence infiltrated Twitter, while it is also a matter of dispute whether protesters in Iran would tweet in English – it is possible that a number of tweets in English may have been written by Iranian exiles. In the end, protests were quashed by force and early 2010 saw the execution of two protesters, Mohammad Reza Ali Zamani and Arash Rahmanipour. So, after all, Twitter did not topple the Iranian regime. But it did give temporary hope that things may change because people want them changed – it offered a window to a country otherwise remote and closed to the rest of the world; it allowed some voices to reach out, and showed the degree of solidarity that can be achieved. To expect a computer application, no matter how sophisticated, to change a political system is perhaps misguided, but the widespread use of social media for political purposes shows that the scales are turning: politicians, even dictators, are facing constant scrutiny by citizens, who do not hesitate to network and demand changes.

The recent revolts in Tunisia and Egypt fed the debate on whether social media can be responsible for toppling long-standing dictatorships in the Middle East and elsewhere. The use of social media, and especially Twitter, were credited with triggering the revolts, so much so that the Tunisian revolt was dubbed the Twitter Revolution. At the height of the mass protests in Cairo's Tahrir Square, the Egyptian government shut down the internet – this act massively backfired, triggering online protests across the world. Soon, the internet was made available again. But can we argue that social media are responsible for these revolts? Not so argue both Joss Hands (2011) and Mejias (2011): the revolts were the result of long-standing discontent, repression and social unrest, triggered by desperate actions such as the suicide of Mohamed Bouazizi in Tunisia. The social media, however, enabled to some extent the coordination of the protests, the organization of a popular resistance front, as well as the galvanization of public opinion. Charles Hirschkind (2010) further argues that, at least in Egypt, social media have paved the way for these uprisings through publishing cases of clear injustice, torture and corruption. For example, a blogger named Wael Abbas, whose blog is titled *al-wa'i al-masri* ('Egyptian Awareness'), posted a video of a man being physically and sexually abused by police officers at a police station in Cairo. The video was apparently recorded by the police as a means of intimidating others, but when it was circulated on YouTube and elsewhere, it offered the legal ammunition necessary to pursue the case through the courts. In addition, such cases were further taken up by newspapers, which then helped circulate this kind of information further, thereby galvanizing public opinion. While the debate is still on, it is clear that social media's capacity to voice discontent, coordinate action, galvanize public opinion, and elicit global solidarity is certainly a new dimension in political struggles and must be taken into account. Figure 5.5 shows an image in solidarity with the Egyptian and similar protests in the Middle East and elsewhere.

Returning to the mainstream, another famous user of social media for political purposes is US President Barack Obama. A report by Edelman Digital Public Affairs offered a detailed analysis on the extensive use of social media by Obama. In *The Social Pulpit: Barack Obama's social Media Toolkit* (Lutz, 2009), Lutz identified the kinds of online media uses that Obama and his team had embarked on, as well as the kinds of results they ensured. Figure 5.6 summarizes this 'toolkit', but for Edelman the crucial thing to understand is that social media allowed the President's team to engage with people directly, and to offer them a series of possible ways in which to contribute to the campaign. An equally important dimension was that the campaign

Figure 5.5 Image circulated on the internet during the 2011 Egyptian revolt

By Numbers	
E-mail	13 million people on the email list who received 7,000 variations of more than 1 billion emails
Donors	3 million online donors who contributed 6.5 million times
Social Networks	5 million 'friends' on more than 15 social networking sites; 3 million friends on Facebook alone
Website	8.5 million monthly visitors to MyBarackObama.com (at peak)
	7.2 million profiles with 400,000 blog posts
	35,000 volunteer groups that held 200,000 offline events
	70,000 fundraising hubs that raised $30 million
Video	Nearly 2,000 official YouTube videos watched more than 80 million times, with 135,000 subscribers
	442,000 user-generated videos on YouTube
Mobile	3 million people signed up for the text messaging program
	Each received 5 to 20 messages per month
Phone calls	3 million personal phone calls placed in the last four days of the campaign

Figure 5.6 Obama's social media toolkit

Source: Lutz, 2009

made room for and in fact positively encouraged user generated content – this ended up being one of the most positive dimensions of the campaign, as reports tell us that voters are more likely to find information credible if it comes from a person like them. This combination of personal address and the offer of several levels of involvement multiplied the support the President had.

During his Presidency, Obama has often addressed US citizens through social media, most notably through YouTube, in scheduled interviews, where he took questions by users. Of course, these events are very carefully managed, but nevertheless allow for a kind of direct communication that would have been inconceivable during the reign of the mass media. On the other hand, how much has this changed politics and the political process? We need to keep in mind here that although Obama's social media use was very successful, its success was measured in terms of strategic advantage rather than democratization or gains for citizens. From the point of view of politicians, bypassing the mass media and addressing citizens-voters directly, clearly offers an advantage as they are more in control of the process of communication. However, the extent to which this translates into actual democratic gains (more equality and justice) is unclear.

Blogging and Political Subjectivities

Another contribution of blogs and other social media to the political process may be a more subtle one. It may be that blogging, and generally participating in online social media introduces changes in the person themselves. We already know that new media introduce important changes in the ways in which our identities and subjectivities are constructed. We will discuss this in more detail in a later chapter, but the important thing here is to note that often these changes are associated with political changes. In his work on the novel, the theorist Georg Lukacs (1974 [1914]), argued that the medium of the novel, exemplified by Cervantes' Don Quixote, signalled the development of a new kind of subject and consciousness, differing substantially from the subject of the Greek and Medieval worlds. This new subjectivity attempted to make sense of the alienated and fragmented world associated with modernity, through the imposition of a single narrative, based on reason. Similarly, Habermas (1989 [1962]) argued that the 'audience-oriented subjectivity' associated with the rise of the moral novel was a necessary development for the function of the public sphere – this subjectivity was undermined by the rise of the mass media. For Guy Debord (1967), the rise of the mass media is linked to the society of the spectacle: subjects therein are passive, inasmuch as the focus is on the consumption rather than the production of images, but also plural and dispersed across signs and images: no single sign or image is capable of capturing them. Mark Poster (1995) follows similar lines positing that the arrival of the internet as a new communicative form signals a new shift in subjectivity, associated with the rise of the digital author. The digital author points to the situation in which producers of online (hyper) texts are radically separated from their text, unable to control its multiple meanings as well as the uses to which it is put. At the same time, readers are unable to point to a single author, and attribute meaning to the intention of authors.

If we therefore begin with the premise that the blog constitutes a new form of communication, we can expect an associated shift in subjectivity, in the ways in which people understand themselves and the world around them. I have suggested elsewhere (Siapera, 2008) that the blog may be associated with a kind of 'authorial subjectivity', which may be conceived as positioned yet plural, separate or autonomous from others, yet collaboratively produced. The main idea here is that through blogging, and more broadly by participating in social media, people become more attuned to the external world, they are more able to articulate thoughts, problems and opinions, as well as to connect to others and deal with oppositional views. In short, they become a person able and willing to participate in politics. This is because participation in social media leads to an engagement with the external world and with others, it leads to position taking vis-à-vis issues that can also be political. In addition, such participation provides people with a platform in which they articulate and refute arguments, albeit not always with the same degree of eloquence. However, these possibilities remain possibilities, provided by the architecture of the social media. For these possibilities to be realized and to lead to political action, blogs must actively engage with questions of power – this dimension corresponds to the actual contents of social media. Secondly, through blogs and other social media, people should link with others – they should build coalitions, mobilize resources, and also compete with others in order to create a critical mass, able to introduce changes in the political landscape. Although shifts in subjectivity introduced by social media entail a powerful new promise, any changes are likely to be slow and subtle – a gradual shift of power from established political centres to the widely diffused networks of politically active people.

It is clear from the above that it is too early for a definitive critique. There is little doubt that Web 2.0 contains a democratic promise and potential but the extent to which it will be realized in a sense depends on us, users of the web, and what in the end we choose to make of it.

Conclusions

What kind of general conclusions can we draw regarding the relationship between the new media and politics? Box 5.2 summarizes the main points of this chapter. In general we can see that the new media have introduced some changes into the political process, but until today, these have not really contributed to any major political shifts. Politics in the new media age is still very similar to politics in the mass media age.

On the other hand, as we have seen in the chapter, the new media have provided more and new opportunities for political participation, revolving around: (i) the provision of information; (ii) promotion and advocacy; (iii) linking and connecting to others, building alliances and coalitions; and (iv) engagement in direct political action (protests, petitions, civil disobedience and so on). In addition, the new media allow for a continuous engagement and political involvement far beyond what is formally expected of citizens in representative democracies. It can therefore be argued that the new media can be seen as leading to a new kind of citizenship: one understood as ongoing civic engagement, beyond voting in election time. However, there is little evidence that this new idea is widespread as most new media use, as we shall see, remains personal and social. After all, political involvement is not a function of new media and technologies, but a function of able and interested citizens.

5.2

Summary of Main Points

New Media and Formal Politics

- Ambiguous relationship
- Spill-over of offline formal politics in online environments
- New media 'normalized'?

New Media and Activism

- Activist gains in strategies and tactics
- But: wider political changes not yet accomplished

Web 2.0 – Social Media and Politics

- Social media contribute by complementing political journalism
- They contribute by allowing the formation of public opinion and direct communication
- They contribute by introducing subtle yet important changes in political subjectivities

E-tivity: Exploring Online Politics

This e-tivity seeks to critically engage readers with shifts in political practices. Through this e-tivity, readers should be able to understand and explain further the political gains (and losses) involved in the use of the internet. Readers will choose one or two websites belonging to each of these categories: government and/or opposition sites; activist sites; websites of supranational institutions (e.g. UN, EU). They will then be invited to examine carefully these sites and address the following questions:

1   How is information presented in these sites? How interactive are they? How do they address readers? What type(s) of communication are they engaged in? Is the communicative type argumentative, persuasive, descriptive, declarative, or narrative? What are the implications of the choice of communicative type?

2   Can you identify any Web 2.0 features? Which sites tend to make more use of these? How do Web 2.0 features differ to other web-related features? What do you think they add to the sites?

3   On the basis of the above, how is citizenship changing in the age of the internet? Refer to both continuities and transformations.

Further Reading

This collection of articles aims to show the various issues and debates surrounding the new media and their democratic promise and potential. The first article, by thee of the most well known and respected political scientists of the media, examines the new media political landscape and suggests some ways which can contribute to the realization of the new media democratic promise. The article by De Zúñiga et al., looks at the changes from the point of view of citizens and their participation in the political process. Like Gurevitch et al., they assume a positive, optimistic perspective on the new media and their relationship to politics. Similarly, Natalie Fenton's article represents an attempt to understand how new media have reconfigured politics and specifically the concept of resistance. While Fenton is primarily focusing on informal, bottom up politics and social movements, Aeron Davis looks at the relationship between political parties and citizens in the new political context created by the new media: paradoxically, argues Davis, the enlargement of participation has yet to reach the outer edges of the citizenry, who emerge as left out of the new media political ecology.

Gurevitch, M., Coleman, S. and Blumler, J.G., 2009, Political Communication – Old and New Media Relationships, *The ANNALS of the American Academy of Political and Social Science,* 625(1): 164–181.

De Zúñiga, H.G., Puig-I-Abril, E. and Rojas, H., 2009, Weblogs, traditional sources online and political participation: an assessment of how the internet is changing the political environment, *New Media & Society,* 11(4): 553–574.

Fenton, N., 2008, Mediating Hope: New Media, Politics and Resistance, *International Journal of Cultural Studies,* 11(2): 230–248.

Davis, A., 2010, New Media and Fat Democracy: The Paradox of Online Participation, *New Media & Society,* 12(5): 745–761.

CHAPTER 6

SECURITY, SURVEILLANCE AND SAFETY

Learning Objectives

- To learn the negative aspects of the articulation between technology, society, economics, and politics
- To understand the significance of the expansion of surveillance
- To develop an understanding of issues relating to security
- To learn about online safety and protection against fraud
- To understand the relationship between new media, extreme porn and sexual aggression
- To critically apprehend the underlying dynamics of surveillance, security and safety

Introduction

For most people, the internet and the new media are associated with a host of positive developments, as they represent technological progress. Technological progress, one of the most central characteristics of modernity, signals improvements of almost all aspects of life, and entails the promise of more just and equitable distribution of wealth and power. This view, which we can term techno-optimistic, is very widespread in society, with public money going into technological innovation and the spread of technologies among people. But in fact we know that technology, its 'essence' as Heidegger would have it, or at least its uses, as other thinkers would insist, is much more ambiguous. This chapter will focus not only on this inherent ambiguity of technology, and hence of the new media, but also on some of its negative sides.

In discussing the negative aspects of technology and the new media, we need to first clarify the status of technology, and its relationship to people and society. The main question here is the following: are any negative outcomes the result of the way in which technology functions or are they the result of problematic use of technology? In other words, is the logic or 'essence' of technology responsible for negative outcomes or are we, our societies, to blame for the misuse of technological resources? There are three possible answers to this question, which mobilize a different version of what technology is. This is based on Darin Barney's (2004) classification of theories of technology into three categories: instrumentalism, substantivism and social constructivism.

Instrumentalism views technology as neutral, a tool that is employed by people in ways that reflect each society's goals, values but also its problems and limitations. Technology itself cannot be assessed on moral or political terms, as it is seen as a neutral device. While we can examine and judge the ways in which technology is used, technology as such can only be judged on the basis of how efficient it is. Following this logic, as long as technology is efficient then it is also in a sense 'good'. This logic underlies the kind of technological optimism referred to above, which holds that technological innovation signifies progress and must be thought of as good (Barney, 2004). If technology is made to serve bad ends, then it is not technology that should be blamed but rather those who used it in these ways. Negative outcomes are never the fault of technology, according to this position, but rather the result of problematic uses of technology.

In contrast, substantivism holds that technology is ruled by a certain logic, which implicates not only our societies, but also our subjectivities and our very being. For this school of thought, represented by the works of the sociologist Max Weber (1958) and the philosopher Martin Heidegger (1977), technological outcomes reveal the logic and essence of technology. This, in turn, is considered to be that of instrumental rationality, involving the logic of standardization, homogenization, and the mastery of nature and society (see also Barney, 2004: 38–39). For substantivism, using technology also implies using human beings, or rather producing a certain kind of human being and a certain kind of society. All technological outcomes entail this logic, and there is no way to distinguish between 'bad' and 'good' ones: they are all more or less equivalent and all display the dominant technological logic of instrumental rationality and efficiency.

Finally, social constructivism questions the focus of substantivism on technology alone, arguing that it disregards human agency and the role played by contingency and random factors. In actual empirical cases, we can observe that technological outcomes are not always the most technological or efficient, while we can also see the failure of certain technologies to take hold, although they are both efficient and 'technological' – genetically engineered food or nuclear power may be two cases in point. The point here is that technological outcomes must be seen as the products of a complex interplay of social, political, cultural, economic but also technological factors. Each technology interacts with its context, and the artefacts produced and the uses they are put to feed back into technologies, leading to other directions and new artefacts. This is the argument put forward by the social constructivist school of thought, associated with the work of Wiebe Bijker and his colleagues (e.g. Bijker, 1995; Bijker, Hughes and Pinch, 1987). Given the plurality and heterogeneous character of our societies, we can infer that technological uses and outcomes will be as plural and as heterogeneous: while some might be considered 'progressive' in the sense that they contribute to a more equitable and just distribution of wealth, status and power, others may be seen as politically problematic, socially destructive or psychologically pathological. This is not only a reflection on the uses themselves, but also the result of the interaction and articulation between certain political, social etc. characteristics with some elements of the technology itself.

In this chapter we will assume a social constructivist approach, holding that technology, its uses and outcomes, must be thought of as an articulation between certain 'local' factors, such as the political, socio-cultural, and economic conditions within specific historical contexts, and the specific 'affordances' or dimensions of the technology at hand. We will then look at the 'dark' side of the new media, assuming a case study approach. In sections that will cover society, politics, economics and culture, we will follow a case study approach which will examine surveillance, cyber-conflict, fraud and porn pathologies respectively. Our goal here is not only to describe some of the 'darker' aspects of the new media, but also to find out the specific articulation of the technological elements of the new media with the specific socio-historical circumstances in the contexts in which they are located. Throughout this discussion, we must keep in mind that the economic, political and social domains are all intermingled, and that the economic has a political and social dimension and vice versa; the current division is only undertaken for analytical purposes.

Society: Surveillance and Control

If by the term society we mean primarily the ways in which people associate and interact with each other, then there is no doubt that the internet and the new media have had a profound effect on these. While the specific changes in sociality – the ways in which we interact – are discussed in other chapters, the goal here is to find the 'dark' side of society online, the problematic aspects which are the outcome of the application of technology in certain ways that in turn reflect the current socio-historical circumstances. There is no doubt that these may be many, depending on how one chooses to define 'problematic'. In the present context, we may understand as 'problematic' those aspects that oppose the very understanding of society in Tönnies' (2001 [1887]) *Gesellschaft* form, that is, as an agreed, self-conscious and quasi-contractual association with others. While Tönnies was to an extent critical of this kind of association, we want to highlight here the reflexive and liberal elements in this understanding. In other words, if societies in an ideal-typical form are voluntary associations based on conscious choice, which preserve people's autonomy and independence, and which allow them to act freely as independent agents, then anything opposing these conditions may be deemed problematic in the current context. While many things can be considered problematic in this manner, in the context of the new media, the focus here will be on surveillance, which as we will see has a long history, but is now taking new forms and becomes more intense in and through the new media.

The rise of continuous monitoring of people and the collection of massive quantities of personal data for all of us have led theorists such as David Lyon (2001) to propose that we are witnessing the rise of a surveillance society. This kind of society refers to the increasing amount of surveillance that is taking place, alongside an explosion in the possible methods and means for observing and monitoring people's behaviours. While to an extent surveillance must be thought of as one of the defining characteristics of modernity, new media and technologies have helped make surveillance a central aspect of late (or post) modernity as well. Surveillance, and significantly also self-surveillance and more broadly what Mark Andrejevic (2005) calls lateral surveillance have now become an inextricable part of modern governance. Without surveillance, the work of governing bodies and bureaucracies would be extremely difficult if not impossible. But surveillance further introduces new divisions, new ways of classifying people and dealing with their behaviour. In so doing, new symbolic meanings are generated alongside new modes of control and often punishment: in short, new forms of power are made possible, and this power is concentrated in the hands of those who collect and control surveillance data. All these may be seen as infringements of personal freedom and as detrimental to the democratic principles according to which our societies are said to function.

Panopticon and Synopticon

Surveillance has a relatively long history as it pre-existed new media technologies. However, as we shall see, it now takes new forms, which are commensurable with current socio-political developments. Specifically, in one of the better known formulations of his relevant work, Michel Foucault has spoken of the panopticon, an imaginary machine designed in 1791 by Jeremy Bentham, a British architect and legal reformer. This contraption allowed for the total and complete surveillance of prison inmates who quite literally inhabited a transparent world with no place to hide. The logic behind this machine, as Foucault (1995 [1975]) tells us, is that prisoners, aware of their complete and total visibility, would regulate their behaviour knowing that they would get caught. For Foucault, this ensures the automatic functioning of power, since it would be internalized by prisoners without the need for any external enforcer to be present at all times. For power to work in this manner, it must be visible, seen by everyone, and unverifiable – it must operate independent of whether there is an enforcer or inspector present at all times.

While the panopticon was designed for prisoners, today's surveillance society has extended its function to society as a whole: for how else can we describe the preponderance of the all seeing CCTV cameras across not only public buildings and banks, but also in shops, squares, open spaces, train platforms, airports? Knowing that we are watched, we must behave ourselves: the visibility of power is evidenced in the ubiquity of cameras, while we almost never see the enforcers, the inspectors behind the cameras, those whose job it is to watch us all the time. The very idea of the Panopticon, argues Foucault, is an ideal form of power, and as such it was destined to spread in society, as it makes power more efficient. Its main principle is that people internalize the surveillance and behave in ways that conform to the requirements of power and the result is not so much a repressed and conformist society, but rather a society whose individuals have been constituted as subjects/objects of surveillance. This means that they are constructed as subjects/objects for whom information can be, and is, collected on a constant basis, analyzed, collated, processed, and even sold. In this manner, individuals are constantly (re)classified and assessed according to the requirements of power. But it is crucial to see the changes in the mechanisms of power involved in the shift from the Panopticon, which was essentially an architectural device or implement of power, to late modern ways of surveillance that primarily use the media.

The social theorist Zigmund Bauman (1999) argues that while the Panopticon created docile people to populate the factories of the industrial era and created an information asymmetry between the owners and controllers of production systems and labourers, current conditions have different requirements. In globalized informational capitalism it is no longer efficient to discipline labour from 'above'. Producing a docile labour force through discipline is no longer necessary as this labour force can be found everywhere in a globalized world. Rather than discipline, Bauman argues, the mechanism is seduction: introduce the stakes through televised broadcasts of celebrities and create new fantasies and new desires. The Panopticon is thus turned into a Synopticon which seduces people into watching. Specifically, Synopticon, a term coined by Thomas Mathiesen (1997), is taken to refer to a new technique of power, exemplified by the mass media, in which people are themselves turned into watchers: the many watch the few, but these few tend to be the global elites, movie stars and celebrities, politicians and star academics, in short, those in power and those whose statements are carefully repeated and all together convey a total way of life that is subsequently admired as the only or the most worthy way of life. Bauman's argument here is that this technique of power, which is implemented by the mass media on the one hand, legitimizes the current state of inequality through giving the impression of transparency and of equivalence between the watched elites and the watchers. At the same time, it stifles any dissenting voices by propagating a certain lifestyle to be emulated and endorsed, in a bid to ensure conformity.

But while Bauman argues that the techniques of power have fundamentally changed under globalization, Mathiesen's (1997) original argument was that panoptical methods, in which the few watch the many, coexist with synoptical methods, in which the many watch the few. Similarly, David Lyon (2001) argues that these two work in tandem, complementing each other as mechanisms of control: for Lyon, the fact that the many watch the few legitimizes and justifies that the few can watch the many. But for Mathiesen, and Bauman, the rise of synoptical techniques take place through the mass media, and especially television, which allows the many to watch the few. The question, however, that emerges here concerns the role played by the new media, which may introduce a new dynamic. Indeed, the new media offer renewed possibilities for surveillance intensifying processes of watching. At the same time, the new media impose a new model of watching, which entails constant surveillance of one another – it's as if the panopticon was outsourced to everyday people, who now act as constant watchers of one another. Mark Andrejevic (2004; 2005; 2007) has extensively discussed surveillance and its mode in late modernity, holding that recent developments have intensified and amplified disciplinary surveillance. He refers to a new kind of lateral surveillance, in which peers watch one another – although this kind of monitoring existed in villages and other, older forms of social organization, new media technologies have introduced new modes of watching, while they have also made these available to many people. For Andrejevic (2005) this democratization of access to investigatory techniques is linked to the rise of risk and uncertainty: anything can happen at any time by anyone. This creates a general culture of insecurity and suspicion which in turn feeds into and sustains the techniques of surveillance. Andrejevic further argues that the spread of surveillance techniques among the general populace reflect broader shifts in governance, shifts that relate to the rise of neoliberalism. On the other hand, this constant watching of one another follows or has contributed to the tendency to dissolve the boundaries between the public and the private: in a world of 24/7 surveillance, there is nothing left hidden, no area protected by the Big Brother gaze. Indeed, the metaphor of the Big Brother, based on George Orwell's *1984* novel, has now become a reality; in television shows, on our computer screens, and in public spaces, we are subjected to others' gaze and scrutiny, while we too subject others to the same scrutiny.

Surveillance and the Expropriation of Information

Summarizing these theoretical elements, we can see that surveillance can be direct and top down (panopticon), used to coerce people into conformity, or indirect, in which the many watch the few (synopticon), implemented through the mass media, using seduction to ensure conformity and the legitimization of existing inequalities. While the former, argues Lyon (2003), results to a system of control through classifying and categorizing people, the latter contributes to what may be called 'soul training'. Based on Andrejevic's work, we can argue that the new media have introduced a new dynamic in which the many watch the many: through the popularization of the new media and associated techniques of surveillance, including digital-web cameras but also Google Earth, following people's accounts on Twitter, Facebook and the like, through search engines and mobile phones we can collect information on others, and they can collect information on us. This lateral surveillance supports and amplifies the previous two forms while intensifying further the functions of control, classification and wilful subjection to power. But apart from the clear socio-political implications here, which include loss of privacy, constant suspicion and a generalized sense of insecurity, surveillance has another dimension as well. This concerns the commercial exploitation of the information collected. Information is not only used for purposes of classification and social control, but is also bought, sold and otherwise capitalized upon.

As we use supermarket fidelity cards, as we shop on e-shops such as Amazon, as we download music from iTunes or vote on talent shows using our mobile phones, we generate more and more information. These data are subsequently collected and used to create massive databases, which are then bought and sold. These databases are used to inform marketers of our choices, tastes and preferences, enabling them to sell or market products and services in more efficient ways. Often unbeknownst to us, the data trail we leave behind is used to classify us, to include us in certain categories which then are used to inform production, marketing and distribution of products and services. This commercial use of such data means that information that previously had no owners is now someone else's property. Already Facebook and Twitter are making money by selling 'analytics', demographic information combined with user online behaviours, which they collect on the basis of what their users disclose and how they move within these applications. This is raising serious questions regarding information ownership, privacy and exploitation. More broadly, it questions the rhetoric on the rising power of the user, a rhetoric that has dominated the debate since the rise of Web 2.0. In taking control over information that we, the users, produce through our media use, new cleavages and new power structures emerge, while more and more domains of life become commodities to be bought and sold. Information is collected by a few private companies, resulting in what Andrejevic (2007) has called a 'recentralization' of information. While those controlling the massive databases created are private companies, they make information freely available to national security agencies, compromising activism as well. What is worrying here is that until recently surveillance techniques were controlled by governments, which whatever their failings they at least represent the broader public and act on its behalf. Now, surveillance techniques have become the property of private companies, who operate for profit: more and more control and power is ceded to them, leaving less and less space for the public, the non-commercial, and the common to operate freely.

In some ways, submitting to this constant monitoring in all its forms is seen as participation – we are doing it willingly, because we want to be part of the online networks, and to take advantage of what they offer. But this kind of participation under conditions such as those described above, argues Andrejevic (2007), is a kind of unpaid immaterial labour (see also Chapter 3), as we produce even as we surf the internet, use our phones, update our social networking account, or download music. Both aspects of new media surveillance, which include the loss of privacy and generalized suspicion as well as the expropriation of information by private companies (Schiller, 2007), are commensurable with neoliberalism. This ideology revolves around ideas of deregulation and privatization (Murdock and Golding, 2001) and is also associated with an emphasis on individual self-regulation and assumption of responsibility for everything – ultimately, this heightened individualism ends up eroding the solidary basis of society. From this point of view, surveillance of the many by many (the lateral kind), which is precisely a reflection of this kind of neoliberalism in that it represents surveillance that has passed on to individuals themselves, ends up undermining the societies in which we live. If therefore in general, we can argue that the flip side of online participation is surveillance and control, then for as long as we, not as individuals but as the public, refuse to take control of the information that we generate, this dark side will remain.

Politics: Cyber-conflict, Terrorism and Security

In our discussion of politics and the new media, we argued that the new media entail important political promises for more democracy, and a more just and equitable distribution of wealth and power. Such a promise for more democracy also entails improvements in the lives of all people across the world. While critical of utopian approaches that considered that new technologies will cure all political evils, we must not overlook the positive potential of more engagement by more people, which may result in important democratic gains. From this point of view, it is surprising that two profoundly problematic political phenomena are encountered in online and other new media environments. These include cyber-conflict and terrorism. The former may be defined as real-world conflicts that spill over to cyberspace (Karatzogianni, 2004), while (cyber) terrorism is understood as politically motivated attacks against information systems that result in violence against non-combatant targets, and which are undertaken by sub-national groups or clandestine agents (Curran, Concannon and McKeever, 2008). Both cyber-conflict and cyber-terrorism may be considered problematic, if not inherently undemocratic, because they involve violence and the imposition of the will of the few to that of the many. From this point of view they do not include cyber-activism which is primarily aiming to change and influence public opinion. Rather, as Karatzogianni (2004) argues, in cyber-conflict antagonists use the internet as a weapon, hurled against each-other. In this section we will discuss some of the methods and effectiveness of the internet when used as a weapon.

In his discussion of the relationship between the media and political conflict, Gadi Wolfsfeld (1997) argued that the effectiveness of the use of the media by political antagonists, and more broadly their ability to control the political environment depends on: their ability to initiate and control events; their ability to regulate the flow of information; and their ability to mobilize elite support. Although Wolfsfeld was referring to the mass media, we can usefully employ his analytical framework in order to gauge the effectiveness of cyber-conflicts and cyber-terrorism. Karatzogianni (2004; 2006; 2009) situates cyber-terrorism primarily within the frame of ethno-religious (cyber) conflict, and holds that its main methods include hacking enemy sites and creating/managing sites for propaganda and mobilization. To these we can add the use of the internet to distribute terrorist know-how on using bombs, explosive devices and so on, while another use includes soliciting financial support. In what follows we will discuss some examples of these methods as well as their effectiveness based on Wolfsfeld's schema.

Hacking and/in War and Conflict

Hacking, also referred to as information warfare, uses information technology tools to attack enemy websites. They use the standard methods employed by hacktivists, but to different ends. These include Distributed Denial of Service (DDoS) attacks, as well as Domain Name Service (DNS) attacks (see Karatzogianni, 2004). In the case of DDoS, websites are prevented from working because they are flooded by a very high number of page requests, usually by 'zombie' machines. In DNS attacks the domain name is severed from its numerical address, preventing users from accessing the site. While these are methods used by hacktivists for purposes considered more acceptable since they are primarily symbolic, in cyber-conflict and terrorism in particular two more malicious methods are used as well: the spread of worms and unauthorized intrusions (Karatzogianni, 2004). Worms may enable hackers to gain control of computer accounts, turning them into 'zombies', which operate without the owners' knowledge and approval. Unauthorized intrusions into computer systems is the perhaps the most widespread form of hacking in popular imagination, spread through early films, in which hacker-geniuses hacked into top secret super-computer systems such as that of the US military, NASA etc.; through their illicit actions hackers can get access to top secret information or otherwise sabotage the system.

These methods can work together as well as separately, and are quite effective weapons in cyber-war. In some cases, they can even herald hostility and forthcoming war. In the summer of 2008, some weeks before the conflict between Georgia and Russia escalated into an armed one, there were extensive reports of DDoS attacks against Georgia (Markoff, 2008). Observers noticed a stream of data directed at Georgian government sites with the message 'win+love+in+Russia'. These attacks effectively shut down Georgian servers, while the Georgian President, Mikhail Saakashvili, saw his website being attacked and rendered inoperable for 24 hours. In response, the presidential site was moved to Atlanta, in the US state of Georgia, hosted by Tulip System, run by a Georgian ex-patriate. In other hacking attacks, just as Russian troops entered South Ossetia, DDoS attacks crippled media, communications and transportation sites, as well as the National Bank of Georgia site (Markoff, 2008). The result, argues Markoff, was that throughout the attack, Georgia had effectively no internet connection, and could not communicate with possible sympathizers abroad. Although those responsible for the attack were never identified, sources cited by Markoff point the finger to Russian nationalists. A group under the name of South Ossetia Hack Crew has claimed responsibility for defacing the Georgian Parliament website with image collages comparing Georgian President Saakashvili to Adolf Hitler (Leyden, 2008). In the meantime, the website of the South Ossetian government was attacked in August 2008, hours before being attacked by the Georgian artillery, while the Russian news agency RIA Novosti was also hit by a DDoS attack. In a combined DDoS and DNS attack in January 2009, the Central Asian Republic of Kyrgyzstan was knocked offline for more than a week, reportedly by Russian cybermilitia (Googin, 2009). In many ways, this kind of cyber-war represents the escalation and/or spillover of conflicts into cyberspace.

Other examples include the ongoing hacking wars between Israelis and Palestinians. In November 2000, an anti-Israeli hacking group, reportedly the Pakistan Hackerz Club, hacked the site of one of the most powerful pro-Israeli lobbying organizations, the American-Israeli Public Affairs Committee (Aipac), replacing it with important emails from Aipac's own database, while they also published credit card numbers and email addresses of Aipac members (BBC, 2001b). According to Gary Bunt (2003), one of the most well-known hacking incidents is the one against Ariel Sharon, then one of Israel's most senior politicians. Sharon's election campaign website was hacked by the World's Fantabulous Defacers, who kept the original format of the site but changed the image and text, posting horrific photos of an injured Palestinian child, and the statement 'Long live Hizballah! Long live Palestine! Long live Chechnya, Kashmir, Kosovo and Bosnia!' (in Bunt, 2003: 43). In the ensuing cyber-war, visitors to the Hamas website were diverted to porn sites, allegedly by Israeli hackers. UNITY, a website which forms part of the British registered *ummah*.net domain sought to attack Israeli ISPs as part of a strategy which would disable Israeli government sites first, followed by financial sites, at the same time crippling Israeli ISP servers and disrupting e-commerce sites.

New Media as Communication Tools in War and Conflict

The use of the new media in propaganda has often had more disturbing consequences. In 2007 a video of a girl being stoned to death by a mob surfaced on the internet. The girl was 17-year old Du'a Khalil Aswad, of Kurdish ethnic origin and Yazidi religion who was stoned to death in an honour killing in the Iraqi-Kurdish town of Bashika, because she had eloped with a Kurdish Muslim boy. This video was replayed in various Islamic and jihadist fora, which reframed it as a crime against Islam, on the basis that the girl was killed because she had converted to Islam, subsequently calling for some sort of retaliation and revenge. This came in April 2007, a few weeks following Du'a's death: several cars with gunmen stopped a bus with factory workers returning to Bashika, abducting all men of Yazidi faith, and then executing them (Cockburn, 2007). Although there is no possible way in which to link the video with the calls for retaliation with the actual executions, we may place it in a context in which offline conflicts continue seamlessly in online environment. Similarly, the many videos of, for instance, Palestinian children in Gaza, or images in war-torn Iraq and Afghanistan, may not contribute directly to the radicalization of young Muslims and others, but must be seen as part of the wider conflict, and as such as tools in the effort to recruit more supporters (Hoskins, Awan, and O'Loughlin, 2011).

Finally, this is the broader context in which we must place other techniques, such as use of the internet to distribute know-how and other kinds of practical knowledge over the internet. Manuals, how-to lessons, as well as detailed instructions are available online to guide prospective terrorists, while terrorists use the internet to make financial transactions, either through money laundering (Castells, 2004) or through seeking donations; Levitt (2002) reports that in 2001, a British internet site called the Global Jihad Fund, which openly associated itself with Bin Laden, provided bank account information for various Islamic fundamentalist fronts and groups to 'facilitate the growth of various Jihad movements around the world by supplying them with funds to purchase their weapons' (posted on GJF's site). Ariely (2008: 9) further reports that Al Qaeda and other terrorist organizations must be seen as 'learning organizations' involved in knowledge transfers, and that includes communication, economic, scientific and practical information and knowledge.

We can see therefore that the use of the internet in cyber-conflict can be very effective: It can be used to initiate events and control their outcome, as in the case of DDoS and DNS attacks; it can be used to regulate the flow of information, as in the propagandistic uses discussed above; and it can be used to mobilize support, both in the form of new recruits as well as in the form of donations. From this point of view, the internet is indispensible in modern cyber-conflict. More broadly, the use of the internet in cyber-conflict and cyber-terrorism provides, it seems, a good example of the mutual shaping of technology and society-politics. In a world which is riddled with conflict, technology can neither be seen as neutral or as imposing its own logic of efficiency. Rather, it seems that new technologies are shaping some of the forms this conflict takes, which are now organized around distributed networks, using sophisticated technological tools, and mobilizing support from across the world. At the same time, the spillover of conflict in technological domains gives rise to antagonistic, aggressive and destructive technological practices. New technologies must therefore be seen as part and parcel of the current world order, actively shaping it whilst also been shaped by it.

Economics: Fraud and Deception

While in cyber-conflict we discussed attacks aimed at political targets, the economic dimension reveals a wide arsenal of cyber-tools all aimed at defrauding and deceiving people for monetary gains. The relationship between new media technologies and economics was discussed in Chapter 3, in which we placed developments in the context of informational capitalism. In this section, however, we will focus on the underbelly of online economics, which shows its vulnerability to attacks motivated by financial gains. Ranging in sophistication from email scams to Trojans and other high-tech tools to defraud, one thing is for sure: online fraud is here to stay and it proliferates even as we speak. Although the techniques of online fraud are far too numerous to list, we will focus on some of the most common examples, which include the '419 scam', phishing and identity theft. In theoretical terms, the main argument here is that although fraud has always been a part of capitalism, its online counterpart is linked to developments concerning the erosion of trust and the rise of risk, thereby feeding into other 'dark' developments such as surveillance and conflict.

The 419 Scam

One of the most widely spread email scams is the so-called '419 scam', after Section 419 of the Nigerian Criminal Code (Capp 777 of 1990) that prohibits advance fee fraud (Longe, Ngwa, Wada and Mbarika, 2009). Typically, scammers write an email to say that due to certain circumstances they have access to a deceased person's bank account. They offer 50% of the funds, provided that email recipients give them their bank and other details. Notwithstanding the crudeness of this scam, the fact that it keeps on running is a testament to its success. Longe et al. (2009) report that this email scam is the continuation of a letter scam which was based on the same premises: you are promised a large amount of money provided you are prepared to give an advance first. People have lost a lot of money with this scam, which has many variations, including posing as victims of some disaster, representatives of charitable organizations, retired politicians and so on. The psychological cost of this kind of fraud should not be underestimated either, as it erodes trust and leaves long-lasting effects on victims.

The '419 scam' works primarily by persuading people to transfer their money, using the new media mainly as a means by which to contact people in large numbers, and to retain their anonymity as they use untraceable email and often pre-paid mobile phones. In other instances, they persuade victims to part with their bank account details, and then empty the accounts. A recent variation of this scam is the lottery email, which informs you that you have won the lottery but you can only access the cash if you forward a sum of money. Most of these email scams originate in Africa, and are low-tech, as they merely use new media as facilitators for their scam. The advance fee fraud is therefore an old scam given a new media makeover.

Phishing and Spoofing

In more recent developments, phishing and spoofing are two widely used criminal techniques that steal personal data with a view to eventually stealing money. Typically, phishing works through an email from a well known company, such as a bank, a social networking site, or paypal, ebay and other e-commerce sites that users do business with. The email asks you to confirm, update or validate your username and password, credit card or bank account number or any other sensitive information. Upon pressing a relevant link, unsuspecting users are directed to a fake website which is virtually indistinguishable from the authentic one, and which acts as a means of reassuring the victim of the genuineness of the request. Upon inputting the information, the fraudsters empty bank accounts, charge credit card or debit card accounts and so on. Spoofing is a similar activity in which fraudsters create a copy of a website, and trick users into thinking it's the real one; they may even use a real site and insert a pop up into which they ask users to input their sensitive information. The upshot is the same: victims have their bank accounts emptied, their credit cards charged to the max, and their personal details stolen and often sold to be used by other criminals. These scams require technical knowledge as they need to be able to create convincing copies of existing websites, or pop ups. In other variations of this scam, fraudsters infect computers with viruses or Trojans, which follow and record users' keystrokes – the so-called key-logger Trojans – and subsequently steal their passwords, and through these their sensitive information. All these contribute to another scam, the theft of one's identity.

On 25 March 2010, in two federal cases in Boston and New York, Albert Gonzalez, 28, was sentenced to 20 years in prison, after admitting that he ran an international identity theft ring that stole more than 40 million credit and debit card details from retailers (Feeley and van Voris, 2010). The scam cost more than $200 million and the US authorities hailed this case as the start of a serious crack down on identity theft. But as more and more economic activities migrate online, identity theft is on the increase and the creativity of criminals, who often combine high and low tech methods, is really astonishing. In the USA alone, the Federal Trade Commission estimates that more than 9 million people have fallen victim to identity theft. Fraudsters steal personal information and details either through phishing, spoofing and key-logger Trojans or through old fashioned theft of wallets, handbags and other personal items which may contain sensitive personal information. They then use the stolen information to empty existing bank accounts, or open new credit card accounts in the names of the victims, or even take out loans and sell the property of their victims. Clearly this is a crime with long-lasting effects on victims, who have not only lost their money, but they can also have their credit rating destroyed and are left with feelings of personal violation.

All these are serious and pernicious crimes that have a series of negative effects on the economy as well as on their victims. The responses to these crimes have been numerous but fraudsters seem to be one step ahead. Legislation can sometimes act as a deterrent, but often identify theft and especially credit and debit card fraud, is conducted from far away and criminals cannot be found and prosecuted. There have also been some attempts to raise awareness among people on how to protect themselves from such scams, and how to remain safe in online environments. The main advice offered is never to part with sensitive information, such as passwords and account numbers, unless steps are taken to ensure the bona fides of the request. In addition, users must be aware of their personal details, and to monitor and safeguard personal information.

Risk, Trust and Security: More Surveillance?

On a more abstract level, however, this kind of economic fraud and deception used to obtain personal information seems to link directly with other 'dark' aspects, such as that of surveillance and control. In proliferating the methods of deception, the new media have fed into the erosion of trust, one of the key characteristics of the risk society. Ulrich Beck, who coined the term 'risk society', summarized neatly the relationship between risk and trust: 'The discourse of risk begins, where trust in our security and belief in progress end' (in Adam, Beck and van Loon, 2000: 213). In these terms, hearing and learning about such fraud and scams damage our trust in the system, and raise the risk associated with online environments. The upshot is that we more than welcome attempts to police such environments, and are prepared to submit to methods of surveillance 'for our own protection'.

Another side of the same coin is that eventually such fraudulent behaviour may actually lead to open conflict. We must keep in mind that although the above discussion was focused on individual victims of fraud there is another more dangerous world of online corporate fraud, which includes industrial espionage and corporate identity theft. Indeed, by spoofing authentic websites, and by scamming individuals who then pass on the costs of fraud to their insurance or to their banks, firms are already involved in online fraud. But there are cases of firms getting involved in fraud not as victims but as perpetrators, using online means to spy on their competitors. By far the largest and most interesting case is the Google vs China affair that took place in late 2009–early 2010. When Google decided to enter China in 2006, it promised to abide by the Chinese rules of the game which included censorship of certain politically sensitive keywords and sites – a practice known as the Great Firewall of China. This lead to Google receiving a lot of flak from people who thought that Google was selling out the internet cyber-libertarian principles of freedom of information for profit. Given Google's compliance with the Chinese government, we can only imagine their surprise when in December 2009, Google fell victim to a cyber attack that was subsequently linked to China. The attack, which contained code linked to China, is said to be of the Aurora or Hydraq Trojan kind, which gives hackers the possibility to run commands on the hacked computers, allowing them to download files and other information stored therein (McMillan, 2010). While the hack attacked other US corporations as well, Google took the attacks personally. It responded immediately by making the attacks public and when in January 2010 the attacks were openly linked to China, the US government via its Secretary of State, Hillary Clinton, called for a thorough investigation into the matter. On 22 March 2010, Google decided to effectively leave China by relocating to Hong Kong and exiting the Great Firewall. The decision, which may prove both an economic (Google's Chinese income stood at $250 million in 2009) as well as a strategic loss for Google given the size of China's market, also reflects an internal dilemma for Google, as Sergey Brin, one of its founders is a vocal advocate for freedom of speech (Johnson, 2010).

This case represents an increasingly complex situation unfolding in cyberspace: an intermingling between strategic and political interests, technological know-how and high economic stakes. In this sense, it is not strictly speaking a case of fraud or deception, but it involves the mobilization of technological know-how for economic and political purposes. While China seeks to control the access of its citizens to cyberspace, the US is seeking to consolidate its position as a global leader in human rights advocacy and protection, and Google to protect its reputation and 'don't be evil' mantra. At the same time, some see China as involved in industrial espionage in a move to ascend into a higher position in industrial design and production (see for instance Homeland Security Newswire, 2010a). All these show the inevitable cross-overs between economics and politics but also directly feed into other practices such as increased surveillance and control. For example, as soon as Google realized it was being hacked it contacted NSA, the US National Security Agency, in order to draft an agreement which includes data sharing between the two (Homeland Security Newswire, 2010b). This may involve Google handing over data upon NSA requests, and this data may include personal emails and other personal information. From this point of view, political cyber-conflict and economic cyber-fraud and espionage feed directly into practices of surveillance and control over cyberspace. Is this the case for 'dark' cultural practices? We will examine this in the next section.

Culture: Online Porn

This discussion must begin with a short justification of the rise of online pornography as one of the negative outcomes of the new media. Pornography has had a long history of being debated within feminist circles as well as more broadly in society: Mightn't porn just represent a human tendency towards appreciation of the erotic? Must we always view women as victims, when some sex workers themselves feel they are in control of their sexuality? What about issues of freedom of speech? These are debates that have not been resolved, and are not likely to be in the near future, but the internet and the new media have in some ways exacerbated these dilemmas by making porn freely available in online environments. Paasonen (2010) found that estimates of the prevalence of online porn vary considerably, ranging from 3.8% to 80% of all internet traffic – the variation is attributed to the different times as well as the different agencies involved in the measurement. Thus, in the early–mid 1990s, online porn was more prevalent while in later years, with a wider demographic found online, the numbers fell. Similarly, filtering software sites or conservative family organizations tend to exaggerate the incidence of online porn, often making no distinction between erotic poems, hardcore porn and sex education (Paasonen, 2010). Moreover, online porn-related contents may range from extreme SM and violent porn to alternative erotica, referred to as altporn (Attwood, 2007; Paasonen, 2010) and porn catering to diverse sexualities, queer, alternative body types and so on, referred to as netporn (Jacob, Janssen and Pasquinelli, 2007 in Paasonen, 2010). Finally, the production of online porn may range from professional and commercialized to artistic and writerly, and may include user-generated amateurish porn contents as found in YouPorn, the pornographic version of YouTube. The extent of this variety in prevalence, contents and production makes difficult any generalized conclusions regarding porn.

But it should be clear that not all of these categories may be seen in negative terms. This section is concerned with online/new media-related practices that introduce a negative, exploitative dynamic that may disrupt and otherwise dislocate flows of culture and cultural expression – in this instance, this translates to a disruption of broadly accepted cultural conventions on sexuality, and/or these cases in which people are seriously harmed in both a physical and in an emotional and psychological manner. Thus, while porn is often linked to moral panics (Kuipers, 2006), the exaggerated view that it always leads to sexism or violence against women or that it undermines the morality of the family is not warranted by all porn contents. On the other hand, there are instances of extremely violent and disturbing pornography in which people are clearly exploited. It is this kind of exploitation that places online porn in the 'dark' side of cyberspace. In a sense this is a modified form of Catherine MacKinnon's *mala in se* (evil in itself) argument that pornography is violence against women, and that women are coerced into this exploitative industry. From this point of view, we will discuss violent and paedophile porn as two instances of problematic porn and examine its articulations with the new media.

In April 2003, police in West Sussex, UK, discovered the body of a 31 year old music teacher, Jane Longhurst, who was strangled with a pair of tights and her body was hidden for weeks before it was found. In March 2004, Graham Coutts was convicted of her murder and sentenced to 26 years. Coutts, a 35 year old musician, admitted he had a neck fetish and that he used internet porn sites involving asphyxial sex and strangulation for about eight years (BBC News, 2004). During his trial it emerged that 86% of the pornographic images found in Coutts' computer were violent, often showing naked women with ligatures around their necks. The prosecution in the trial showed evidence that Coutts had visited websites advertising violent 'snuff movies', just the day before the murder. Although there is no proof that violent porn led to this murder, the victim's mother, Liz Longhurst, campaigned against this kind of internet porn. She argued that the government must 'take action against these horrific internet sites, which can have such a corrupting influence and glorify extreme sexual violence' (in BBC News, 2006a). Furthermore, Liz Longhurst argued that most women appearing in these images are not consenting adults, but trafficked and exploited women (in Murray, 2009). From this point of view, the production of such images is a violent crime. Although in the UK it is considered a crime to produce and distribute violent porn, new laws have made it illegal to possess images that are or appear to be violent or life threatening and which may lead to severe injury. Section 63 of the Criminal Justice and Immigration Act 2008 criminalizes possession of images depicting violent sex, bestiality and necrophilia. While the extent to which this law is justified may be questionable, many see it as a necessary first step towards controlling and punishing violence against women (see Murray, 2009 for the legal arguments).

Another extremely disturbing case concerned a 39 year old nursery nurse from Plymouth, UK, Vanessa George. George worked at a nursery, looking after children from the ages of 0 to 4 years old. In June 2009, George admitted 13 charges which included sexual abuse of children and making and distributing indecent images of children (BBC News, 2009). George had befriended an IT consultant and known sex offender, Colin Blanchard, and another individual, Angela Allen. She then began abusing children in her care, taking pictures of the abuse on her phone, which she would then send to her Facebook friends, Blanchard and Allen, who would do the same for George. There is no doubt that the new media have created new opportunities for child abusers, who can produce, distribute and download abusive images in mere minutes. Although the legal framework for this kind of activity exists, the internet's vast size and geographical spread makes difficult the control of either the production or the distribution of such images.

In yet another disturbing case, Ashleigh Hall, a 17 year old British girl, was attracted by a Facebook 'friend' who pretended to be a teenage boy calling himself Peter Cartwright. 'Cartwright' published a photo of a handsome bare-chested teenage boy, and befriended Ashleigh on Facebook, eventually exchanging text messages and making arrangements to meet in October 2009. In fact, 'Peter Cartwright' was Peter Chapman, a 33 year old sex offender who lured Ashleigh into his car by pretending to be 'Peter's' father. He then raped and killed her, dumping her body in a gully by a fence. Chapman confessed the murder to police the next day and was eventually jailed for life. The murder prompted Facebook to issue a statement urging people not to meet anyone that has contacted them online unless they knew them well, 'as there are unscrupulous people in the world with malevolent agendas' (in BBC News, 2010). In this instance, a new medium allowed a predatory sex offender to contact and lure an innocent girl to her death.

New Media and Sexual Aggression

In general, there is little doubt that new media technologies have created a new environment of opportunities for predators of all kinds. Donna Hughes (2002) argues that the articulation of new technologies with a broader ideology of sexism and violence against women create an explosive combination that leads to violence and other forms of sexual exploitation. This is happening either directly, in cases where women and other vulnerable groups such as children are coerced into having sex, raped and assaulted, and then videos of these acts are sold or posted online for the gratification of others; or indirectly, through the mainstreaming of pornography, which in turn fuels more violence and exploitation. Hughes further attributes this to the pro-liferation of internet porn, which, she argues, intensifies competition leading to the production of even more extreme and degrading sex scenes. Equally, the new media have given rise to a massive growth of child pornography: older media, such as cameras and analogue videos were expensive and difficult to use and reproduce, while the main distribution medium was snail mail. The new media have revolutionized both production (digital cameras, scanners, and phone cameras and other digital recording media are used to capture pornographic images of children), as well as distribution (the internet can reach an unprecedented number of people). Moreover, the new media have offered new opportunities to paedophiles to contact and groom children, who are sometimes accosted in chat rooms, and asked to pose and send photographs or even try to meet them. Finally, pimps and traffickers use the internet to advertise their 'wares' and find customers. Hughes reports the case of 'Logo Center', a 'modelling' agency in Latvia, which used the internet to advertise the availability of young women and children for sex and for the making of pornographic films. According to Hughes' information, 'Logo Center' oper-ated several porn sites, including some with children engaged in sexual activities. They further supplied 'models' for porn production in other countries, while it is estimated that in total they exploited '2000 women, men, girls and boys, resulting in 174 juveniles relying on prostitution for their basic livelihood' (Hughes, 2002: 138). Other disturbing findings by Hughes include a Danish website called 'Slave Farm', which includes pictures of torture and rape, and a Russian site which offers more than 30,000 pictures of rape.

The relationship between the new media and sexual aggression is therefore four-fold. First, it involves the actual physical and emotional harm of persons, who are filmed in extreme scenes. Second, it offers an unprecedented ease of production distribution and access to extreme and violent porn – Hughes cites a consultant who says that before the advent of the new media, sexual predators had to remove themselves from their community by three levels: they had to physically go somewhere, then they had to know where to go and finally to know where to find the extreme images and sensations they sought (Hughes, 2002: 139). Third, the proliferation of extremely violent pornographic images may contribute to the rise in violent crimes against people, such as the kinds of rapes and murders we saw above. Finally, the new media offer the opportunity to sexual predators to contact and groom vulnerable people in online environments such as chat rooms and social networking sites.

Responses: Surveillance Once Again

The response to this kind of synergy created between the new media and sexual aggression and exploitation is in turn two-fold. First, it takes the form of the development of a legal framework that addresses the challenges of the new media. Here for instance, we can place the banning of possessing violent porn images as discussed above. Most countries also ban not only the production but also possession and distribution of sexual images of children. Other developments include a recent amendment passed in 2006 in the UK Data Protection Act, which allows credit card companies to withdraw credit cards from customers who used them to purchase child pornography on the internet (BBC News, 2006b). The second form of the response is a technological one. Special filters and tracking software have been developed with a view to protecting vulnerable people such as children from accessing porn sites, and in order to track consumers and users of online child pornography respectively. NetNanny, Safe Eyes, Cybersitter and others are just some of the filtering software programs that developed with the specific agenda to prevent access to porn, but they may go further than this: they may allow parents to follow their child's activities on social networking sites, to prevent access to P2P sites, such as Gnutella, to block chat rooms and so on. In 2005, Microsoft Canada along with the Royal Canadian Mounted Police and the Toronto Police Service developed CETS (Child Exploitation Tracking Software), which allows police agencies to collect and process large volumes of information, to cross-reference and use social network analysis to identify offenders. More recently, in March 2010, a US software program called the Wyoming Toolkit, allows police to cross-reference millions of illegal images being shared across the internet and create a map of users accessing and using these images (*Herald Sun*, 2010). Clearly, these responses, albeit helpful in containing to some extent the sexual abuse and exploitation of people, are part and parcel of the broader culture of surveillance and security in online environments. In these terms, safety relies once more on surveillance and monitoring.

Conclusions

This chapter explored some of the negative dimensions of the new media understood as disruptive or even destructive of the flows of social, political, economic and cultural flows, resulting in the actual harm of social bonds and/or persons. We have argued that these negative dimensions are not the result of the technology as such. At the same time, although surveillance, conflict, fraud and porn pathologies pre-existed the new media, their articulation with new technologies has given rise to new forms, opened up new avenues and created new opportunities for disruptive and problematic relationships to operate. Some of these articulations are summarized in Box 6.1 below.

In all this we see that the proliferation of surveillance and the appropriation of non-proprietary information; the rise of cyber-conflict and terrorism which creates issues of security; the explosion of fraud and deception which erodes trusts and multiplies risk; and the spread of porn pathologies, which objectifies and exploits human beings can all be linked to a rising culture of control. As these forms spread and multiply, governments and people demand more protection and more control over the new media. This control more often than not takes the form of more surveillance, which in turn often takes the form of internalized self-control and surveillance of others: friends, enemies and even our own children. This in turn feeds into the erosion of trust and feelings of insecurity, creating a kind of vicious circle from which it is difficult to escape. Moreover, all too often control translates in curbs on free speech and invasion of privacy: is this a necessary trade off to ensure safety? This is a pressing question that societies will need to address. For the time being though, our discussion ends with the observation that the dark side is an inextricable part of the new media and one that we must at some point confront head on.

6.1 Summary of Main Points

Society

Surveillance:

- Panopticon: one watches many: e.g. CCTVs
- Synopticon: many watch one: e.g. the mass media culture, watching celebrities
- Lateral Surveillance: we constantly watch each other, e.g. Google Earth, following people on Twitter
- We associate with other people in a context of mistrust and insecurity
- Information that was non-proprietary, i.e. belonged to none, is now commercially and politically exploited

Politics

Cyber-conflict and terrorism:

- Distributed denial of service (DDoS)
- Domain Name Service attacks (DNS)
- Worms and Trojans
- Unauthorized intrusions (hacks)
- Contributes to an environment of increased risk and insecurity

Economy

Cyber-fraud and deception:

- Email scams
- Phishing
- Identity theft
- Articulation of economic with political conflict – the Google China affair
- Feeds into more surveillance and demands for policing and control

Culture

Violent and extreme porn:

- New modes of production and distribution of (extreme) porn
- New media allow sexual predators to groom vulnerable people online
- Internet violent porn may lead to actual physical violence, rape and murder
- People are actually hurt in the production of violent porn
- Increase of reach of legal controls
- Development of filtering and tracking software
- Both feed into culture of control and surveillance

E-tivity: Online Protection

The goal of this e-tivity is to help readers understand that online security is primarily a matter of self-control and limitation. In considering the following scenarios, you will reflect on the ways this self-control and protection represents a significant shift from exclusively relying on crime authorities to deal with illegal activity. This task involves considering encountering several different illegal or criminal activities in online environments:

1   A phishing scam, in which a very convincing email ostensibly from their bank, requests their bank account details. How can we determine the bona fide or otherwise nature of the email? What steps might we take to counter the scam and to prevent it from happening again?

2   Identity theft: reflect upon your own online behaviour: what type of information are you making public, and in what type of sites? What dangers might this entail? What protective measures are you taking?

3   Trojan horse attack: in this scenario, you suspect that your computer
    has become a 'zombie', performing malicious tasks, e.g. spamming
    etc. How can you be sure that your computer is (not) affected? If
    affected, how are you going to proceed? How will you protect your
    computers from such attacks in the future?

4   Encountering online crime: in this scenario, imagine that while blog-
    ging or chatting you come across an illegal activity of some sort. Will
    you get involved? If so, how and under what circumstances?

5   Finally, you should reflect on your answers: what types of protective
    and defensive behaviour are you prepared to engage in? What are
    the common elements emerging? What are the implications of these
    protective measures?

Further Reading

The aim here is to explore the various dimensions of security, surveillance and safety as they emerge through our engagement with the new media. Greg Elmer's article highlights some of the new ways in which panoptic surveillance works through the new media, with users-consumers continuously supplying information which becomes immediately integrated into an information processing system, which then feeds it back to us. The results? Eventually, loss of differentiation and diversity, as well as 'punishment' of any transgressive behaviour. On a somewhat different note, Giselinde Kuipers reminds us that some cultural elements considered dangerous by some are in fact quite acceptable by others. This social construction of digital dangers must be kept in mind before we embark on any kind of moral crusade. Combining insights from surveillance theories as well as taking into account of the constructed-ness of many online threats, Torin Monahan's article, which looks at identity theft, shows that the neo-liberal paradigm leads to more self-monitoring, surveillance and self-discipline. On the other hand, Akil Awan's article shows the all-too-real danger of radicalization through jihadist media, and the multiple ways in which they have managed to legitimate themselves.

Elmer, G., 2003, A Diagram of Panoptic Surveillance, *New Media & Society*, 5(2): 231–247.

Kuipers, G., 2006, The Social Construction of Digital Danger: Debating, Defusing and Inflating the Moral Dangers of Online Humor and Pornography in the Netherlands and the United States, *New Media & Society*, 8(3): 379–400.

Monahan, T., 2009, Identity Theft Vulnerability: Neoliberal Governance through Crime Construction, *Theoretical Criminology*, 13(2): 155–176.

Awan, A.N., 2007, Virtual Jihadist Media: Function, Legitimacy and Radicalizing Efficacy, *European Journal of Cultural Studies*, 10(3): 389–408.

CHAPTER 7

NEW MEDIA AND JOURNALISM

Learning Objectives

- To understand the crisis of journalism and its socio-political implications
- To gain knowledge of the relationship between the internet and journalism
- To learn about the changes in the production, contents and consumption of news and journalism
- To develop a critical awareness of the future of journalism and the new media

Introduction

The rise of journalism in the eighteenth and nineteenth centuries as the Fourth Estate – alongside the other estates, Aristocracy, Parliament, and Church – signalled the rise of a more democratic social and political system in Europe and North America. While print journalism began life as a business, the business of selling news, it soon became a vehicle for ideology, opinion and political position taking. In *The Structural Transformation of the Public Sphere*, Jürgen Habermas (1989 [1962]) discusses the various historical shifts in journalism: the trade in news developed out of the system of private correspondences and for a long time publishers merely collected and organized news for a modest profit. Parallel to these early newspapers, 'men of letters' began publishing scholarly journals in the European continent and political journals and moral weeklies in the UK (Habermas, 1989 [1962]: 182). Habermas refers to this as 'literary journalism' – it was practised mainly by educated middle and upper-middle class men, who sought to publish their rational-critical reflections with the intention to educate readers. This kind of journalism did not make money and it was often financed by the authors themselves. Merging newspapers and literary journalism led to the creation of the editorial function in newspapers, which no longer limited themselves to reporting the news: they also sought to publish their opinions and comments on issues of common interest. The journalism that emerged had the function of being both a transmitter of news and an amplifier of public opinion: it continued in print the debates taking place in the various salons and it acquired an explicit political function. This was the principle of publicity which entails the subjection of political decisions and other matters of common concern to the public use of reason (Habermas, 1989 [1962]).

The third phase of journalism as a commercial enterprise took hold around the middle of the nineteenth century in Western Europe. This occurred because on the one hand constitutional rights had ensured freedom of speech and lifted excessive taxation, while on the other the rise of advertising promised good investment returns. The former allowed the press to become less partisan while the latter allowed it to concentrate on the business opportunities (Habermas, 1989 [1962]). Habermas quotes Bücher, who argued that under these circumstances 'the paper assumes the character of an enterprise which produces advertising space as a commodity that is made marketable by means of an editorial section' (1917 in Habermas, 1989 [1962]: 184). This meant that the success of a newspaper in selling advertisements depended on the kind of editorial stance it assumed and the numbers and demographics of the readers it attracted. This, for Habermas eventually led to the structural transformation of the public sphere, with journalism becoming the Trojan horse through which private interests invaded the public sphere.

While this is perhaps far from ideal for the public sphere, journalism as business thoroughly boomed. Newspapers acquired huge profits and massive power, especially in the early twentieth century with the rise of the 'press barons' – Lords Rothermere and Northcliffe in the UK, Hearst and Pulitzer in the USA – with the trend continuing until very recently. Rupert Murdoch, the owner-majority shareholder of News International was credited with winning elections in the UK, influencing media policies, and having a say in international politics, all the while making News International one of the most powerful and rich corporations in the world. Yet in the late twentieth–early twenty-first century, things began to change. Circulation figures show sharp drops year after year – for example August 2009 figures show an average 4.5% drop in circulation of all daily newspapers in the UK (*Guardian*, 2009), while the Pew Project for Excellence in Journalism reports a decline of about 13% in the circulation of US daily press, with a 5% fall just in one year (2008). Income from advertising dropped as well, with Pew reporting a drop of about 23%. It is estimated that in the USA, one in five jobs in journalism has been lost since 2001. At the same time online news sites report record numbers of visitors, with the (UK-based) *Guardian* and *Telegraph* online sites reporting an excess of 37 million visitors! It does not come as a surprise that theorists talk of a profound crisis in journalism, a crisis in which the new media are directly involved. This chapter will review the evidence and arguments regarding the crisis, and will then move on to discuss the changes in the production of journalism and the news, the contents of online news sites, and the audience or consumption side of online journalism.

The Crisis of Journalism

Although the word 'crisis' is overused, as Todd Gitlin points out (2009), it is, in the context of the current stage of journalism, a very apt term. In fact, Gitlin goes on to suggest that journalism suffers from many crises and he identifies no less than five. Drawing on the condition of American journalism, he argues that (i) the fall of circulation; (ii) the fall of advertising income; (iii) the diffusion of attention; (iv) a crisis in authority; and (v) the inability or unwillingness of journalism to question structures of power – all contribute to bring about a profound crisis of journalism, one from which it is unlikely to survive unscathed.

But what does it mean to be in or to face a crisis? The term goes back to Ancient Greece, in which *krisis* meant judgement in both its juridical and everyday sense. To be or to face *krisis* then implied that a disorder was introduced that needed rectification. *Krisis* was at the same time the outcome of this situation, which proposed ways of restoring the disorder. In this manner, *krisis* was inextricably bound to the notion of critique, as the latter includes both the identification of a problem as well as the remedial action (Brown, 2005). While in early modernity the terms critique and crisis became separate and quite distinct (Koselleck, 1998), we can hold on to their historical linkages, as they imply that any exit from crisis is precipitated by a thorough and clear critique. From this point of view, a crisis implies a certain impasse in which things cannot move forward unless decisions are made, and changes introduced – a crisis is therefore a hidden opportunity for changes, a means by which systems retain dynamism, and feed off critiques that introduce shifts that allow them not only to survive, but to move forward. The crisis of journalism therefore includes both a diagnosis of a series of problems that journalism faces as well as an opportunity for all interested parties to apply their judgement – critique – in order to enable journalism to move forward. But a clear diagnosis of the problems or crises is the first step towards the formulation of an effective critique. Reworking Gitlin's five problems, we can propose the following four crises that journalism has to deal with: time, money, autonomy and cultural changes. We will deal with each in turn and discuss the role played by the new media in these crises.

Time and Journalism

The ways in which new media have altered the conception of time have been discussed by Castells, who developed the notion of timeless time, as characteristic of the network society (Castells, 2000 [1996]; see also Chapter 1). Time is timeless precisely because it can no longer be divided, measured and compartmentalized into specific slots. In the network society, time is ongoing, continuous as the rhythm is 24/7. This rhythm has entered journalism and transformed the cycle of news into a 24/7 one. Time has always been a constitutive dimension of news – the very concept of 'news' entails a conception of time, as only the most recent events qualify as 'news'. But the flow of news followed the flow of time that suited each medium: the news cycle for newspapers typically ends in the early morning, while in television it follows the regular news broadcasts, for instance at 12, 6 or 10 o'clock – although some allowances were made for extra editions or breaking news. Equally important for news is the speed by which it is conveyed – this is indeed one of the most well established dimensions of the news (Chalaby, 1998). Consider, for instance, that the first Marathon was run by an Athenian warrior, who ran 40 kilometres to give Athens the news of victory in the battle of Marathon. But the new media have ushered in timeless time, and the news cycle became dislodged from these schedules – the new news cycle is constant, never-ending, with newness and speed of publication being the main criteria, over and above any other considerations. Thus, while the traditional news cycle allowed for some research, selection and processing of news, the continuous rhythm of timeless time leads to a pressure for constant updates with speed taking precedence over all else.

The implications of the rise of timeless time for journalism are multiple. The most important one concerns the shift from journalism as investigation or analysis to journalism as immediate publication. This in turn leads to shifts in journalism as a profession: the emphasis is placed on techniques for hunting the most recent news, rather than on painstaking research, in-depth analysis and informed commentary. Online news has to be updated several times a day, if it is to attract more readers, or to get the same readers to visit more than once. This is typically accomplished through harvesting anything as long as it is recent, regardless of whether its actual news value is minimal. The overall result is a decrease in the quality of news as well as a decrease in credibility, as there is no time to go through the necessary relevant checks on stories often resulting in extremely trivial or even inaccurate stories (Dimitrakopoulou, 2005). While the 24/7 rhythm associated with the new media has no doubt made this kind of competition for the newest updates an important part of journalism, the broader framework of competition within which journalism operates is the result of the logic that the market imposes (Bourdieu, 1998).

Journalism and the Market

Indeed the pressure of the market on journalism has been unmistakeable. As mentioned earlier, income from sales as well as advertising revenue and revenue from classifieds is in steady decline. Newspaper bankruptcies and closures are becoming increasingly common with some famous titles falling victim to the financial crisis. Hearst publishers, the owners of *San Francisco Chronicle*, said that unless drastic cuts are introduced, this historical newspaper is likely to close or go online only (*Time Magazine*, 2009). The *Seattle Post-Intelligencer*, also owned by Hearst, ceased its print edition in 2009, shedding more than half of its workforce. *Ann Arbor News* as well as *The Christian Science Monitor* followed a similar path, and are now only published online. But newspapers keep bleeding money, with the inevitable result that some will close for ever. *Time Magazine* reported in 2009 that the Boston Globe was losing $1 million per week, while the *Guardian* reported the closure of about 50 local newspapers in the UK. These trends are global, with newspapers suffering across the world.

On the other hand, a 2009 study by the Pew Project for Excellence in Journalism reported that journalism is still a viable industry, with US journalism earning $38 billion in 2008. Yet these profits were down 14% in the year 2008 and in the previous two years, revenues were down by 23%. Although still not experiencing overall losses, large media organizations sought to protect profits by cutting down expenses. Inevitably this meant cutting down journalistic jobs: Pew estimates that in 2008 about 10% of newsroom jobs were lost, with a total of 25% of all newsroom jobs that existed in 2001 lost. Yet these findings may actually reflect problems with financing journalism rather than an overall decline of interest in journalism.

Thus, the Pew study reports that in the USA, cable news thrived in 2009, which saw ratings increase by 38% and respectively profits rise up by 33%. Although to an extent this reflected the increased interest in politics – the mainstay of cable news – in an election year, audiences after the election still remained at a 5% higher level compared with the same month the year before. Moreover, traffic to the 50 top news websites rose by 24%, which, according to Pew is triple the pace of the year before. Although the number of newspaper readers (34%) and radio news audiences (35%) and television news audiences (39%) is still higher compared to online news consumers (29%) the gap is steadily declining. Interpreting the Pew study's findings it seems clear that people are still interested in news and journalism, but had a wider choice of media wherein to consume journalism. But the problem for actual journalism is that this diffusion of audiences or readers resulted in loss of revenue. One of the most widely cited explanations is that journalism is losing money because people are no longer willing to pay subscription fees, or for newspaper copies since they can get the news online for free. At the same time, although online news consumers increased revenue from online advertising actually flattened while in newspapers advertising declined (Pew Project for Excellence in Journalism, 2009). To an extent, this loss of advertising income reflects the uncertainty felt because of the financial crisis, although it also reflects the somewhat problematic relationship between the new media and advertising. Given the levels of interactivity, and the wide diffusion of users across many sites on the web, advertisers are unwilling to spend a lot of money online as the return might be minimal. In fact, according to a measure referred to as ROAS (return on advertising spend), the average online user is worth only about 35–55% of a newspaper reader, although it should be noted that this figure represents an increase from earlier years. Nevertheless, although in general, advertising spend on the internet has increased in the last few years, the lion's share has actually gone to Google and other search engines such as Yahoo!. In addition, while the new media, as we shall see, present exciting new opportunities for journalism, it has not found a way to 'monetize' them, or to secure a steady income from them.

In short, the financial crisis of journalism may to an extent be attributed to the internet, as on the one hand it has introduced a new medium for publishing the news, thereby fragmenting journalism's audiences, while on the other, it diverted advertising income, depleting journalism from its traditional source of revenue. The remedial actions taken by large news organizations seem to hurt journalism even more. The tendency to protect profit by cutting down on journalistic jobs resulted in the repetition of the same news across different journalistic outlets. At the same time, cost cutting has also meant the cutting of expensive news, which is mainly international news that relies on correspondents, as well as investigative journalism that requires a relatively high number of hours spent investigating. Again the result is a loss of diversity in the news, and an over-reliance on news or even on PR agencies for news.

Journalistic Autonomy

Although the financial crisis may have been precipitated by the new media, the very structure of journalism signalled potential problems. Structurally, journalism is located in-between the market, since it relies on it for survival; and politics, since it relies on it as its primary subject matter, although it is said to serve the people (c.f. Habermas, 1989 [1962]). However, the problem with journalism is that in fact it is dominated by the market, while in our media-saturated age, it tends to dominate other fields, such as science, law, politics, etc., dictating the conditions under which they operate. This is the argument put forth by Pierre Bourdieu (1998), who further holds that journalism with its emphasis on publicity and its links with the market, has taken over most other fields, which now have to operate on the basis of publicity as well, while also making them subject to the laws of the market. The price for journalism however was its credibility, precisely because it does not act autonomously but adopts the rules of the market. From this point of view, journalism ought to safeguard its autonomy and to be able to function as other professions do. Typically, for this to happen, journalism must set criteria for entry and costs for exit. Just as medicine and law control who enters the profession and how they behave as practitioners, so should journalism dictate what is necessary for one to be a journalist and how they must act as professionals.

But journalism never had clear criteria as to who qualifies as a journalist, as the profession was traditionally open to all kinds of people, regardless of whether they had university degrees or any other kind of training. This is probably because journalism does not actually posses a kind of specialist knowledge as such, although of course it requires drive and motivation, interest in the commons, as well as some kind of talent and knowledge of writing. In addition, laws on free speech are in essence prohibitive of any kind of prohibition from publishing or writing by people, regardless of their profession. This difficulty in professionalizing journalism is not necessarily a negative thing. Journalism has always stood in-between people and politics, and its remit is to serve the public good: as a closed profession, journalism would not be accountable to the people nor would they be able to write and criticize journalism. On the other hand, this kind of professionalization could perhaps protect journalism from encroachment either from the market or from politics, allowing it to perform its public duties according to a binding code of ethics and practices. If ever this was possible, the new media has made journalistic autonomy-as-professionalization well nigh impossible. The new media have opened up the floor to everyone who wishes to write or otherwise state their opinion, criticize, publish news or investigations, comments and analyses. Although most of these people may not qualify as journalists, they in fact perform more or less the same job, albeit perhaps not to the same standard. In any case, there is no means or indeed any justification to prevent them from writing or voicing their opinions and views. While therefore journalism's lack of autonomy might contribute to the crisis it is facing, autonomy-as-professionalization does not seem likely to produce a solution.

Cultural Shifts

A final aspect of the crisis of journalism relates to what we can term cultural changes. As we shall see later, these changes include a shift in the ways in which journalism is consumed. While traditionally people read their morning newspaper over breakfast or on the train to work, and they watched the evening news at 8 or 9 o'clock, the consumption of online news has introduced a new pattern which is mainly to steal quick looks at the headlines at several intervals while at work. Additionally, the new media have introduced an important shift from consumption of the news towards producing the news, or at least writing and commenting on news. As opposed to journalistic autonomy, what we see is a turn towards collaboration, collective effort and cooperative production. Notions such as wiki-fication and crowdsourcing reflect precisely this shift towards a collaborative culture, in which we rely on each other and build on our respective contributions.

Although these changes towards a participatory and collaborative culture have been around for some time now, traditional journalism has, on the one hand, failed to respond to these changes, while on the other, it seems to be in denial about them. The production of news, comments and analysis by non-journalists leads to an inflation of online news and information, resulting in effect in their depreciation and overall devaluation. At the same time, this participatory culture developed to the point of either replacing or considerably enriching journalism. All the while journalism seems unable to respond effectively, because it appears set in defending its traditional role as the sole mediator in-between politics and the people. Its focus seems to be on its glorious past of investigative and watchdog journalism, sending it in denial over the profound cultural changes since the heyday of traditional journalism.

The Internet and Journalism

So what is the relationship between the internet and the crisis in journalism? The relationship between the internet and journalism certainly seems to be a troubled one. On the one hand we find the internet featuring as the catalyst if not the very cause of the crisis: time, money, heteronomy, as well as cultural changes are all due to the advent of the new media. At the same time, the internet seems to have ushered in a new, direct relationship between people and the news, as well as between people and politics. As John Hall (2001) has put it, we have entered the phase of disintermediation – we no longer need journalism to mediate between us, the people, and politics or other events as they are reported directly by those involved and seen by people in an equally direct and immediate manner. This certainly raises important questions regarding the very role and raison d'être of journalism.

On the other hand, theorists turn to the internet looking for a solution to this crisis. For instance, Jo Bardoel (2002) considers that the internet will lead to the development of a new kind of journalism, online journalism, which will make effective use of the internet's main attributes, leading to a renewal of journalism. Interactivity, multimediality, hyperlinks, and the asynchronous nature of news and information online, offer new possibilities for journalism. These attributes allow journalism to extend in space, in depth and breadth through hyperlinks and hypertext, as well as through the participation of users, who may be found in different geographical locations. Moreover, they allow journalism to expand in time as the internet can operate as an enormous and accessible archive. Although Bardoel is optimistic regarding the future of online journalism, he points out that journalism needs to embrace and make full use of the attributes of the new media. Others, such as Pavlik (2001) consider that the internet restructures journalism across four dimensions. First, it changes the contents of journalism; second the skills necessary for journalists; third, the structure of news organizations and newsrooms; and finally, the relationship between journalism and all its publics, including the people, its sources, politicians and so on. These changes are seen in positive terms by Pavlik, who finds that this kind of restructuring of journalism will not only lead it out of the crisis, but to effectively improve it, modernize and democratize it.

So are we to hold the internet, and more broadly the new media, responsible for the crisis of journalism or should we regard them as potential saviours of journalism? Perhaps a way out of this somewhat polarized discussion could be found in the actual empirical changes we can observe in journalistic practices. The next section will look at how production, contents and consumption of journalism change in online environments. We will then return to the role of the new media in the conclusion.

Changes in Journalism

In mapping the changes in journalism, we can look at three different levels: the level of media organizations, in which we can trace the changes in the ways in which journalism is produced in online environments and more broadly the changes that have occurred at the organizational level. Second, the level of news contents, in which we can observe the changes in the ways that contents are structured. And finally, the level of the public, in which we can look at the changing patterns of news consumption. In all these we will draw on relevant empirical studies before trying to synthesize the findings and reach some conclusions regarding the relationship between the new media and journalism.

Media Organizations

This level mainly refers to changes in the various organizational routines and practices involved in producing the news, as well as to some broader changes that news and media organizations have had to adopt in the light of new technological developments. In general, new technologies have ushered in new modes of producing the news. But which has been the most important change? For many, the most important series of transformation in the production of news have been brought about by convergence. Convergence refers to the process which blurs the lines between media, even those point-to-point communicative media, such as the post and the telephone, as well as between mass media, such as television, radio and the press (de Sola Pool, 1983: 23). Ithiel de Sola Pool primarily referred to the convergence of media technologies which further allows the convergence of both media organizations as well as products. Thus media organizations, such as for instance newspapers, may convergence with online news sites, and/or with broadcasting companies. Their products, already digitized, can appear in audio, text or video form on a computer terminal, a television, or even a mobile phone. However, we can also observe a converging process in the internal processes of media organizations. Processes that were previously separate, performed by different people and perhaps even in different departments have now converged. Henry Jenkins (2006c) discussed convergence as taking place between production and consumption of media, arguing that we now find ourselves in the beginning of a new era in communication, which relies more on participation than on passive reception. In the first place, this kind of convergence signals only a need to revise our theoretical models of communication; it further implies, however, that there are a series of changes in the practices of media organizations, and in the ways in which media products are produced, distributed and consumed.

Convergence

The main question here therefore concerns the effects of convergence in the production, as well as in the distribution and consumption of news and related communicative materials. To begin with, convergence in news production points to technological developments, such as digitalization, which allows the same material to circulate and appear in different media platforms, without the need for any major re-writing or adaptation (Flynn, 2001, in Saltzis and Dickinson, 2008). The motto here seems to be 'write once, publish everywhere' (Saltzis and Dickinson, 2008: 3). In practice, this kind of convergence means that we can have just one journalist or news producer for all media platforms, as well as the same contents for all these media. At the level of distribution, convergence means that one device could combine all media. While initially the industry supported the idea of a super medium that would replace computers, televisions, radios and so on, today the dominant idea is that we can receive the same material in all kinds of platforms ranging from HD televisions to mobile phones. However, this in turn implies that these media that do not allow for this multi-platform kind of delivery may end up obsolete; the most endangered medium seems to be print, with newspapers and books considered too old fashioned and inflexible to survive in a convergence era. Different platforms that may replace them are currently in development, with the most popular currently being Kindle, Amazon's portable reader, which can download a vast number of books, replacing not only books but whole libraries. Finally at the level of consumption, convergence emphasizes the increased reader or better, user participation, and the role they play in the process of production. In practice, this means that a media organization must make sure to keep open channels for communication between media and their publics, as well as to offer users the possibility to get actively involved in the production of news, and to find ways to integrate the materials they produce.

Convergence is really appealing to most media organizations, because it allows them to extend themselves across different channels, gaining in growth and reaching more publics, while at the same time cutting their costs, something that is indeed necessary if they are to remain competitive. Saltzis and Dickinson (2008) argue that to ensure competitiveness and cost effectiveness, media organizations may follow four strategies. First, they move towards the organizational and technological integration of newsrooms; sometimes this entails the actual merging of different departments, and more often than not a few redundancies of staff judged to be superfluous. Second, they hire and use journalists or specialists that have knowledge and skills across all media; again, this may signal more job losses especially for those that specialized in only one medium. Third, the application of flexible and user-friendly technology at all levels of production; this clearly makes the production process more efficient. Lastly, media organizations actively pursue the extension of their services in new media; they seek to find ways to grow and to use more platforms.

In practice, convergence in news production is translated in the creation of a fully digitized newsroom that uses a server-based system of news and other media content production. This means that contents and news are available to all news personnel, who are then instructed by their editor as to how to deal with it. The UK-based *Daily Telegraph* is a good example of this kind of convergence. To begin with, *The Daily Telegraph* defines itself as a media group rather than a newspaper or a website group. Damian Reece, *The Telegraph*'s City editor, in describing the integrated newsroom reports that editors meet at the 'hub', placed in the centre of the newsroom and decide on the areas to work on. Then key editors, e.g. sports or media editors, decide which themes to pursue, and they have to design the news from the point of view of not only text, but also video and audio material, as well as to think of the hyperlinks that will appear in the online version (*The Daily Telegraph* Newsroom, 2007). These are just some of the changes taking place in converged newsrooms from a practical point of view.

More broadly, however, we need to understand convergence not only as a growth strategy but also as an important cost-cutting tactic. But does all this mean that convergence has spread across all newsrooms? The short answer is no. There is little doubt that convergence is one of the most clear and dominant trends, but it is not yet fully adopted. The reasons for this vary. There is some resistance from journalists themselves, who feel threatened and whose expertise and special skills in one medium are not recognized and appreciated. In addition, some organizations may lack the technological know-how as well as the technological means and may not have funds to invest in training and acquisition of the necessary equipment. This may be common in developing countries, which additionally deal with the problem of limited diffusion of broadband internet. A final problem concerns the quality of the news contents: can it be of the same high standard found in a single medium? Notwithstanding these issues, convergence represents the future of media organizations because of its increased efficiency.

Multi-skilling

From the point of view of journalists, they need to develop a range of skills across all media. This is the notion of multi-skilling, and while it is certainly a good thing, as people are allowed to learn several skills, it is in the end more ambiguous for the profession of journalism (Saltzis and Dickinson, 2008). For example, we have journalists that work for two or more different media, for television, newspapers and the web, and also journalists who record and edit their own footage. The BBC, under John Birt (1992–2000), encouraged its journalists to become multi-skilled, but in the end, this practice appeared to backfire. In general, in the BBC the impression was that a good radio journalist is not necessarily a good TV journalist. Currently, the BBC does not expect its journalists to produce contents for both media, although most have the skills to do it. From this point of view, they are interested more in the quality of their output rather than in controlling costs. On the other hand, to be multi-skilled is a positive attribute for most journalists, at least in the sense that it allows them a more in-depth understanding of the process of news production. Moreover, some kind of editing and processing of audio, video and textual material was always an informal part of the job of a journalist. But to have it officially as part of the job description further allows for more control over the final product that goes out there. Broadly speaking, however, the full implications of convergence on journalism are not yet known and cannot be fully appreciated at this stage. However, insofar as it is primarily experienced as a cost-cutting measure, convergence may be faced by resistance both by journalists as well as by publics, who may raise questions concerning the quality of converged journalism, and complain about the lack of diversity in the news. But this concerns more the actual contents of journalism, and we will examine these next.

Contents

We can divide the discussion of online contents in two parts. The first comprises changes that derive from the technical characteristics of new media, while the second derives from actual empirical observation of news contents. This distinction is necessary because for a relatively long time, theorists tended to focus on the potential offered by the technical characteristics of the new media rather than on the actual empirical reality of what people (and journalists) did online. At some point it is likely that the two will converge. Indeed, as more and more people go online, they use the new media in more imaginative ways, and they expect and demand more. On the other hand, content provision is shaped by the very pragmatic requirements of efficiency and cost cutting imposed by the logic of convergence discussed above, as well as more broadly by the economic environment in which journalism operates. It should be pointed out however that it is not a simple case of good but unrealized potential versus 'bad' reality; rather, the ways in which the technical characteristics of the new media have impacted online contents are more equivocal. As new forms arise we have not yet had the chance to assess them properly. At the same time, online practices dictated by the logic of convergence and efficiency might provide innovative and unlikely solutions to problems faced by online news and other media content. Thus, we shall review the new dimensions of online contents and the changes in the narrative structure of the news as well as some practices employed by news and media organizations, and other content providers.

Techological Affordances and Contents

In their discussion of the technical aspects of the new media, Lister et al. (2009) hold that their main characteristics include digitality, interactivity, networking, hypertextuality, as well as virtuality and simulation. Most of these may have important implications when articulated with online news and media contents. We can think of this articulation as giving rise to four broad new dimensions for online contents. We may list these as: hypertextuality, multimediality, interactivity and collective authoring. At the same time, these technical characteristics as well as their articulation with media contents introduces important shifts in the narrative plot of the news. We can summarize these as personalization and customization of news, games-as-news, and multi-perspectival news. These will be discussed in turn.

Hypertextuality can be defined as introducing a kind of database in which users have direct access not only to the information on their screens, but also to information associated with that on their screens (see Manovich, 2001). The resulting text, which combines both information that is present as well as that to which it is linked, can be understood as hypertext, and it is usefully thought of 'as a particular trajectory through a series of texts rather than merely the texts themselves' (Hall, 2001: 66). Embedding and using links, which essentially make up hypertext, constitute the basic components of online news and contents. Steve Paulussen (2004) argues that effective use of links is an essential part of good online news production because it enables journalists to include background and further information on the subject they are writing. At the same time, it can also be used to increase the credibility of the article since links can be used to back up and support claims made in the article, as well as to refer readers directly to sources (Gahran, 1998 in Paulussen, 2004). Links can clearly add depth and breadth to online contents, extending them in time and space, in ways unimaginable in print journalism, which had to deal with strict time and spatial limits. From this point of view, online contents need to be thought of as archives, raising issues of ease of access and search.

However, hypertext, and the embedding of links, places further demands on the structure of news stories. John Hall (2001) argues that the classic 'inverted pyramid' model of news, which prioritizes the most important bit of news first, and providing details and background later on in the article, is no longer appropriate for online news. But since hypertext with its extension in space and time requires a different, non-linear means of story-telling, online news items should be structured differently. Hall (2001) suggests a version of online news story that could be thought of as a matrix, containing different chunks of information ('lexia') which are all linked to the main story. In this manner, the news story we see on our screens is linked to a number of other relevant articles or information, often combining video footage, interactive charts, or other means for enriching the story and keeping readers interested. The embedding of other media formats into the story points to the next dimension of the news, multimediality.

Specifically, multimediality refers to the integration of different media formats, audio, graphics, pictures and text, into a single media form, made possible through the digitalization of the media (see Dahlgren, 1996; Paulussen, 2004). In the first instance, multimediality places important demands on journalists who need to be familiar with all these media formats, and subsequently decide which media format goes where. The clear linear structure of a print or broadcast news item is clearly disrupted by the convergence of media forms, and journalists need to develop new ways for integrating multimedia material into their news stories (see Hall, 2001; Pavlik, 2001). As we saw earlier, newsroom convergence transforms newspaper or broadcast organizations into multimedia ones – more often than not, websites of newspapers include video files, summarizing, extending, or taking further the text part of the article. It is important to note that these video files are produced in house on behalf of these organizations. Thus, while in the early days of the internet, broadcast organizations such as the BBC had an advantage in terms of multimediality, as they already had video footage to post online, more recently most online news sites embed video and audio files into their sites and in specific news stories.

Another dimension of online contents, perhaps one of the most important ones, is interactivity. While a lot has been written about interactivity, it is a difficult concept to define. Most definitions focus on users and their ability to have an impact on the contents and information they see. For instance, Steuer (1992: 84) defines interactivity as 'the extent to which users can participate in the modification of the form and content of a mediated environment in real time', pointing to the role of interactivity in empowering users and allowing them to have some control over contents. A second definition, by Newhagen and Rafaeli (1996), holds that interactivity refers to the process by which communication reflects back on itself, and responds to the past. This definition highlights the shift that has taken place in communication, a shift from a linear, monologue-style communication to a dialogical model, in which feedback is one of the most important aspects.

Interactivity places a set of further demands on online contents. Paulussen (2004), drawing on Massey and Levy (1999) suggests five parameters of interactivity that find or should find their way in online contents. These include complexity of choice available, responsiveness to the user, facilitation of interpersonal communication, ease of adding information, and immediacy of content. Complexity of choice refers to the available options to users, which should be offered at least a few choices, enabling them to pick and chose what they want from the site. Second, responsiveness to the user refers to the extent to which users' feedback is actually appreciated and put to use. The more responsive a site is, the more likely it is for readers to remain there, as they will have acquired a kind of personal relationship to it. However, more often than not, it is other users who respond rather than journalists or other content providers. This kind of responsiveness points to the third parameter, facilitation of interpersonal communication, which refers to the extent to which a site allows users to interact with one another. Again, this is an important dimension of online contents, as it enables direct, often synchronous interaction and communication among people reading the same information. Fourth, ease of adding information refers to the extent to which users are allowed to publish information. In recent years, the comments section adopted by most online news sites, employs at least the latter three, more 'communicative', parameters, as they allow for a kind of dialogue between journalists and readers, as well as allow readers to interact and communicate with each other, and to publish their own comments and information. From this point of view, the early awkward kind of limited interactivity has been replaced by a more complex model, in which user feedback plays an important role and is often integrated in the online contents. Often, the length of the comments far exceeds those of the news story or article itself, shifting the balance and centre from the actual news story to the users' views and comments on it. Finally, the issue of immediacy is a crucial one. The extent to which a site updates its contents is frequently a determinant of user for those users who, as we shall see soon, read the headlines at least four or more times a day. While traditional journalism, as we discussed earlier, had to deal with time limits, online news extend through time, operating on a 24/7 rhythm, which demands continuous news updates. The issue of interactivity, especially those aspects that emphasize the role of the users, points to the development of another dimension of online news, which we can term collective authoring. This dimension refers to, or rather dissolves, the distinction between authors and readers, as well as between journalists and publics. It depends on, and revolves around interactivity, but it takes it a step further. Rather than merely allowing readers or users to interact on the basis of more or less limited choices, collective authoring refers to the exclusive reliance on users for contents. Articles are written by users themselves, although some of these users may be trained journalists. This dimension refers both to cooperation in writing an article, as in Wiki news, as well as to writing and posting an article or news story in a news site. Clearly collective authoring seeks to capture the participatory dimension of news, and it refers to participatory news sites such as Indymedia, some news blogs, Wiki news, and so on. This dimension has important implications for online news, not necessarily positive: on the one hand, it raises issues of credibility, as often there is no first hand investigation or cross-checking of sources. Collective authoring may not necessarily use the professional guidelines employed by journalists. Similarly, it raises questions of ethics, as sometimes articles may undermine reputations or use erroneous and fraudulent information that offends or hurts people. Equally damagingly, not knowing who has posted an article precludes readers from knowing what kind of interests lie behind a story; thus, adverts may be disguised as news or research, as so-called advertorials are made to appear as bona fide news. On the positive side, collective authoring bypasses problems of access to the media, as it has a very low threshold for publication. Thus, while traditional media organizations use strict guidelines and 'news values' to help them decide what is news (c.f Gans, 1980), collective authoring allows for the direct and immediate communication of issues of concern.

News Narratives

But for many people, the most pressing question concerns the extent to which the narrative plot of online news has been affected by these dimensions and more broadly by the migration of news online. We can observe at least three kinds of changes: personalization and/or customization of news (linked to hypertextuality and interactivity); the increasing integration of games with news (linked to multimediality); and finally, a shift towards multiperspectival news (linked to both collective authoring and mulitmediality).

There are two sides to the personalization of online news and contents. The first has to do with the increased importance of personal testimonies, experiences and views in online news, while the second refers to the ways in which users plan their own trajectory through the news, picking and choosing those aspects they find most interesting and relevant for them. The latter aspect may be thought of as customization. In general the web and more specifically Web 2.0 applications follow but also impose a personalized way of relating to others and to the world around us. Priority is placed on the personal experiences users have, on possible testimonials and subjective perspectives of those who witnessed events. If we consider Twitter for instance, and the way in which it has been used in journalism then we can see the ways in which the news becomes more of a personal narrative. For example, the *Guardian*'s Charlie Skelton reported and tweeted his attempts to 'infiltrate' the secretive Bilderberg group when they met in Athens in 2009, writing his personal experiences of the kind of security and secrecy surrounding the group. While he never managed to get in, his reports and tweets were widely read and provide a good example of personal experiences as news report (*Guardian*, 2009). In general, we can conclude that there is a clear shift from objective, detached news towards more involved, 'lived' news, as experienced either by journalists or by members of the public who write about them.

One of the direct results of technological convergence and multimediality has been the ability to present news in different formats, including in 3D, but also with real video footage and sound.

This points to the idea of 'immersive news' (Pryor, 2002), an early idea, according to which readers will be able to immerse themselves in the news, hear the sounds and view the images of news events, often as they unfold. More recently, most news sites make extensive use of multimedia, providing audio and video files as well as interactive features, such as maps and so on. Users often have control over the use of these multimedia files, and they can chose when, if and how to make use of them. It is in this manner that online news resembles virtual reality, simulations and digital games. On the other hand, online and digital games have entered the 'real' world. An example of such a game is Peacemaker, which presents the situation in Israel and Palestine and offers users the possibility to make peace. Peacemaker makes use of real footage from Gaza and elsewhere, while it also informs users of the international treaties and other agreements that apply in the case of Palestine. Often the increasingly blurred lines between games and reality are the result of the convergence of the games industry with news organizations. For instance, Vivendi, which owns War of Warcraft, one of the most successful digital games, controls about 20% of NBC Universal, which in turn broadcasts NBC news and so on. When games and news meet, the emerging narrative resembles games in many ways: the use of interactive features controlled by users, the options for navigation offered to users, the adoption of so-called 'game mechanics', which include points systems and feedback, are all characteristics of online games which have entered the process of news reporting (see Muthukumaraswamy, 2009). While the use of features that essentially make news more interesting, especially to younger people, is not necessarily negative, there are some ambiguous elements in this kind of convergence. Nolan (2003) argues that often the emphasis is placed on impressive graphics without any corresponding emphasis in the essence of the story. In addition, games are played with the goal of obtaining some sort of reward, while in news the process of information provision is the ultimate goal – to provide rewards to users for consuming the news is ethically problematic (Nolan, 2003).

Finally, online news no longer adopts a single perspective, ostensibly that of objectivity, but rather includes several points of view (Gans, 2003; Bruns, 2006). This creates a kind of journalism that makes room for all kinds of views, even the most marginalized ones. Until recently journalism was produced in newsrooms by journalists considered authorities and experts in their job, who in fact wrote the news from their perspective, and through the adoption of certain professional news values (c.f. Galtung and Ruge, 1965). This, however, changed with the migration of news online, because it introduces a direct relationship with the public, who in turn demand that their preferences and viewpoints are taken into account. This essentially changes the structure of the news which can now be considered a dialogue. Dan Gillmor put it like this: 'if […] journalism is a lecture, what it is evolving into is something that incorporates a conversation and seminar' (2003: 79). The upshot of this development is that the news is never a finished product, but rather an ongoing process, which includes not only what journalists and other experts write, but also the comments, feedback and reactions of the multiple publics that consume the news. While this is certainly a positive development, we need to consider some of the problems associated with the adoption of a multiperspectival kind of journalism. The most pressing problem is that subjective views and opinions often found in the comments sections do not necessarily count as quality journalism. In addition, the existence of many viewpoints does not necessarily guarantee exchange of ideas and opinions, as readers may in fact stick to opinions and articles they agree with – this can contribute to a kind of cyber-fragmentation, in which people get to interact only with similar others (Sunstein, 2001). Finally, to what extent are all viewpoints really represented? Issues of power inevitably creep in and must be taken into account.

While all the above point to largely positive developments in terms of changes in the contents of online news, a word of caution must be inserted here. Although the online environment offers great possibilities for journalistic contents, in practice we often see a remarkable similarity of contents not across different news sites, but also across different media, both online and off. This can be explained by what is known as the repurposing of contents: this refers to the use of contents in different ways or in different media. For example, a book may be repurposed as an audio CD. This is in many ways the result of convergence, which allows the transformation of contents into different media formats. Media companies then find it easier and certainly cheaper to reuse contents, often only very slightly changed, rather than produce new contents altogether. Thus, a newspaper may be repurposing its contents online, blogs may be repurposing other blog posts, and video footage may be repurposed and reused in many different ways (Deuze, 2006; Erdal, 2009). Alongside content repurposing we have the practice of remediation, in which new media change but also reproduce the contents and practices of older media, while the latter adapt their ways to the new media (Bolter and Grusin, 1999). Deuze (2006) also argues that remediation is not always done on purpose or at least in a deliberate fashion, but people remediate contents in ways commensurable with their own interests and experiences. A good example of remediation is that of blogs, which remediate (reproduced in a changed form) print and broadcast journalism: they often reproduce articles which they then comment upon, frame in their own ways, or combine with other information to produce an altogether different product. The outcome of these processes is not clear: for some, there is an overall lack of diversity of news across all kinds of media (see for example Fenton, 2009), while others, like Mark Deuze, see promise in these new practices, and even the possibility for subversion in some instances. While we cannot determine yet which side is right, it may be useful to note that any changes in the contents of online news must be seen in conjunction with the practices of users, or those that Jay Rosen (2006) calls the people formerly known as audiences. To them we turn next.

Consumption/Use of Online News

The main questions here include the issue of the quantity of online news users as well as their demographics: who are consuming online news and how many are they? In general there are not a lot of studies on online users, but the studies we have indicate first that there is a steady increase of those who consume news online, and that their use varies as a function of age. Thus, while typically older generations used to read the morning newspaper and watch the evening news on TV, this is no longer common among younger people under 30 (Couldry, Livingstone and Markham, 2007). This points to the increased importance of the internet as a source of information and news. A 2008 study by the Pew Center on people and the press, conducted in the US, shows a steady increase of online news consumption in recent years (Pew Research Center for the People and the Press, 2008). Table 7.1 shows details of this growth, which on average was 24% in the decade 1998–2008 among the general population and a slightly less 20% among internet users. We can also see that men, those with higher education, and those aged 30–49 are more likely to go online for their news.

But what are the practices among those who consume the news online? The same study by Pew classifies online news users into four types. First, the traditionalists, who comprise about 46% of the news users (Pew Research Center for the People and the Press, 2008). They use almost exclusively traditional media and go online for their news less than three times a week. They are of a relatively low socio-economic background and most of them are women (52%). Then, there are the integrators, who are about 23% of the total number of users. They use traditional media, but also go online over three times a week, and they tend to be rather young and rather well educated. The net-newsers are the next category, who comprise about 13% of online news consumers; net-newsers rely exclusively on the internet for their news and information, and they are the youngest and best educated of all online news consumers. Finally, the disengaged, who make up about 14% of the sample, report that they are not interested in the news at all – they tend to be the least educated of the sample. Tables 7.2a, 7.2b and 7.3 offer a better idea not only of these types but of their behaviours online.

Table 7.1 A decade of growth in online news

Regularly go online for news*	General puplic			Internet users		
	1998 %	2008 %	Change	1998 %	2008 %	Change
Total	13	37	+24	35	55	+20
Men	17	40	+23	42	59	+17
Women	8	34	+26	27	51	+24
Black	8	24	+16	24	45	+21
White	13	38	+25	36	54	+18
18–29	18	42	+24	33	54	+21
30–49	16	45	+29	37	59	+22
50+	5	27	+22	32	52	+20
College grad+	24	61	+37	39	67	+28
Some college	16	44	+28	35	57	+22
HS or less	7	19	+12	30	39	+9

* Go online for news at least three days a week

Source: Pew Research Center for the People and the Press, 2008, http://people-press.org/report/444/news-media

All these tell us that there is an increased migration not only of news but of news readers online. As more and more people go online, their news habits change as well. In their study, Couldry et al. (2007) found that people actually consume the news through a combination of media, including offline, online and broadcast media. But the ways in which they consume the news are qualitatively different especially when compared to previous decades. Most online news consumption tends to be quick and superficial. The so-called news grazers tend to graze or merely scrape the surface, quickly glancing the headlines or checking their RSS feeders a few times throughout the day. So although people consume the news more often during the day, the time they spend on average reading the news has in fact decreased. This is an interesting finding which actually contradicts earlier positions which focused on hypertextuality and the extension of online news in depth. From the point of view of news

Table 7.2a

Regularly get *news* from...	Total %	Traditionalists %	Integrators %	Net-Newsers %	Disengaged %
Local TV news	52	61	61	35	30
Nightly network news	29	36	37	18	11
Network morning shows	22	25	27	14	15
News magazine shows	18	22	23	9	7
Sunday political shows	13	15	17	9	4
Daily newpaper	46	52	56	42	19
Cable news	39	41	53	43	14

Table 7.2b

Regularly get news from...	Total %	Traditionalists %	Integrators %	Net-Newsers %	Disengaged %
NPR	10	8	15	15	1
BBC	5	4	6	11	3
News magazines	12	10	19	16	2
Technology magazines	4	1	5	12	–
Business magazines	5	4	7	12	–

Source: Pew Research Center for the People and the Press, 2008, 2008, http://people-press.org/report/444/news-media

Table 7.3 Online news behaviours

% who regularly...	Total %	Traditionalists %	Integrators %	Net-Newsers %	Disengaged %
Watch news online	9	2	16	30	3
Listen to news online	5	–	10	19	2
Read political/ news blogs	10	3	19	26	2
% who...					
Sent news email in last week	9	2	18	27	3
Got news email in last week	18	8	32	39	8
Have RSS reader with news	7	2	13	19	3
Have used a news ranking site	3	1	5	10	1

Source: Pew Research Center for the People and the Press, 2008, http://people-press. org/report/444/news-media

organizations, this kind of user behaviour shows the necessity for frequent news updates, and less focus on analysis and commentary.

In general, from a user perspective, online news tends to have credibility issues, mainly when it comes from blogs or other non-established sources. This tends to privilege established media organizations and known brands, such as the BBC, CNN, Reuters and so forth. Thus, research has found that the majority of people who go online for news actually rely on mainstream media sources (Horrigan, 2006). More recently, the rise of social bookmarking engines, which classify the news according to tags offered by readers and according to readers' interest and ratings, have all the marks of a growing online trend. This is the trend towards personalization and customization of consumption, prioritizing users or readers and their interests, as opposed to what is considered to be big or important news. But this ordering and classification of news from below, as it were, shows that more and more of the news is becoming a collaboratively produced process, in which consumption can also be seen as production of news.

'Produsers'

This is precisely the argument made by Axel Bruns, who coined the term produsage to refer to this kind of consumption or use that is in fact productive. This idea draws on Alvin Toffler's (1970) idea of prosuming, which refers to the notion that consumers are also producers, and their input in the process is far greater than merely that of passive consumption. In its more recent uses, this idea refers to the production of user generated contents, and the ways in which they undermine the distinctions between news production and consumption. Bruns (2007: np) actually defines produsage as 'the collaborative and continuous building and extending of existing content in pursuit of further improvement'. For Bruns (2008), the term producing is no longer applicable for the kind of processes that occur online, because the term denotes a sharp distinction between those who produce and those who use or consume. This distinction is no longer applicable in spaces such as Wikipedia or Flickr, in which users upload and download materials, which they often reuse, edit or otherwise change. Clearly Bruns has in mind the open source or peer-to-peer logic which is found online – while this to some extent may appear romantic or even utopian, Bruns's term usefully points to a fundamental shift that has occurred online, which shows that the distinction between production and consumption in the media is no longer clear. Similarly, the term crowdsourcing (Howe, 2006), which refers to the application of open source principles to journalistic contents, shows the increased role and significance of collaboration in the process of making online contents.

Conclusions

This chapter explored the changes in news and journalism associated with the new media and especially the internet. Although we cannot really do justice to a complicated process that involves not only dealing with new media and technologies, but also with a shifting socio-political and cultural landscape, this chapter attempted to provide a general overview of some of the challenges faced by traditional media and journalism. Journalism is undoubtedly facing a crisis. This crisis can, to some extents, be linked to the new media. Time, finances, lack of autonomy and cultural shifts have all created issues for journalism and they are all linked to the new media, although the relationship is more complex than a uni-directional causal one, in which the new media are responsible for the crisis in journalism.

The changes in journalism can be thought of as spanning across three levels or dimensions: the level of media organizations and the processes of production, the level of contents, and the level of use or consumption of online journalistic contents. Box 7.1 summarizes these changes.

7.1

Summary of Changes in Online Journalism

Media Organizations and Production

- Convergence: the meeting and merging between different media and media forms
- The rise of multimedia journalism and the multi-skilled journalist
- Organizations think of themselves as multimedia rather than single medium organizations

Contents

- New media characteristics interacting with contents: digitalization, interactivity, hypertextuality, multimediality, collective authoring
- Narrative structure: customization and personalization of news, games as news, and multiperspectival news
- Practices: repurposing and remediation of contents

Consumption/Use

- Steady growth of online news consumption
- Users tend to be men, younger and better educated
- The rise of 'produsage' (Bruns, 2007) or the convergence of production and use in online environments

How might we assess these changes and the role of the new media? There is little doubt that the new media became a catalyst for journalism, which has to rethink its functions and the ways in which it operates in a new media environment. In many ways, the new media have ushered in a new mode of journalism, one which relies much more on collaboration rather than independent reportage, and which removes authority from traditional journalistic sources. Journalism must face up to the reality of these changes, and seek to readjust in a shifting environment while maintaining its specificity as journalism. Rather than seeking ways to regain its monopoly over news through paywalls, it has much more to gain from reasserting its role in democracy through creating synergies with the new media, through helping to give voice to the voiceless, enabling citizens to make informed choices, safeguarding the public good and checking political authorities. A relevant example here may be that of WikiLeaks. WikiLeaks, the celebrated whistleblowing site, may be thought of as an example of crowdsourcing: it invites people, political activists, civil servants, citizens, anyone with sensitive information they wish to make public but without facing any sanctions for bringing about this publicity. WikiLeaks then publishes the information without revealing the source. In July 2010, WikiLeaks published online a cache of US military records on the Afghan war, known as the Afghan War Diary. It included about 91,000 reports, spanning from 2004 to 2010, on military incidents, which revealed a high number of civilian casualties, and in general painted a bleak picture of the war and the coalition forces. In this manner, sources may publish information without fear of being compromised. On the other hand, sifting through thousands of documents is a Herculean task that citizens are unlikely to undertake on their own: here the contribution of professional journalists, who have the abilities, skills and time to read and summarize these documents, extracting their significance and their future implications, shows the continued relevance and need for professional journalism. Both technological innovation and traditional journalistic values can and should be put to use in the service of democratic goals.

E-tivity: Assessing Online News

This e-tivity seeks to further familiarize readers with some of the issues involved in online journalism, and to engage them in critically thinking about the changes in news cultures. For this e-tivity, readers will choose three different news sites: a news blog, an online-only news site, and the online counterpart of a print newspaper. Exploring each of these sites, readers should reflect on the following questions:

1   What constitutes good and bad practice in online news?

2   Who has written the news article? Is news authorship clear? Equally, is it clear that some news articles may have appeared somewhere else first?

3   To what extent are online news readers allowed to comment on news articles?

4   How should online news be evaluated in comparison to traditional news?

5   Which sites would readers recommend to other people and why?

6   In addition, readers can perform the following task: choose a mainstream news story as it emerges in the print or broadcast media. Then, trace the story as it is reported in the blogosphere. What are the differences and similarities in reporting? Which type of coverage do readers prefer and why?

Further Reading

The relationship between journalism and the new media is explored in the following articles, which study different aspects of journalism as it is articulated in the new media. First, Sue Robinson reviews three books which examine online news, offering a succinct account of what is important when considering the production and circulation of news on the internet. Similarly, the two articles by Eugenia Mitchelstein and Pablo Boczkowski focus on the processes of news production and consumption, reviewing past research in these areas and suggesting new ways forward. Finally, the dimension of contents is explored in the article by Neil Thurman and Ben Lupton, who looked at storylines from the point of view of convergence between different media.

Robinson, S., 2006, Journalism and the internet, *New Media & Society*, 8(5): 843–849.

Mitchelstein, E. and Boczkowski, P.J., 2009, Between tradition and change: A review of recent research on online news production, *Journalism*, 10(5): 562–586.

Mitchelstein, E. and Boczkowski, P.J., 2010, Online news consumption research: An assessment of past work and an agenda for the future, *New Media & Society*, 12(7): 1085–1102.

Thurman, N. and Lupton, B., 2008, Convergence Calls: Multimedia Storytelling at British News Websites, *Convergence: The International Journal of Research into New Media Technologies*, 14(4): 439–455.

CHAPTER 8

MOBILE MEDIA AND EVERYDAY LIFE

Learning Objectives

- To learn about the history and development of various kinds of mobile media
- To explore the spread and diffusion of mobile media across the world
- To understand the implications of mobility and portability for socio-cultural and political life
- To critically apprehend the significance of portability and the changes it has introduced in everyday life

Introduction

When the originators of *Star Trek* introduced the 'communicator' in the plots of the cult 1960s TV series, they had no idea of how popular their gadget would become some forty-odd years later. Figure 8.1 shows the 'communicator' while next to it is Martin Cooper, the inventor of the first mobile phone holding an early model, often referred to as the 'brick'. Cooper developed a prototype and made the first call on a handheld mobile telephone in April 1973, but the invention did not take off commercially until the 1980s. Given its price, the mobile phone was reserved only for the rich and/or the busy businessmen – the yuppies of the 1980s.

The revolutionary idea behind the mobile phone is that it provides a means by which people can communicate with one another regardless of their geographical location. They no longer need to be attached to certain fixed places in order to communicate. They can be in touch with others on a permanent basis regardless of where they find themselves. Perhaps because of this, the rates of diffusion of the mobile phone have been astonishing. But mobile phones are only part of the picture. Along with wireless internet and MP3 players, as well as pagers, mobile games consoles, digital cameras and global positioning or satellite navigation systems, portable media players and other mobile media, they represent a new and in some ways radical feature of

Figure 8.1   *Star Trek* communicator (left); on the right, Dr Martin Cooper in 2007 in Taipei

Source: left: photograph by David Spalding in Wikipedia, Creative Commons License. Right: photograph by Rico Shen in Wikipedia, GNU Free Documentation License and Creative Commons Licence.

the new media: portability. Perhaps for the first time in history, human beings are able to communicate with one another without the restrictions imposed by fixed devices. This portability further introduces an element of continuous availability, as mobile media make us available across boundaries of space and time. As such, they are definitely part of an increasingly mobile network society. But what are the implications of the portability of the new media? What kinds of changes have mobile media introduced into the fabric of social and political life? What broader conclusions can we draw? This chapter will attempt to sketch some answers to these questions. Beginning with the spread and diffusion of the various kinds of portable new media, it will move on to discuss their political, economic and socio-cultural implications.

Mapping Mobile Media

While there is little doubt that the mobile media have introduced a new radical dynamic into our relationship with the media, we should not overlook the broader historical context into which they are located. This section will discuss the three dominant kinds of mobile media: the mobile telephone, MP3 players and wireless internet. It will discuss their history and development and then map their diffusion across the world. Much of the power of these mobile media depends on their diffusion: the more diffuse they are the more their usability increases. In this sense, they represent a clear instance of the network society at work: as different networks of users emerge, the uses and advantages of these mobile media increase. But such increases in the diffusion of mobile media must be understood within the context of aggressive marketing, built-in obsolescence and media convergence. This section will follow the development and diffusion of these media with a view to eventually identifying their political, economic and socio-cultural impact.

Mobile Phone

While for many, the roots of the mobile phone may be traced to popular science fiction of the 1960s, the history of the mobile communicator is a longer one. In fact, we may trace the ancestry of the mobile phone back to Marconi and the invention of the radio in 1894: the mobile may be thought of as a combination of the radio with the telephone. Mobile radios could send and receive signals and were used experimentally in the US police force as early as the 1920s. These two-way radios were seen as only useful for the emergency services and there were no plans to exploit the technology commercially. According to Lacohée, Wakeford and Pearson (2003), commercial use of mobile telephones began in 1947 in the USA, when AT&T offered a radio-telephone service between New York and Boston. In 1956 in Sweden, Telesoniera and Ericsson created the first fully automatic mobile phone system, allowing calls to be made and received in a car, while using the public network telephone system. These phones were operating through the car's battery and were weighing no less than 40 kilos! The invention and spread of the transistor allowed for the development of lighter phones, but they were still too big to carry around. From then onwards the developments are typically discussed in terms of the different 'generations' of mobile phones: 1G, 2G and 3G.

1G is the first generation of mobile phones, which used analogue technology. It was based on the creation of a cellular network that included a series of base stations which in turn provide radio coverage over large geographical areas. This is essentially what allows mobile phones to operate. In 1977, AT&T received a licence from the Federal Communications Committee to start building a cellular network in the USA. Given the size of the USA, this was not an easy task. In the meantime, in the north of Europe, such networks were being developed since the late 1960s by the Nordic Mobile Telephone Group (NMT), and by 1981 Sweden already counted 20,000 mobile phone users (Lacohée et al., 2003). Spain, Austria, the Netherlands and Belgium used NMT services while bigger countries such as Germany, France, Italy and Britain designed their own systems (Lacohée et al., 2003).

In the late 1980s, as digital systems were gaining more and more currency, there was a move to combine mobile phones with digital technology. This led to the development of the second generation of mobile phones. 2G technology, at least in Europe, rested on the global system for mobile telecommunications (GSM), and provided several benefits to users. Contents, the

Figure 8.2 A 1980s 'brick' phone: Motorola Dynatac 8000x

Source: photo by Redrum 0488, Creative Commons Licence, posted on www.retrowow.co.uk

phone conversations, are digitally encrypted, which provides more accuracy and is more effi-cient in power usage, thereby allowing for smaller batteries, and therefore smaller telephones. In addition, 2G phones offered some new services, such as SMS text messaging, which became quickly one of the most popular features of the mobile phones. Digitalization led to the lower-ing of costs, and the mobile phone soon spread across the population. Lacohée et al. (2003) reported that by 2000, 50% of the UK population owned a mobile phone.

The third generation of mobile phones, the well-known 3G, was launched in the early 2000s, amid much hype regarding their potential. Governments in Europe auctioned off licensces and generated vast amounts of money – for instance, in the UK the licence auction generated £22.5 billion and in Germany £30 billion, which led telecoms companies to incur massive debts and eventually crashing, leaving thousands of people unemployed (Keegan, 2000). Licensee telecom companies were responsible for providing the infrastructure relying on optical fibres to ensure for more efficient and quicker data transfer. 3G phones allow for increased speeds and data capacity, eventually allowing for more services, such as digital photographs, MP3 files and multimedia text messages. At the same time, 3G (or perhaps 3G+) telephony offers innovative designs, such as phones with a touch screen as well as QWERTY keyboards.

The fourth generation (4G) is meant to provide quick and easy wireless access to the internet, as well as services such as video streaming. Some 4G phones, such as Sprint and Apple iPhone 4G, were released in the summer of 2010. However, for these phones to deliver their promises for internet speeds comparable to PCs, a new network needs to be provided, as at the moment hardly anyone in the USA has access to 4G coverage (Ludwig, 2010). Sprint's 4G will rely on the wireless network coverage service WiMax, an alternative to WiFi, while Verizon and AT&T are building 4G LTE networks to be launched in 2010 (Segan, 2010).

This brief history of the mobile phone shows its astonishing transformation from an emergency services tool to a sci-fi gadget then to a business and glamorous lifestyle accessory and finally to an everyday ubiquitous artefact. The diffusion of this artefact across the world and across different users is equally astonishing. Figure 8.4 shows the rates of diffusion for the years 1999–2008 in various geographical areas. In Europe, subscriptions in 1999 were covering about 35% of the population, a rate which more than trebled by 2008.

Figure 8.3   A genealogy of mobile phones (from left to right): Ericsson SH888 (1998); Ericsson T39m (2001); Sony Ericsson T610 (2003); Nokia 6630 (2004); and Nokia E70 (2006)

Source: Photo by Barnoid on Flickr, Creative Commons Licence, available at: http://www.flickr.com/photos/barnoid/299512707/

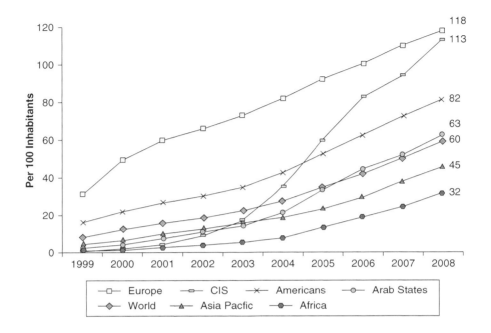

Figure 8.4   Mobile phone subscriptions 1999–2008
Source: ITU (International Telecommunication Union)

The rates above the saturation level of 100% show the so-called double SIM effect, whereby users own more than one mobile phone number. This in turn is attributed to the various uses of the mobile phone for business as well as for personal-social purposes. Nevertheless, there is a considerable degree of inequality in the diffusion of mobile technology. Globally this is clear in the subscription rates of the world in general. The average subscription rate for the whole world is placed at 60%. If we consider that Europe and CIS have rates of 118% and 113% respectively, and the USA about 88.5% in 2008 (Ortiz, 2008), then we can see that the rest of the world has much lower rates, which pull the overall rates down to 60%.

It doesn't come as a surprise to see that the lowest rates are found in Africa, with only 32% of the population having a mobile phone subscription. Perhaps for the same reason we can expect to see in Africa some of the highest growth rates: in the years 2003–2005 the growth rate was 550% and users grew from 54 to 350 million (Smith, 2009). Within Africa, the differences are vast, manifesting the huge diversity within the continent: South Africa has a rate of 100% while Burundi, Djibouti, Eritrea, Ethiopia and Somalia only about 10%. On the other hand, Uganda, with a penetration rate of 23%, has more mobile than landline phones.

Smith reports that Ugandan street vendors offer mobile access on a per-call basis, while they also invite those without electricity to charge their phones on car batteries. Given the lack of infrastructure in Africa, it is not surprising to find that people may have had their first telephone conversation on a mobile. According to Smith, at the end of 2007, the least developed countries had eight times as many mobile phones as fixed lines. At the same time, the number of fixed lines in the world has remained frozen at 1.2 billion since 2006 and even declined slightly in 2008. More broadly, research reports that GDP, income per capita, investment on infrastructure, low tariffs, and large user base are among those factors influencing the rates of mobile phone diffusion.

The high numbers of subscriptions in the developed world, however, shouldn't mask the various inequalities that exist. Figure 8.5 shows the different rates of mobile use among people of high, middle and low income. It is not unexpected to see that the higher the income the more the likelihood of a mobile phone subscription. On the other hand, we can also see the rates tending to become more equal in recent years. This is due to the wider availability of mobiles and the lower tariffs that exist.

In an article on the mobile divide, Stump, Gong and Li (2008), argue that the mobile phone digital divide often reflects a country's overall wealth, measured in terms of GDP and development levels. However, as the world is converging, we see the growth rates of mobile phone subscription reach the level of saturation both for developed as well as for developing countries. An additional divide has been an age one: while mobile communication is typically more

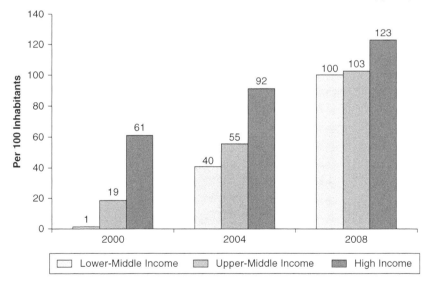

Figure 8.5   Income and mobile phones
Source: ITU

popular among the young, older people have now caught on, and most of them own a mobile phone. However, an age gap seems to be present when it comes to other mobile technologies, such as the MP3 player. To this we turn next.

MP3 Player

More than 30 years ago, in July 1979, Sony Corporation released the Sony Walkman, a portable cassette player with headphones – see Figure 8.6. While the technology for portable cassette players existed since at least the 1960s, there were no commercial applications until, as the story goes, Masaru Ibuka, one of Sony's founders and a frequent traveller, grew tired of dragging around a bulky cassette player. He asked Sony executives to design an ultra portable player with headphones. When the prototype was designed Ibuka brought it to Sony Chairman Akio Morita, saying: 'Try this. Don't you think a stereo cassette player that you can listen to while walking around is a good idea?' (Haire, 2009). The device was named 'Walkman', and proved a huge success: it sold more than 50,000 in the first two months of its release. Its unique combination of portability and privacy offered users the possibility carrying and listening to their music outside their home, but also in relative privacy.

As the technology moved on, and the digital replaced the analogue, vinyl and cassettes gave way to compact disks as storage devices. Portable cassette players were replaced by portable CD players – Sony introduced the 'Discman' – but their success was limited. The next revolution came when Apple launched the iPod in October 2001 – see Figure 8.7. While the portable CD player offered a means of listening to digital music, it was bulky and not very user friendly. The iPod had a revolutionary design, combining a small size with a friendly user interface and a great storage capacity of 5–10GB. Despite its hefty price tag at $400, and its incompatibility with Microsoft Windows, the iPod sold beyond expectations, and revolutionized the way in which we listen to music.

Figure 8.6   *The original 1979 Sony Walkman*

Source: photo by Grant Hutchinson, 2010 on Flickr, http://www.flickr.com/photos/splorp/4251803169/in/photostream/. Creative Commons Licence

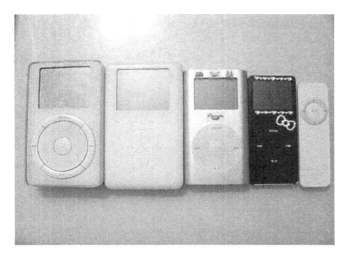

Figure 8.7   'All my iPods', from left to right, the iPod 5GB 2001, 20GB 2003, iPod mini 4GB 2004, iPod nano 2GB 2005, iPod Shuffle 1GB 2005

Source: photo and collection by Kelly Chan, posted on Flickr in 2005, available at http://www.flickr.com/photos/kelly_chan/51478079/. Creative Commons Licence

Figure 8.8 overleaf shows the sales of the iPod in the years since its launch. In 2009 alone, more than 60 million units were sold worldwide, but this is really the tip of the iceberg for MP3 players. While the iPod relied on its exclusive design and software such as iTunes, other electronics producers flooded the market with cheaper but ultimately functional MP3 players.

A relatively early study by the Pew Internet and American Life Project reports that by 2005, 22 million American adults, or 11% of the adult population owned an MP3 player (Rainie, 2005). This number is an indication of the spread of MP3 players, but the survey did not include teenagers under 18 years of age, who are very likely to own an MP3 player. In terms of the demographics of the (adult) users, they are more likely to be men (14%) than women (9%). In terms of age, 19% of those aged under 30 have MP3 players; 14% of those aged 30–39 and 14% of those aged 40–48 own one. The Pew study also points out that it is primarily the higher income people who are more likely to own a player, with almost 25% of those with an income over $75,000 having one. More recent findings from the UK reveal the rising extent of the diffusion of the MP3 player. A study by the Entertainment Retailers Association (2009) shows a slow but steady increase of the MP3 players bought in the UK, alongside a somewhat more impressive increase in the consumption of digital music.

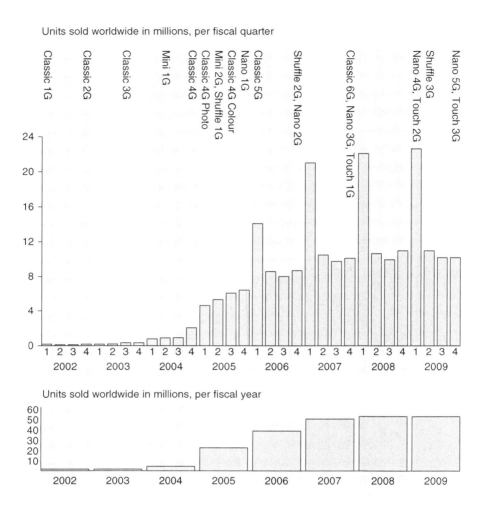

Figure 8.8 iPod sales per quarter and fiscal year

Source: Wikimedia Commons, Creative Commons Licence.

The dominance and continued proliferation of the MP3 player must be thought of as a given. Table 8.1 shows the rates of MP3 diffusion in the UK. The affordability, ease and increasing speed by which one can download music and other audio files, makes it an indispensable tool. But, more crucially from our point of view, the portability of the MP3 player has significant

Table 8.1 MP3 players in the UK

	2007	2008	2009
Total MP3 players (millions)	17.4	19.1	19.6
Personal penetration	29%	31%	32%
Digital single sales (in millions of units)	78	110.3	149.7

Source: Futuresource Consulting, Official Charts Company, in the ERA site at: http://www.eraltd.org/_attachments/Resources/yearbook.pdf

socio-cultural and to an extent also political implications. But before we go into these, we shall look at the development and diffusion of wireless internet.

Wireless Internet

The technology of the radio, as well as the mobile phone, relies on signals that get transmitted through the air rather than through cables. Indeed, in the early twentieth century, radios were called wireless. Broadcast and electronic media, such as the television, made the 'wireless' appear old-fashion. But the rise of the mobile phone soon changed this, as it opened up the road for the establishment of wireless internet connections. In terms of technology, wireless networks operate on a grid that divides geographical areas into smaller cells, which can cover a maximum of 250 square miles. As people move across the city, they get out of one cell's frequency and enter another. Each cell has a base station, comprised of a wireless antenna, which can link callers to the internet. Because of the relatively limited geographical area covered by these antennas, they need not be mounted on tall buildings; most are no bigger than a stereo speaker. Rural areas, however, require taller antennas as larger geographical areas need to be covered. (For more detailed technical information, see the site of CTIA, the International Association for the Wireless Telecommunications Industry at www.ctia.org.)

In short, wireless internet is a way of using radio waves instead of cables to send and receive internet data. Such waves were used in broadcast media to transmit radio sounds or TV pictures. But, unlike radio and TV, wireless internet is typically used to send signals only over relatively short distances with low-power transmitters. Then other transmitters pick up the signals and transmit them further and so on. This network organization is typical of both mobile and internet wireless connections. Wireless signals are received by a device called a router – see Figure 8.9 – which can send signals to any computer within a range of about 90 metres. The area covered by the router provides internet access to any computer within this range and is known as a hotspot. While routers such as the one in

Figure 8.9   Linksys WRT54GS wireless router

Source: photo by Pedro Lourenco Venda, posted on Flickr on 9 Aug, 2009, available at: http://www.flickr.com/photos/pjvenda/3863641126/. Creative Commons Licence

Figure 8.9 provide wireless connectivity at home, their public equivalent, governed by the protocol IEEE 802.11, is called a WiFi Hotspot.

The term WiFi – short for wireless fidelity – is in fact a trademark, belonging to the WiFi Alliance, and is used to describe all products that are compatible with the IEEE 802.11 standards. Often understanding wireless internet as a public service, university campuses, airports and city centres offer wireless access to visitors and clients. While a number of cities wanted to provide wireless access to cover all their citizens, their plans proved difficult to fulfil. Obstacles are not only or primarily technical: for instance, New York provides free access through free hotspots in parks and other public places through municipal and non-profit groups like NYC Wireless; people can also use paid-for services offered by commercial outposts such as Starbucks. On 15 April 2010, however, Cablevision, Comcast and Time Warner made an agreement offering their customers access to any of the wireless areas they cover, thereby extending the reach of the New York WiFi network. Existing customers of these companies will now be able to roam across the WiFi hotspots owned by these companies without any additional cost: all they need to do is use their password. Other cities similarly offer a variety of free and paid-for hotspots but the New York example shows the increasing value of WiFi internet as a commodity. Table 8.2 shows some recent statistics from April 2010.

On the other hand, wireless networks as a whole are lowering the costs of internet connection as they do not require expensive network equipment and cables to be laid out. From this point of view, they are lowering the cost of the internet across both richer and poorer countries. Additionally, in countries of the developing world, which often lack a

Table 8.2 WiFi hotspot statistics, 12 April, 2010: 294,205 free and paid-for WiFi locations in 144 countries

Top ten countries

Rank	Countries	Locations
1	United States	69,553
2	China	37,690
3	United Kingdom	26,935
4	France	26,631
5	Germany	14,848
6	Russian Federation	14,708
7	South Korea	12,816
8	Japan	11,939
9	Sweden	7,525
10	Switzerland	5,545

TOP ten location types

Rank	Type	Locations
1	Hotel/resort	67,583
2	Other	54,183
3	Cafe	42,097
4	Restaurant	41,395
5	Public space/public building	22,436
6	Store/shopping mall	15,324
7	Office building	10,265
8	Hotzone	6,670
9	Pub	5,078
10	Airport	3,547

Source: JiWire, http://v4.jiwire.com/search-hotspot-locations.htm

telephone cable infrastructure, wireless internet can be the only way in which they can have access to the network. In general, wireless internet diffusion is proportionately higher in the developing world due to several factors. Subramanian et al. (2006) list lower costs, ease of deployment, and reliable substitute for local communications infrastructure as three of the main factors for the success of wireless internet in developing regions. Specifically, wireless internet access is much cheaper than having to lay down new cables and telephone lines. They require a relatively small capital investment, allowing local entrepreneurs to set them up thereby supporting local economies. Similarly, wireless networks are much more easily deployed at a local level, because they do not depend on a tower or other means of expensive signal transmission, such as satellite. Networks built on the unlicensed spectrum are providing an easy and economic solution for local communities and grass roots organizations. Finally, wireless internet often offers an alternative means of communication, in the absence of reliable telephone lines. In short, wireless internet offers both a kind of public service, by lowering the costs of access to the internet, as well as a fertile ground for commercial use and profit making both for small, local entrepreneurs as well as for larger corporations. This discussion of three examples of wireless artefacts and technologies will turn now to examine the wider socio-cultural and political implications of mobility and portability.

Mobile Media: Politics and Society

Are mobile media more or less democratic than other media? What might their contribution to politics be? What kinds of new social relations do they give rise to? How do they alter existing social relations? What is their impact on cultural processes? These are some of the questions that have arisen following the growth of mobile media. The responses to these questions have been variable; different theorists concentrate on different aspects, making it very difficult to develop a sort of theory of mobile media. In this section we will try to group together some relevant findings and arguments, positing that, as with the new media more broadly, the positive potential of mobile media for politics, culture and society may be squandered or prevented due to systemic constraints. But this requires us to examine first what this potential is and second the constraints imposed on it.

To begin with, the very argument that mobile media bring about societal changes points to a kind of deterministic position, whereby these kinds of media determine societal and political processes. We must therefore clarify here that, following Castells et al.'s (2007) work on mobile media, we consider their use as a social practice. It is not therefore the media as such that 'cause' any kind of effects, but rather their use, as embedded in existing socio-cultural and political contexts. At the same time, as Castells et al. put it, technology extends the domain of what is feasible (2007: 238). It opens up new opportunities that may or may not be picked up by users. It is therefore the combination of technological 'affordances' – or what the technology of mobility in this instance 'creates', what kinds of 'action possibilities' it offers – and the distinct characteristics of the socio-cultural and political environment in which the use of mobile media takes place. Katz and Aakhus (2002) refer to something similar using the term 'apparatgeist' or the spirit of the artefact: for them, to understand mobile media we must understand the kind of 'spirit' or 'essence' the technological artefact has, and the various but specific ways in which it interacts with its environment.

Mobile Politics

In political terms, the articulation of the mobile media with the political environment offers new possibilities for democratization (Rheingold, 2002; Agar, 2003; Lasica, 2008).

For others, such as Yochai Benkler (2006), the commercial mobile media are juxtaposed to the open and free character of the internet. Who is right? Perhaps there is no right answer here – rather we must see the mobile media in a tension with existing power structures – but this tension does not always or necessarily lead to more democracy, more equality and justice.

For Yochai Benkler (2006), open wireless networks alongside other forms of the new media have opened up new opportunities for the creation and exchange of information, and have increased the role of non-market and non-proprietary production. But for this collaborative framework to lead to more democracy, the network and its infrastructure must be governed not by commercial and market-based interests but by a commons type of governance (Benkler, 2006; Goggin, 2008). Benkler juxtaposes wireless networks to the mobile phones, which are seen as seeking to impose a market-driven regulatory scheme on networks that should be free. In other words, given that telecommunications networks are controlled by telecommunications companies, they clearly control access to these networks. For Benkler, the new media must be governed as a commons, that is, in a manner similar to natural resources to which all of us have a stake (c.f. Lessig, 2001). But since mobile phones, the actual devices, their applications and technologies are all controlled through patents, and other means of ownership, the idea of networks as a commons is seriously undermined. Moreover, this is now spilling over to other new media, such as the MP3 players as well as wireless internet. The commercialization of the new media commons may prevent them from fulfilling their democratic potential. On the other hand, theorists such as Goggin (2008) suggest ways which will make mobiles part of a new media commons. More broadly, this concerns the governance of mobile networks and not their potential and actual contribution to politics. Do they contribute to an increase or deepening of democracy? If so, how?

Agar (2003: postscript) argued that the mobile phone is seen in various ways: as 'a way of rebuilding economies in eastern Europe, an instrument of unification in western Europe, a fashion statement in Finland or Japan, a mundane means of communication in the USA or an agent of political change in the Philippines'. But through all this, he highlights a common theme emerging. This, for Agar, has to do with the development of horizontal social networks that, in political terms, are critical of central authority. This is because the mobile phones of today follow upon the culture of the CB radios, which created alternative communication networks in the 1970s, as well as the early use of the mobile phone for the organization of rave parties in the UK of the early 1990s. It's not, though, the case that mobile telephony is inevitably opposing centralized power. Rather, it is in constant tensions with it. While mobile phone users may use their phone in ways incommensurable with established power, the multinational corporations that control mobile services are very much part of this establishment. Examples abound: the use of mobile phones for political organizing and coordination is notorious. The most well known example comes from the Philippines, where the ousting of Joseph Estrada was largely due to protests organized and coordinated through SMS messages (Castells et al., 2007). In other examples, mobile phones have been used in, among others, the Seattle WTO protests in 1999, in Gleneagles for the G8 summit in 2005, and the Athens riots in December 2008. The rise of internet-enabled mobile phones and the synergies created between mobile phones and social media add new political dimensions to mobile telephony.

On the other hand, authorities may seek to control such organizing – for example, following the riots in Athens, the government made name registration for pay-as-you-go mobiles compulsory. The anonymity of a mobile phone is no longer possible in this context. In other cases, mobile phone text messages have also been used as a form of direct political marketing, targeting prospective voters with direct SMS messages. Meanwhile, in China, text voting on TV talent shows has been banned, perhaps because it may encourage people to demand more democracy (Lee, 2007). Agar (2003) further refers to the example of the Vatican, which refused to host mobile phone masts, as they were 'alien to the sanctity of the church'. At the same time, the Catholic Church seem to have no problem accepting the Vatican radio masts – a symbol, argues Agar, of broadcasting and its centralized authority and hierarchy. In all these we see the tensions between mobile phones as a bottom up, grass roots practice and attempts by politicians, governments and corporations to control them.

Howard Rheingold (2002) refers to this kind of organizing as a smart mob, or an intelligent swarm: mobile phones encourage a horizontal, network-style organization, characterized by the lack of a central authority and by the autonomy of the 'subunits' that make up the network. Such smart mobs are driven by the 'nonlinear causality of peers influencing peers' (Rheingold, 2002: 178). In other words, individuals using mobile phones remain autonomous, but their choices, motives and decisions, influence the rest of the network to which they are connected; in this manner, the mobile network can exist and have a shape without being led by a central authority. Rheingold's perspective on mobil(e)zation – the term is by Joss Hands (2010) – although interesting is not without its problems. Hands (2010) argues that it still operates within the confines of liberal individualism, with politics seen as the outcome of individual preferences and decisions – and underneath it all, one can see the maximization of profit, utility, or reputation as the prime motivator. From this point of view, the smart mob still operates within the logic of the market: indeed, this is evident in the sometimes successful attempts by advertisers to utilize smart mobs for marketing purposes. But, more broadly, the political implications of the mobile phone may be seen as providing an alternative form of political organizing that is more egalitarian, direct and personal than other mediated forms.

Digital cameras, often embedded in mobile phones, have also fed into this articulation of mobility and politics. The most widely known political use of digital cameras is that of witnessing. People have the opportunity to act as witnesses of a political event, which is recorded by digital cameras and subsequently posted online or sent to mainstream broadcast media. In a recent case in Athens, a witness recorded soldiers and other members of the Greek military shouting racist and anti-immigrant chants; the short video was then sent to a newspaper which posted it online, resulting in severe sanctions for those involved (Enet, 2010). In other cases, videos or photographs taken by citizens have disputed official accounts of events by the authorities: an example here is Ian Tomlinson's death in the G20 protests in London in 2009. A video showing that Tomlinson was attacked from behind by a policeman while he was just walking past, was shot by a New Yorker who happened to be present (*Guardian*, 2010). The possibility offered by mobile media not only to witness but to immediately record events as they happen introduces a shift in the mediation of politics: rather than decided upon and recorded by mainstream media alongside politicians, politics is becoming more grass roots, mediated by citizens-witnesses who happen to be in a given place at a given time when a politically significant event takes place. This witnessing, recording and crucially also publishing by citizens with mobile media, feeds into this model of a more direct or 'disinter-mediated' (Hall, 2001), more personalized and experiential kind of politics – a kind of politics that is also less hierarchical and more diffused, since the power for the mediation of politics is now shared by citizens with mobile media. Can this type of politics be considered more democratic? It seems that it is not politics as such that is democratized by mobile media in the hands of citizens, but its *mediation*. In other words, while, at least formal, politics remains as hierarchical and closed as always, its mediation, or the ways in which we acquire information and form opinions about politics, can be seen as democratized in the sense that it is no longer the exclusive monopoly of mainstream media, but is shared by citizens. Clearly, though, we must insert here a caveat: while citizens can and do make use of mobile media for political purposes, they cannot be seen as equivalent to mainstream media – the latter still have a greater control over visibility and setting the agenda, given their resources and professionalism.

Mobile Society and Culture

But it is in society and culture that mobile media have brought about the most profound changes. While there are many descriptions and examples of changes associated with the mobile media, it is difficult to order them and identify the most important ones. From a social point of view, as we shall also see in other chapters, the crucial aspect is that of living or being together. From a cultural point of view, of crucial concern is the ways in which creativity, knowledge and cultural output is changing. When it comes to the former, Castells et al. (2007) argue that the main outcomes of the use of mobile media include the enhancement of individual autonomy, the creation of networks of choice, the blurring of the social context of individual practice, and the association of identity markers with mobile media. To these we may add Katz and Aakhus' (2002) arguments on the rise of tensions between public and private. Considering these together we may conclude that mobile media contribute to the rise of a personal communication society (Campbell and Park, 2008), or as Castells et al. put it, a strengthening of the culture of individualism. When it comes to mobile culture, Castells et al. (2007) note that mobile media give rise to instant communities of practice, while also the blurring of production and use is also clear here: users produce new contents and services, either in the form of shifts they introduce in the language or in developing mobile phone applications, which can be downloaded and used. Additionally, mobile media such as

MP3 players create new forms of experiencing and storing cultural output such as music, while the customized mobile artefacts display, in some ways, the dazzling creativity of both users and mobile media designers. In cultural terms, therefore, we may argue that mobile media lead to a renewed cultural creativity but not one without any costs: associated with consumerism, privatized consumption and display rather than the avant garde, mobile culture does not seem to share the radicalism and criticality of other forms of art. As with mobile politics, the picture that emerges here is equivocal.

While the diminished importance of locality is a development common to both globalization and the network society, mobile media seem to further amplify this trend. Castells and his colleagues (2007) write that mobile media enhance individual autonomy primarily vis-à-vis space, time and cultural norms. Whereas other media allow us to communicate across distances, mobile media allow us to completely detach ourselves from locales and communicate at will and across different localities. We are no longer connected by wires that seek to fix us at one place, but through the various wireless networks that have developed, communication is possible across most of the world regardless of where we find ourselves. Moreover, the wide availability of mobile technology across space has allowed us more and more autonomy over time as well: communication is no longer limited to certain times, but as with other new media it can take place on a 24/7 basis. Additionally, the very concept of time changes in and through mobile media: for instance, Katz and Aakhus (2002) refer to mobile phones as leading to 'perpetual contact', while most of us will have experienced empty time – e.g. waiting for our train or bus – filled in through texting or otherwise fiddling with our mobile phones or MP3s. At the same time, this constant movement results in increased autonomy vis-à-vis socio-cultural norms specific to places: the conventions of communication and inter-personal contact are changed through mobile communications, which allow people to transgress them precisely because they move from space to space.

It must be noted, however, that this kind of autonomy vis-à-vis time and space varies as a function of technological infrastructure (after all, not all spaces are covered by wireless networks); affordability (after all, not everybody can afford expensive devices and subscriptions); and literacy (after all, not all of us are equally well-versed in the ways of mobile communication) (see Castells et al., 2007). Assuming, however, that these parameters – and others, such as the legal environment and regulations – are present, then mobile media enhance the control of the subject of communication over the process of communication (Castells et al., 2007). Campbell and Park (2008) argued that since the individual is placed at the centre of the mobile communicative process we can speak of the rise of a personal communication society: this refers to the idea that society revolves more and more around interpersonal communication, which is seen as the evolution of the mass mediated and network society. While the network society introduced the concepts of space of flows and timeless time to refer to shifts in our understanding of space and time, mobile media introduce a variation in these, which now are personalizing this experience of space and time. Mobile networks allow people to become autonomous nodes, independent of space, in freeing them from the confines of specific places and allowing them to communicate with their personal networks whenever they wish. This, however, produces an effect which Gergen (2002) described as absent presence: people are there, present, in a given space, but at the same time they are absent as they communicate not with those they see, but with others that may be many miles away. This kind of dislocation is in many ways characteristic of mobile media. In his work on the Walkman and subsequently the MP3 player, Michael Bull (2006) found a similar effect: people with their headphones on elect to cut themselves off from their environment, they are physically there but at the same time they are not really present.

The notion of timeless time is also amplified through mobile media. The idea of constant touch, or perpetual contact, as Katz and Aakhus (2002) put it, refers to the ways in which mobile media have enabled us to stay in touch with others regardless of time. Time is no longer divided into personal, work-related, leisure and so on; rather, we can get in touch whenever it makes sense for us. But this perpetual contact and more broadly the 'personal communication society' have also introduced a series of changes in the ways in which we connect to others. To begin with, Katz and Aakhus (2002) describe how the mobile phone has introduced new points of orientation in our discussions: phone conversations typically begin with 'where are you' as opposed to 'how are you' – our new home seems to be within ourselves. Second, it has added to the tensions between public and private: while a telephone conversation is private – indeed, it is legally protected as such – it takes place in public spaces – most of us will have overheard fragments of private telephone conversations taking place on buses, trains or in restaurants. Similarly, while most of us had to work in offices, mobile media and specifically wireless internet mean that we can work from home, from a coffee shop, airport and so on: work and leisure are no longer as rigidly separated, but seem to converge. On the other hand, the idea of constant connectivity associated with mobile media has certain oppressive qualities, particularly the dissolution of boundaries between work and leisure, the possibility of surveillance, where your exact location is always known, and your phone calls recorded, while being out of reach is no longer easily achieved. The new excuses used to account for being out of reach, such as 'my battery is low' or 'I have signal problems', indicate the need to account for or justify not-communicating.

This, in turn, has given rise to a new set of ethics, rules and regulations regarding the use of mobile phones. For instance, Campbell (2006) reports that students and faculty members are disturbed by and dislike the use of mobile phones in the classroom or lecture theatre, supporting the formal ban against them. Sorensen (2006) reports some emerging mobile phone norms, such as, for instance, 'it's rude to speak on the phone when with another person'. Other studies refer to norms in different countries. For example, Ito (2005) in Japan reports that it's rude to take voice calls on the underground, and Yoon (2003) reports that Korean schoolchildren consider it unacceptable to use their phones in class. Similarly, the use of cameras in the public domain is covered not only by informal rules but also laws against terrorism as well as laws protecting our privacy. The development of this kind of etiquette but also a set of regulations reflects the need to embed mobile media in our everyday lives in ways that require mutual adaptation of the socio-cultural environment to mobile media use and vice-versa.

Another significant implication here concerns the use of mobile phones by young people, who strive between becoming autonomous and the continuous monitoring of their parents. Indeed, while the mobile phone was initially introduced to young people as a means for becoming more independent while being safe, it is increasingly becoming a tool for parental control with some parents continuously monitoring their children. The use of mobile phones by young people has had other, parallel implications – these concern the creation of youth subcultures and the associated development of a mobile phone vernacular, used primarily in text messages. The changes in language take us to the domain of culture, and the ways it has changed in conjunction with the rise of mobile media. To be sure, we have all come across some fairly incomprehensible abbreviations in the style of text messages, but it seems that these are becoming like a second language for young people. While there exist a lot of criticisms aimed at this emerging language or dialect, mainly centring on its paucity, it must also be seen as an indication of the creativity of young people. Thurlow and Brown (2003) argue that text messaging is in fact serving the socio-linguistic principles of brevity and speed, paralinguistic restitution and phonological approximation, showing that young people's messages are both linguistically unremarkable and communicatively adept. Thurlow and Brown show that messages are intended to be short and quick, but that senders also make sure they compensate for the lack of tone and other linguistic cues that would clarify to readers the meaning of the message – the use of capital letters, e.g. 'LOL', or multiple punctuation, e.g. 'wow!!!' indicate emphasis. Finally, the language of text messaging is based on principles of phonological approximation – that is, the abbreviations are based on sounding similar to the actual words. For example, txt, for text, l8r (later), 2morrow, evr1 (everyone) and so on are phonetic renderings of everyday words. These tactics, argue Thurlow and Brown, show that texting is part and parcel of everyday life, woven seamlessly into the communicative environment of young (and not so young) people. '…[T]ext-messagers', Thurlow and Brown conclude (2003: np) 'manipulate conventional discursive practices with linguistic creativity and communicative competence in their pursuit of intimacy and social intercourse.'

Language is not the only creative practice associated with mobile media. Customized colours, 'skins', applications, ringtones and phone accessories show the embeddedness of mobile media in everyday contexts, as well as their links to identity formation. Through choosing a mobile phone or MP3 model, its colour, its 'skin', but also its contents, ringtones, playlists, wallpapers and so on, mobile media serve as identity markers, much in the same way as clothes or other forms of cultural consumption mark people's identities. MP3 players, in particular, offer a good example of the links between identity processes and mobile media. Michael Bull (2005) argues that mobile listeners create their own auditory and aesthetic environment, which isolates them from their ambient environment. Thus, contrary to the always in touch, always connected sociality of the mobile phone, MP3 players operate on the opposite premise. Seeing someone wearing MP3 headphones means you cannot approach them, and that you mustn't speak to them, as they are not socially available.

Bull (2005) further argues that MP3 players offer unprecedented opportunities for controlling one's experience of time and space. As he puts it, MP3 users: 'achieve a level of autonomy over time and place through the creation of a privatised auditory bubble' (2005: 344). This, for Bull (2005), has two related implications: First, people create and control their own environment, resisting imposed auditory experiences, such as muzak etc. Second, they re-orientate their spatial environment on the basis of their moods and aesthetic preferences – people become wrapped up in their own personalized experiences, brought about by their play lists. The physical space around them becomes reconfigured as personal space corresponding to psychological moods.

In general, it is clear that mobile media contribute to the rise of a personalized culture, or as Castells and his collaborators put it, the intensification of individualism. But this kind of individualism does not reflect the rise of an authentic individualism which, as Theodor Adorno has argued, reflects critical consciousness and is manifested in avant garde modernist art. Rather, it is a pseudo-individualism based on consumer choices that appear different but which in fact represent variations of the same theme (Adorno, 1978 [1938]). Indeed, to the extent that mobile media practices, such as texting, mobile music listening and so on, do not critically apprehend the world around us, they merely reproduce the same or only slightly different social relationships. From this point of view, mobile media are just the latest development within consumer culture. The long queues and all-night stays of people anticipating the latest release of an iPhone or an iPad cannot be seen as representing any sort of critical stance vis-à-vis society and culture, but merely an obsession with the newest and the trendiest that is part and parcel of consumer culture. From this point of view, the socio-cultural outcomes of mobile media may be seen as proliferating and amplifying the trends more broadly associated with the network society, while also at this stage they seem to reproduce rather than undermine dominant socio-cultural patterns.

Conclusions

In this chapter we reviewed the main developments associated with mobile media, focusing on mobile phones, MP3 players and wireless internet. The main points and arguments are summarized in Box 8.1 overleaf. Overall, we have seen mobile media introduce important changes in the ways in which we relate to our physical, socio-cultural and political environment. These changes fall within the patterns identified within the network society, but are amplified and intensified through mobile media. The extent, however, to which these changes may lead to improvements in political and socio-cultural life, is debatable.

What might the broader conclusions be here? Mobile media must be seen as firmly embedded in our lives. They have offered us the unique possibility of transcending the confines of space and located-ness, allowing us to communicate with others regardless of where we are. In doing so, they transformed the way in which we understand space, and disrupted the boundaries we had placed between private and public space, and between working life and social-private life. Whether the emerging highly mobile, personalized, atomized, hybrid work-social life will offer us more contentment if not happiness is still under discussion.

8.1 Summary of Main Points

Mobile Media – Main Characteristics

Mobile phones:

- Exponential growth of diffusion
- Rates of more than 100% in some developed countries
- Age and wealth divides in mobile phone ownership

MP3 players:

- Diffusion about 20% in developed countries
- Dominant form of digital music consumption

WiFi internet:

- Average of about 20,000 wireless hotspot locations in the top ten countries
- Wireless internet more popular in developing countries

Political Outcomes of Mobile Media

- Tensions between wireless internet and mobile telephony (Benkler, 2006)
- Development of horizontal social networks, critical of authorities but:
- Pressure of commercialization and control of mobile media
- A democratization of political mediation?

Socio-Cultural Outcomes

- Enhancement of individual autonomy
- Personalized space and time
- Tensions between private and public space
- Blurring of boundaries between work and leisure
- Renewed creativity and use of imagination but:
- Dominance of consumer culture

E-tivity: Mobiles and Everyday Life

This e-tivity requires a focus on our own patterns of use of mobile media in order to be able to understand their implications. The main idea here is to attain a more in-depth understanding of the changes introduced by the mobile media, as well as their ubiquity in our everyday lives.

You will observe and monitor the instances of using a mobile medium for a week (including a phone, a laptop, an MP3 player, and a digital camera). On the basis of this diary, address the following questions:

1   What is your average use of mobile media every day?

2   When do you typically use an MP3 player? Why?

3   When do you typically access wireless internet? Why?

4   What types of uses did you observe (e.g. social, work, family etc.)?

5   Can you recognize a change in the pattern of media use (e.g. the blurring of lines between work, leisure, and family commitments)?

6   How do you assess the always-on element of mobile media? Is it necessarily a positive aspect? What are some of its advantages and disadvantages?

Further Reading

The various uses and functions of mobile media are explored in the following three articles. Janey Gordon's article on the mobile phone examines its dual aspect as both a personal medium of communication as well as its public-political dimension, highlighting the element of mobility as a new factor that is worthy of more detailed examination and study. In her article, Miriam Simun traces the ways in which individuals reconfigure their auditory and perceptual environment through their MP3 players, thereby creating a new kind of autonomy and subjectivity – compare this to the concept of networked individualism discussed in Chapter 10. Ralph Schroeder's article represents an attempt to conduct a mulit-level kind of comparison both between different nations and their uses and functions for mobile phones, as well as a comparison between different kinds of mobile media: he suggests the concept of multimodal connectedness as a way in which to understand the role of mobile media in maintaining relationships. The final article, by Mary Griffiths, is a review of three different books on mobile media. Griffiths provides a neat summary of the main points of these books and a good introduction to some of the issues concerning mobile media.

Gordon, J., 2002, The Mobile Phone: An Artefact of Popular *Culture* and a Tool of the Public Sphere, *Convergence: The International Journal of Research into New Media Technologies*, 8(3): 15–26.

Simun, M., 2009, My Music, My World: Using the MP3 Player to Shape Experience in London, *New Media & Society*, 11(6): 921–941.

Schroeder, R., 2010, Mobile Phones and the Inexorable Advance of Multimodal Connectedness, *New Media & Society*, 12(1): 75–90.

Griffiths, M., 2007, Review Article: Future Assemblies: Theorizing Mobilities and Users: Manuel Castells, Mireia Fernández-Ardèvol, Jack Linchuan Qiu and Araba Sey, *Mobile Communication and Society: A Global Perspective*, Cambridge, MA: MIT Press; O. Groebel, Eli M. Noam and Valerie Feldmann (eds), *Mobile Media: Content and Services for Wireless Communication*, Mahwah, NJ and London: Lawrence Erlbaum Associates, 2006; and Mimi Sheller and John Urry (eds), *Mobile Technologies of the City*, London and New York: Routledge, *New Media & Society*, 9(6): 1029–1036.

CHAPTER 9

NEW MEDIA AND IDENTITY

Learning Objectives

- To learn about the relationship between the new media and the construction of identity
- To understand the shifts in identity associated with the new media
- To critically apprehend the changes to gender and ethnic/racial identities as a function of the new media
- To critically evaluate the new kinds of subjectivities that emerge through our association with the new media

Introduction

'Blogito ergo sum' appears to be the new rendition of Descartes' famous dictum 'Cogito ergo sum' – 'I think therefore I am'. In Descartes' original formulation, the point was to show that if one thinks this is proof that they exist. While thought was the means by which one could ascertain one's existence in the early Enlightenment, blogging is the twenty-first century way of supporting and showing one's existence on the web. The connections between new media and people's existence and identity are strong: if we use the media to communicate, they, in turn, enable us to fashion ourselves out of the materials or affordances that they offer us. This may be considered to be one of the medium's messages, to quote McLuhan (2002 [1962]). But the new media may be even more directly involved in processes of identity and subjectivity because of the ways in which they engage with subjects.

But what exactly do we mean by the term 'identity'? In social psychology, identity is defined as all the answers to the question 'Who am I?' along with the specific meaning and significance these answers have for the person (Tajfel, 1981). Tajfel understood identity in terms of a continuum ranging from personal identity to social identity. Personal identity includes all those identifications derived from individual personality traits and interpersonal relationships, such as, for example, 'I am organized, sociable, caring' etc. Social identity includes all those identifications derived from group memberships, e.g. 'I am a woman', 'I am Chinese' etc. Identity is therefore plural, contains both personal and social elements, is always accompanied by evaluations and has important psycho-social implications for the person. From this point of view, the involvement of the new media in processes of identity, both at the level of its constitution and at the level of its expression, has important ramifications both for the types of identities constructed and expressed, as well as, ultimately, for the person's well being. In these terms we need not only to examine how the new media are involved in identity work, but also to evaluate this involvement.

In doing this, the present chapter will look at the ways in which this relationship has been theorized, in order to provide an insight into any relevant shifts or transformations. The main argument pursued here is that while the internet may be associated with novel means of constructing identities, ultimately these must be assessed in terms of their contribution to self-actualization, liberation and recognition. At the same time, these new identities entail the development of new patterns of inequality and discrimination that have to be taken into account.

The chapter will be divided into three parts: first, it will look at personal identity, or subjectivity and the internet, reviewing classic work, such as Turkle (1995) and Poster (1995) but also looking at how new internet genres, such as blogs, might be linked to new types of subjectivity (Siapera, 2008). Second, the chapter will cover debates on gender and the internet, examining the relevant body of work, and showing the ways in which technologies interact with gender and sexuality. Finally, the chapter will examine the relationship between race/ethnic and religious identity and the new media, discussing the rise of transnational links and networks, but also struggles over control of identity and visibility.

Identity, the Self and the New Media

If we accept the broad definition that self-identity includes all our personal and social identifications along with their evaluation and their significance for us, the question of how we acquire such identities still remains. Are we born with certain dispositions, which may or may not be developed further, are we wholly made due to our environment, or are we endowed with some identities? While there is a multitude of theories on this subject, here we will take it for granted that identities are constructed through the various materials we have in our disposal. But how do these materials influence or shape identities? In order to understand the relationship between the (new) media and identity, this section will first discuss relevant theories and then seek to identify the role of the new media. It will then conclude with a discussion of blogging as a technology that constructs identities.

One of the most influential theorists of identity, Michel Foucault (1988), argued that identity, especially subjectivity, that is, the ways in which we become unique individuals and selves, is constructed through certain techniques, or practices. These are referred to as 'technologies of the self': the practices by which we get to understand and shape ourselves. These technologies are, in turn, constituted through power discourses. The Christian confession is an example of such a technology. Foucault considered that these technologies worked through configuring identities in certain ways: they allow certain things to be experienced, discussed, felt, and they prohibit others altogether. In this manner they condition us as persons, while also following the requirements of power: after all, our identities must be compatible with the broader socio-political system in which we live. Thus, for Foucault, individuals actively construct their own identities, but using discourses and practices which are already steeped in power relations. To paraphrase Marx, people make their own identity but not out of their choice; rather they fashion it 'under the given and inherited circumstances with which they are directly confronted' (Marx, 1852). We can only be who we are because of the very specific socio-historical circumstances in which we find ourselves, and in being who we are, we can only use the materials and technologies available to us.

While Foucault was at pains to show that while identities are constructed they are not constructed under circumstances of liberty and free will, Anthony Giddens (1991) considered identities as dynamic, ever changing and evolving. For Giddens, self identity is linked to processes of modernity, such as reflection. While in pre-modern times, and even in early modernity, identities were given and static, in late modernity, the self is an ongoing project that we are constantly modifying, updating, safeguarding and so on. This reflexive project is built on the basis of local reflection on global events. Giddens argues that we constantly create and revise our personal narratives, our 'life histories', on the basis of information from our environment. This processing is undertaken through the resources that we have at our disposal. In this manner, in constructing our identity we take into account any feedback we receive from our environment, and this includes both what is happening in our immediate physical environment, as well as in the broader socio-historical context in which we find ourselves. In other words, identities are not static, acquired once and for all, but exist under conditions of permanent ongoing construction – in a perpetual beta phase, to use new media terminology. From this point of view, the materials we use for their ongoing construction as well as the circumstances under which this construction takes place, acquire an increased significance.

The historical and social circumstances of identity construction are at the heart of Castells' theorizing on identity. For Castells (2004 [1997]: 10–12), identity construction in the network society acquires different dimensions because of the distinct reconfiguration of the global/local and time/space dialectic. He therefore argues that the search for meaning is no longer local or with reference to locally shared frameworks, but *defensive*, i.e. obtained in opposition to global discourses threatening local and communally shared values. Castells then moves on to make a distinction between project and resistance identities. Project identities are those identities constructed in order to change the world: in other words they are built around a certain ideology. Resistance identities, on the other hand are stigmatized identities that seek recognition – these are identities that do not enjoy a high symbolic and material status, and they are typical of identity politics. In the network society, argues Castells, all identities tend to become resistance identities, they seek to defend and safeguard their own position. This is why, more broadly, the network society revolves around identity politics.

Conceptualizing Identity and New Media

If these are the broader theoretical frameworks within which we can conceive identity, then what is the relationship between new media technologies and identity? There are three main ways, associated with these theories in which we can think of this relationship. Firstly, drawing on Foucault, the new media can be clearly thought as new technologies of the self. They can be seen as instituting new practices for self-construction always within existing power discourses. In other words, we can, and in fact do, construct ourselves using blogs, social networking sites, MP3 players, mobile phones and so on. Second, based on Giddens, new media may be understood as offering the opportunity for reflection and the ongoing construction of the self. As contents, on the one hand, the new media confront our selves with global discourses which in turn force us to rethink who we are; on the other hand, as forms, the new media reposition ourselves, by requiring that we rethink ourselves in relation to specific new media, such as mobile phones, emails, blogs, social networking sites and so on. Third, following Castells, new technologies can offer new channels both for the collaborative construction of communal identities beyond territories, as well as the means by which such identities organize and act upon their demands. These identities cannot exist outside networked technologies.

Castells then posits a fundamental break in identity processes in the network society, while the other two would probably understand new technologies as primarily technically implicated in identity construction – as practices, platforms and opportunities for reflection. Identities change and evolve all the time, but they would find no reason to assume any radical changes in the ways in which identity is constructed. For Castells, however, the shifts in time and space characterizing the network society introduce a fundamental break, such that the construction of identity has moved beyond geographical constraints, and also because of this, it may elude or at least confound power discourses which operate in specific localities. We will see this more clearly in our discussion of ethnicity and identity, but in terms of personal identity, the implications are clear: it is no longer limited or determined by the immediate socio-cultural context of values, requirements and expectations. Does this mean that we end up with an emancipated self?

Theorists such as Donna Haraway and Sherry Turkle also posit a fundamental break in identity processes associated with the new media, arguing for a cyborg self and a fractured, fragmented but ultimately freer self respectively. The term cyborg refers to a kind of hybrid, a mixture between humans and machines. Popular cyborgs in fiction range from Tin Woodman in the *Wizard of Oz* to Darth Vader in *Star Wars*: all cyborg characters display a mixture of human and machine characteristics, and cannot be thought of as either entirely human or entirely machines or robots. But the term can also be used metaphorically to refer to self or human-made creatures. This is the way in which Haraway uses the term. For Haraway (1991), just as cyborgs mix and chose nature and biology, so do people. Women and men reinvent themselves using various technologies to improve, correct or otherwise alter themselves – they can use various technologies, ranging from the simplest (e.g. wearing glasses), to the most complex (such as having implants or pacemakers). Haraway's main argument is that all of us use technology to reinvent ourselves and that identities undergo constant revision and reinvention through technology. The point, argues Haraway, is that identities are neither given nor essential, unchanging blocks characterized by the same attributes across time. She was primarily arguing against essentialism, or the idea that identities are characterized by a set of fixed qualities or an essence that remains the same. Since we can, and do, continuously undergo changes using technologies, then there is nothing in our identities that can be considered fixed or stable. As we shall see later, Haraway's work is of great significance for gender identity and its relationship with new technologies and media.

In terms of personal identity, the work of Sherry Turkle, and especially her book *Life on the Screen* (1995), has been valuable in helping us understand the specific implications of networked technologies in the construction of identities. Multiplicity, plurality and choice are at the centre of Turkle's understanding of identity: people have many identities and are happy to juggle between them while they are seen as making informed choices regarding the appropriateness of certain identities in certain contexts. Her study of MUDs (Multi-User Domains), online environments connecting many users together, showed that people are happy to operate with a number of identities. Moreover, the multiplicity and plurality of these identities may also have a therapeutic value, as people are able to reveal aspects of their identity otherwise hidden. Freed from the confines of social conventions, embarrassment and norms, people may express themselves in different ways. In these terms, the anonymity and disembodiment of online subjects lead to identities liberated from past concerns – online no one knows who you are, so for Turkle you can be anyone you want. At the same time, there is no 'real' you, your identity cannot be reduced to one of your 'avatars' or online personas. An example of this juggling of multiple identities can be seen in Second Life, the user-created virtual community, in which people assume an 'avatar' and live a 'second life'. What is the relationship between second life and 'first life' – are identities similar or diverge and if so in what ways? While this is an empirical question, it is likely that for some people their Second Life avatar may differ dramatically from their actual life: if we follow Turkle's arguments, this may enable individuals to live a more complete life, as they have the opportunity to experience, albeit virtually, different, complementary or antithetical identities. 'Be yourself, free yourself' is one of the injunctions of Second Life, and indeed for many participants their experience of this virtual world may offer them precisely this kind of freedom.

However, although plurality and multiplicity, as well as construction, are generally accepted as conditions of identity in late/post modernity, the assumption that online selves differ radically from the offline ones, or that people can really be who they want to be online are not always warranted. Castells (2001) argues that this type of experimentation is mostly limited to young people, who are yet to construct a core identity. Certainly, most of the participants in Turkle's study were younger people, whose identities were perhaps not as consolidated as those of, for example, people over 25 years old. Similarly, Wynn and Katz (1998, in Baym, 2006) report that in web pages people still maintain a coherent overall identity. This implies that even when given the chance to be someone else, or to express all the multiple facets of their identity, people still seem to stick to one identity which is characterized by a set of more or less stable characteristics. Indeed, we need to have some sort of continuity and stability in our identity if only for others to recognize us and to be able to interact with us. Even the most extravagant avatar in Second Life needs to display some stability across time and across the Second Life environments in order to be able to participate in the game or virtual world, to make friends, and to experience this kind of online environment. More broadly, it is not that actual norms and rules don't exist in online worlds; they do. However, they are negotiated in common with others and made to fit new environments and requirements. Some of these norms, e.g. politeness, may be 'inherited' but are modified when online. We cannot live our lives outside of rules and norms, but we can reinvent rules and norms to fit new circumstances.

In more political terms, the danger is to overlook the ongoing material and symbolic inequalities in favour of an aestheticized perspective which views identity exclusively as a voluntary choice. Are we really liberated or emancipated because our Second Life avatar seems to be? More broadly, however, the general point made by all these theorists is that identities are not inscribed in stone, even if they are involved in power discourses and hierarchies, and that technologies offer new and exciting possibilities to rebuild our identities because online there are no set rules or norms, and because of the ways in which we can play with offline aspects of our identity. But how exactly are new media involved in the construction of identities? To this we turn next, using blogging as a case study.

Technologies of the Self: Blogging

Perhaps the clearer articulation of the relationship between new media and identity is that of new media as technologies of the self. Technologies of the self, Foucault tells us, 'permit individuals to effect by their own means or with the help of others a certain number of operations on their own bodies and souls, thoughts, conduct, and way of being, so as to transform themselves in order to attain a certain state of happiness, purity, wisdom, perfection, or immortality' (1988: 18). In these terms, these technologies allow us to construct ourselves in very specific ways, circumscribed by these technologies, which give shape and form to our very core. Foucault discussed some of these technologies, more notably the exploration and constant examination of the self contained in the Ancient Greek injunction 'Know Thyself' and the Christian confessional. Through this constant reflection of trying to find and 'know' ourselves, argues Foucault, we construct a very specific kind of self, a reflexive, inner-directed self, a self who, as a result, has an internal life, as it were, which we can access through examining and monitoring our thoughts and actions. At the same time, this examination also has as its object the body and the self in its 'external' as it were dimensions: taking care of ourselves. By occupying themselves with themselves, argues Foucault (1988: 19), people can learn and cultivate their selves. Similar principles are found in early Christian religious practices, which involved 'soul searching', the

constant monitoring of each thought and act, in order to ensure compliance with God's requirements. The main point of technologies of the self is to produce a kind of self or identity that is
compatible with social, cultural, religious, and political norms and requirements. In this manner, the techniques themselves were an inextricable part of identity construction.

If letters, self-examination, and confessions were the technologies of the self in Antiquity,
what are today's technologies of the self? What kind of subjects or identity do they produce?
Since Foucault's technologies of the self are all forms of communication perhaps we could
turn to communication and media forms. This question follows a long line of enquiry into the
relationship between media forms and subjectivity. Examples of this line of thought abound in
social and political theory. As we have seen in Chapter 5, different media of communication
are linked to different kinds of selves and subjectivities. For example, Georg Lukacs, in *The
Theory of the Novel* (1974 [1914]) argued that Cervantes' *Don Quixote* introduced a new kind
of consciousness, which is not the same as that of antiquity, found in tragedy and epic poems;
it further differs from the subjectivity associated with the Medieval Christian world, in which
subjects were in the hands of God. Rather, in the modern novel, subjects are confronted by a
fragmented and alienated world, where neither gods nor God can offer help or support. They
must therefore find and impose their own narrative, which is based on reason, to explain and
make sense of this world. A similar argument is pursued by Habermas (1989 [1962]), for whom
the rise of the 'moral novel', such as Richardson's 1740 *Pamela*, led to the creation of an inner
self – this is the so-called 'audience-oriented subjectivity', in which we imagine our life as
narrated to others. The advent of the mass media led to important changes in subject formation. Guy Debord (1967) documented the rise of the society of the spectacle, in which images
proliferate and subjects are positioned through consuming these images. The multiplicity of
these images, however, is fragmenting subjects, who cannot be identified with any single sign
or image. The changes introduced by the advent of the digital world are discussed by Mark
Poster (1995), whose idea of the digital author refers to the kinds of subjects who may produce
text, but are not in control of it: their texts may acquire different meanings and may be put to
different uses as they traverse cyberspace.

If we turn now to blogs, as one of the most widely available means of online communication,
and we consider it as a technology of the self, then what kind of subject does it produce? To
begin with, we must note that blogs offer persons the opportunity to re-imagine themselves and
to become subjects – as opposed to merely playing with identities, as one finds in virtual environments such as Second Life, and also as Turkle suggested. Becoming a subject requires the
acceptance of difference and multiplicity within oneself, but also to manage to retain a sense of
precarious togetherness. The technical characteristics of blogs (archives, categories, links etc.),
the ability to shift between modes of address (to readers, to friends, to oneself), the discretion
enjoyed by the blogger over their blog (they can write about whichever subject they choose,
they can post photos, poems and so on), all point to the construction of a different kind of subjectivity that differs from the one cultivated by letters, confessionals, novels and mass media.
Elsewhere I have referred to this as an 'authorial subjectivity' (Siapera, 2008): in this mode and
through blogging (including microblogging and social networking blogging), a person acquires

ownership and responsibility over what they say (and hence what they are), thereby becoming autonomous. But autonomy here is not seen as radical separation from others; rather, it refers to the ability to judge, evaluate, think and act through self-instituted and self-assessed modes. And this kind of autonomy is a collaborative one: through looking at other blogs and posts we take a position, we 'like', 'dislike', comment, link to and so on, while others do the same to our blogs. In this sense, blogging creates a self who is in constant revision alongside and through others. It is different to letter exchanges, as these take place between two people and are private; to self-examination, as it is a reflection performed by one on one; to the confessional, as this is done in the privacy of the church or the psychoanalytic couch; to novels, as these are written by others and internally projected; and to the mass media, as blogging is not a spectacle prepared by others for mass consumption. As a result, in and through blogging, subjects emerge as autonomous, that is different from others in specific ways, but this is a social kind of autonomy, as it takes place in the virtual presence of others and involves a kind of exteriorization of one's 'inner' thoughts, ideas, opinions, experiences and so on.

Other aspects of blogging include the identification of the blog with the self (Reed, 2005). The blogger's self becomes the text they are writing, changing and shifting across topics, themes, categories and time. The archival aspects of blogs means that they can act as depositories of memories, ideas, thoughts, but also their existence, to a degree, constrains the blogger, as archived content potentially remains there for ever. In some ways, blogging operates on the dialectic between control, as bloggers have almost absolute discretion over their blogs, and loss of control. This loss of control is epitomized in the following: the moment posts go live, they can be used and quoted out of context, and in general acquire a life of their own beyond the narrow confines of the blog – similarly with comments: opening up the blog to comments implies relinquishing control, as visitors can write whatever they wish. In this manner, blogging identities appear to be both gathered in their blogs/profiles and so on, as well as dispersed across the web, (re)posted or re-tweeted, they can form part of a broader network or conversely they can fragment larger networks into smaller and more targeted communities of users, 'friends' or 'followers'. This 'authorial subjectivity' emerging from blogs and social media practices appears to be as fragmented and dispersed as the one discussed by Debord and Poster, but it differs from them in that blogging and social media activity attempts to refocus and re-centre subjects in given online spaces. However, we may argue that it is precisely this dynamic of centrifugal and centripetal power that characterizes subjectivity in the era of the new (and social) media.

At the same time, we should also point to the kind of power struggles involved in this subjectivity. Blogging and social media activities open up at least two inter-related types of new struggle: one is that of visibility (Thompson, 2005) and the other is that of popularity. Being visible as a blogger is important to some bloggers, as readership and connection to others is part of blogging's appeal. Equally, popularity, understood as the extent to which posts are liked and linked to, is an important aspect of blogging as it offers a kind of reward and recognition to bloggers. But these two dimensions have led to the rise of blogging hierarchies, alongside the emergence of strategic or tactical blogging seeking to increase visibility and popularity. For instance, Technorati, the blog monitoring site, publishes the names of the 100 most popular blogs, ranked in terms of 'authority', which refers to links from other blogs/sites to them: the more the links to a blog, the higher its 'authority'. Social bookmarking sites, such as Digg and Del.icio.us allow for the ranking of posts through popularity, as they allow people to repost items they liked. From this point of view, blogging activities may be strategically aimed at increasing popularity rather than blogging for blogging's sake.

If we are to assess this kind of subjectivity, what kind of criteria can we use? To be sure, theories such as Foucault's go beyond any simple assessment of good versus bad. For Foucault, power, which is inscribed in all technologies of the self, is both oppressing and enabling: it fashions individuals and selves in given ways, but in making them subjects it allows them to act; in so doing people actively modify and rewrite the conditions of their existence. However, here the problem is more pressing: if we take blogging as a certain activity that produces a certain self, then what is its potential in terms of our current levels of happiness and self ful-filment? In psychological theory, one of the most widely known theories has been Abraham Maslow's (1954) hierarchy of needs, in which he argues that having fulfilled their basic needs for food, and safety, as well as their social needs for companionship, and their needs for esteem, achievement and approval, people will seek self-actualization. This refers to the quest to real-ize one's potential, to gain a deeper understanding of the world and to be able to help others in their quest for self-actualization (Maslow, 1954; Maslow and Lowery, 1998). Does blogging enable people to self-actualize? We may venture here that if all other needs are met, blogging as a technology of the self, which is both autonomous and social-collaborative, may contribute significantly to personal growth, understanding, exploration of ideas and events, as well as 'self-transcendence', going beyond one's self and seeking to help others. It is an activity that is both inner-directed towards the self, as well as outer-directed towards the external world; at the same time it is performed in public, with others not only watching but being actively involved through comments and so on. From this point of view, blogging, if not strategically oriented, can be seen in positive terms. But if blogging enables us, at least in principle, to go for self-actualization, to what extent do the new media more broadly contribute to the emancipation and liberation of social identities, such as gender and race/ethnicity? To this question we turn next.

Gender Identities and New Media

If we accept that self identities or subjectivities are constructed then where does this leave gender (and other ascribed) identities? Since at least Simone de Beauvoir's *Second Sex* (1953) we know that women are made, not born. That is, that gender is an identity that is constructed rather than one we are born with. While we are born girls or boys, the meanings, behaviours, values, desires and expectations formed on the basis of our gender are constructed on the basis of dominant discourses and gender ideologies. In other words, we are conditioned to be male or female, women and men, and to act in ways commensurable with these gender identities. As with self identities, we make these identities out of the materials available to us, but in the case of gender these materials are much more limited and prescriptive: gender roles must be strictly adhered to.

Indeed, most feminist theorists theorize gender identity in terms of precisely the restrictive and prescriptive gender discourses while also seeking to identify ways of undermining and changing these discourses. It is in this dynamic that we can locate the role of the new media: in enabling or creating new opportunities for the articulation of gender identities, which may in the end prove less oppressing and more liberating for people who embody them. In discussing these issues, this section will begin with a short discussion of gender, before examining the ways in which gender is articulated in the new media. We will then discuss cyber and techno-feminist theories and the extent to which the new media contribute to more equal gender relations.

Theories of Gender and Technology

Judith Butler (1993) described the process by which gender identities are generated and become consolidated as a process of repetition and reiteration: this is the concept of performativity. We acquire our gender identity through repeating what is expected of us, what we see others doing, and what we have been taught as acceptable for our gender. But these gender performances in different contexts also contain the grains for change and for undermining dominant discourses on gender. We perform or act on the basis of pre-existing expectations and norms but in the process we end up modifying such expectations. According to Butler, this modification is based on the mismatch between contexts and performances. When a 'wrong' or inappropriate gender performance takes place, then it opens up the way for a new interpretation of gender; for example, drag is a kind of inappropriate gender performance, because it is the 'wrong' gender, but in this exaggerated performance, room is created for a different imagining of gender.

Following Butler, new technologies may be articulated with gender in at least two ways: first, as a different context for performances of gender, which in turn help institute a new kind of gender interpretation. For example, acting as a woman or a mother in an online environment contributes to changing the meaning of womanhood and motherhood, because it articulates the discourses of motherhood or womanhood with those of the new technologies. In acting as a mother online we reinstitute a gendered identity and at the same time we change this identity, which now may have another set of values or expectations attached to it. Second, gender may also be performed differently in online environments. This refers to the virtuality of online environments, which do not require strict adherence to the norms and conventions of face-to-face encounters and allow for different, more playful, gender performances to take place. In practice, this means that we can pretend to be any gender we want in online environments, and/or to attach to gender any kind of behaviour we see fit. Thus, just as drag undermines conformist gender identities, so gender masquerading in online environments may radicalize gender to an unprecedented extent: it may allow for an understanding of gender identity that is disembodied from our actual bodies and their biologies, while following this, it may transgress the binary male/female, through leading to the creation of fluid identities (Rodino, 1997; O'Brien, 1999; c.f. van Doorn, van Zoonen and Wyatt, 2007).

In the early days of internet research, in the mid to late 1990s, these gender plays were discussed as one of the ways in which new media would revolutionize gender and contribute towards eradicating the gender divisions that have for so long plagued the world. For instance, Danet (1998: 130) argues that gender masquerading online may 'contribute to the long-term destabilization of the ways in which we currently construct gender'. Discussing research on text-based multi-user domains (the so-called MUDs and MOOs), Danet reports the extent of experimentation that went on there as quite extensive. Two of these domains, LambdaMOO and MediaMOO, listed no less than ten different genders, including gender categories such as 'neuter', 'either', 'royal' (the 'we'), plural and so on, and research identified that 31.8% of users actually listed an unconventional gender, that is, other than male/female.

But does this actually translate to actual changes in gender identities? Lori Kendall (1996) is pessimistic about this: in her work on MUDs she found that in the end most people were pressed to reveal their 'real' identity. Perhaps more problematically, people tended to reproduce gender stereotypes when they assumed the identity of another gender. In similar research, Leslie (1993 in Danet, 1998: 140), described how when men masqueraded as women, they tended to act as 'late adolescent males wish they would, responding with enthusiasm to all sexual advances'. Others argue that in any case this masquerading offers at best temporary respite of the oppressing qualities of gender rather than lasting change.

More recent research on blogs and gender has shown that on the one hand blogs tend to focus on 'real', everyday life, unlike the often imaginary, virtual world of MUDs, such as Second Life, and as such they relate directly to bloggers' lives (van Doorn et al., 2007). From this point of view, there is little room for gender experimentation and the creation of unconventional or alternative, gender-bending identities. On the other hand, it is often said that technology is gendered, that it has a given gender, and this is the masculine one: technology serves ends devised by men, it is developed and used by them, and for them (see Wajcman, 2010). Feminists have long tried to identify the ways in which gender is actually written in technology. Blogs, as a technological artefact, are meant to be equally gendered, but their personal, experiential, confessional style is meant to be more feminine than masculine. On this basis, van Doorn et al. (2007) argue that in fact blogging may be contributing towards opening up feminine discourses and allowing the plural expression of gendered identities.

Gendered Technologies

However, in arguing that technologies and artefacts are gendered, the implication is that genders and their identities are somehow already written and unchanged through time. The point of these arguments was to show the gender inequality inscribed on technologies and media, but it inadvertently ended up essentializing identities, as it ascribed certain characteristics as their core, essential, unchanging ones. And here the work of Donna Haraway acquires an increased significance. It is as a response to this kind of essentialism that Haraway suggested the concept of a cyborg, arguing that all of us are 'human made', we integrate our lives with technological objects and other artefacts, and as such we can be considered 'cyborgs', hybrids of humans and machines. Haraway was also writing against a particular type of feminism which grouped all women together on the basis of a shared identity. Her arguments for gender mean that we cannot assume that all women share the same identity just because they share certain biological commonalities. Politically, this means that groups traditionally put together because of perceived biological similarities (e.g. sex, race etc.), must now find new means of connection, based on choice – the politics of affinity: 'related not by blood but by choice' (Haraway, 1991: 155). In terms of technology, Haraway recognizes that technology is ambiguous: on the one hand it subverts nature, helping people to overcome limits and boundaries set, but on the other hand it may become a tool for control. More broadly, Haraway's ideas represent the position that technology, especially online media, with their emphasis on the virtual, may enable women (and men) to free themselves from bodily limitations. Sadie Plant (1998) holds that technology effectively blurs the boundaries between humans and machines and this has the potential to liberate them from constrains associated with their gender.

On the other hand, as Wajcman (2010) has observed, the implication here is that everything that is digital is necessarily positive, something that is unfortunately far from the truth. Even if we accept Manuel Castells' argument that patriarchy is dead, and although women do participate in almost equal numbers in digital worlds, the reality of the new media is that they are still tied to stereotypical gender identities. Although the idea of cyber-feminism is that gender identities can be transgressed through or in digital culture, the reality is that gender identities remain as defining identities in both the actual and virtual worlds. This is evidenced in both material and symbolic domains of digital cultures. Concerning the former, Rosalind Gill (2002) reports that women are bearing the brunt of the ad hoc project work associated with the new media. They tend to get less offers for work, they are in general paid less, and suffer from job insecurity. Gill attributes these differences to the informality of this kind of work which tends to favour men and their 'old boy networks', as well as to the discourse of flexibility which effectively means working at all hours of the day. Another kind of issue, as Gill notes, concerns the ways in which this kind of project-based digital work actually individualizes the risks associated with work, and ultimately leaves women worse off, as they have to pay for social security contributions, maternity leaves, pension schemes and so on, on their own. In the domain of the symbolic, the domination of overly sexualized, exaggerated body parts, and quasi-pornographic aesthetics of some female avatars is emblematic of the ways in which stereotypical and male-oriented understandings of women are embedded in digital domains.

Where does all this leave the relationship between gender identity and technology? If we take Judith Butler's arguments seriously, gender is a performance: it comes into being through the ways in which it is performed. Similarly, if we follow closely a social constructivist understanding of technology, then we must see it equally shaped in and through its various uses. Bringing these two strands together, it can be argued that gender relations are materialized in technology, while gender identities acquire meaning through their involvement in and use of technologies (Wajcman, 2010). As Wajcman (2010: 150) puts it: 'the materiality of technology affords or inhibits the doing of particular gender power relations. Women's identities, needs and priorities are configured together with digital technologies'. Both technology and gender are moving targets, involved in a fluid relationship in which they co-constitute each other (although they are also co-constituted by other elements). Because of this we cannot know in advance if certain new media are 'good' for gender relations or liberating for women: rather this becomes both an empirical question for feminist scholarship and a political one for feminist praxis. The former aims at observing the ways in which certain new media forms may contribute to more equal gender relations, while the latter seeks to come up with new media actions and practices through which to institute more equal gender relations.

Ethnic and Religious Identities in the New Media World

So far we have seen that the relationship between new media and identities, self and gender identities, is a complex and ambiguous one. Perhaps in the case of ethnic and religious identities the situation may be different, as we know from Castells that new media erode territorial boundaries and minimize the importance of geographical divisions. In discussing this relationship, this section will begin with a brief discussion of Castells on the relevance of ethnic identities in the network society, and a short discussion of Giddens on religious identity in late modernity. We will then discuss the various articulations of ethnicity with the new media and finally assess the role of the new media in contributing to emancipatory practices for ethnic and religious identities. For a more detailed review of this area see Siapera (2010).

In sociological theory, ethnicity is understood in many ways; some, such as Clifford Geertz (1973), hold that ethnicity is based on historical continuity, which in turn is linked to commonalities of culture, traditions, language and so on. Others, such as Ernest Gellner (1983) find that ethnicity and the nation-state, which he views as the political organization around ethnicity, have been brought to prominence because industrial capitalism required a culturally and linguistically homogeneous workforce. From this point of view, commonalities and ethnic traditions are modern inventions that helped capitalism to function (Hobsbawm and Ranger, 1983). In both cases however, ethnicity is circumscribed by geographical borders and shared territories, while it is underpinned by some sense of historical continuity, albeit for some this is invented or imagined (Hobsbawm and Ranger, 1983; Anderson, 1991 [1983] respectively). Regardless of the provenance and function of ethnicity, its role in providing meaning to people's lives is generally acknowledged. Throughout history, ethnicity formed the basis of cultural attachments, differentiations as well as for outright discrimination in some cases. Now, given the radical ways in which new technologies transform space and time, what is the relevance of ethnicity and ethnic identities in a globalized world? If we accept Castells' arguments on the space of flows and timeless time, then it follows that ethnicity cannot be defined either by geographical boundaries or by historical continuity. Where does this leave ethnic identities?

Theorizing Ethnicity and Religion in the Network Society

Castells (2000 [1996]) accepts that ethnicity and race still exist in the network society, but argues that they do not any longer have the power to provide strong common identities. This is because their territorial basis is no longer relevant as space has become delinked from territories; at the same time, their historical significance is undermined precisely because of the lost relevance of territories, which provided the context to common ethnic bonds. In short, we no longer understand ourselves as rooted in particular territories, as we take meaning from participation in different networks, which are not bound to geography, but which create their own space. Confronted with this reality, argues Castells, ethnicity has two options. The first is to attach itself to broader cultural communes, such as religion, and in this manner to operate as a 'statement of cultural autonomy' (Castells, 2000 [1996]: 63). In other words, ethnicity gets grafted on other communal identities which then lend their appeal and significance to it, and enable it to survive albeit in a different form in the network society. A second option is to function as a kind of territorial identity but rooted in local communities, gangs or turfs as Castells put it. In either case, the meaning of ethnic identities is changing as a result of their role and function in network society. To paraphrase Gellner, ethnic and racial identities now operate in terms of the requirements of informational and globalized capitalism.

The shifts and changes undergone by identities that have their roots in earlier historical periods are found at the root of Anthony Giddens' (1991) work on identity. As we discussed earlier, for Giddens, identity in late modernity is understood as a project and a process: dynamic and evolving on the basis of reflecting upon itself and making use of the information it receives. Religious identities, from this point of view, are incompatible with modern identities as they are based on dogma, a set of unchanging and unquestionable beliefs and practices. Giddens' argument is that we may see some resurgence of religious identities, but this is a reaction to the lack of clear guiding ethic and moral principles for modern identities. In addition, they may be seen as reactions to the broader environment of risk and uncertainty associated with late modernity. Understood as reactionary, religious identities appear at odds with both the liberal environment of the internet/new media and its high tech credentials which point to a dynamic relationship with the everyday rather than to any kind of metaphysical transcendence.

Race/Ethnicity Online

Notwithstanding the many contradictions in the conceptualization of ethnic and religious identities, the empirical reality of the media is very different. Online, both ethnicity and religion proliferate and even profit significantly through their association with the new media. Upon looking closely at the articulation of ethnic and religious identities with the new media, we can observe both continuities and transformations. Although continuities include the function of these identities as markers of difference, their articulation with the new media has deeply affected their structure and wider role in society. To begin with the continuing role of ethnic and religious identities as markers of difference, statistical evidence suggests some differentiation in the use and consumption of new media in terms of ethnicity. While this will be explored in more detail in other chapters, this kind of evidence points to the function of ethnicity and religion as the bases not only for difference but also for discrimination. The work of Lisa Nakamura is instructive. Nakamura (2002) argues that ethnicity and race in online environments is 'coded' differently, reflecting the different and changing roles of various ethnicities in the division of labour within informational capitalism. She uses the term 'cybertyping' to refer to these new kinds of ethnic and racial coding in the new media environments. Her work shows that Asians are considered to be very technologically capable, while blacks are seen as 'techno-primitive'; in the 'normal' middle one finds the whites. This kind of techno-Orientalism reflects a continuing fascination with the Orient, whose 'mysterious' and 'exotic' ways are in this case projected to the future. In her discussion of cyberpunk fiction, Nakamura captures this continuing mystification of race and ethnicity: in a futuristic world, inhabited by cyborgs, humanity is still understood as white.

However, as with gender identity, when online people can pretend to be someone else. This practice is referred to as 'passing', and because of it and more broadly because of the lack of any physical and bodily presence online, it is suggested that race and ethnicity may be stretched and changed, thereby eschewing racist and discriminatory practices. This argument is based on Turkle's (1995) work, which proposed that experimenting with different identities may increase understanding. Lisa Nakamura disagrees: for her, this kind of 'identity tourism' views identities in a very superficial manner, as mere aesthetic add-ons, overlooking the structural dimensions underpinning such identities. In addition, pretending to be someone else does not necessarily question and undermine the assumptions and stereotypes associated with some ethnic and racial identities, while often it just replicates them. On the other hand, the online circulation of many kinds of ethnic and racial identities, even imaginary ones, as found in Second Life, shows that multiculturalism thrives, at least in online environments. However, Nakamura urges caution, as these identities are only acceptable insofar as they are 'all singing the same corporate anthem' (2002: 99). In other words, the practice of passing is neither subversive nor emancipatory as it is confined on the most superficial aspects of identity without challenging the structural conditions upon which these identities are founded and operate.

On the other hand, research has documented many positive aspects in the articulation of ethnic, racial and religious identities with the new media. The new media allow for dispersed diasporic communities to get together and pursue political goals. In her work, Franklin (2007) found that diasporic Tongans met in online fora and discussed the political situation in the Pacific archipelago of Tonga. Similarly, Muslim online spaces offer the opportunity for diasporic Muslims to 'meet' and discuss aspects of common concern. In an article on Muslims and the internet, Siapera (2007a) found that some Muslims used the internet for political empowerment. The low threshold for publication means that members of minority cultures, ethnicities and religions are able to find their own voice, and to acquire higher visibility, eventually promoting goals such as equal rights and recognition (Georgiou, 2002; Siapera, 2005; 2007b). Similar findings are reported by Parker and Song (2007), who found that the development and use of ethnic websites by British Chinese enable this low key and almost invisible minority to articulate its political demands. At the same time, this kind of development and participation in ethnic sites familiarizes minority members with political debates and processes, thereby preparing them for political participation in the mainstream political environment (Siapera, 2004). A final aspect concerns the bridges that some ethnic and religious minority sites throw to their majority counterparts: as long as they don't only or exclusively address their in-group members but the broader public they promote understanding and contribute to better inter-group relations.

Another dimension, however, within ethnic and religious sites, may not prove as positive. Two main problems emerge: the first concerns the internal functioning of ethnic sites, and the extent to which they tolerate and recognize intra-community diversity and difference. The second refers to the extent to which ethnic and religious sites contribute to the fragmentation of society. As far as the former issue is concerned, some ethnic and religious sites understand themselves as custodians of the community's history and tradition, thereby seeking to police behaviours and impose certain practices, values and understandings as the only ones. They do this by prescribing appropriate behaviours, interpretations of tradition, and by outright condemnation of those practices deemed inappropriate. Some religious sites, for instance, openly condemn homosexuality, while other sites offer prescriptive advice to women on aspects such as relationships and motherhood. Yet other sites, such as for instance the US-based Hot Ghetto Mess (www.hotghettomess.com), display and comment on photographs depicting 'inappropriate' styles and attitudes by black Americans, acting as a kind of cultural police. From this point of view, while on the whole we can argue that the articulation of ethnic-religious identity and the internet has a positive potential, to ensure that this potential is realized ethnic-religious sites must allow for internal diversity and difference to emerge. When it comes to fragmentation, the main argument is that by operating a series of different ethnic sites and by users primarily using the ones corresponding to their in-group, society is further fragmented across ethnic and religious lines. This argument, first put forth by Cass Sunstein (2001), points to the tension between the need to have a common space where everyone comes together to discuss and exchange views on matters of common interest, and the reality of the internet, which fragments audiences or users into small groups and communities sharing identities or interests. A society fragmented across these lines, argues Sunstein, is in danger of being indeed a society, that is, common to all. Moreover, the development of online ethnic enclaves may form a 'breeding ground for group polarization and extremism' (2001: 67, 71). From this point of view, ethnic websites may contribute to the erosion of social cohesion and to the fragmentation of society. Some of these arguments are disputed by Dahlberg (2007), who argues that such enclaves may have benefits in redressing some of the power asymmetries involved in current multicultural pluralistic societies.

Nevertheless, these issues highlight the very real implications of the articulation of ethnic-religious identity with the new media. These are even more pronounced in the case of Islam: Gary Bunt (2000; 2003; 2009) who has worked extensively on Islam and the internet has found that Islamic religious websites have managed to alter the very structure of religious authority in Islam. Bunt shows how the internet creates new centres for Islam, especially among Muslims living in Muslim minority countries, bypassing the traditional authorities of the madrassas (religious universities) in Egypt and elsewhere. Through electronic fatwas (or opinions on religious matters), diasporic Muslims acquire not only a new sense of how to practise their religion, but they also contribute to bypassing traditional religious sources found in the Middle East. In broader terms, Bunt (2009) argues that the internet is perfectly suitable for Islam because it is geared towards a constant reinterpretation and 'rewiring' of its principles. From this point of view, the internet has offered Islam a new lease of life. Similar effects may be observed for other religions as well: as Christians, Evangelical, Catholic, Pentecostal and so on, gather more and more in online spaces and less and less in churches, the traditional Church authorities may become either weaker, or else they may feel compelled to go online in order to congregate with the faithful. In addition, the possibilities offered by the new media for propagation and apostolic missions are too important to be ignored. It seems therefore that when traditional sources of power, such as religion, become articulated with the new media, their structures may shift and change, but they are also infused with new life and new potential.

This appears to hold true with ideologies such as nationalism, which the new media have to some extent altered, but also strengthened. This argument is made by Benedict Anderson, who has written extensively on the relationship between media and nationalism (Anderson, 1991 [1983]), holding that print capitalism and the spread of the mass media in early modernity are associated with the rise of the nation-state and the ideology of nationalism. On the one hand, the new media undermine the nation-state because of their links to globalization and their lack of respect for geographical borders. On the other hand, however, they allow members of diasporas to come together in virtual spaces, to consume images and narratives of their home countries, and to lobby, pressure, and to some extent dictate politics in homelands, which often lie thousands of miles away. In his work, Zlatko Skrbis (1999) notes the ways in which Slovenian and Croatian Australians become involved not so much in Australian but in Slovenian and Croatian politics through the new media. In this manner, the new media sustain rather than undermine nationalism and the resulting strong ethnic-national identifications. Some of the cyberwar interventions we discussed in earlier chapters further support this argument: thus, malicious hacking of Georgian sites by suspected Russian ultra-nationalists, of Israeli sites by Palestinian supporters, or of US sites by Chinese hackers may be seen as denoting the existence of this kind of dynamic in which new media somewhat paradoxically strengthen ethnic and nationalistic bonds.

Conclusions

This chapter reviewed the literature on the relationship between identity and the new media. In broad terms, we found that identity is constructed on the basis of materials available to us. New media and technologies may be seen as offering some such materials, but they do so in a context of both historical continuity as well as change. It does not come as a surprise that notwithstanding the positive potential of the articulation of identities with some new technologies and new media forms, which may be seen as contributing to the emancipation and liberation of identities from constraints of the past, the new media cannot, on their own, be seen as causing this. Box 9.1 summarizes the main points.

9.1

Summary of Main Points

Self-identity

- Foucault: the new media as technologies of the self
- Giddens: the new media offering opportunities for reflection and the continuing project of identity
- Castells: the self constructed under radically different conditions
- Is the new self-identity more emancipated?
- Haraway: the cyborg as a prototype for a new kind of identity offers new possibilities for emancipation
- Turkle: online environments allow for identity play and can be seen as liberating

Blogging subjectivities:

- autonomous but in a collaborative manner, may contribute to personal growth if not strategically oriented

Gender Identity

- Butler: performativity and new media: a new context for gender performances contributing to the dynamism of gender, while also identity playing may lead to transgression of gender norms
- Haraway: cyborgs point to constructed-ness of gender out of (also) technological materials. An ambiguous relationship: freedom from gender constraints but also instruments of control
- Cyberfeminism: the transcendence of gender through or in digital cultures (Sadie Plant)
- Just as new technologies, gender identities are fluid and dynamic – together they form a moving target
- To view the new media as 'good' or 'bad' for gender relations overlooks the dynamism of both

Ethic-Religious Identity

- Castells: space and technology de-linked from the formation of ethnic identities
- Ethnic identities lose meaning and significance and operate now in terms of the requirements of globalized informational capitalism

- Religious identities seen as reactionary and their relationship to new media as ridden with tensions and contradictions

- Some evidence for emancipatory potential of new media: increased visibility, ability to voice concerns, to participate in the political process and articulate political demands

- However: evidence of ethnic stereotyping in new media environments: cybertyping and techno-orientalism (Nakamura)

- More negative aspects: community policing and cyber-fragmentation

- Religious identities reformed in new media environments

- Long distance nationalism (Anderson): the paradoxical strengthening of ethnic bonds

Overall, we can see that we are in fact trying to keep pace with a moving target: identities are both fluid and dynamic, in constant evolution, much in the same way as new technologies develop and evolve in constant interaction with socio-political, economic and cultural factors. When put together, their articulations are manifold and unpredictable. From this point of view, it would be wrong to insist that the new media are necessarily a positive or negative influence on identities. On the other hand, specific instantiations may be shown to be good in terms of specific effects, such as increased political participation or visibility, symbolic value and so on. In these terms, any assessment of the relationship between identities and the new media must be an ad hoc one, referring to specific instances, and valid mostly for these.

E-tivity: Online Selves and Identities

The point of this e-tivity is to help you understand the ways in which technologies positively contribute towards new formations of self and identity, but that these new formations entail new dangers and new hierarchies. You should choose one or two examples of three types of sites: a personal blog; a women's group site or a gay group site; and a site linked to a particular ethnicity. You should then address the following questions:

1   With reference to the group sites, based on gender/sexuality/ethnicity: Who do these sites primarily address? Who are included and excluded from the users? Who is allowed to participate and how? How do these sites deal with dissent and disagreement both from users and guests?

2   With reference to the personal blogs: What are the main features of the blog pertaining to the self? How do these blogs present and maintain the self/blogger's identity? What type of interaction do they allow, and who may be the main readers of such blogs?

Further Reading

This collection of articles focuses on the relationship between new media and identity, and explores its many facets. The article by Yangzi Sima and Peter Pugsley explores the ways in which the Chinese blogosphere contributes new ways of identity construction, influenced more by individualism and consumerism rather than by traditional Chinese values – compare their findings and arguments with our discussion of global culture and new media in Chapter 2. Jenny Davis' article looks at 'architectural' features of a social networking site, and examines the ways in which they circumscribe the construction of self. The following two articles look at gender and ethnicity respectively. Niels van Doorn looks at online gendered and sexualized performances, while Parker and Song rework the notion of social capital and its applicability to how members of ethnic minorities use the internet. The final article is one of the first attempts by Castells to articulate the relationship between the internet and the self: presenting and summarizing the main components of his network society, Castells concludes by examining the shifts in the ways in which the self is (re)constructed in and through new media technologies: this constant reconstruction is a necessity in a kind of society that prioritizes flexibility and immediate response to information flows.

Sima, Y. and Pugsley, P., 2010, The Rise of A 'Me Culture' in Postsocialist China: Youth, Individualism and Identity Creation in the Blogosphere, *International Communication Gazette*, 72(3): 287–306.

Davis, J., 2010, Architecture of the Personal Interactive Homepage: Constructing the Self through MySpace, *New Media & Society*, 12(7): 1103–1119.

van Doom, N., 2010, The Ties that Bind: The Networked Performance of Gender, Sexuality and Friendship on MySpace, *New Media & Society*, 12(4): 583–602.

Parker, D. and Song, M., 2006, Ethnicity, Social Capital and the Internet: British Chinese Websites, *Ethnicities*, 6(2): 178–202.

Castells, M., 1996, The Net and the Self: Working Notes for a Critical Theory of the Informational Society, *Critique of Anthropology*, 16(1): 9–38.

CHAPTER 10

SOCIALITIES AND SOCIAL MEDIA

Learning Objectives

- To learn about theories of sociality and association with others
- To understand the relationship between sociality and the new media
- To critically apprehend the shifts in sociality introduced by social networking sites
- To develop a critical understanding of the concept and implications of networked individualism

Introduction

How many 'friends' do you have on your social networking site(s)? How many 'contacts' on your mobile phone? How many 'followers' on Twitter? Facebook statistics reports that the average number of 'friends' Facebook users have is 120, while mobile phone SIM cards can store about 200 contacts. Out of these, with some we communicate often, with others very rarely, while some of these 'friends', 'followers' and contacts we haven't even met! Just a few years ago things were very different, as proximity seemed to determine our social life: we met and socialized with people in our immediate environments, at school, work, or leisure activities. Friendships were sustained by regular face-to-face contact, although telephone calls and letters were used to keep in touch with those living elsewhere. In sociology, being and/or living with others are mediated through ethical ideas about how life should be lived, and by physical space. Ethical ideas, such as individualism, i.e. the primacy of the individual and his/her freedoms over community life, or conversely collectivism, the primacy of community – or alternatively ideas regarding safety, protection, or a needs-based social organization might permeate social structures, and seep through our everyday lives. Both ethical ideas and our notion of space are profoundly affected by the new media because they generate new ideas about how life should be lived and because they provide a different, virtual space in which people come together. But how can we think of these developments in a more systematic and theoretically fruitful manner?

What does it mean, more broadly, that the ways in which we socialize and interact with others tend to be increasingly mediated by the internet and other new media? How might we understand the shifts and changes in sociality associated with the new media?

Some of the answers, this chapter suggests, are to be found in theories of sociality and community. The question of being together with others – what we term here sociality – has concerned theorists for a long time. One of the first interrogations of sociality came at the dawn of the previous century, when massive urbanization uprooted people from villages and relocated them in cities, producing profound changes in how people are together. Yet if we accept, as Aristotle suggested, that humans are social animals, then we would expect that certain elements of sociality are characteristic of our species. Nevertheless there is little doubt that the new media have ushered in radically new ways of being with others – this clearly necessitates some new theorizing of the new relationships and new socialities that have emerged. This chapter will examine these issues by discussing some of the older theories of sociality, beginning with the work of Ferdinand Tönnies on society and community. The chapter will then review more recent theorizing on new media socialities, through the works of Barry Wellman, Manuel Castells and others on social networks and networked individualism. The final section will look at the social media explosion and discuss their relationship to networked individualism.

Society and Community in the Age of the New Media

We can just imagine Ferdinand Tönnies walking in the newly paved streets of the sprawling German metropolises, wondering about the massive and profound changes in social life. For most of the nineteenth century, most people lived in small villages, knowing not only each other, but each other's parents and grandparents, children, cousins, uncles and aunts! Closely-knit communities, relying on face-to-face contact were the main form of social organization in traditional and early modern societies. And then, with the advent of the industrial revolution, more and more people left their villages and went to the cities, looking for work in factories. Towns became proper cities, accommodating more and more people, who were strangers to each other. What held this kind of society together? How was society even possible, given that it concerned more and more association between strangers? These were partly the questions that Tönnies posed. But he was also interested in the historical changes that societies undergo as they evolve: how might we understand such historical changes? To understand the historical process of shifts in the ways in which we associate, Tönnies (2001 [1887]) suggested we need concepts which will help us theorize these changes. In this section we will discuss his main concepts and examine their applicability in the context of the new media.

For Tönnies, Aristotle's understanding of humans as social animals is seen as corresponding to a psychological mechanism that concerns human will. Societies, argues Tönnies, can only exist because people want to associate with others. But human will is of two kinds: there is the essential, organic will that is almost instinctive – this is referred to as the natural will. On the other hand, there is a rational will, which is purposive and goal oriented. While natural will leads people to form associations as an end in themselves, rational will leads them to associate with other people in order to attain some goals. Community (*Gemeinschaft*) is formed around this organic, natural will and it includes all these associations in which we partake out of our own choice and volition, while membership is self-fulfilling: friendships, neighbourhood groups, voluntary organizations, families and so on are examples of communities. The bonds that bind us to other community members tend to be affective ones. Conversely, society (*Gesellschaft*) is formed on the basis of rational will, and membership takes the form of an instrumental association, that leads to certain goals: for example, membership in a city or state as citizens (rights, protection etc.), or in private companies (profit etc.). While community represents the romantic ideal of association that is organic and meaningful, society represents the rational component of association, which fulfils the needs of modern society. Tönnies' argument is that while early societies relied on a *Gemeinschaft* type of social organization, modern societies must rely on a *Gesellschaft* organization, which binds people together through the application of rationality, the rational management of being and living together, all of which stem from the operation of rational will.

Thinking about what precipitated the shift from community to society, Tönnies holds that it was trade, mercantile capitalism which subsequently led to industrial capitalism – his idea was that the desire to use money more profitably ushered in trade on a larger scale, and this in turn led to capitalism (Loomis and McKinney, 2002). From this point of view, while he was influenced by Marx, he did not think that technology had any contributory role, and hence his theory cannot be used to understand the role of the new media in social change. On the other hand, his theorizations of society may provide fruitful ways of thinking about shifts in social organization linked to the new media. The main question emerging from Tönnies' work, which can guide us in rethinking society and sociality, is this: if we accept that early societies were mostly functioning as communities and modern societies as societies, then what do late modern, informational societies function as?

While Tönnies devised these concepts as ideal-typical formulations to enable us to understand shifts in society, there is an undercurrent of nostalgia. The shift from organic communities towards impersonal societies is associated with a loss of human contact, a loss of the unity and solidarity of the community in favour of an instrumental pursuit of profit or other goals. Do the internet and the new media continue this trend of erosion of community or, do they, as Rheingold (1993) argued, breathe new life into a new form of community? In his groundbreaking study on communities in the age of the internet, Howard Rheingold, who is online since 1985, wrote about his experiences and attempted to rethink the way in which people relate to one another in online environments. His experiences with his own 'virtual' community, WELL (Whole Earth 'Lectronic Link), led him to argue that such communities are decentralized, autonomous in the sense that they make their own rules, and diverse. More specifically, Rheingold defined virtual communities as: social aggregations that emerge from the Net when enough people carry on those public discussions long enough, with sufficient human feeling, to form webs of personal relationships in cyberspace' (1993: 5). Such virtual communities, mediated and sustained by electronic communication technologies, exist independent of geographical location and without necessarily any face-to-face contact between their members. Virtual communities come together on the basis of sharing information, ideas, feelings and desires (Calhoun, 2002). The rise of virtual communities is due on the one hand to the loss of more traditional public places in which people came together, and on the other on the pioneering spirit of the first 'netsurfers' who were attracted to the idea of interacting with others on a completely different level (Rheingold, 1993). The ability of the new media to bring about and sustain such communities is thought to radically change the ways in which we live our lives in late (or for some post-) modernity. If the trend was towards more and more isolation and atomization, more *Gesellschaft* and more instrumentalism, then virtual communities represent a shift towards a new kind of community, based not merely on proximity and relations made possible by sharing a given space, but common ideas, beliefs, experiences and so on.

In general, virtual communities are characterized by lack of physical proximity, they are based on shared interests rather than shared location, and there are weaker ties between their members although the relationships formed can be quite intimate (Wellman and Gulia, 1999; Katz, Rice, Acord, Dasgupta and David, 2004). Because they are primarily based on shared interests they eschew the repressive side of physical communities, while they can also permeate boundaries of all kinds: geographical, ethnic, racial, gender and so on (Katz and Rice, 2002). As Katz et al. (2004: 327) put it, 'virtual communities are based on shared social practices and interests whereas physical communities are based on shared social and physical boundaries' and this is precisely where their novelty and potential is located. While typically communities operate in a more or less conservative manner, safeguarding and often imposing certain traditions on their members, virtual communities allow individuals to meet like-minded people, to express their identities without any fear of exclusion or ostracism, and they can therefore escape the boundaries of their local communities. Furthermore, while these virtual communities set up their own rules and norms guiding their behaviour, they are decentralized, in the sense that they do not have established community leaders. From this point of view they can be considered more egalitarian and hence democratic than their offline versions. Another relative advantage of virtual communities is the ease of their creation and their openness. While traditional communities are often sceptical towards newcomers, virtual communities tend to be more open, happily welcoming new members. In addition, even if people cannot find a virtual community that can accept them, they can easily set up a new one (Castells, 2004). Rheingold locates the specific contribution of virtual communities to their decentralizing tendencies and their ability to bypass both 'malevolent political leaders' as well as the power of centralized broadcast networks and the corporations that own them. They can therefore contribute to the reinvigoration of the public sphere as well as to the development of an electronic democracy. However, Rheingold is quick to point out that this potential can only be realized if the new media can escape both governmental control and commercialization.

Loss of Community? .

On the other hand, there are those who view these new communities with a high degree of scepticism. Their potential is seen as ambiguous at best, since they can serve to further isolate and fragment people, leading to a further loss of community as well as of 'social capital'. Bourdieu and Wacquant (1992: 119) define social capital as 'the sum of the resources, actual or virtual, that accrue to an individual or a group by virtue of possessing a durable network of more or less institutionalized relationships of mutual acquaintance and recognition'. In other words, social capital refers to the people we know and the relationships we have with them, and to the kinds of benefits we get out of being associated with these people. In a ground breaking essay, Robert Putnam (1995), based on data generated by surveys from the 1950s until the mid-1990s, concluded that social capital in the USA is eroding: less people get involved in social activities, and do less things together compared with previous generations. Putnam's metaphor is bowling: although more Americans are bowling, he says, less of them are bowling in leagues – this for Putnam shows the degree of social disengagement in the USA and more broadly in Western societies. The result is a society that is not much more than a collection of individuals, meeting and socializing occasionally but who do not share any strong bonds or any sense of common purpose. And if we do not meet and engage with other people, social trust and the social fabric that holds society together will eventually dissolve. Putnam attributes this loss of social capital to, among others, new technologies. He argues that technological trends, such as occupying our time with television, are individualizing our time off work, thereby disrupting opportunities for the formation of social capital (Putnam, 1995: 75). In other words, the more time we spend at home watching television, the less time we have for socializing, for forming neighbourhood or other groups, for meeting people and so on. In addition, he argues that electronic technologies satisfy individual tastes, but this occurs at the expense of other 'positive social externalities' associated with older forms of entertainment. For Putnam, new technologies use up our time in ways that do not allow us to form meaningful social associations with other people, and in satisfying our personal interests, they also remove our motives for associating with others. While Putnam was not directly referring to the internet and other new media, his arguments imply that not only do they not contribute to a renewal of sociality, but they end up eroding what little social capital television has left us! In his 1995 essay, he refers to the 'virtual reality' helmet, which he says will be worn by most of us in the future, as a symbol of this growing isolation. Although this hasn't happened yet, looking at people walking in the streets wearing headphones almost all the time seems to support Putnam's contentions: even as we walk among other people we are increasingly alone, increasingly isolated and retreating to the worlds offered or created by the new media.

Cass Sunstein in his *Republic.com* (2001) offers a somewhat different criticism. The ability of the new media to offer customized information, their interactivity, which makes us able to choose and filter what we see, are leading us, argues Sunstein, to a perfectly egocentric, atomized world, in which the 'Daily Me' prevails. In most societies, we end up having some form of unanticipated encounter with others, who may be completely different to us, and this diversity, argues Sunstein is crucial in keeping us aware of other points of view, of disagreement, conflict and difference. The new media, for Sunstein, in fact offer limited opportunities for a truly public forum in which we are all brought together and exposed to each other. While the new media may encourage the formation of some communities, these tend to be closed groups of like-minded people. This polarization is not good for society, which ends up becoming fragmented, less a society and more a collection of polarized groups that share little if anything with each other. This, argues Sunstein, is divisive and breeds extremism. When online, we tend to stay in the confines of our in-group of like-minded members, rarely venturing 'out' and rarely coming across to the vast diversity of the world. Thus, although the internet is astonishingly diverse, users tend to go to places where they are likely to meet others like them thereby ignoring this diversity to the detriment of society at large. In an updated version of his book, Sunstein (2007) speaks of the effects of Web 2.0 applications and especially the blogosphere: blogs, he argues, rather than bringing forward a bottom up 'revolution' and allowing for wider participation, have ended up creating 'information cocoons' and 'echo chambers' repeating and echoing the same information and arguments over and over. While Sunstein's arguments were intended as political critique on the relationship between the internet and democracy, they have important implications for understanding the kind of society and community supported by the new media. It is indeed quite disappointing that instead of the liberal and free-minded virtual communities described by Rheingold we end up with closed, polarized groups, which contribute to the fragmentation, or as Sunstein put it, the (cyber)balkanization of society.

Where does this discussion leave us? Do the new media breathe new life into communities, which were in a slow decline since the industrial revolution? Or do they in fact put to rest the idea of closely knit communities? Calhoun (1998) argues that the debate on virtual communities rests on different understandings of the term community, and we should produce more precise definitions if we are to understand not only the transformations in sociality associated with the new media but also their impact on democratic societies. In principle, communities can be understood as the extension of people's personal relationships and community life is understood 'as the life people live in dense, multiplex relatively autonomous networks of social relationships' (Calhoun, 1998: 391). For Calhoun, community denotes not only a place or a small-scale population aggregate, but a mode of relating to each other, which is variable in extent. In other words, we can consider communities as offering a way for relating to others. Now the internet, argues Calhoun, can do little in the way of producing community, or 'binding people to each other in dense, multiplex networks' (1998: 392). It can prove useful in organizing and coordinating communities that operate offline, but does not seem to be able to initiate the ties, rights, and obligations understood as part of community life. Calhoun then seems to draw a line separating online from offline communities, implying that the former can only supplement but never replace the latter. Since Calhoun's essay, however, the new media have become more firmly embedded in our lives, and the distinction between off- and online is becoming more and more blurred – we seem to combine being on- and off-line in a seamless way, while for more and more people their online conduct is an inextricable part of their lives. Does this mean that we no longer experience community life or enjoy the dense bonds that communities can provide us?

It seems that there is little agreement between theorists regarding the existence, functioning and evaluation of 'virtual' communities. In his assessment of this debate, Castells (2001) argues that most of it took place in the early days of the internet and may therefore not be relevant any longer. In addition, the debate took place before we had any substantial research evidence regarding sociality on the internet, while, third, it was polarized between two simplistic extremes: harmonious communities and lonely, atomized 'netizens'. More broadly, it seems that the organic entities described by Tönnies are long gone, and no degree of nostalgia can bring them back. On the other hand, if the ways in which we relate to others have changed we need to understand the direction of this change, before we are able to evaluate it, notwithstanding Putnam's and Sunstein's important critiques. The debate on virtual communities shows us more than anything that the concepts we have may be inappropriate for describing the kinds of relationships ushered in by the new media. A promising line of thought has been developing over the last few years most notably by Barry Wellman and his collaborators. Although relying on theorizations of community, Wellman suggests that we can better understand shifts in sociality in terms of networks. These new theoretical developments will be discussed next.

Networks and Sociality

While most of the debate on community is characterized by nostalgic undertones, Barry Wellman has attempted to specify the stakes of the 'community question' in an entirely pragmatic and rigorous manner. For Wellman (1999), the community question concerns essentially the way in which social systems affect the ways in which people relate to each other, as well as, conversely, how specific kinds of interpersonal relations affect the large-scale social systems within which they are embedded. Wellman argues that the question of the community is not a matter of preserving some ideal form of community, but understanding its dynamic nature and its historical embeddedness. His understanding of the 'community question' is not so much to see if communities still exist, but to find out how a social system is integrated: how people relate to each other, how they manage their life alongside other people and what implications this may have for society more broadly. Because of this more abstract understanding of community, Wellman was able to decouple it from specific locales, the village, the neighbourhood or the city, and to seek its structural dimensions. He argues that while once communities were associated with densely knit groups, they are now seen as loosely bounded social networks of relationships (Wellman, 2001a). Such networks are seen as characteristic of the society of the new media, representing therefore the shifts in sociality in late modern, informational societies. This section will discuss the main characteristics of networks, their relationship to the new media, and some of their implications (networked individualism).

Redefining communities as networks, Wellman holds that communities can now be understood as 'networks of interpersonal ties that provide sociability, support, information, a sense of belonging and social identity' (2001b: 227). In his earlier work, Wellman defined a network 'as a set of ties linking social system members across social categories and bounded groups' (1988: 21). As with all kinds of networks, social networks consist of nodes, ties and flows. Nodes are the people who are connected, ties are the ways in which they are connected, and flows refer to the contents of their connection (Barney, 2004). On the basis of these main structures that characterize networks, network analysis has mainly looked at: (i) the density and clustering of a network; this refers to how the people are connected, in direct or indirect ways, and how concentrated were their connections (clusters); (ii) how tight connections are, for example if they are multiple or singular, reciprocated or not and so on; and (iii) the size and heterogeneity of networks (Wellman, 1999). While networks can be dense and tightly bound, recent empirical studies have found that in general they tend to be loosely knit, and frequently changing, although they remain broadly supportive (Wellman, 1999). Another important characteristic of social networks is that their power does not rest on the strength of their ties, but rather on the extent to which they allow for weak ties. In an important essay, Mark Granovetter (1973; 1983) found that weak ties, for examples acquaintances rather than close friends, in a network provide bridges to other networks and other people. Were it not for such weak ties, argues Granovetter, we wouldn't be connected at all. Indeed, a group of people very closely but exclusively connected to each other are more an enclave rather than a network. Thus although networks have a number of weak ties, this does not diminish their power to offer support and social capital, but rather increases it, as such weak ties offer connections to other networks. Most networks tend to be characterized by homophily, that is, a tendency to link to similar others (McPherson, Smith-Lovin and Cook, 2001), and from this point of view weak ties emerge as even more significant for providing connections to other networks – the so-called 'bridging social capital' (Putnam, 2000; Gittell and Vidal, 1998: 15; see also the discussion in the next section). In other words, such weak ties generate an important network resource that brings together people or groups who did not know each other (Granovetter, 1983; Gittell and Vidal, 1998).

New Media Affordances and Changes in Sociality

If these are the general characteristics of social networks, what is their relationship to the new media? Wellman argues that although networks pre-dated the new media, 'recent technological developments have afforded their emergence as a dominant form of social organization' (2001b: 228). Within this context, Wellman (2001b; Wellman et al., 2003) looked for the social affordances of the new media and the internet in particular, that is, the possibilities they create for social relationships and social structure. In other words, Wellman and his colleagues examine the room or space created by the technologies of the new media for social relations. Four broad parameters emerge as relevant: bandwidth, personalization, wireless portability and global connectivity.

Broader bandwidth – the rapid expansion of the amount and speed of data we can exchange online – has important implications for online social networks. On the one hand, broader bandwidth can foster 'telepresence' (Buxton, 1992, in Wellman, 2001b): most of us will have experienced skype calls with friends and family, and can testify to the importance of being able to have this kind of relationship, especially when distance is an issue. On the other hand, as Wellman reports, for most people, broader bandwidth is associated with the 24/7 availability of network connection; the implications of this is that we are always connected with our networks. In Hampton and Wellman's (1999) study of 'Netville', a suburban development in Toronto equipped with high speed internet, respondents found this continuous connectivity very important as they could access and share thoughts or information at any time.

Personalization is the outcome of the possibilities offered by the new media for customization as well as personal communication. Customization offers people the possibility to pick and choose who and what they like, as well as how they want it to appear. For instance, the choice of certain people as 'friends' in a social networking site, as well as the choice to disclose only part of one's profile are some examples of this customization. Filtering, the process by which people select their interests in online environments, and by which they evaluate services, products, films, books and sites, is an important means by which people locate similar others (Wellman, 2001b). At the same time, the new media often operate as personal communication media: this is the case with email, as well as Twitter, instant messaging and even status updates on social networking profiles. This allows for interaction with selected others when and if one chooses. The clear tendency of online social networks to form communities of choice can be seen as afforded by the personalization element of the technology.

Portability, as we have already seen, is an important element of the new media. While the significance of locality was already diminishing in late modernity, the new media, and especially the element of portability amplified this trend. Taking our media with us allows us to be completely independent of locality. This results, as Wellman (2001b) argued, in both the embracing and the negation of ubiquitous globalization: if all localities can be the same or equivalent at least as far as new media access is concerned, then they no longer have any meaning in terms of communication. The person becomes an autonomous communication node, while space, as Castells put it, is becoming a space of flows. Moreover, contextual sense and lateral awareness lose their significance, as people lose their touch with the specificity of certain locations, as well as their sense of space. This is because while they are physically in different locations, by accessing and having their more or less standard interactions with their social networks, the meaning and significance of this difference in locality is diminished. Portability therefore liberates people from the confines of locality, and turns them into autonomous communication nodes.

As computer, but also mobile phone and satellite networks continue their expansion, they create connections across the world, even in countries that lack the infrastructure of highly developed countries. The new media support what Wellman refers to as global connectivity: connections are created and operate even in the most remote parts of the world. The spread of network technology leads to a dispersion of nodes across the world: there is no central node but distributed ones which allow for dispersed communication flows. Given the networked organization of society, global connectivity allows for the creation of ties between everyone. All can be connected to all, either through being part of the same network or indirectly through others who play the role of 'weak ties', building bridges between diverse networks.

Networked Individualism

Taking the above into account, how might we understand the changes in sociality? The diminished role of physical space, personalization and connectivity in space and time all contribute, argues Wellman (2002), to a shift towards networked individualism. This represents a transition from a social organization based on groups – Wellman uses the metaphor of 'little boxes' to denote the closed boundaries and self-sufficiency of these closely-knit communities – to one based on 'glocal' networks, which connected people from place to place. But this place-to-place transition soon gave way to another shift, this time involving a change to a social organization in which social networks are person-to-person ones – the metaphor used by Wellman is the 'switchboard': people operate as switchboards, managing and switching between their different networks or nodes within these networks (Wellman, 2002; Wellman et al., 2003). To understand this transition and its significance Wellman focuses on two main characteristics: that people connect directly to other people and that they are involved in specialized relationships with specific others, with whom they share common interests. In short, in networked individualism, connectivity depends on the person, rather than the locality, household or group – the individual is the primary unit of connectivity. Networked individualism can therefore be defined as the patterns of networks created by individuals on the basis of their preferences, skills, knowledge, background and so on. Castells (2001) takes the idea of networked individualism further, arguing that it represents the privatization of sociability, but it must not be seen as a psychological attribute. Rather, it is rooted in a host of changes, such as the individualization of the relationship between capital and labour; the demise of patriarchalism, urbanization, and the crisis of political legitimacy – he understands it as the upshot of developments that seem to undermine the role of collective organizing or being-together as groups. Networked individualism is not therefore brought about by the new media, but the new media provide the means by which it is diffused as the dominant form of sociality in informational capitalism.

Networked Individualism: An Evaluation

Where does all this leave notions such as community and society? Does networked individualism increase or decrease social bonds and social capital? In other words, how might we evaluate networked individualism? This evaluation can be theoretical, based on an analysis of theoretical concepts and aspects surrounding networked individualism, but it can also be empirical, based on actual research findings on the kinds of relationships people develop and manage in and through the new media. In theoretical terms, networked individualism represents a balance between individuation and the interconnectedness. As Castells (2004: 223) has argued, networked individualism is the synthesis between the affirmation of an individual-centred culture, and the need and desire for sharing and co-experiencing. As the development of sociality takes this form, we can see its compatibility with other changes within informational capitalism: for instance, (immaterial) labour becomes on the one hand more autonomous (individuated) while it relies more and more on ad hoc networks. To some degree, this may be seen as a positive development: Wellman notes that networked individualism offers important advantages compared to the group enclaves and 'little boxes' of previous forms of social organization. The choices afforded to individuals, their disentanglement from physical space, and the ability to manage sociality are all seen as positive aspects of networked individualism. On the other hand, as Wellman (2001b) has noted, to be able to build and manage their own networks, individuals must have the skills to do so and hence to know how to connect with others, as well as to whom to connect.

However, there are also some more damaging issues: Willson (2010) argues that to view networked individualism as supporting choice overlooks the ways in which, first, people are caught up in power structures and existing socio-cultural frameworks, while second, it overstates the case for the availability of free choice as well as the degree to which people are free floating, atomized agents. In focusing on the individual, points Willson, we end up overlooking the ways in which other social configurations and patterns are mediated by the new media. An example here is the mediation of transnational communities or diasporas. Such communities are mediated in ways that may enhance and strengthen bonds between their members, as well as between second and third generation transnationals and their 'mother country' (c.f. Anderson, 1992). Participation in these is not so much a matter of choice, and it is difficult to reconcile the atomized view of net-worked individuals with loose bonds to each other with the strong bonds that bind transnational communities and diasporas. The question here is that although there is no doubt that socialities are changing, probably towards a more individuated variant, more traditional communities and socio-cultural frameworks not only exist but are often given a new lease of life through the new media.

Another issue concerns the extent to which networks and networked individuals are caught up in structures of power. Both Wellman and Castells have pointed out that networks can operate as resources, while within networks people can enjoy considerable power as hubs, but they can also be marginalized. As social organization within (informational) capitalism is riddled with inequali-ties, these are also expected to be found in networks. In contrast to images of individual free agents exercising choice, networks are embedded in existing power structures, which in turn position people differently. Not all of us can have access to the same networks, and the ones we have access to typically reflect our socio-cultural background. Moreover, if we understand networks as resources, then participation in (some) networks does not only reflect the unequal distribution of resources in capitalism, but also puts pressure on people to cultivate the 'right' networks which will then allow them to be upwardly mobile. In this manner, networked individualism may be seen as encouraging a primarily instrumental, goal-oriented attitude to sociality. As we will see in Chapter 11 on games, informational capitalism blurs the boundaries of work and play – in the same manner, it can be observed that networked individualism with its emphasis on the instrumental acquisition of networks blurs the distinction between work and social-personal life. An example here includes the ways in which we manage our online networks of 'friends' in social networking sites. For most of us, these include personal friends, relatives, as well as work contacts; this makes our updates a combination of personal alongside work-related information and self promotion. Typically, young people are advised to mind the kind of information they post online, lest any potential employers see them in an unflattering, unprofessional context, compromising their chances for finding work. Others choose strategically who to ask to be a 'friend' and whether to accept or decline requests on the basis of how useful and desirable these new contacts may be. This blurring of personal and working life ends up prioritizing the latter over the former, and signals a clear shift towards an instrumental understanding of social and personal networks. Networked individualism appears to be a means by which we acquire, manage and administer our public profile rather than a more lib-erating form of sociality. While these lines of critique cover networked individualism as a concept and a theory, the rise of social media introduced a new, more empirically oriented element to this discussion. How do they relate to sociality? This question is approached in the next section.

Social Media and Sociality

While researchers and theorists such as Wellman and Castells have been interested in the social-ity of networks for a long time, more recent developments led to a new momentum in this area.

Specifically, Web 2.0 and especially the rise of social networking sites offered new possibilities for conducting one's online social life, while at the same time providing ample empirical evidence for researchers to examine online socialities. At the same time, the almost unprecedented popularity of the so-called social media may have introduced further changes in network socialities. This section will review the evidence for the 'effects' and influence of social media on sociality; it will begin with a discussion of what social media are, and then move on to look at empirical studies, before finally commenting on the theoretical construct of networked individualism on the basis of the empirical evidence.

Social Media Definitions and Characteristics

When Mark Zuckerberg launched Facebook from his dorm room in Harvard in 2004, no one could have guessed the impact that this kind of combination of technology with social interaction would have on our lives. The technology and similar ideas have been there long before Facebook: sites such as SixDegrees, which was launched in 1997, LiveJournal (1999), Friendster (2001) and MySpace (2003) have ushered in a new kind of online relationship (boyd and Ellison, 2007). The main idea was that they enabled people to publicly list their profile – interests, hobbies, background and so on – as well as their 'friends', 'contacts', 'fans' or 'followers'. Through these lists, other people could join in, becoming 'friends' with other friends of their friends, creating in this manner a network of people with whom they had ties of various strengths. At around the same time, in the early to mid-2000s, the rise of sites allowing the posting and sharing of user-generated contents, such as Flickr and YouTube, led to the integration of social networking sites with content sharing sites, which began to function themselves as social networking sites, listing user profiles, friends, favourite contents and so on. boyd and Ellison (2007: np) define social networking sites as web-based services that '(1) construct a public or semi-public profile within a bounded system, (2) articulate a list of other users with whom they share a connection, and (3) view and traverse their list of connections and those made by others within the system'. Some years later, the term social media is used as an umbrella term for all these sites that integrate technology, social interaction and user-generated content. In definitions of social media, researchers variously prioritize their communicative aspects (boyd, 2008), their openness and participatory elements (Mayfield, 2007) and their connectivity and community-creation (Smith, Borash, Getoor and Lauw, 2008; Mayfield, 2007). In general, we can identify three main characteristics of social media: they allow users to create, download and share contents, to publish their profile and personal information, and to connect with others.

The popularity of social media is beyond question. A 2009 study by Nielsen reported that two out of three people who are online visit social media sites, which makes this activity the fourth most popular online activity, ahead of emailing – searching is the most popular activity. Nielsen estimates that about 10% of all time spent online is spent on social media, while Facebook statistics reports that its users exceed 400 million – if this were a country, it would be more populous than the USA, overtaken only by China and India. Moreover, social media are still rising in terms both of their popularity as well as the volume of contents and information exchanged. In 2009, Twitter grew 577%, Facebook 188.6% and LinkedIn 89% (Liss, 2010), while by mid-2010 they still hadn't reached a plateau. In fact, the social media trend continued to affect other new media areas: mobile phones, especially internet-enabled ones, entered the equation, with applications integrating mobile phone and social media technologies.

Research in Social Media

While these are very suggestive of the hold social media have on people, what do we actually know about the impact and more broadly about the mediating role of social media? Relevant scholarship, argue boyd and Ellison (2007), is divided in four main areas: research on how people manage their identities and reputation; research on social networks and/in social media; research on the relationship between online and offline networks; and privacy. Research on identities and reputations in social media has focused on the ways in which users manage their profiles in public, and mediate between reality and imagination, using aliases, avatars and the like. To a large extent this strand of research reflects the problematic of online identity as studied by Turkle and others, and discussed in Chapter 9. It is mostly research on social networks, their relationship to the offline world and issues of privacy that are the most telling for how sociality changes in the age of social media. Most research, as boyd and Ellison (2007) suggest, has shown that online networks are an extension of offline networks. Studies by Ellison, Steinfield and Lampe (2007) as well as Choi (2006 in boyd and Ellison, 2007) and boyd (2008) found that online social networks in social networking sites are formed primarily on the basis of existing online contacts, acquaintances and friends, and users compile these networks in order to maintain and reinforce their ties with people they already know. If this is indeed the case, then the question of the relationship between social media and social capital still remains. Following Sunstein's and Putnam's arguments, it may be that social media lock people into pre-existing networks, effectively creating enclaves, ending up at best keeping social capital stable and at worst diminishing it.

In a well known early study, Barry Wellman and his colleagues (Wellman, Quan Haase, Witte and Hampton, 2001) found that the internet supplements what they refer to as network capital (our relations with friends and family), and increases participatory capital (involvement in politics and voluntary activities). Do these findings hold for social media as well? In a relevant study, Ellison, Steinfield and Lampe (2007), follow Putnam's (2000) distinction between two forms of social capital: bonding social capital, which refers to the kind of close bonds and solidarity which exists between close friends and family, and bridging social capital, which refers to the 'weak ties' that bind acquaintances, friends of friends, work contacts and so on. Examining the relationship between these kinds of social capital and social networking sites, Ellison et al. found that Facebook use actually increased both bonding and bridging capital, as well as what the researchers referred to as 'maintained social capital', or the ability to hold on to social capital even when frequent face-to-face contact is no longer possible. However, Ellison et al. report that intensity of Facebook use was not associated with the creation or maintenance of bonding capital. Moreover, this study also found that Facebook use led to larger increases in bridging social capital than bonding capital. A similar suggestion was made by Donnath and boyd (2004) who argued that social networking sites would increase the weak ties in networks, because of the ease by which the technology allows us to include acquaintances and people we do not know very well. Another significant finding of this study was that these effects did not hold for the 'internet' at large, but only for Facebook use. In other words, it looks as if social media, but not the new media in general, may help people maintain and increase their social capital.

If these findings suggest an overall positive relationship between sociality and social media, research on privacy shows a more ambiguous relationship. One of the key ideas of modernity, the division between the public and private spheres delegated social life and sociality to the private sphere, while participation in the public sphere typically involved a bracketing of identity and private interests, and in general includes what is of concern to the public as a whole. However, social media upset this division, by mixing public and private elements: information included on profiles can include some of the most intimate details, such as date of birth, relationship status, while research suggests that people, especially teenagers, use social media with no clear idea of their publicness (Barnes, 2006). At the same time, privacy policy is ranked as one of the most important concerns of social media users (Acquisti and Gross, 2006). Raynes-Goldie (2010) attempted to resolve this privacy paradox (Barnes, 2006), by arguing that we need a multi-level understanding of privacy, which she then distinguishes between institutional and social privacy. The former refers to concerns about how social media companies use personal information, and the latter refers to the publishing and control of personal information. The ways in which new media corporations monetize personal information has been discussed already in earlier chapters, but what is important here is to understand some of the dilemmas posed by social media for the ways in which we associate with others. One of the main problems here is that if indeed social media are creating more and more 'weak tie', heterogeneous networks of people who only share a few similar interests, then the kind of information one posts must be very thought through: as one of Raynes-Goldie's (2010) informants put it, you do not want your teetotal boss to see the same information as your party animal friend. Raynes-Goldie refers to this as 'context collision' and some of her informants' strategies for avoiding such collision included the use of aliases and operating multiple accounts. Similar findings were also reported by boyd (2007b), pointing out the ways in which social media users seek to circumvent privacy concerns over social media use.

More broadly, these issues reflect a shift in sociality that marks it as both private and public: the blurring of these boundaries has been characteristic of the new media (Weintraub and Kumar, 1997). In a study on social networks on YouTube, Lange (2008) reports that there are effectively two kinds of networks, those labelled as publicly private and those understood as privately public. The former consist of people who are disclosing personal and technical information while also uploading videos on popular contents; they may also choose popular tags for their videos, making them accessible through Google searches – people in these kinds of networks choose to make private information public. On the other end, privately public networks seek and make public connections, while withholding private information, often using aliases and/or masks to hide their identities in shared videos. Lange's point is that both kinds of social networks operate with private and public formats, but they choose different paths as to what they choose to keep private and what to make public, using both symbolic and technical means. As sociality becomes more and more a hybrid form between publicness and privacy, such findings seem to support the theory of networked individualism, in which the individual is at the centre, negotiating and implementing their own choices regarding the kind of networks they choose to belong to.

At the same time, however, the ambiguous dimensions of this new kind of individualized network sociality are ever present. For example, even accepting that social media increase social capital, this still imposes an economic model of sociality which understands it in terms of capital and costs. It follows that network sociality becomes yet another field of competition for scarce resources, for the best contacts or friends, for participation in the most valuable or prestigious networks. Moreover, as boyd's (2007a; 2008) research has shown, class and other divisions still operate in social media networks, which seems to negate the more individualistic and liberal elements of networked individualism: if it is a matter of free choice, then why are class differences reflected in network participation? Similarly, negotiating the symbolic and technical means by which network choices for friends, privacy, uploading contents and so on are made online requires familiarity with these codes, something that points to the different kinds of choices available to different people. One the other hand, the pressure more and more people feel in order to join such online networks and to use social media is mounting, confronting people with the dilemma: either participate or risk becoming invisible. Another issue here concerns the kinds of relationships we end up having: the inclusion of all kinds of personal contacts, ranging from our family to our professional contacts, implies that any boundaries between different parts of our lives are broken down. Personal, professional and family life all slide into each other, with results that may not necessarily be positive, as instrumentalism may take over from any kind of altruistic need for friendship. As we have seen time and again, the network society is no respecter of boundaries set in earlier kinds of society: work, play, leisure, privacy and publicity, community and society are all mixed together, placing the individual at the centre. The conclusion we can draw here reiterates Manuel Castells' argument that network individualism reflects the individuation of the relationship between capital and labour and more broadly, the dynamics of the network society, in which social structures, as well as the ways in which we relate to each other undergo a series of changes.

Conclusions

The main question this chapter sought to address concerned the changes in the ways in which we associate with others. These changes, as we have seen, take the form of a sociality that combines elements of individualism, already present in the pre-new media social organization, with the deep human need to share with others. The result is a sociality that has been described as networked individualism. Box 10.1 overleaf summarizes the main points of the chapter, and the different ways in which sociality has been theorized.

Where does all this leave us? Should we understand networked individualism as an overall positive development, or as limiting and problematic as other forms of association? While we must remain critical, we do not yet have enough evidence on the basis of which to come up with a definitive evaluation. At best, we should understand networked individualism as equivalent, although we should also be aware that there cannot be a perfect way of connecting with other people and managing our life in common. But we must also be aware of the costs that new forms of sociality may entail: as Castells (2001: 133) put it, the costs of networked individualism for society are not yet clear, but there will be costs.

10.1

Summary of Main Points

Community and Society

- Community: revolving around the will to be with others and constitutes a tightly knit association bound together with affective bonds. Examples: neighbourhoods, families etc.

- Society: instrumental, goal-oriented membership, stemming from the rational will, bound together by rationality. Examples: the state, private companies etc.

- Does the internet/new media resurrect or completely destroy communities?

- Rheingold: the rise of virtual communities, based on shared interests rather than shared physical space can be more democratic and egalitarian, less oppressive

- But, contra Rheingold, Putnam argues that overall social capital is diminishing (at least in the USA) and the (new) media may be responsible

- Sunstein argues that atomization, fragmentation and polarization rather than community emerge out of our engagement with the new media

Networks and Society

- Not communities but networks: loosely knit sets of ties that provide sociability, support, information and belongingness (Wellman)

- Networks characterized by 'homophily', the tendency to include similar others, but also by weak ties (e.g. by including acquaintances or friends of friends) which provide links to other networks

- New media have created the material environment that supports networks

- Bandwidth, personalization, portability and global connectivity emerge as the new media affordances that circumscribe social networks

- All these contribute to the rise of networked individualism: a social organization that is no longer based on close groups or networks connecting place-to-place, but networks connecting person-to-person on the basis of preferences, skills, knowledge and so on

Critical points:

- Overstates availability of free choice

- Emphasis on choice overlooks embeddedness in power structures

- Networks are resources and hence are unequally distributed
- Imposition of instrumental, goal-oriented logic on associating with others

Social Media

- Defined as sites/media that integrate technology, social interaction and user-generated contents
- Main characteristics:

  Communicative

  Open and participatory

  Provide connectivity

  Support community

  Actively encourage and rely upon the creation and sharing of contents
- Research on social media reveals that networks are mostly formed on the basis of existing offline ones
- Social media increase primarily bridging social capital but not linked to the creation and maintenance of bonding capital
- Privacy concerns: while users are concerned with privacy, they do not appear to appreciate the public nature of social media
- A new sociality that blurs the boundaries between private and public
- An economic model that understands sociality in terms of capital and costs
- Divisions of class and others operate in social media
- Boundaries erode, with the professional meshing with the personal, the public with the private and work with play

E-tivity: Exploring Online Socialities

Much of the controversy surrounding the social use of the internet concerns the extent to which it does in fact offer a new kind of social connection, the extent to which it leads to a new kind of community, and the extent to which this is a positive or negative development. This e-tivity aims to help understand further some of the issues involved in the relationship between social life and the internet. With reference to concepts such as 'community' and 'society' (Tönnies), 'social capital' (Putnam), or 'networked individualism' (Castells, Wellman), this e-tivity requires that you carefully examine and explore sites belonging to: a self-help association; a social networking site; a gaming/virtual reality site (e.g. Second Life); and a locally-based network site (e.g. a parent association etc.). You will then be asked to consider the following questions:

1   For each of these sites, consider the type of community they give rise to. How closely does it approximate any of the above understandings ('community', 'society', 'social capital')? What do you think keeps these groups together?

2   For each site list what you consider to be the positive and negative aspects with respect to how they connect people together.

3   For each site, consider the opportunities offered or created for connection beyond the virtual, online world. Do you consider the provision or lack of such opportunities positive, negative or equivocal?

Further Reading

Following up on the theme of identity, the articles here explore the social dimension of new media lives. Jill Walker Rettberg looks at how social media frame lives and feed these narratives back to us. Ulises Mejias, on the other hand, launches a critique of networks as a means of understanding the social, on the basis that these models often develop and reinforce a privatized notion of sociality. The last two articles, by Ellison and her colleagues, and Zizi Papacharissi are applied research studies in aspects of online socialities. While Ellison et al. look at social media users' online strategies as a means of amassing or converting social capital, Zizi Papacharissi looks at the ways in which the different structural dimensions of social media such as Facebook and LinkedIn condition different kinds of socialities.

Walker Rettberg, J., 2009, 'Freshly Generated for You, and Barack Obama': How Social Media Represent Your Life, *European Journal of Communication*, 24(4): 451–466.

Mejias, U.A., 2010, The Limits of Networks as Models for Organizing the Social, *New Media & Society*, 12(4): 603–617.

Ellison, N.B., Steinfield, C. and Lampe, C., 2011 (published online before print), Connection Strategies: Social Capital Implications of Facebook-enabled Communication Practices, *New Media & Society*.

Papacharissi, Z., 2009, The Virtual Geographies of Social Networks: A Comparative Analysis of Facebook, LinkedIn and ASmallWorld, *New Media & Society*, 11(1–2): 199–220.

CHAPTER 11

GAMES AND GAMING

Learning Objectives

- To critically understand the games industry, and the ways in which gaming practices and contents are shaped by economic requirements
- To find out the kinds of representations and narratives encountered in games
- To learn the various gaming practices and their implications
- To develop an understanding of the formation of gaming communities and their characteristics

Introduction

About 70 years ago, the Dutch theorist Johan Huizinga (1938) published a book titled *Homo Ludens* or Playful Man. The main argument in this book was that play is not merely a superfluous activity to be undertaken by children and the idle, but a necessary condition for culture. Through play, cultures established themselves, but also evolved and changed. For Huizinga, play comes first, before culture, and culture derives from it. In this sense, it may be argued that within a given historical context, the most prominent games define the logic and core of a culture. If we introduce computer games into this equation, and accept that their rising popularity and quick spread across the world is turning them into one of the most prominent forms of play, then our culture is by and large characterized by these kinds of games. The question then that emerges here concerns the changes and shifts that gaming is introducing to our culture. While this is a question that needs to be addressed empirically, this chapter takes some initial steps to examine some of the main characteristics of games and more broadly play.

More specifically, Huizinga argued that play is characterized by certain key features. First, play is freedom in the sense that one is not forced or morally obliged to play but it is an activity one chooses to do out of enjoyment – it is not a task, says Huizinga (2003 [1938]: 8), but done at free time. Second, play is not 'ordinary' or 'real life', but involves 'stepping out of real life into a temporary sphere of activity' (ibid.: 8). Games create their own worlds, parallel to 'real life'. This, in turn, is linked to another characteristic, that play takes place in a different locality and has a certain duration: games have limits of time and place, they begin and they end. Fourth, while in play mode, games have their own rules of what can and cannot be done: in this sense, games introduce order. If the rules are broken, the game is over. From this point of view, order and the rules of the game tend to be quite rigid. To the extent that some initiation to the rules is necessary, play creates divisions between those in the game and those outside it. Huizinga argues that play therefore promotes the formation of social groupings that tend to surround themselves with secrecy and often use a special code to differentiate the insiders from the outsiders. Finally, play is seen as an activity that is not connected to any material interest, and Huizinga tells us that no profit can be extracted from it (ibid.: 13). To what extent do computer games share these characteristics? Or, put differently, to what extent do the new media introduce changes in the main characteristics of play?

To begin with the last feature, that of material gain, while most gamers do not play for profit, computer games form part of a growing billion dollar industry. This industry needs to be properly understood, as its interests may shape the ways in which computer games get developed and marketed. The first section of this chapter will therefore look at the games industry from a political economic perspective, seeking to outline the economic parameters that shape gaming practices and contents. Second, how is the non-ordinariness of games and their rules determined and expressed? This requires an examination of the contents and representations of games, to determine if indeed they mark a departure from ordinariness. Third, Castells has told us that in the network society, time becomes timeless and geographical space becomes a space of flows: how does this affect the duration and place limits of games? This requires a combination of an analysis of games structure as well as of gaming practices. A final issue here concerns the formation of quasi-exclusive communities around games, an important characteristic of play according to Huizinga: what are gaming communities, how are they formed and what are their main characteristics? In addressing these issues, this chapter will be divided into three sections: a section on the political economy of games; a section on the contents and representations of games; and finally, a section on gaming practices, which will look at gamers and gaming communities.

The Political Economy of Games

The games industry is first and foremost just that: an industry. But beyond this, it is also, as Aphra Kerr (2006) argues, a cultural industry. The term cultural industry was suggested by Adorno and Horkheimer (1997) to denote the ways in which culture has become industrialized and commodified, and as such it has become a fundamental part of capitalist life, unable to stand in opposition to it. For critical theory, the issue here is that culture should be left outside the realm of the economy so as to be able to criticize it and through this critique to improve the economic and political system, making it not only more equitable and just, but also more meaningful. But since the economic realm has colonized culture, the latter has lost its critical edge, and now merely serves the interests of the current political and economic order. As cultural theory and political economy evolved, the critique went even further. It is not only that culture has lost its edge, but it is produced, managed and marketed in ways that seek to maximize profit. In so doing, they turned culture from a public good to effectively a private commodity. Clearly, as Kerr (2006: 45) argues, the games industry is a cultural industry, characterized by high risk in its production, by high production but low reproduction costs and by the semi-public good nature of its products. The task of this section is to outline the ways in which games have become part of a growing industry, and how this has affected the ways in which they are produced, distributed and subsequently consumed. It will begin with an examination of the industry in terms of numbers and income, and then look at its structure and business strategies. The overall argument here is that the games industry is seeking growth and higher returns, and in pursuing those it may sacrifice originality and creativity. More broadly, following Kline, Dyer-Witheford and De Peuter (2003), it will be argued that the computer games industry is a fundamental part of digital capitalism, relying on its networking logic and distributed creativity for profit.

Games Industry: Size and Income

As Kerr (2006) has noted, it is very difficult to estimate the size of the games industry for several reasons. First, there is no doubt that the industry is internally diverse: it includes not only games consoles, such as Wii and PlayStation, but also handheld devices such as Nintendo. Games can also be released for PCs, or they can be played online. The most successful games are marketed and sold globally, making the industry a global one. While size estimates are difficult, one thing appears certain: this, unlike the recording industry, is an industry with a future and it keeps on growing. Figure 11.1 shows a 2005 estimate of growth prepared for the OECD. According to this, the global games industry was worth more than $35 billion by 2008. As a comparison, we can say that the recorded music industry totalled $32 billion in 2003.

And what is more, the growth of the industry is considered to be healthy – the US Bureau of Labor estimates a growth of about 14% between 2010 and 2018 in the USA. The industry is not only growing in the USA but in Asia as well: South Korea's gaming industry, which accounts for the 56% of the entire Asia Pacific market share, was growing at 20% at least until 2008 (Jin and Chee, 2008). Not to be outdone, the Chinese games industry was measuring 31 million users by 2006, generating 6.5 billion ren min bi (about $1 billion) but growing at a very rapid rate (Ernkvist and Ström, 2008). To these we may add the Japanese games giants: Sony has sold about 143.8 million PlayStations worldwide retailing at $50 each, Nintendo has grossed $15.75 billion in 2009, while Sega's 2009 revenue was at $1.65 billion. In 2010, as the world was sinking deeper into an economic crisis, the industry seemed recession-proof. However, the *Economist* notes that it, too, is hit by the recession. In June 2009 the US sales were 31% lower than in June 2008 and in July 2009 the sales were down by 26% (*Economist*, 2010). The industry bounced back in December 2009, however, with a record breaking income of $5.53 billion, a rise of 4% from December 2008 (Cnet, 2010), but worldwide losses were reported for the whole of 2009: 9.3% in the USA, 3.5% in Europe and 2% in Japan (*Economist*, 2010). As the *Economist* notes, these losses reflect the widening popularity of gaming which makes it susceptible to economic cycles: as long as it had been the domain of a few dedicated players, it remained impervious to the economy. Since, however, it has

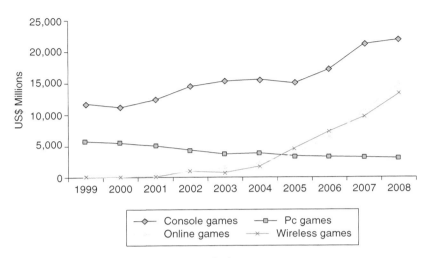

Figure 11.1   The computer games market

Source: OECD (2005: 8)

now become mainstream, it is part of the wider economy. In another explanation, it may be that 2009 was not a very creative year for games releases – at least this is what an industry insider, the game designer Shigeru Miyamoto of Nintendo, told the *Economist* – and perhaps this was reflected in the lower sales. Despite these losses, the games industry is looking forward to a bright future.

Development, Production and Informationalized Labour

What has made this industry so successful? What kinds of production processes and strategies have led to this success? Kline et al. (2003) argue that the industry has embraced the kinds of production values and processes associated with the shift towards a digitalized, informational capitalism: flexible, networked-organized production along with intensified marketing processes (see also Chapter 3). In fact, it forms an exemplary case of informational production, relying on creativity, 'perpetual upgrades', and saturation marketing (Kline et al., 2003: 74). The profitability of the industry depends on how it balances technological innovation, cultural trends and marketing strategies. Given its reliance on informational strategies the digital game may in fact be something beyond a mere commodity: it may be an ideal-typical commodity form. Kline et al. (2003) elaborate on Martin Lee's (1993) argument that each phase of capitalism is exemplified by a certain commodity, which acquires an ideal-typical form, condensing the defining characteristics of this historical phase. Just as the car was the ideal-typical commodity of Fordism and industrial capitalism, computer games, argue Kline et al. (2003; see also Dyer-Witheford, 2003). Indeed, as Dyer-Witheford (2003) has argued, we shall see that the digital game is a perfect illustration of production under conditions of informational capitalism.

In another article, Dyer-Witheford and Sharman (2005) divide the production process into four distinct stages: development, which refers to the creation and design of a game and its software; publishing, which involves the whole management of the game commodity, including its financing, manufacturing, packaging and marketing; licensing; and distribution, which refers to the actual shipping of the gaming hardware and software to retail stores. We will look into those in some detail.

How are games developed? Kerr (2006: 64) distinguishes between three types of development companies: (i) first party developers, which are in-house production teams, integrated into publishing companies and developing games for them; (ii) second party developers, who are contracted to develop games from concepts; and (iii) third party developers, who develop games independently and then try to sell them to publishers. The majority of games, reports Kerr, are developed by first party developers who are directly employed by publishers. Game development, as Dyer-Witheford and Sharman (2005) put it, is the wellspring of gaming. It is a costly, work intensive process that can take anything between 12 months and three years, it can cost several million dollars, and it relies on collaboration between 20 and 100 people, depending on the scope of the project (ibid.).

While game developing is the result of intense collaboration, there is an ideal form of a game developer, who resembles an auteur: Deuze, Bowen Martin and Allen (2007) refer to names such as Will Wright, Shigeru Miyamoto and John Carmack, who developed *The Sims*, *Mario Brothers* and *Quake* respectively, as having reputations similar to those of Kubrick, Kurosawa and Polanski in earlier generations. Game developing is seen as exciting and creative, making full use of talent and offering great opportunities for success. This involvement of talent, as well as effort and personality or vision in the process of creating a game is a perfect example of Lazzarato's concept of immaterial labour (1996, see Chapter 3), which allows a lot of discretion and creativity to workers, and which entails the involvement of knowledge, both formal and cultural, as well as a great deal of creativity. On the other hand, the reality of work is often much more prosaic. As Kerr (2006) notes, game developers are under pressure by publishers for more profitable and commercial products. In addition, licensing laws and contract agreements seek to own and control the products of this kind of immaterial labour. These pressures have resulted in adverse working conditions: the most well known case is the lawsuit against Electronic Arts, one of the largest game publishers, who employ over 4,100 game developers in the USA, Canada, Japan and the UK (Deuze et al., 2007). Exposed by a blogger, EA_Spouse, who reported that during 'crunch time' (game testing periods) workers often work 80-hour weeks, often without any compensation. While EA settled the case, this resulted in laying off about 5% of its workforce. More broadly, as Deuze et al. (2007; c.f. Kline et al., 2003) report, game publishers tend to move to areas or countries which offer tax incentives and have deregulated workers' rights. In addition, outsourcing game development (the so-called second party developers) is becoming more frequent with the result that the workforce of gamers is in fact dispersed across the world. In their description of this workforce, de Peuter and Dyer-Witheford (2005), report that it is overwhelmingly male and young, between their late teens and early thirties. Based on interviews with developers they identify several positive aspects of this kind of work, including creativity, flexibility and more broadly its 'work-as-play' outlook.

On the other hand, in its dark side, they report the existence of passionate pay slaves, precarious global developers and free networked labour, referring to instances where the positive aspects of autonomy and creativity turn into 'forced workaholism' (IGDA, 2004: 6 in de Peuter and Dyer-Witheford, 2005), to the precariousness of working as outsourced labour and to the ways in which the free labour of gamers is appropriated by publishing companies.

While all these show what it means to be part of an informationalized workforce, the links between the games industry and informational capitalism are even more apparent in the cases of game publishing, licensing and distribution. Publishers face the '90:10' dilemma, which points to the high rate of game failure: only 10% of the games developed are successful, while the remainder sink without a trace (Dyer-Witheford and Sharman, 2005). This puts them under enormous pressure to find ways to produce games that work and will be successful: game 'clones' or sequels of proven hits, such as for example *World of Warcraft*, which has released four editions, or games that emerge from film blockbusters, such as *Matrix* (*Enter the Matrix*) or books such as *Harry Potter*. In doing so, game publishing becomes more and more entwined with the entertainment and media industry: development, licensing and promotional activities involve rising costs, and small independent companies are unlikely to survive in a massively competitive media environment. This has led to a consolidation within the game industry, which involves vertical, horizontal and diagonal integration (Kerr, 2006). In the simplest terms, this means that a small number of very large firms dominate the market. The objective of these kinds of integration is to minimize costs, by exploiting economies of scale and to maximize profit by increasing global sales and controlling distribution. Publishers such as Sony, Nintendo and Microsoft own both consoles and software, while they also seek to expand diagonally across different market segments, for instance through developing online multiplayer games. In addition, in what is known as vertical integration, they create synergies with retailers, thereby controlling distribution as well. On the other hand, this kind of near monopoly is tempered by the very nature of games development, which is innovative and creative: games publishers need to stay alert and able to pick up any hits by independent developers (Dyer-Witheford and Sharman, 2005). However, as Dyer-Witheford and Sharman (2005) point out, the growing number of independent developers often absorb labour and other costs for the big games publishers, who end up scooping up most of the profits. As we also saw earlier, these firms operate in a global market, and seek to expand to lucrative markets, such as China, Latin America and Eastern Europe. It is within this context that games are produced, constituting, as Dyer-Witheford and his colleagues have argued, the ideal-typical commodity of informational capitalism. But games are not only the ideal commodity because of their conditions of production, but also because of the semiotic elements they mobilize – to understand this further we need to look into the actual contents of games.

Games: Contents, Narratives and Semiotic Power

Dyer-Witheford's (2003; Kline et al., 2003) historical analysis of games reveals their provenance: they were not created in playgrounds or by geeky teenagers, but, just like the internet, are a spin-off of the military-industrial complex. The first digital game is generally accepted to be *Spacewar*, a military simulation 'hacked' by defence-related workers at MIT (Dyer-Witheford, 2003: 125). Even today, military simulations cross over to games, while the military frequently enters into partnership with games publishers thereby making digital games one of the most clear instances of the so-called 'military-entertainment industrial complex' (ibid., 125; the term is MacKenzie Wark's, see Wark, 2006). Given these close synergies between the military and entertainment industries, it does not come as a surprise that games are heavily influenced by the military: a look at some of the most popular games in 2010 reveals several war-related games, such as *Call of Duty: Modern Warfare*, *Bayonetta*, *Assassin's Creed*, not to mention old time classics, such as *World of Warcraft*, *Delta Force: Black Hawk Down* and so on. There are an increasing number of people voicing concerns regarding games as training tools for the military and their relation to violence. Indeed, in a recently released shocking video from Iraq, in which US pilots shoot unarmed people on the ground, both the image and the words exchanged between the soldiers clearly point to relevant war games. The point here is that the games' plots and storylines end up naturalizing war and justifying violence. Analyzing the contents of games will therefore provide us with important insights into dominant and powerful cultural narratives.

But the issue proves far more complex than that. Often referred to as the ludology versus narratology debate, a dilemma has emerged concerning games as texts (Kerr, 2006; Raessens, 2006). In simple terms, this concerns the extent to which games can be analyzed in the same terms as other texts, such as film for instance (i.e. through a narrative analysis of characters, plot etc.), or whether in fact they constitute a different non-linear, interactive kind of 'cybertext' that requires new modes of analysis (Aarseth, 1997). Games, argue 'ludologists' such as Espen Aarseth (2004), must also be analyzed in terms of their rules, the material/semiotic world they create ('gameworld'), and in terms of the actions taken when players follow the rules within the gameworld ('gameplay'). Of these, the semiotic element, which corresponds to the narrative, is one of many, and not the most important. While Aarseth (2004) has vocally argued against the employment of literary-based narrative theory on games, others, like Raessens (2006) prefer to combine insights from both narrative analysis and 'ludology', employing innovative combinations of methods, including observation, interviews, the use of diaries, as well as discourse and textual analysis. Following Raessens, this section will present some findings from studies that have focused on textual-narrative analysis, as well as those which looked at other areas, such as the 'game' elements. We will seek to understand this part of digital games and the ways it is linked to their wider significance in informational capitalism.

Genres

In approaching the analysis of game contents, we must somehow attempt to understand and map their diversity: from Wii's physical games, to *Guitar Hero* and *Second Life*, there is a great variety of games' genres. Analysts such as Poole (2000) have identified no less than nine genres, including Shoot-em ups, Puzzles and Sports. Others, like Apperley (2006) condense them to four main genres. Apperley is following Aarseth (1997) and Wolf (2001) arguing that games genres must be understood not in terms of differences in their aesthetics, but in terms of their 'ergodicity' – the term 'ergodic' is suggested by Aarseth (1997) to refer to the work undertaken by 'readers' or players in co-creating the game. On this basis, Apperley refers to the following genres. First, simulation games, which are characterized by realism and simulate real world environments; *SimCity* and *Second Life* can be considered simulation games, as well as racing, and other sports games. Second, strategy games, in which players typically assume a god-like perspective, and must gather and process information before making decisions in order to win the game; *Civilization* and *Age of Empire* are two examples of strategy games. Third, action games, which can be first person, in which players undertake directly the action – shooting, fighting and so on – or third person, in which the action is undertaken by an avatar; *Doom*, *Quake*, and *Mortal Kombat* are all action games. Fourth, role playing games, in which a fantastic magical world is created and players assume a character and contribute to the game through acquisition of new skills, solving puzzles and so on; *Dungeons and Dragons*, *Legend of Zelda*, and *Final Fantasy* are examples of this genre. While each genre is characterized by distinct background, tasks and goals, which are accomplished by players in distinct ways, they all share elements of each other: thus, some game environments make use of simulations, while action is common in both strategic and role playing games. Information processing and puzzle solving are required in action games as well. More broadly, the notion of game genres is suggestive of the differences between games in terms of what is expected of players as well as in terms of their aesthetics and background.

Looking more closely at background storylines, the analysis often takes a form that echoes the analysis of films and other media texts. On the one hand, games are too many and diverse to draw any definitive conclusions. On the other hand, however, analysis of some games reveals their habitual use of gender, ethnic and other stereotypes as well as the employment of formulaic narratives. Given the political economic context of gaming and the links between gaming and the military, it is not surprising that dominant and over-simplified narratives regarding 'good' and 'bad' guys emerge in most games. We will explore some of these themes through a case study of an action game, Novalogic's *Delta Force: Black Hawk Down*, which has been studied by David Machin and Theo van Leeuwen (2005).

Delta Force: Black Hawk Down – Exploring Games Narratives

In their analysis of *Delta Force: Black Hawk Down*, Machin and van Leeuwen (2005) point out the links between the military and entertainment industries and the ways in which they shape game contents. The result is that military interventions not only appear justified and necessary but that they are normalized and accepted as solutions to political problems. The game *Delta Force: Black Hawk Down* was produced by Novalogic in 2003, as part of their series Delta Force. Novalogic has a subsidiary called Novalogic Systems, which works with the US Army's Training and Doctrine Command Analysis Centre as well as with Lockheed Martin Aeronautical Systems producing simulations for their training needs (Machin and van Leeuwen, 2005). In addition, it donated part of its profits to the Special Operations Warrior Foundation, which offers scholarships for children of soldiers killed on duty. The game is based on the film *Black Hawk Down* (Ridley Scott, 2002) which portrayed the events that transpired when President Bush decided to send US troops to Somalia during Operation Restore Hope in 1992. Somalia had suffered years of instability, a brutal dictatorship, and clan wars which led to famine and other hardships for its people. The US special operation had the goal of helping to restore order, deliver food to Somali civilians and help the UN in their operations. In reality, as Machin and van Leeuwen note, they ended up causing disruption and unsettling agreements that the Red Cross had reached with clan leaders.

The game is based on the same events, and the film. Between its launch and 2005, it had sold over a million copies, grossing over $30 million, but this does not include all the pirated copies. It was distributed globally with virtually no changes, even in the US accents of the soldiers. The goal of the game is to ensure that the Red Cross humanitarian operations are not disrupted, by capturing the 'bad guy', Mohammed Farah Aidid, a clan leader. Aidid was a real person, involved in the conflict, but did not have the power or stature attributed to him. Players in the game assume the role of soldiers of Delta Force, the special operations unit of elite soldiers, looking at the screen just above the barrel of their 'gun' and shooting 'bad guys' in order to capture Aidid. There is no opportunity to play any Somali characters, and while Delta Force soldiers are shown to experience emotions, for instance when their comrades get shot down, none of the Somali characters show any kind of emotion. While US soldiers are represented as a team, this is not the case with Somali militia or civilians – they are represented as a group or collective but in generic terms, and players cannot actually see their faces or characteristics. The only individual Somali is Aidid, the 'despotic' leader of the Habr Gedir clan. One of the most interesting elements of Machin and van Leeuwen's analysis is the identification of a 'special operations', which depicts US soldiers as professionals, doing a job, which is to protect society. This discourse acts as a frame for the legitimation of war, at least at the level of soldiers. They do not mobilize any kind of argument about what is moral or just, but focus on the application of their skills and on following orders. While Delta Force is seen as highly trained, organized and efficient, the 'enemies' are seen as ill disciplined and untrained.

This formulaic narrative of good versus evil has been an integral part of recent discourse on the war on terror. Do games have a role to play in this? Given these differences in the representation of the two parties it is easy to conclude who is right and who is wrong, who has the moral right to intervene and who must be destroyed. It is also easy to conclude that in the case of any kind of conflict, the solution lies in a quick and efficient military intervention. But these kinds of games serve another purpose as well: they globalize these kinds of discourses, which are now widely used, and therefore becoming more and more acceptable in different parts of the world. In their analysis of Arab and American games representing the conflict in Lebanon and the role of Hezbollah, Machin and Suleiman (2006), found that the same special operations discourse was used in both Arab and American games. While in the Arab games Hezbollah represented the good guys and US/Israeli soldiers the bad guys, the basic premises of the special operations discourse remained the same. On the other hand, in the Arabic game *Special Forces*, fighters were represented in terms of their beliefs and their will to fight. Despite some differences, the broader point here is that the form and basic narrative of action games are becoming global discourses and spread their simplified versions and explanations of complex political events, thereby justifying and glamorizing military conflicts. It is mostly against this type of action games that popular interventions are aimed: such violent games end up, according to this view, desensitizing people and even causing real violence (Anderson, 2003). We will discuss this controversy in the section on gamers.

The Architecture and Structure of Games

Other games' genres, however, rely on different narratives, the fantastic and magical, the virtually real, the strategizing. What do they accomplish? Aarseth's (1997) argument was that game narratives differ from other media texts because the player has a say over what goes on. This is the same across genres, but perhaps more so in role playing and strategy games, but despite this, Carr (2006) argues that most games incorporate straightforward elements of narrative, in that they have a given story line, with characters whose attributes are already 'written'. On the other hand, players have the ability to manipulate characters, thereby to an extent subverting or altering the narrative. However, as Carr notes, this flexibility has limits: in the end you need to score points and win the game, and your character can and will only do things that enable the game to proceed – otherwise, it's game over! But the broader argument here is that we cannot think of the contents of games in the same way as we think about other media texts: the built-in interaction on which they are premised does not allow us to draw conclusions regarding games just from analyzing their contents. Rather, we must think of these contents and game plots as part of a cycle in which gamers are directly involved. From this point of view, the semiotic power of games is limited by the 'consumers' or players themselves: they choose not only which games to play but also how to play them – which characters to choose, which tools to use, and so on. As we noted earlier, game publishers operate on the 90:10 rule: for every hundred games produced, only about ten will be successful. Offering gamers what they want, as well as more flexibility and the possibility to 'write' the game themselves, are two ways which safeguard the success of the game.

But games, as we have argued, are not only narratives: they involve rules and a structure that guides players in specific ways. What does this gaming architecture accomplish? Dyer-Witheford and de Peuter (2009) discuss the ways in which games are used by multinationals to test and train their employees as simulation games are integrated with psychometric and cognitive skills tests alongside personality tests. Cosmetics giant L'Oréal has come up with an online simulation game in which players/employees make strategic R&D investments, marketing plans and cost-cutting procedures (Johne, 2006 cited in Dyer-Witheford and de Peuter, 2009). Cisco, the ideal-typical networked enterprise according to Castells, prepares its management for dealing with crises through a game in which they repair a network in a Martian sandstorm (Dyer-Witheford and de Peuter, 2009). Firms such as Minerva Software (Cyberlore) hone the skills of their servicepersons through games such as Playboy Mansion in which they try to persuade models to pose topless (ibid.). In similar developments, Stanford University has found that the attention and concentration exhibited by players of Massive Multiplayer Online Games (MMOG) of *Star Wars Galaxies* is such that they could be used to check real medical scans for cancer inside the game (Hof, 2007 in Dyer-Witheford and de Peuter, 2009). But this is not all: most computer games follow closely the employment paradigm of career progression, management of assets and accumulation of capital (Poole, 2008, in Dyer-Witheford and de Peuter, 2009).

Almost 100 years ago, at the beginning of the twentieth century, Walter Benjamin observed that '[w]hat the Funfair achieves with its Dodgem Cars and other similar amusements is nothing but a taste of the drill to which the unskilled labourer is subjected to in that factory' (1969: 176). How different from this is the way in which games train players/workers for multitasking, flexible role playing, inventive problem solving, persistence and quick decision making? Games, as Dyer-Witheford and de Peuter persuasively argue, are training the new global 'cyber-precariat', turning work into play and play into work. 'Amusement' insisted Adorno and Horkheimer (1997 [1947]: 137), 'under late capitalism is the prolongation of work'. The architecture of games is directed towards the production of subjectivities, along with cognitive abilities and skills that serve informational capitalism. But are we to consider gamers 'docile bodies', unwilling and unable to resist, playing obediently the game? We will examine this next.

Gamers: Practices and Communities

While for many years media research was debating on the role of the reader, and the extent of their involvement in the production or eventual decoding of any text, it is clear that games require active involvement, not only in interpreting the game but in actually moving or playing the game. What gamers do is understood as configurative rather than interpretive activity (Eskelinen, 2001 in Sihvonen, 2009). Indeed, the work required by players is such that many have spoken about the popularity of games as representing a shift towards a participatory culture (Jenkins, 2006a). Specifically, Henry Jenkins has developed a passionate and persuasive account of a new culture that has emerged out of engagement with the new media. In a recent publication, Jenkins and his colleagues (2009), defined participatory culture as:

> a culture with relatively low barriers to artistic expression and civic engagement, strong support for creating and sharing one's creations, and some type of informal mentorship whereby what is known by the most experienced is passed along to novices. A participatory culture is also one in which members believe their contributions matter, and feel some degree of social connection with one another. (Jenkins et al., 2009: xi)

Keeping this in mind, games are an integral part of this participatory culture, especially some of the multiplayer games, in which the gameplay develops as a result of collaborative playing practices. On the other hand, we have identified games as the ideal-typical commodity of informational capitalism – do these gaming practices subvert this role or do they in fact reinforce it? For yet others, gaming is very far from being either participatory or subversive: gamers are seen as passively reproducing norms and practices learned during gaming, often resulting in violence spilling over from the virtual to the actual world. This section will summarize relevant arguments and findings on gaming practices, the communities that emerge and their role within informational capitalism. It will begin with a discussion of the controversy surrounding gaming as a problematic activity possibly leading to violence; move on to discuss counterarguments on participatory culture, and again some counterarguments concerning gaming as reinforcing existing structures. It will then finish on a more optimistic note, discussing the potential of gaming to generate radically new collaborative practices.

Games and Violence

On 20 April 1999, Eric Harris and Dylan Klebold, two high school students, entered Columbine High School in Littleton, Colorado, armed with shotguns and began shooting at students and teachers. By the time they had finished, 12 students and a teacher were dead. Why did they do it? While both students had been in trouble before, it was their video game playing that attracted the most interest. Popular accounts in the media focused on the hours these students played *Doom* and *Quake*, and noted the fact that one of them (Harris) was creating new levels for *Doom* (Brown, 1999). An article in the *Washington Post* describes one of these levels in some detail. Apparently, Harris had created a level, called 'U.A.C. LABS', which he described as an all-out war between humans and demons on the planet Phobos. The goal of the game is to get to the planet's teleporter. Harris' further instructions read: 'The platoon guarding the teleporter out is VERY large, so beware. Good luck marine, and don't forget, KILL 'EM AAAAALLLL!!!!!' (*Washington Post*, 1999). Parents and relatives of those killed filed a lawsuit against 25 games makers, seeking damages on the basis that they had contributed directly to the massacre (BBC News, 2001a). Although the lawsuits were eventually dismissed, the rejection of liability was not on the basis that computer games were not responsible, but on the premise that accepting the lawsuit would lead to problems with the First Amendment on freedom of speech.

The wider problem here is that of the links between violence and computer games. Although there is a burgeoning body of research on violence and the media more generally, the research has failed to come up with any conclusive evidence pointing to a causal relationship (see Jenkins, 2006b; 2007). The main arguments involved here are first that computer or video game violence causes real violence, and second, that it desensitizes people to violence, thereby making it more acceptable (Anderson, 2003; Funk et al., 2004). Problems with this research are both theoretical and methodological: on the one hand, there is the assumption of a simple behaviouristic understanding of how children and young people learn, and on the other, most methods are quasi-experimental ones, conducted in laboratories and focusing on the short-term effects of playing violent computer games or watching violent images. But also in meta-analytic studies, that is, on studies that analyze other relevant studies, there is no evidence of a causal relationship such that playing video games leads to real life aggression and violence (Ferguson and Kilburn, 2010). Moreover, as Jenkins (2007) reports, there is no evidence of increased violence in society, which is what we would expect as violent computer games increased in recent years. Finally, violent games are rated: in the USA, the rating body, the Entertainment Software Rating Board (ESRB), provides no less than six classifications: early childhood (EC), everyone (E), teen (T, 13 years old and above), mature (M, 17 years old and above), adult only (AO, over 18), and rating pending (RP) – see the ESRB site at: http://www.esrb.org. Concerned parents should make sure their children access and/or purchase only appropriate games.

Games and Participatory Culture: Collaboration and Co-optation

While this controversy still persists, theorists such as Henry Jenkins (1992; 2006b) have focused on the participatory elements of games, emphasizing their potential to mobilize resources, to collaborate, to form communities which act as prototypes for a new, more open, participatory and creative culture and society. Role playing but also other games' genres, allow the player not only to enter but also to co-author a fantasy world. Perhaps the clearest example of the participatory qualities of games is modding. Modding refers to activities that modify the original game in various ways, such as for example by offering more weapons, by creating new characters or levels. Often mods can be equally and even more popular than the actual game, leading to a new game, referred to as total conversion (Sihvonen, 2009). Modding is incorporated into the logic of game production, with game developers releasing game software that is non-proprietary and allows for modification. An example is Fireaxis, the makers of *Civilization*, who have not only allowed mods, but have also incorporated them in versions of the game. Moreover, modding has led to the emergence of communities, offering instructions, help as well as the possibility to discuss modding online – see for instance, http://www.civfanatics.com/. Modding can therefore be seen as an instance of what Axel Bruns (2007: np) refers to as produsage: 'the collaborative and continuous building and extending of existing content in pursuit of further improvement'. Drawing upon the open source principles, this kind of collaborative production of games-related content effected by players themselves opens up possibilities for the creation of a culture and society that are based on collaboration and participation, on the use of all our abilities and our collective intelligence (c.f. Benkler, 2006). While this kind of activity is supported and even reinforced by game developers, it has led to some controversial moments: when modders introduced an 'Alien vs Predator' mod in *Quake*, they were confronted by 20th Century Fox with demands to cease production, remove websites and disclose the names of modders (Coleman and Dyer-Witheford, 2007). But modding and more broadly this kind of gamer activity is not necessarily politicized: in his comparison between culture jamming and fan/gamer activities, Jenkins pointed out that the latter is 'dialogic rather than disruptive, affective more than ideological, and collaborative rather than confrontational' (2002: 167).

This idea of collaboration and sharing is central in gaming communities that revolve around specific games, while it is also built-in in several kinds of games, ranging from Massive Multiplayer Online Games (MMOGs), such as *World of Warcraft* and *EverQuest*, to *Mafia Wars* and *FarmVille* on Facebook. Such communities belie the popular understanding of gamers as lone teenagers, enabling community members on the one hand to unleash their creativity and on the other to make the most of collaboration (Taylor, 2006a). Furthermore, such communities, often referred to as 'guilds' can be thought of as autonomous, in the sense of setting and operating with their own rules and regulations. Taylor (2006b) has referred to a kind of mutual surveillance which is used in order to regulate players' conduct (c.f. Chapter 6). The active and continuous input by gaming networks and communities contributes to making games open and unfinished texts, which in turn may subvert the idea of a production cycle as understood by game publishers (Humphreys, 2009). Such communities in fact operate in ways not only limited to 'synthetic worlds' (Castronova, 2005).

In his analysis of MMOGs, Malaby (2006), using Pierre Bourdieu's concept of capital, argues that game networks on the one hand operate on the basis of economic, cultural and social capital, while on the other, they blur or mix the divisions between synthetic and 'real' worlds. Specifically, by being part of a game network or guild, players acquire a certain identity, which accumulates a certain cultural capital, according to what they do, and a certain social capital, according to who they associate with. These kinds of capital, as Bourdieu has shown us, can be translated into economic capital. In addition, players already possess some form of cultural, social and economic capital before participating in a gaming network – they then mobilize it when they become part of such a network. Simply put, online players as community members acquire and accumulate certain competencies, know-how as well as a reputation – these can subsequently be capitalized upon in terms of being exchanged for other objects of value. Malaby (2006) uses the example of Kermitt Quirk, who has made a trading card, Tringo, for *Second Life*. His card generated a lot of interest among players, resulting in its being bought by Donnerwood Media. Quirk already possessed some cultural capital, as he is a computer programmer, while he is also in possession of social capital, as he has a network of people. In producing and circulating his Tringo card, he mobilized these kinds of capital, eventually translating them to economic capital. In more broad terms, what goes on in MMOGs has a real world counterpart: game currency, armour, tools and so on sell for real dollars in online auctions: Castronova (2001) estimated that Norrath, the imaginary EverQuest continent, was in fact the 77th stronger national economy in the world! In *Second Life*, players are assigned copyright over their avatars and productions – they can also choose a creative commons licence – while they can trade any items they want. As Coleman and Dyer-Witheford (2007: 946) put it, such activities involve 'the validation and encouragement of player-created content, but within the boundaries of fully commodified system'. Far from creating new and alternative worlds, these communities, their members and their activities, operate in ways that reproduce dominant socio-cultural and economic values.

Based on similar arguments, Humphreys (2009) argues that gaming must be understood as affective labour – that is, as part of immaterial labour which produces relationships. This kind of affective labour produces value that becomes attached to products as well. From this point of view, most participation in this context can be understood as affective labour (see also Hardt and Negri, 2000). The point Humphreys is making is that we must be cautious when thinking about collaboration and participation as necessarily subversive activities. We must understand them as part of wider shifts that occur and become integrated into the existing system of informational capitalism. Insisting on caution and scepticism, and perhaps even with a touch of pessimism, McKenzie Wark argues that games in fact form an allegory of our societies. In his *GAM3R 7H30RY*, Wark (2006) argues that any form of choice and creativity is either already predetermined, just as games' outcomes are predetermined by programming algorithms, or already co-opted and integrated into society/game (much in the same way that the flip side of participation is affective labour, already an integral part of cultural and material commodities). The whole world is understood as gamespace, defined and controlled by algorithms that offer only the illusion of choice, but also structuring the space around us: all possibilities are already predetermined in advance. Even mastery of these algorithms, as in the case of modding, does not constitute escape or exit: but more than anything, this signifies deeper subjection and conformity to the rules of the game. From this point of view, gamers are the exact opposite of hackers whose creativity lies in the production (and destruction) of new possibilities – gamers, in contrast, enable existing (mostly commercially created) worlds to fulfil their potential – in this sense they are the ultimate collaborator of the military-entertainment complex that has spawned games.

Is there any way out? Sarah Coleman and Nick Dyer-Witheford (2007) argue that although there is much in gaming that not only resonates with, but outright supports informational capitalism, there are certain activities based on gaming which to the extent that they are riddled with ambiguity may be seen as contributing to shifts associated with the development of a digital commons. This digital commons is understood as a non-proprietary space and resources that all members of a community can use but no one can own (Coleman and Dyer-Witheford, 2007: 934). Such activities include piracy, modding and machinima – the creation of films out of games – and the development of MMOGs. All these activities, they argue are situated in-between commodification and the commons, revealing tensions and the creation of autonomous zones. Specifically, piracy on the one hand undermines game and other publishers, but on the other contributes to black and other markets. The practice of 'warez', the free circulation of broken copyrighted works, participates in a kind of gift economy. Modding, as we already discussed can be supportive of the gaming industry, but it can also be unruly and out of control, and the same can be said of machinima. Coleman and Dyer-Witheford (2007) refer to the example of a player who used the simulation game *The Movies* to create a machinima film called *The French Democracy*, which presented a highly critical view of racism and political authority in the Paris riots of 2005. MMOG activities, finally, oscillate from the outright commercial, as in *Second Life*, to pushing the boundaries of creativity, imagination and collaboration. For Coleman and Dyer-Witheford, MMOGs are at the same time commodities and commons, as they must rely on the activity of players for their continuation – as more and more gamers organize into clans or guilds, they actively contest and resist publishers' decisions regarding the game: in an incident, Blizzard, the owners of *World of Warcraft* were forced to lift a ban on the publication of gay and lesbian guilds. This hybrid arrangement points to a curious and unstable co-existence of the commercial and the commons, which, for Coleman and Dyer-Witheford, may be seen as presaging a 'yet-to-emerge "commonist" mode of production' (2007: 948). It seems that gamer activities are in fact much more unpredictable than perhaps Wark had assumed: as Coleman and Dyer-Witheford argue, the relationship between commodities and the commons is at present 'fluid, fertile, and unresolved' (2007: 948).

Conclusions

Our discussion of games took us very far from Huizinga's analysis with which we began this chapter. The 'innocence' of playing as freedom, unconnected to material interests, is for ever lost in a world in which the gaming industry is worth billions, and in which gamers can themselves earn money not only from developing new games, but also from trading in gaming artefacts and tools. This so-called ludocapitalism (Dibbell, 2006) has not only 'tainted' playing, but is also considered emblematic of informational capitalism. Dibbell (2006) gave a fascinating account of a year in which he lived solely out of income he generated by trading in virtual goods on the

MMOG *Ultima* Online. In an article in the *New York Times Magazine*, Dibbell (2007) wrote about the life of about 100,000 young Chinese who work in factory-like conditions: their job is to play MMOGs such as *World of Warcraft* for hours and hours, earning about $0.30 per hour. What they do is to harvest virtual goods, armours, coins and so on, which they then give to their employers who then sell them for real money. What they are doing is blurring not only the boundaries between play and work (c.f. Kline et al., 2003), but also between the virtual and real and between the material and the imaginary. But this gaming activity is further involved in blurring the boundaries between production and consumption; through modding and similar practices, gamers not only play but also produce (new) games, which are subsequently (re)sold by game publishers. At the same time, viewing games as texts or representations reveals their links and connections to dominant cultural values and ideologies. No wonder Nick Dyer-Witheford and his colleagues suggest that games are the ideal-typical commodity of informational capitalism or the Empire, to use Hardt and Negri's (2000) term. Box 11.1 summarizes the main points in this chapter.

What kinds of conclusions can we draw? Are games the ideal-typical commodity of informational capitalism or the Empire, exemplifying its core characteristics of 'banal war, endless work and monetized labour' (Dyer-Witheford and de Peuter, 2009)? Or can we find something more positive to say about gaming? The redeeming quality of games, argue Dyer-Witheford and de Peuter (2009), are to be found in the contradictions and tensions they are involved in. Although modding and other bottom up gaming practices appear already co-opted by the game industry in its quest to minimize costs, they still involve a radically different mode of production, while the products of this new mode are not always so easily palatable to the industry. Any potential of gaming therefore emerges from its two 'warring' aspects: 'creative dissidence and profitable compliance' (Dyer-Witheford and de Peuter, 2009).

11.1

Summary of Main Points

The Political Economy of Games

- Industry worth in excess of $35 billion
- Reliance on flexible networked production and extensive marketing. Profitability depends on technological innovation but also compatibility with cultural trends
- Games as the ideal-typical commodity of informational capitalism
- Game development: precarious immaterial labour
- Game publishing: relentless competition leads to consolidation and integration

Games as Text

- Games as cultural texts are more complex than other media texts
- Aarseth: games as cybertexts characterized by 'ergodicity', i.e. by co-creation through players' actions

- Games genres:

  Simulations, e.g. *SimCity*

  Strategy, e.g. *Civilization*

  Action, e.g. *Mortal Kombat*

  Role playing, e.g. *EverQuest*

  Most games combine elements of all

  Games narratives operate through stereotypical representations of 'them' and 'us' but semiotic power mediated by gaming practices

Gaming Practices

- Gaming as a configurative and not (only) an interpretive activity (Eskelinen)
- Gaming as leading to violence: the Columbine controversy
- Modding: activities that modify and repurpose games – often modding is already included in the games' design, hence already co-opted by the industry
- Gaming communities: ranging from loose networks to tightly-knit, hierarchical 'guilds' or 'clans'
- Ludocapitalism (Dibbell): the generation of real capital through gaming and trading in virtual goods.
- Gaming as affective labour (Humphreys) producing relationships and affective value that becomes part of the game's overall value
- McKenzie Wark: gaming as collaboration rather than subversion – the anti-hacking
- But: gaming practices are ambiguous – could they form a prototype of an application of 'collective intellect' (Dyer-Witheford, 2003)?

E-tivity: Understanding Gaming

This e-tivity seeks to enable you to understand games in a holistic, non-reductionist manner, realize their embeddedness in existing political economic structures and power discourses, while also considering the unpredictable outcomes that gaming might have. You should visit and engage with at least two types of games, choosing one of the four genres identified in the chapter (simulation, action, strategy, role playing). Then, consider the following questions:

1   Who developed, owns the copyright, and distributes these games? How readily available is this information?

Further Reading

The industry of games and its socio-cultural and political implications are explored in this series of articles. The first article, by Dal Yong Jin and Florence Chee focuses on the Korean games industry, and examines its socio-cultural specificity as well as its economic determinants. Second, the article by Dmitri Williams and his colleagues examines the dimension of game contents and representations: through looking at representations of gender, race and age, the article concludes that these are similar to the representations emerging from mainstream media. James Newman explores the dimensions of game consumption, looking at gamers' activities in online environments. John Banks and Jason Potts look into the involvement of gamers in the production of games, arguing that this kind of coproduction must be thought of not as transcending but as part of the games market. The final article by Jonathan Corliss is a review of the relevant games research from a social scientific perspective – this review provides a good entry point to some of the debates and questions concerning online games.

Jin, Y.D. and Chee, F., 2008, Age of New Media Empires: A Critical Interpretation of the Korean Online Game Industry, *Games and Culture*, 3(1): 38–58.

Williams, D., Martins, N., Consalvo, M. and Ivory, J.D., 2009, The Virtual Census: Representations of Gender, Race and Age in Video Games, *New Media & Society*, 11(5): 815–834.

Newman, J., 2005, Playing (with) Videogames, *Convergence: The International Journal of Research into New Media Technologies*, 11(1): 48–67.

Banks, J. and Potts, J., 2010, Co-creating Games: A Co-evolutionary Analysis, *New Media & Society*, 12(2): 253–270.

Corliss, J., 2011, Introduction: The Social Science Study of Video Games, *Games and Culture*, 6(1): 3–16.

CHAPTER 12

THE FUTURE OF THE NEW MEDIA

Learning Objectives

- To understand commonalities and regularities in the articulation of the new media with different fields of life
- To learn about new initiatives and their future implications
- To understand the struggle for control over technological resources and technological futures
- To develop a critical awareness of the relationship between the future of technology and the future of the society
- To comprehend the difficulties and complexities of governing the internet/new media governance

Introduction

About 100 years ago, sponge divers in the Aegean Sea discovered a strange bronze object lying among the remains of a cargo ship close to the tiny island of Antikythera. The mysterious object, named the Antikythera Mechanism, is thought to have been constructed towards the end of the second century BC, and it represents the world's oldest computing mechanism. Research has shown that the mechanism was used to calculate celestial information, including lunar cycles while it also included a luni-solar calendar (Freeth et al., 2006). Freeth et al. suggest that the mechanism incorporated an application of a theory on the Moon's irregularities, developed by Hipparchos in the second century BC. This does not merely show the technical prowess of the Greeks at the time, but also more broadly the human development of, and reliance to, technology, a good illustration of Stiegler's arguments (see Chapter 1) on technology being coeval with humanity. On the other hand, it has emerged that the Antikythera Mechanism was in fact more sophisticated than technology produced much later, and it turns out that this kind of technology was not replicated until the Renaissance, some 1,500 years later. This, in turn, suggests that the development of technology does not follow a single line from the least to the most sophisticated, neither can we speak of a continuous technological progress, as there are clearly regressions, but also cycles and dead-ends. This is the point made by Bijker (1995) and his colleagues of the social constructivist approach to technology (see Chapter 6). From this point of view, predicting the future and the direction it will take is a futile exercise. On the other hand, thinking about the future may help us understand the world around us as it is now, and perhaps also it may contribute to steering or governing it in ways that may offer improvements in our lives. It is further useful in helping us identify some dominant trends and thus to evaluate them, asking ourselves if this is really the direction we wish to follow.

This chapter will therefore be concerned with the future as it appears through the lens of today, seeking to identify and critically apprehend the main techno-social trends that characterize our world. The first section will begin with a summary of the main arguments encountered in the course of this book, seeking to find the regularities that suggest the existence of a set of common threads, which may be considered as trends. It will then move on to discuss some future scenarios as they appear in the literature, before discussing some of the means by which to evaluate all these and also, crucially, discussing what is to be done. The final section will therefore discuss issues of governance of the new media and the internet in particular.

The Story So Far: Emerging Trends

The main remit of this book was to examine the articulation of the new media with various aspects of our lives, to map the changes and understand some of their consequences. The theoretical position regarding new media and society prioritized in this book follows Stiegler in holding that technology neither determines humanity nor is it determined by it: instead it is understood as emerging alongside the rise of humanity, as an inextricable part of it, an exteriorization of the human ability for symbolic thought. This exteriorization, and the unique way in which we can pass it along to our descendants, implies that technology can in turn shape and condition humanity and the conditions within which we live. We can understand this relationship as one of dynamic mutual composition (Stiegler, 2006, see also Chapter 1). The dynamism of this relationship implies an unpredictable outcome or, better, a lack of determination when it comes to the shape of things to come. If we understand the new media as relying on technology, we can posit the same kind of indeterminate relationship. But indeterminate and unpredictable does not mean directionless. In fact, technologies, and human societies and actions, are rooted in history: they are found in certain historical circumstances that give priority over certain ideas, logics and behaviours. They become, in this sense, articulated with what has preceded them, both in technological as well as in socio-economic and political terms. While we cannot determine the shape of this articulation, we can certainly observe it and seek to understand its underlying dimensions and logics. Thus, although we observed and traced different areas of life, such as politics and gaming, subjectivity and globalization, in their articulation with the new media, insofar as the new media remain as a common denominator we can seek to identify the common threads that are found in all these different articulations. To be sure, Castells has already identified the logic of the network as the dominant logic and emerging historical trend. Yet this overarching logic must be complemented with more details from the various facets of life. To isolate these details, this section will revisit the themes covered in this book, seeking to identify any commonalities, continuities and discontinuities that may subsequently lead to some suggestions of emerging trends.

Theories of the New Media

Chapter 1 followed the work of an eclectic set of thinkers on the (new) media: McLuhan, Kittler, Stiegler and Castells have all enriched our understanding of the new media, the role of technology, and the ways in which they are involved in our lives. McLuhan's insistence on the primacy of the media is suggestive of the importance of the media for social, political, and economic life: so much so that McLuhan held that the media determine the kind of life we lead. Kittler cross-fertilized McLuhan's arguments with those of Michel Foucault, positing that the media construct specific kinds of subjects: those constructed by the new media are understood as 'end-users', as opposed to 'readers' and 'audiences' characteristic of previous media. Stiegler, on the other hand, avoids accusations of determinism by holding technology and humanity as co-evolving: technology is what makes us human, and in turn, we make technology. As argued earlier, this dynamic relationship implies that we cannot predict the direction of future technology, but this does not mean that we cannot steer technology in ways commensurable with political principles, such as those of democracy and its quest for equality and justice. More concerned with empirical reality, Manuel Castells describes the sociological changes that have taken place in the last few decades, seeking to extract trends and meanings from these historical shifts. This book attempted to combine Castells' interest in empirical reality with Stiegler's explicit politics of technology/new media. While we need to approach the world in terms of facts, data and information, we also need to be able to take a political stance vis-à-vis these facts. It is with these two aspects in mind that we can proceed to discuss the remaining themes.

New Media and the Economy

One of the most important discussions in the book concerns the political economy of the new media, as well as more broadly, the relationship between the economy and the new media. Production under conditions of informational capitalism assumes a network organization, whereby enterprises do not own all parts of the production, but assign these to other companies as and when they need. Just as enterprises are no longer represented by large factories and mass production, employment is no longer characterized by stability and permanence. Instead, flexibility at all levels is the key characteristic of employment, as it becomes more and more informationalized. Tele-working and project work are more and more common, while the tendency is for former employees to work as independent 'project managers', whereby they become responsible not only for the delivery of services, but also for the communication and coordination of all activities relating to these services. This kind of employment is very different to wage labour, in that it affords a greater degree of autonomy to workers while it is also much more creative than the kind of work associated with industrial production. On the other hand, it is insecure and uncertain, as workers no longer know if and when they will have another contract or project – this is the 'precariat', informational capitalism's answer to the proletariat (Tarì and Vanni, 2005). Consumption in informational capitalism is no longer the passive buying of mass produced commodities, but a process which involves, mobilizes and produces, meaning and identities. As such, this process, which has merged with production, must be understood as an individualized process, since produsers – to use Axel Bruns' (2006) neologism – do not easily fit into patterns of class or other social divisions. But this does not mean that workers-consumers are now freer or that they live in markedly better conditions. Rather it reflects a change in the relationship between capital and labour. Using a phrase by Castells (2001), we can refer to it as the individuation of this relationship. In working, in producing and in consuming we do something more than the application of knowledge or skills: these processes involve meaning, interpretation, communication, and often innovation, thereby individuating us, dividing us into units with unique skills, abilities and aptitudes. Work no longer takes place in the factory: tele-working shows the expansion of work outside of the factory or the office. But this individuation comes with a high price: on the one hand whole lifeworlds are sucked into the production no longer of commodities but of worlds, as Lazzarato has argued (2004). Lazzarato refers to workers as monads to indicate the new conditions under which labour takes place: the new conditions 'affirm workers' autonomy, independence and singularity (individual substance)' (2004: 194), but Lazzarato holds that this does not represent an improvement over Taylor's and scientific management's fragmented work movements – rather it denotes a change and, we may say, offers a clue as to a current trend in labour. This may be summarized as the individuation or singularization of labour.

Network organizing and informational – singularized – labour constitute the key characteristics of the new media industry. Where (new) media firms cannot merge or integrate, they build synergies with other companies along the chain of production and distribution. However, new media companies, despite the huge hype that surrounds them have, for the most part, failed to come up with a successful business model, relying instead on older models, such as generating income through advertising and subscriptions. To an extent, this failure to come up with a model for 'monetization' may be due to the elusive nature of user-generated contents, which represent a substantial part of new media contents. The free circulation of contents has on the one hand led to an increase of available online contents often relying on user contents, while on the other it has put a lot of pressure on corporations and governments to come up with effective means for maintaining a monopoly over contents and their distribution. Consumption or use of new media involves in many ways the production of contents, which is what we do when we use social networking sites and mobile phones, or when commenting on blogs. But production and consumption in informational capitalism is premised on circulation of these goods, and therefore also on collaboration: in producing/creating, we use and mobilize knowledge, input, and feedback from others, we require that our 'creations' are seen by others, who often offer this to us in the form of consuming and commenting on our 'products'. This collaboration shows the difficulties lying ahead for firms seeking to capitalize and monetize new media and their contents – so far successful monetization of ultimately collaborative products is premised on the acquisition of a monopoly, often taking the form of 'intellectual property rights'. The new conditions of production-consumption are therefore based on a tension between the individuated or singularized form of labour, and the necessity for collaboration between these singular producers-consumers. The emerging, or rather continuing trend in this case, is the rise and rise of immaterial labour. This is a kind of labour that strips workers from the possibility of unionization, as it isolates and individuates them, but which on the other hand offers them both autonomy and the possibility for collaboration.

Globalization and New Media Diffusion

This tension may be seen as the dominant thread and/or trend running across many of the domains of life covered in this book. On the other hand, we must keep in mind that our era is more likely a transitional one, in which change coexists with continuity. Thus, although the diptych individuation-collaboration may appear as an emerging trend, there are still a number of persistent patterns associated with industrial capitalism. Chapter 2, on Globalization shows the unequal spread of the new media across the world: these follow along lines of development, such that the more developed a nation or region the more likely it is to have high rates of diffusion. At the same time, Chapter 4, on Consumption and Divides, showed that patterns of internet diffusion follow divisions corresponding to class, gender and ethnic cleavages within nations. These two chapters provide evidence that patterns of inequality linked to previous stages of capitalism continue to prevail in informational capitalism as well. On the other hand, both chapters show that the diffusion of the new media accelerates and there is a tendency to equalize divisions. This, on the one hand, will precipitate the spread and dominance of informational capitalism, while on the other it is likely to create new divisions and patterns of inequality, as well as pathologies and abuses. Such new divisions may not necessarily follow age, gender and ethnic/racial lines, but they may interact with these and other factors, pertaining to the 'habitus' of each of us: to the unique dispositions, knowledge and attitudes we have acquired as a result both of our particular socio-cultural and economic status, as well as our personalities, cognitive abilities and preferences (see Bourdieu, 1977; Bourdieu and Wacquant, 1992). Again, this shows the tendency towards an individuation of our relationship to the new media. However, the dynamic of the spread of the new media is such that their diffusion leads to more diffusion: in other words, it seems that it will be difficult to escape the new media, as more and more people use them. We can see the reliance of the new media on collaboration: after all, to whom can you tweet if there is no one online? Who can you call, if no one has a mobile phone? It seems that while collaboration, or at least concerted acquisition of new media takes place in terms of their diffusion, individuation takes place in terms of patterns of use: divides here may fall across a continuum, ranging from 'grazers' – those who occasionally use the new media in simple ways – to 'engaged' – those who are actively and continuously employing the new media. Here, we should also insert a note of caution: the line separating 'engagement' from 'addiction' is a thin one. The trend here is the continuous expansion of the new media, an ongoing diffusion that covers old divisions of gender, ethnicity, development, but which creates new ones of competence and literacy.

Politics

On the other hand, engagement is the key to understanding the relationship between politics and the new media, as we saw in Chapter 5. The somewhat passive involvement in politics in the form of voting every four years or so is certainly intensified in the days of e-government. Political parties seek to develop a disintermediated relationship with citizens, in which they have more control and in which they can communicate directly with citizens. Social movements have profited immensely from the new media, which allow them to reach and mobilize people. At the same time, the new media and the internet in particular have created their own politics, which centre on the idea that information should be free. In addition, new Web applications, especially the so-called social media, have created a new momentum, allowing citizens to participate, organize and mobilize for political causes. But the 'effects' or impact of the new media on politics are harder to detect: can it be argued that we now have more democracy, more equality and justice because of the new media? Much as we would have liked to say yes, inequalities and injustices still prevail. On the other hand, it may be that the new media introduce subtler changes that may shape the political process in the years to come. For sure, there is a greater demand for accountability, as political actions and statements are scrutinized in the blogosphere. But bloggers themselves are getting used to thinking about and commenting on aspects of the world which can also have political significance: blogging may therefore be seen as an activity shaping a new kind of political subject, one who is tuned to the world, who thinks, blogs and comments, thereby assuming a political stance and asserting their own political views. In this sense blogging may be seen as reaffirming an authorial subjectivity, which is the result of positioning oneself vis-à-vis the (political) world, but which is at the same time the result of a collective effort and a collaboration with others: posting, commenting and receiving comments or feedback for posts allows social media users to constantly reposition themselves. The mobilizing dynamic is, as we have seen in the domain of the economy, a tension between the individuation of our relationship to politics, as more and more ideologies and political parties lose their hold on the citizenry, and the collaborative elements that are both native to social media applications and necessary for a political subjectivity to develop. The emerging trend in politics has to do firstly with the continued disintermediation of politics as more and more politicians and political activists rely on the new and not on the mass media in order to communicate. Second, people acquire a new kind of political identity, which allows them to continuously comment upon and in a sense participate in politics through blogging, microblogging and other social media applications.

Surveillance and Security

In some instances, the collaborative and collective elements of the new media may take on a nightmarish form. The technical capabilities of the new media for surveillance, alongside the increased threats to security and safety, have given rise to a culture of control and constant monitoring. In Chapter 6 we discussed some of these aspects, focusing on case studies such as war and conflict, online fraud and extreme pornography. Following arguments by Lyon and Andrejevich, we traced the rise of a surveillance society, in which we continuously monitor ourselves and others. Caught in a vicious circle of insecurity, risk and more surveillance, this culture of generalized suspicion, where anything can happen at anytime by anyone feeds into a heightened individualism, in which we stand as isolated units, suspicious of all others. While the new media have been used in war and conflict, in defrauding and actually harming people, the solution to safety and security risks appears to be equally risky and equally threatening. Is surveillance the only way by which to exorcise security and safety risks? While this is a political question, this kind of tension between surveillance, security and safety may be seen as yet another instance of the underlying dynamic of the individuation of our association to others alongside the necessity to collaborate and collectively address threats and risks. At the same time, the trend towards more surveillance and the collection and collation of more and more personal data is unmistakable. These are also related to attempts to profit from them, through selling 'analytics', or demographic and other relevant information to those interested.

Journalism

Earlier, we saw the various changes that the political process has undergone as a function of the new media. But how do traditional institutions of modern democracies fare in the new media environment? Journalism may be thought of as one of the most important institutions of (representative) democracies, functioning as the public sphere in which citizens can come together, discuss matters of common concern and develop an informed public opinion (see Habermas, 1989 [1962]). But the new media have precipitated a crisis which goes to the heart of journalism threatening its very survival. The rise of the new media has changed the time frame within which it operates, undermined its autonomy, dried up its revenue sources and drastically changed the habits of its consumers-readers. How has journalism responded? It has sought to adopt more efficient production processes, through convergence; it has made use of the new media technological affordances, introducing changes in its contents and narrative structures; while, finally, it has merged production with use/consumption, adopting open source practices such as crowdsourcing. There is no doubt that these practices have revolutionized journalism, which is now found not only in respected broadsheets and popular tabloids, but also in blogs, on Twitter and Facebook, making use of a wide range of materials and sources, ranging from text messages to testimonial mobile phone pictures. This has rendered journalism a collaborative process, in which readers are actively involved in the production of journalistic output, but at the same time it has undermined journalistic credibility. In a provocative book, Andrew Keen (2007) argued that the amateurism of user contents ends up creating 'a digital forest of mediocrity' (p. 3), in which readers cannot and do not distinguish between professional journalism, which relies on facts and analysis, and personal opinion appearing on blogs. At the same time, the customization of news and journalism means that we are not all part of the same public sphere, but occupy little areas of specialist interests. This inevitably results in the fragmentation of the public sphere. The tension here between the opening up and 'democratization' of journalism and the requirement for some limits over what qualifies as journalism shows that collaboration is not a necessary and sufficient condition for an improved journalism. On the other hand, the individuation and customization prevalent in the consumption of journalism does not allow us to participate in a common public sphere, thereby undermining its operation and ultimately its democratic functions. The tendency towards disintermediation has clearly damaged journalism, and as this trend continues, journalism needs to reinvent itself and (re)claim its continued usefulness in the new media environment.

Mobile Media

Perhaps this fundamental tension between the collaborative and individualizing aspects of the new media is more evident in areas that deal with cultural and social life. We can understand mobile media as forming part of the fabric of our everyday lives and as an important part of our culture. Indeed, the global spread of mobile phones shows that they have become a ubiquitous everyday artefact. Moreover, as MP3 players converge with mobile phones and with the internet, media portability is a reality. Wireless networks have spread across most developed urban spaces, providing internet access to mobile phone and portable computer users, and freeing the internet from the confines of the office and the home. Moreover, the spread of wireless internet is proportionately higher in developing countries which find it a cheaper alternative to laying a cable infrastructure. The commercial character of the mobile media is often juxtaposed to the network character of wireless internet (Benkler, 2006), and it shows the tensions between the tendency within informational capitalism to exploit media for profit and the tendency of information and communication to operate freely and without constraints. But here we also see the tension between the individualizing effects of portable media such as the mobile phone and MP3 players and the collaborative aspects of wireless networks. While the former allow and even encourage users to exist and operate within their own little 'bubble', they rely on wireless networks, which require a collaborative and common effort for their operation. Additionally, we see a tension between the individualization associated with portable media and some of their political effects, such as smart mobs or sms-based coordination, which show the results of collaboration. In socio-cultural terms, mobile media, especially mobile phones, manage to isolate individuals from their surrounding space and time, while allowing them to connect with distant others. Mobile media then display in full the pull towards individualization and atomization and the pull towards the opposite direction, that of communication, collaboration, and collective effort. The trend towards more mobility and more portability is continuing unabated, as new hardware devices, such as Kindle and iPad, offer more and more possibilities to users.

Identity and Sociality

The relationship between the new media, sociality and identity reveals not only changes and shifts, but also a dynamism and fluidity that makes it difficult to pin them down. Already in modernity identity is no longer seen as fixed or given, but a project, constantly changing on the basis of people's experiences and choices. For theorists such as Foucault, identity is constructed out of the materials that comprise our culture: these technologies of the self have in the past managed to construct an inner self, concerned with self examination and monitoring. If we consider the new media as technologies of the self, the emerging self can be seen as constructed through blogging, 'friending' others on social networking sites, tweeting, texting, gaming and so on. To the extent that these activities are initiated and controlled by the individual, the resulting self is atomized and autonomous; to the extent, however, that these new media activities rely on others for feedback, communication, recognition and reflection, this emerging self is a kind of collaborative project. But how do ascribed identities, such as gender and ethnicity/ race fare in the new media world(s)? While the individualized elements of identity offer a more liberal and free environment for these identities, there is evidence showing the perpetuation of stereotypes and inequalities in online and other new media environments. The ambiguous relationship of the new media with ascribed identities indicates that there is no easy solution to inequalities and injustices, although the tension between individualization and the collective elements in the new media variably supports in some environments the playful (de)construction of gender and ethno-racial identities while in others it contributes to phenomena such as techno-orientalism and long distance nationalism.

This idea of a collaborative yet autonomous self resonates with Barry Wellman's and Manuel Castells' concept of networked individualism. The new media, they argue, allow people to connect to others beyond the confines of place, they allow them to choose their social contacts on the basis of common interests, and to coordinate the intensity and frequency of these contacts in ways they see fit. In these terms, the individual is the unit of connectivity, and not family, locality or group. For Castells (2001), networked individualism is the result of a series of broader changes, such as the demise of patriarchy and political ideologies, which lead us to relate to each in different ways, prioritizing interests, skills, individual preferences and so on. In some respects network individualism overstates the element of free choice in relating to others, overlooking the limits set to networking by differences in access to networks, in abilities, and indeed in knowledge and skills. These power differences are reflected in studies of social media and their relationship to social capital: although there is evidence that social capital may increase through social media, the economic logic of accumulation, profit and loss prevails even in the social domain. If we accept that networked individualism forms the dominant sociality of the new media, this individuation of sociality, which at the same time retains and reproduces some of the most pernicious social divisions, such as class (but also gender and ethnicity/race), must be understood in critical terms. Similarly, the erosion of other boundaries, such as the public-private one, appears to undermine what Habermas would call the autonomy of the lifeworld. The emerging trend in the relationship between identity and the new media seems to be that identity is more and more reliant on personal choice and preferences, albeit these choices and preferences are themselves shaped in an environment which is still characterized by persistent socio-economic and cultural divisions. Equally, the trend towards the spread of an economic logic in domains such as identity and sociality and the blurring of personal and working life may perhaps not be directly attributed to the new media, but it certainly coincides with the rise of the network society, informational capitalism and immaterial labour.

Games and Gaming

Games have been shown to be the ideal-typical commodity of informational capitalism (Kline et al., 2003), a commodity whose informational nature, and conditions of production and consumption display in condensed form the main characteristics of informational capitalism. While big media companies compete for the production of games, they are considered to be high risk products, as there is a very high rate of failure, when the development costs are very high. In other circumstances, games are produced by independent developers and then sold to media or gaming corporations. In the mythology that surrounds game development, developers are themselves ardent players, who consider their work a kind of play. But research has shown that working conditions are gruelling, with game developers working for hours on end, especially in the beta phase of development, where games are tested, often receiving only minimum payment. The narratives of games clearly show the links games have with the 'military-entertainment complex' (Wark, 2006), globalizing simplified good-vs.-evil explanations for complex political events. At the same time, the architecture and structure of games is successfully training informational workers, turning play into work. But games, and gamers in particular, have been involved in other kinds of controversies as well: games are, for some, directly linked to violence and violent practices. The stereotypical image of a gamer is that of an anti-social loner, who ends up committing random acts of violence. On the other hand, theorists such as Henry Jenkins have shown the participatory and collaborative elements of games, in which gamers collaborate in creative and imaginative ways, often forming their own communities, and creating new games or levels. 'Modding', in which gamers modify existing levels or parts of a game, is one such creative activity. But gamers can also participate in gaming practices that end up generating income for them, thereby contributing to a so-called ludocapitalism, in which gaming by itself is a kind of employment, while gamers can trade credits, cheat codes and gaming objects in online auctions. For McKenzie Wark (2006), gaming practices and activities are already predetermined through the game's algorithm, and all gamers do is to follow the instructions. Nevertheless, Coleman and Dyer-Witheford (2007), point to the ambiguous potential of practices such as modding, piracy, machinima and the development of MMOGs, arguing that they are located in-between commodification and the development of a digital commons, which does not belong to anyone, and which provides resources that anyone can use. The image of the gamer as a lone, alienated 'geek' spending hours in front of a screen is complemented by a set of gaming practices which require participation in communities, collaboration, and which contributes to the creation of a set of common resources. This is typical of the tension between individuation and collaboration which underlies games and gaming practices as well as other new media forms. The emerging trend here is the spread of the gaming logic in other domains, most notably that of employment, and the resulting dissolution of the boundaries between work and play. To the extent that this gaming logic is associated to the capitalist logic of competition and profit accumulation, games help (informational) capitalism to spread in other domains as well.

Throughout this section, we identified a series of continuities and discontinuities, emerging and continuing trends, as well as an underlying tension between the individualizing and collaborative elements of the new media. Throughout, these developments were linked to capitalism as the dominant political-economic form of organization. To this extent, the logic of accumulation and profit seeking as well as certain forms of inequality, mainly linked to our position vis-à-vis the means of production of informational commodities, prevail in informational as they did in industrial capitalism. On the other hand, the above mentioned tension creates a dynamic field, leading to changes which mark a clear departure from previous practices: examples here include immaterial labour, the kinds of identities and socialities created in and through the new media, mobile media and gaming practices, and so on. These changes are, in most cases, ambiguous: to this extent they may be seen as entailing a promise. Will this materialize in the future? And what can we do about it? The next section will examine the question of the future of the new media, followed by a discussion of internet governance as an example of political intervention that may enable the fulfilment of the progressive promise of the new media.

Thinking of the Future

Innovation and creativity are the two concepts more often associated with the future new media, as well as the future *of* the new media. The links between the new media and the technologies that support them are such that it is expected that new technological developments will lead to new media. Thinking about the form the future may take involves therefore thinking about the kinds of technological innovations that will give rise to newer versions of the new media. On the other hand, we have seen in this book that technological innovation and novelty does not guarantee success: more often than not, new media and/or other technological innovations succeed because they managed to resonate with socio-cultural, as well as economic and political developments. We must therefore incorporate culture, society, economy and politics when we think about the future.

Technological Innovation

The built-in obsolescence of the various technological devices requires that we acquire new devices every so often. In fact, a characteristic of the new media era is that the life cycle of technology is becoming shorter. Just as we got used to our 3G phones, smartphones came up. No sooner had we got used to our laptop computers than netbooks came up, followed by iPads. It is clear that the new media are driven by innovation both in terms of devices as well as in terms of applications. We wouldn't be buying all these devices if they didn't have anything new to offer, and indeed the novelty claims of devices and applications are continuous. One of the characteristics of Web 2.0 is the so-called beta phase, an ongoing development and testing phase, often driven by user feedback (O'Reilly, 2005). How can we understand these innovations and what can we learn about the future?

Clayton Christensen (1997), writing on innovation, came up with an influential classification scheme. For Christensen, not all innovations are the same: we have disruptive and sustaining innovations. Some innovations are incremental, building on previous innovations, but improving them or slightly changing their direction. These are understood as sustaining innovations. At the same time, some innovations completely annihilate what preceded them, disrupting and ultimately destroying previous innovations. These are understood as radical innovations. Drawing on the work of the economist Joseph Schumpeter, on the cycle of production and creative destruction, authors such as Anderson and Tushman (1990; see Latzer 2009) argue that innovation occurs in cycles. First we have some sort of disruptive, radical innovation that breaks the previous cycle of innovation; then this new innovation becomes established, triggering a competition for the dominant form or design of the innovation, followed by series of imitations leading to ferment. This in turn triggers some incremental changes (sustaining innovations), while the cycle is disrupted yet again by another radical innovation.

Radical innovations are those which are seen as disrupting the previous state of affairs, introducing a discontinuity, as they often do not have a predecessor (Latzer, 2009). In addition, they rely on new technology, rather than improving old technology, and require substantial re-training and re-education. The internet clearly constitutes such a radical innovation, alongside digitalization and the invention of computers, and especially PC. They have all introduced radical changes, leading to major restructuring, a new economic cycle, and the need for re-education and training. But if we focus on the disruptive effects of radical innovations, as Christensen (1997) did, then we can see that they are often not much better than their predecessors, and sometimes they can even perform worse: a case in point may be digital photography, whose quality is worse than its analogue counterpart. In addition, they may lead to lower profits, at least until a new business model emerges; an example here is journalism as well as the music industry, which have suffered considerable loss of income when their contents became digital and began circulating in online environments. As Latzer (2009: 609) points out, the effect of these radical disruptive technologies may be that in destroying an older business model, they may enable less skilled or wealthy groups of people to do things that once were done only by specialists (e.g. journalists or photographers).

Although the concept of disruptive innovation appears to usefully account for developments in the field of the new media, it is not without its problems. Specifically, Latzer notes that when we look at the actual applications of this concept to technological innovations such as WiFi and VoIP (Voice over Internet Protocol), the results are mixed: often these new technologies, although radical, have little or no disruptive potential. In addition, it seems that disruption is typically considered from the point of view of incumbents, while what is disruptive for some, is sustaining for others. For example, although user-generated contents may be disruptive to journalists and mass media outlets, they may actually empower users. While the internet may be disruptive to the music industry, this is not the case for pharmaceutical companies (Latzer, 2009). As Latzer suggests, the concept may require some fine tuning, and it has limited applicability. On the other hand, however, we may use the distinction between radical-disruptive and sustaining innovations to question the future of the new media.

Following Isenberg's (1999) argument, the internet is the 'mother of all disruptions' but in the sense that it includes various radical, new technologies. The different trajectories of these new technologies pull the internet towards different directions. Some of these may be radical-disruptive, some may be sustaining. We can think of Tim Berners-Lee's invention of the World Wide Web as a radical innovation, since it dramatically changed our relationship to the internet. Although it rests on more or less the same technology, we could also think of Web 2.0 as disruptive, since it has led to important shifts in the logic and use of the internet. Thinking, for example, of the web as platform and the shift towards a dynamic, peer-to-peer, collaborative internet, exemplified by applications such as blogging and wikis, shows a disruptive effect on previous dominant applications, such as Netscape. On the other hand, developments such as cloud computing, that is, the use of virtual servers on the internet, and the ability to work on shared files, denote a kind of sustaining innovation. Cloud computing, exemplified by Google Apps, which includes gmail, Google Docs, Picasa and so on, essentially represents an improvement on, and fine tuning of the logic of the web as platform, which is characteristic of Web 2.0. Similarly, innovations such as tablet PCs, the iPad for instance, improve but do not radically change nor do they disrupt the logic of portable personal computers, exemplified by laptops and netbooks. If we accept Anderson and Tushman's cycle of innovation, then we should expect that these new designs will eventually flatten out, reaching a plateau, before a new radical-disruptive innovation occurs.

Semantic Web

Could it be that Tim Berners-Lee's Semantic Web – or Web 3.0 – will lead to the next radical innovation? While in popular thinking radical innovations occur suddenly and unexpectedly, more often than not they are the culmination of years of planning and research. Thus, Berners-Lee and other members of the World Wide Web Consortium have been working on a new kind of web. They believe that the next phase of the Web should be a semantic one, revolving around meaning rather than simple keywords. For Berners-Lee and his collaborators, the web should be able to do more than keyword searches, and data or search findings should be integrated. In technical terms, this requires the possibility that 'data is shared and reused across applications, enterprise and community boundaries' (see www.w3.org). The problem with Web 2.0 is that it is getting larger and larger with data flooding in from all directions. Ordering this in terms of keywords is becoming less and less efficient. The semantic Web is looking for ways in which to integrate data with the context in which they occur, specifying a qualitative relationship, and relying on the actual meaning of data. As Berners-Lee has put it, this web will be capable of reading and understanding context and content together. It will be able to filter contents and present users with those that are the most relevant, come from the most relevant sources and are the most recent. To accomplish this, users will have to provide information on the context of the contents they produce; tagging is one form of doing this, while voting on the most relevant may be another. The idea is that the web will make use of the users' input and characterization of content, which will subsequently enable semantic, meaning-based qualitative searches. The underlying technology, which is currently developed by W3C, relies on the development of a new protocol, Resource Description Framework (RDF). Every kind of information or data on the web will be coded or described through this protocol, which includes not only a description of the data but also of relationships between data, developing a common language, which can then make qualitative searches possible. In contrast to Web 2.0 which basically employed the same Web 1.0 technology, Web 3.0 requires technological innovation, which will combine user input with a new protocol for classifying web data. W3C considers that the Semantic Web will be developed and operational by the year 2020. There is little doubt that this has the potential to lead to radical and perhaps also disruptive changes to the web and computing as we know it. But will this innovation succeed? To be able to gauge this, we need to understand the social aspects of innovations.

The Social Life of Innovations

We have argued throughout this book that technologies and media are not driven by technological sophistication but by socio-economic, political, and cultural factors. Their success is the result of a combination of these factors, and appears often to be random. For instance, when the feature of texting was included in mobile phones, no one expected its huge success. In fact, it was also quite slow in the uptake, with mobile phone users in 1995 sending less than one SMS text message per month. However, it soon became very popular with US users alone in 2008 sending over 75 billion text messages every month (Cell Signs, 2008). Texting has also triggered a series of changes in language and in communication more broadly, with brevity becoming a dominant feature. Its success cannot be seen as the result of the cutting edge technology that it used; rather we must understand it as the result of initially economic factors, as texting was – and still is – considerably cheaper than voice calls. The more people used it, the more popular it became, creating a culture of its own, especially among young people. It was then only a matter of time before it spread further. Other innovations are not so successful: Leah Lievrouw (2006) showed the diverging fates of email and videotext – an application similar to teletext, linking television sets to computer databases: while the first is considered one of the most successful applications of all times, videotex has been consigned to history. Various reasons are to account for this: the degree of institutional support of an innovation; the kind of distribution mechanism employed; the actors involved in producing and managing the innovation and so on. As Lievrouw (2006) points out, the success of an innovation is the result of a complex interplay between different moments of technology development, and the extent to which they are determined or contingent.

It is precisely this kind of uncertainty that makes it difficult to predict the success and degree of diffusion of an innovation. From this point of view, the success of any kind of future innovation, such as Web 3.0, will be the result of a series of factors. On the one hand, Web 3.0 has the potential to succeed as there is considerable investment, both in terms of financial capital as well as in terms of the human contributors to this project. Second, some aspects of it resonate with the existing culture of folksonomies, sharing and collaboration, which implies that people may find it easier to understand and employ it. On the other hand, people may not be particularly convinced by the Semantic Web, as they are not sure what it will accomplish. Moreover, there is always a degree of resistance to change as most people are set in their ways. Part of the problem may be that while Web 2.0 was a bottom up organic development, the Semantic Web is driven from the top. In addition, at this stage it is very technologically oriented, and comes across as relevant more to computer engineers than users. This means that the technological innovation behind the Semantic Web must first be developed and then 'marketed' or 'sold' to users, making it difficult for at least some users to grasp and adopt it. At the same time, parts of the Semantic Web, especially those relying on data sharing, need to deal with issues of control over data, privacy, and copyright. We have seen that these issues are at the heart of Web 2.0, and part of an ongoing struggle – the Semantic Web has to face this struggle as well. A final issue here concerns the disconnection between the technology and people. This points back to Kittler's criticism that as long as we are ignorant of the algorithms employed, we will be at the mercy of those who produce and own these algorithms. But will these issues lead to the failure of the Semantic Web? One thing is for sure: unless people find ways to creatively appropriate and embed the Semantic Web in their lives, it is probably doomed to fail.

New Media Governance

The previous discussion concerning the future of innovations and the future of the new media more broadly, focused primarily on the technological and social aspects that may influence the future. But in considering the future we must also think of the possibility for conscious and deliberate efforts to steer it towards certain directions. We have seen, for instance, that the dominance of questions of security has led to a rise in surveillance. We have also seen that in some instances, the internet may cause addiction, or that violent games can be associated with real world violence. What are we, as society, going to do about these issues? How might we regulate the internet/new media and how can we ensure a positive future for them? At the same time, the internet, as we have seen, relies on a set of very dynamic technologies, whose operation relies, in turn, on the agreement and collaboration of those who produce them. But how can we make sure that this agreement and collaboration will represent the interests of all involved? This is the political aspect of the present and future of the new media: how best can we manage and steer the new media, and especially the internet? Clearly, many different ideas compete here for the definition of 'best': how might we define 'best'? 'Best' for whom? There are no easy answers here, but this section will discuss the history and the main issues regarding internet governance, concluding with a discussion of the various proposed models of policy, regulation and governance.

Most discussions of internet governance adopt a technological perspective, based on the assumption that existing legal codes and political positions regulate the social, behavioural, and political aspects of the internet. Thus, theorists such as Solum (2008: 50) define internet governance as 'the regulation of internet infrastructure, its current operation and the processes by which it develops and changes over time'. On the other hand, Solum recognizes that when content and conduct go through the internet, they may introduce changes that cannot be effectively dealt with within the existing legal framework. Thus, internet governance needs to encompass the policy questions that arise when content and conduct is communicated and acted upon through the internet (Solum, 2008: 50). What is at stake here is both the present and the future of the internet and the new media. How have they been managed so far?

In 1998 the UN received a proposal for a world summit to deal with the so-called information society, and especially with concerns regarding the divide between developed and developing countries (see Wu, Dyson, Froomkin and Gross, 2007). In general, internet regulation and governance of the so-called root servers, controlling domain names, was left to a private organization, ICANN (Internet Corporation for Assigned Names and Numbers). This rather secretive US-based organization decided on name allocation and the management of domains, such as .com, .org and the like – the main criticism faced by ICANN was that it is unclear whose interests are served by the organization, that stakeholders do not participate in the decision process for name allocation, and that it is not accountable. Eventually, the UN organized two world summits to deal with the information society more broadly and to tackle the issue of internet governance. The first one took place in Geneva in 2003, and the second in Tunis in 2005. In the Geneva summit, delegates accepted a declaration of principles, which asserted the principle that information society must be accessible to all, but ultimately failed to reach any agreement on more controversial issues concerning in particular the role of the private sector in governing the internet. David Gross, a US ambassador and responsible for international communications and information policy, rather cynically described how the US diverted efforts to exclude ICANN (Wu et al., 2007). Gross did not want to assign internet governance to an international organization, such as the International Telecommunications Union or the UN, for fear that some countries would exercise their veto powers and perhaps compromise US interests.

The Tunis summit followed along similar lines, eventually leading to the development of the Internet Governance Forum, with a consulting role, while ICANN and the USA retained control of the root servers. While this certainly prioritized what can be seen as a (neo)liberal approach to regulation and governance of the internet, we must not disregard some important gains, since regulation must follow the US constitution and the First Amendment, concerning freedom of speech. More recently, ICANN adopted a different, more open and transparent approach, which acknowledges the right of all stakeholders to be involved in its decision-making processes.

This multi-stakeholder model essentially draws on the work by the Internet Governance Forum, as well as from others who may express their views and opinions, which are then integrated and taken into account in the development and steering of the internet. ICANN claims that its latest projects, such as the Internationalized Domain Names and the Domain Name System Security Extensions, emerged through a series of consultations which showed that stakeholders prioritized an all-inclusive, unified and secured internet (see www.icann.org). On the other hand, to the extent that the input of these stakeholders is only consultative, and they have no veto or other means of appealing or changing ICANN's decisions, ICANN remains a top-down hierarchical organization.

Models of Governance

How might we assess these regulatory efforts? Rather than assessing them on the basis of their outcomes, theorists seek to evaluate them on the basis of the decision-making process. In other words, the better the decision-making process, the more likely for its outcome to be acceptable. Malcolm (2008) focuses on the Internet Governance Forum, which is emerging as a key network for the governance of internet, and discusses four models of governance, or organizational forms that shape and influence IGF's decision-making process. The first is the anarchistic model, which is based on the lack of a formal hierarchy of authority, and which assumes a structure of equality, a discussion among peers. This model appears to be especially compatible with the culture of the internet, its networked, polycentric structure, and its peer-to-peer model of exchange and communication. Malcolm discusses Wikipedia as an example of an anarchistic governance model, albeit a limited one, since all participants must operate within a set of guidelines and rules. But how would that work as a model for internet governance? Malcolm holds that it would involve all stakeholders in the process, but forbid them from coercing each other, even if they make democratic or meritocratic claims. This means that the structure of internet governance is not predetermined, but emerges out of this 'cacophony of voices' – eventually the success of any policy is determined by its adoption by the community (Reagle, 1998 in Malcolm, 2008: 192). Decentralized collective action then determines both the rules of the decision-making process, as well as their outcome. All stakeholders in internet governance would participate and through cooperation determine the procedure to be followed as well as its outcome. While there is no doubt that this is an attractive framework, Malcolm finds that its fluid structure does not guarantee that all stakeholders will be involved at all stages of the decision-making process, while there are also issues of transparency and effectiveness. The anarchistic model hinges on an idea of cooperation motivated by notions of what is best. However, rational choice theories note that people or groups plan and move strategically, seriously undermining these anarchist ideas. Given that the main stakeholders in internet governance are governments, NGOs and the civil society, it is likely that it will move strategically to ensure their interests. Malcolm then concludes that an anarchistic governance structure may be appropriate to other forms of decision making, but not when it comes to internet governance, as the stakes are high and we must ensure that all are involved.

The second mode, the hierarchical one, although incompatible with the internet's architecture and culture, may prove an efficient way for governing the internet. Based on a top-down ordering, it may take a bureaucratic, oligarchic or meritocratic form (Malcolm, 2008). A bureaucratic-hierarchical organization would mean that participants would have a unique role in the hierarchy, and would conduct their role on the basis of its formal requirements rather than on the basis of their interests. Since however, internet governance requires that stakeholders represent the interests of their group, this kind of anonymity is not appropriate. An oligarchical organization would require that the number of participants is drastically reduced, thereby making the decision-making process quicker and more efficient. However, this makes the process less representative and less transparent – in fact this is the way in which ICANN functions. Former ICANN board member, Karl Auerbach has described ICANN as an oligarchy, arguing that it operates with impunity, deriving its power from government projects (Koman and Auerbach, 2002 in Malcolm, 2008). Notwithstanding its efforts to include the community, ICANN remains an oligarchy since it does not allocate a formal and binding role to stakeholders. A meritocratic hierarchical organization would require that only the best qualified would take part in the decision-making process. However, the decision of who indeed may be chosen as the best qualified is an arbitrary one. Malcolm (2008) argues that the Internet Engineering Task Force (IETF), one of the first regulatory bodies of the internet, governing the development of its standards, may be considered as a meritocracy, or a technocracy, given its technical character. Similarly, the open source movement can be seen as a meritocracy. The merit of members is evaluated by their peers, but in this sense it cannot qualify as a hierarchy (Malcolm, 2008). There is little doubt that merit must play a part in internet governance, but the delegation of essentially political decisions to bodies of experts, strips power from stakeholders and is undemocratic. To assume that experts have all the answers, moreover, contradicts the arguments we have pursued earlier, that technological developments are the complex result of a number of factors, not only technological ones.

A democratic form of organization may prove to be the best, since it is based on the premise that all stakeholders are represented, and that this representation is based upon the consent of those that are represented and governed. Two issues therefore are central here: representation and consent. The difficulty by which we can ensure proper representation as well as the often hegemonic ways of getting consent however present important hurdles. First, there are different approaches to the notion of representation with participatory, deliberative, representative and direct models proposing different ways. Second, consent varies as a function of these models. Moreover, transparency and accountability are not as fundamental to democracy as representation and consent, while inclusion, at least in the typical liberal model is seen minimally as the aggregate of all preferences. In other words, different democratic models offer different solutions to issues of representation, consent, transparency, accountability and inclusion, but they nevertheless take them into account. One of these models that has gained currency in online environments is that of deliberative democracy associated with the work of Jürgen Habermas (Habermas, 1996a; 1996b; for the internet see Dahlberg, 2001; Dahlberg and Siapera, 2007). Thus, despite the problems and difficulties of pinning down which democratic model may be more appropriate for internet governance, they seem to offer considerable advantages over previous models. Following a deliberative model would require that all stakeholders would be included in the decision-making process and deliberate on the basis of rational arguments until a consensual decision is made. However, the focus on rational arguments excludes other forms of discourse, based on irony, story-telling, rhetoric and so on (Young, 1996). Moreover, the assumption that power does not play a part in deliberations appears somewhat naïve. At the same time, in seeking to ensure inclusion and deliberation in online environments we encounter the problems of fragmentation and the polarization of views (Sunstein, 2001), while rational discourse often deteriorates to flaming and abusive comments. Malcolm further points out that the digital divide is prohibitive of inclusion of those with no access to online media, and, we may add, computer literacy skills, thereby undermining efforts to implement a deliberative democratic model on internet governance. There is also a conceptual double bind involved here: if the object of internet governance is to include those with the least access to the positive outcomes of the information society, then finding a solution to digital divide issues involves finding a solution to internet governance.

Malcolm further discusses the consensual model (2008: 291–318) but since there is considerable overlap with the deliberative model, we will here jump to his final model, that of multi-stakeholder governance. In fact this is a hybrid model, drawing upon the strengths of the previously discussed models. From anarchism, Malcolm takes the fluid structure but since this is also the source of problems, he suggests a combination of this fluid structure with some form of hierarchical ordering. Given that meritocracy was found the most attractive form, it may be included, provided that selection of those with merit is based on agreement or consensus, and that some form of entry and exit criteria are agreed upon. Finally, given that deliberative democracy fulfils some basic criteria for inclusion, deliberation and agreement, it too can contribute to a hybrid model. Malcolm then concludes that an appropriate framework for internet governance should comprise:

> an open and transparent forum within which members of all stakeholder groups deliberate with the aim of reaching consensus, led by a meritocratic executive council, to which each group appoints its representatives using consensual or democratic means, and which would be required to ratify all decisions of the forum by consensus. (2008: 320)

While ICANN and the IGF are a long way from approaching this ideal structure, this model can help manage the different ideologies and political positions that feed into internet governance. On the other hand, there is still the possibility that this structure may present problems, especially since in the end all decisions are subject to ratification by experts. We must keep in mind that all such decision-making procedural models must be open to change and reform. Thus, even if we cannot agree upon which direction the future of the internet should take, this governance structure can at least ensure that most if not all interests, as well as political positions are represented.

Conclusions

What kinds of conclusions can we draw from all this? Box 12.1 summarizes the main points of this chapter. We have seen the various trends, and discussed the continuities and discontinuities introduced by the various new media in the multifaceted aspects of our lives. While some elements appear promising, others appear almost nightmarish, making it difficult to draw any definitive conclusions. However, although in the past, inventions and know-how have been lost, it is unlikely that this is possible to happen in our current historical juncture: what has been thought, what has been invented, cannot be un-thought and cannot be taken back. The new media, whether we like it or not, are here to stay. The best, if not the only, option we have is to contribute to their steering and governance in ways that promote ideas of justice and equality for all. From this point of view, we must remain critical, but also optimistic regarding the future of the new media and more broadly our future.

We began this book with two epigrams by McLuhan and Kittler on the media's determination of our lives. Perhaps a fitting epilogue would be Stiegler's call for a new politics of the new media, which he calls a new politics of memory, an injunction for re-appropriation of the media, time and memory in ways commensurable with humanity: a new way of life in which as Stiegler put it, 'economizing means taking care' (undated, online text). Stiegler's point is that we must resist control of the (new) media, which operate not only as communicative media but also as storage and memory devices, by corporations, governments and other self-interested parties. The centrality of the new media is such that we must in the end view them, especially the internet, as a kind of commons, a resource collectively belonging to all of us, and which has to be governed in ways that reflect our equal rights over them.

12.1 Summary of Main Points

Current Trends

- The main underlying trend: a fluid and dynamic tension between individualizing and collective-collaborative elements of the new media

More specific trends:

- Economy: autonomization of (immaterial) labour
- Consumption: a trend towards a wider and deeper spread of the new media across all demographic categories and across developing countries
- Politics: disintermediation and the creation of new political subjectivities
- Surveillance: more and more surveillance offered as a solution to questions of security and safety
- Journalism: under pressure to reinvent itself and justify its continued usefulness

- Mobile media: more mobility, more portability
- Identity and sociality: the individuation of sociality and the spread of an economic logic on the domains of identity and sociality
- Games: the dissolution of boundaries between work and play

Future Innovations

Sustaining innovations:

- Incremental changes
- Struggle for dominant design
- Eventually leading to ferment

Radical and disruptive innovations:

- Introduce discontinuities
- Often lack predecessors
- Lead to restructuring
- The internet as the 'mother of all disruptions' (Isenberg, 1999)
- Web 2.0: a radical innovation?

Semantic Web: the future of radical innovation?

- Based on a qualitative relationship between data
- Requires that we all collaborate in tagging and describing data
- But top down rather than organic development
- Its success hinges on the extent to which it can become embedded in people's lives

Internet Governance

- Internet Governance: deals with the regulation of the internet infrastructure, its present and future operations, as well as with the policy questions that arise out of the migration of content and conduct online.
- Two World Summits (Geneva, 2003, and Tunis, 2005) essentially retained the role of ICANN, a US-based private corporation, while creating new structures, such as the IGF

Models of governance (Malcolm, 2008):

- Anarchist: fluid structure and discussion among peers
- Hierarchical: while the bureaucratic and oligarchic forms are problematic, meritocracy relies on the most qualified (as judged by their peers)

- Democratic: based on the principles of representation and consent. Deliberative democracy offers an attractive and convincing model
- A synthesis of the above leads to a multi-stakeholder model that combines elements of the above, involving deliberation between all stakeholders and eventual ratification by a meritocratic group of experts

Further Reading

Thinking of the future paradoxically requires us to rethink the past as well as what precisely do notions of the future entail. Nick Couldry's article theorizes concepts and narratives of the future of 'the media', holding that technological, political and social forces will make this a site for intensified struggle. Looking back to the past, Michael Zimmer's article focuses on the concept of renvois (references or footnotes) in the Encyclopedia of the French philosopher Denis Diderot. This mode represents an active way of structuring knowledge, and according to Zimmer, it features prominently not only in Web 2.0 and the concept of folksonomies, but also in the Semantic Web to come. Shifting the focus to the issue of new media governance, George Christou and Seamus Simpson examine two relevant actors, the EU and ICANN from the perspective of rational action, showing not only what is at stake, but also how relevant decisions are pursued and secured. The final article by Michael Latzer looks at the concept of innovation in the field of the new media and examines the applicability of concepts such as disruptive innovations in a field that is increasingly characterized by convergence.

Couldry, N., 2009, Does 'the Media' Have a Future?, *European Journal of Communication*, 24(4): 437–449.

Zimmer, M., 2009, Renvois of the Past, Present and Future: Hyperlinks and the Structuring of Knowledge from the Encyclopédie to Web 2.0, *New Media & Society*, 11(1): 95–113.

Christou, G. and Simpson, S., 2007, Gaining a Stake in Global Internet Governance: The EU, ICANN and Strategic Norm Manipulation, *European Journal of Communication*, 22(2): 147–164.

Latzer, M., 2009, Information and Communication Technology Innovations: Radical and Disruptive?, *New Media & Society*, 11(4): 599–619.

BIBLIOGRAPHY

Aarseth, E., 1997, *Cybertext: Perspectives on Ergodic Literature*, Baltimore, MD: Johns Hopkins University Press.

Aarseth, E., 2004, Genre Trouble: Narrativism and the Art of Simulation, in N. Wardrip-Fruin and P. Harrigan (eds), *First Person: New Media as Story, Performance, and Game* (pp. 45–55), Cambridge, MA: MIT Press.

Abramson, J.B., Arterton, F.C. and Orren, J.R., 1988, *The Electronic Commonwealth: The Impact of New Media Technologies on Democratic Politics*, New York: Basic Books.

Acquisti, A. and Gross, R., 2006, Imagined Communities: Awareness, Information Sharing, and Privacy on the Facebook, in P. Golle and G. Danezis (eds), *Proceedings of 6th Workshop on Privacy Enhancing Technologies* (pp. 36–58), Cambridge, UK.

Adam, B., Beck, U. and van Loon, J. (eds), 2000, *The Risk Society and Beyond: Critical Issues for Social Theory*, London: Sage.

Adobe, 2009, Press Release, available at: http://www.adobe.com/aboutadobe/pressroom/pressr eleases/200903/030309AdobeTimeWarner.html

Adorno, T., 1978 [1938], On the Fetish Character in Music and the Regression of Listening, in A. Arato and E. Gebhardt (eds), *The Essential Frankfurt School Reader* (pp. 270–289), Oxford: Blackwell.

Adorno, T. and Horkheimer, M., 1997 [1947], *Dialectic of Enlightenment*, London: Verso.

Agar, J., 2003, *Constant Touch: A Global History of the Mobile Phone*, Cambridge: Icon Books.

Althusser, L. and Balibar, E., 1970, *Reading Capital*, London: New Left Books, available at: http://www.marxists.org/reference/archive/althusser/1968/reading-capital/ch03.htm

Anderson, B., 1991 [1983], *Imagined Communities: Reflections on the Origin and Spread of Nationalism*, London: Verso.

Anderson, B., 1992, Long Distance Nationalism: World Capitalism and the Rise of Identity Politics, The Wertheim Lecture, Centre for Asian Studies, University of Amsterdam, available at: http://213.207.98.211/asia/wertheim/lectures/WL_Anderson.pdf

Anderson, B. and Yitri, B., 2007, Telework Transitions and the Quality of Life, in B. Anderson, M. Brynin, J. Gershuny and J. Raban (eds), *Information and Communication Technologies in Society* (pp. 136–149), London: Routledge.

Anderson, C., 2003, Violent Video Games: Myths, Facts, and Unanswered Questions, in American Psychological Association, available at: http://www.apa.org/science/about/psa/2003/10/anderson.aspx

Anderson, C., 2004, An Update on the Effects of Playing Violent Video Games, *Journal of Adolescence*, 27: 113–122.

Anderson, P. and Tushman, M.L., 1990, Technological Discontinuities and Dominant Designs: A Cyclical Model of Technological Change, *Administrative Science Quarterly*, 35: 604–633.

Andrejevic, M., 2004, *Reality TV: The Work of Being Watched*, Lanham, MD: Rowman & Littlefield.

Andrejevic, M., 2005, The Work of Watching One Another: Lateral Surveillance, Risk, and Governance, *Surveillance and Society,* 2(4): 479–497.

Andrejevic, M., 2007, *iSpy: Surveillance and Power in the Interactive Era*, Lawrence, KS: The University Press of Kansas.

Appadurai, A., 1990, Disjuncture and Difference in the Global Cultural Economy, in M. Featherstone (ed.), *Global Culture* (pp. 295–310), London: Sage.

Appadurai, A., 1996, *Modernity at Large*, Minneapolis: University of Minnesota Press.

Apperley, T.H., 2006, Genre and Game Studies: Toward a Critical Approach to Video Game Genres, *Simulation Gaming*, 37: 6–23.

Ariely, G., 2008, Knowledge Management, Terrorism and Cyber Terrorism, in L. Janczewski and A. Colaric (eds), *Cyber Warfare and Cyber Terrorism* (pp. 7–16), Hershey, PA., and London: Information Science Reference.

Attwood, F., 2007, No Money Shot? Commerce, Pornography and New Sex Taste Cultures, *Sexualities*, 10(4): 441–456.

Bardoel, J., 2002, The Internet, Journalism and Public Communication Policies, *International Communication Gazette*, 64(5): 501–511.

Barnes, S., 2006, A Privacy Paradox: Social Networking in the United States, *First Monday,* 11(9), available at: http://www.firstmonday.org/issues/issue11_9/barnes/index.html

Barney, D., 2004, *The Network Society*, Cambridge: Polity Press.

Bauman, Z., 1998, *Globalization: The Human Consequences*, New York: Columbia University Press.

Bauman, Z., 1999, *In Search of Politics*, Cambridge: Polity Press.

Baym, N. K. (2006). Interpersonal Life Online, in S. Livingstone and L. Lievrouw (eds.) *The Handbook of New Media, Student Edition* (pp. 35–54), London: Sage.

BBC News, 2001a, Columbine families sue computer game makers, 1 May, available at: http://news.bbc.co.uk/2/hi/science/nature/1295920.stm

BBC News, 2001b, Hamas hit by porn attack, 7 March, available at: http://news.bbc.co.uk/1/hi/world/middle_east/1207551.stm

BBC News, 2004, Murder accused speaks of 'neck fetish', 23 January, available at: http://news.bbc.co.uk/2/hi/uk_news/england/southern_counties/3423221.stm

BBC News, 2006a, Mother wins ban on violent porn, 30 August, available at: http://news.bbc.co.uk/2/hi/uk_news/england/berkshire/5297600.stm

BBC News, 2006b, MP wins battle against web porn, 30 August, available at: http://news.bbc.co.uk/2/hi/uk_news/england/derbyshire/5299576.stm

BBC News, 2009, Spotlight on trio of child abusers, 1 October, available at: http://news.bbc.co.uk/2/hi/uk_news/8282764.stm

BBC News, 2010, Facebook murderer to serve at least 35 years, 8 March, available at: http://news.bbc.co.uk/2/hi/uk_news/england/wear/8555221.stm

Beardsworth, R., 1996, *Derrida and the Political,* New York: Routledge.

Beer, D., 2008, The Iconic Interface and the Veneer of Simplicity: MP3 players and the reconfiguration of music collecting and reproduction practices in the digital age, *Information, Communication and Society*, 11(1): 71–88.

Bell, D., 1973, *The Coming of Post-Industrial Society: A Venture in Social Forecasting*, New York: Basic Books.

Bell, E., 2009, Digital media cannot be contained by the analogue rulebook, *Guardian*, 23 March, available at: http://www.guardian.co.uk/media/2009/mar/23/regulating-digital-media

Benjamin, W., 1969, The Work of Art in the Age of Mechanical Reproduction, in H. Arendt (ed.), *Illuminations*, trans. Harry Zohn (pp 217–250), New York: Schocken.

Benkler, Y., 2006, *The Wealth of Networks: How Social Production Transforms Markets and Freedom*, New Haven, CT and London: Yale University Press.

Bennett, L. W., 2003, Communicating Global Activism: Strengths and Vulnerabilities of Networked Politics, *Information, Communication and Society*, 6: 143–168.

Bijker, W., 1995, *Of Bicycles, Bakelites and Bulbs: Toward a Theory of Sociotechnical Change*, Cambridge, MA and London: MIT Press.

Bijker, W., Hughes, T. Pinch, T. (eds), 1987, *The Social Construction of Technological Systems*, Cambridge, MA: MIT Press.

Bolter J. D., and Grusin, R., 1999, *Remediation: Understanding New Media*, Cambridge MA, MIT Press.

Bourdieu, P., 1977, *Outline of a Theory of Practice*, Cambridge: Cambridge University Press.

Bourdieu, P., 1997, The Forms of Capital, in A.H. Halsey, H. Lauder, P. Brown and A.S. Wells (eds), *Education: Culture, Economy, Society* (pp. 46–58), Oxford: Oxford University Press.

Bourdieu, P., 1998, *On Television and Journalism*, London: Pluto Press.

Bourdieu, P. and Wacquant, L., 1992, *An Invitation to Reflexive Sociology*, Chicago: University of Chicago Press.

boyd, d., 2007a, Viewing American class divisions through Facebook and MySpace, available at: http://www.danah.org/papers/essays/ClassDivisions.html

boyd, d., 2007b, Social Network Sites: Public, Private, or What?, *Knowledge Tree*, 13, available at: http://kt.flexiblelearning.net.au/tkt2007/edition-13/social-network-sites-public-private-or-what/

boyd, d., 2008. *Taken Out of Context*, Doctoral Thesis, University of California, Berkeley.

boyd, d.m. and Ellison, N.B., 2007, Social Network Sites: Definition, History, and Scholarship, *Journal of Computer-Mediated Communication*, 13(1): 210–230.

Boyne, R., 1990, Culture and the World System, in M. Featherstone, (ed.), *Global Culture*, London: Sage.

Brabham, D., 2008, Crowdsourcing as a Model for Problem Solving: An Introduction and Cases, *Convergence: The International Journal of Research into New Media Technologies*, 14: 75–90.

Brabham, D., 2009, Crowdsourcing and Governance in Confessions of an ACA Fan: The Official Blog of Henry Jenkins, 10 August, available at: http://henryjenkins.org/2009/08/get_ready_to_participate_crowd.html

Brown, J., 1999, *Doom, Quake and Mass Murder*, in Salon.com, available at: http://www.salon.com/technology/feature/1999/04/23/gamers/index.html

Brown, W., 2005, *Edgework: Critical Essays on Knowledge and Politics*, Princeton, NJ: Princeton University Press.

Browning, G., 1996, *Electronic Democracy: Using the Internet to Influence American Politics*, Wilton, CT: Pemberton Press.

Bruns, A., 2006, Wikinews: The Next Generation of Online News, *Scan Journal*, 3(1): np.

Bruns, A., 2007, *Produsage: A Working Definition*, available at: http://produsage.org

Bruns, A., 2008, *Blogs, Wikipedia, Second Life and Beyond: From Production to Produsage*, New York: Peter Lang.

Brynin, M. and Haddon, L., 2007, What Does Telework Tell Us About Teleworkers?, in B. Anderson, M. Brynin, J. Gershuny and J. Raban (eds), *Information and Communication Technologies in Society* (pp. 222–232), London: Routledge.

Bull, M., 2005, No Dead Air! The iPod and the Culture of Mobile Listening, *Leisure Studies*, 24(4): 343–355.

Bull, M., 2006, Investigating the Culture of Mobile Listening: from Walkman to iPod, in K. O'Hara and B. Brown (eds), *Consuming Music Together: Social and Collaborative Aspects of Music Consumption Technologies* (pp. 131–149), Dordrecht, NL: Springer.

Bunt, G.R., 2000, *Virtually Islamic: Computer-Mediated Communication and Cyber Islamic Environments*, Cardiff: University of Wales Press.

Bunt, G.R., 2003, *Islam in the Digital Age: E-Jihad, Online Fatwas and Cyber Islamic Environments*, London: Pluto Press.

Bunt, G.R., 2009, *iMuslims: Rewiring the House of Islam*, Chapel Hill: University of North Carolina Press.

Butler, J., 1993, *Bodies that Matter: On the Discursive Limits of Sex*, London: Routledge.

Buxton, W., 1992, Telepresence: Integrating shared tasks and person spaces, paper presented at the Graphics Interface Conference, Vancouver, May.

Calhoun, C., 1998, Community without Propinquity Revisited, *Sociological Inquiry*, 68(3): 373–397.

Calhoun, C., 2002, Virtual Community, in C. Calhoun (ed.), *Dictionary of the Social Sciences*, Oxford: Oxford University Press, available at: http://www.oxfordreference.com/views/ENTRY.html?subview=Main&entry=t104.e1764

Campbell, S.W., 2006, Perceptions of Mobile Phones in College Classrooms, *Communication Education*, 55: 280–294.

Campbell, S.W. and Park, Y.J., 2008, Social Implications of Mobile Telephony: The Rise of Personal Communication Society, *Sociology Compass*, 2(6): 203–240.

Carlson, N., 2009, Everything You Wanted to Know About Facebook's Revenue but Didn't Know Who to Ask, in *Business Insider*, 2 July, available at: http://www.businessinsider.com/breaking-down-facebooks-revenues-2009-7

Carnoy, M. and Castells, M., 2001, Globalization, the Knowledge Society, and the Network State: Poulantzas at the Millennium, *Global Networks*, 1(1): 1–18.

Carr, D., 2006, Games and Narrative, in D. Carr, D. Buckingham, A. Burn and G. Schott, *Computer Games: Text, Narrative and Play* (pp. 30–44), Cambridge: Polity Press.

Castells, M., 1996 (second edition 2000), *The Rise of the Network Society, The Information Age: Economy, Society and Culture Vol. I*, Cambridge, MA and Oxford, UK: Blackwell.

Castells, M., 1997 (second edition 2004), *The Power of Identity, The Information Age: Economy, Society and Culture Vol. II*, Cambridge, MA and Oxford, UK: Blackwell.

Castells, M., 1998 (second edition 2000), *End of Millennium, The Information Age: Economy, Society and Culture Vol. III*, Cambridge, MA and Oxford, UK: Blackwell.

Castells, M., 2001, *The Internet Galaxy*, Oxford: Oxford University Press.

Castells, M., 2004, Afterword: Why Networks Matter, in H. McCarthy, P. Miller and P. Skidmore (eds), *Network Logic: Who Governs in an Interconnected World?* (pp. 221–225), London: Demos.

Castells, M., Fernandez-Ardevol, M., Linchuan Qiu J. and Sey A., 2007, *Mobile Communication and Society: A Global Perspective*, Cambridge, MA: MIT Press.

Castronova, E., 2001, Virtual Worlds: A First-Hand Account of Market and Society on the Cyberian Frontier, *The Gruter Institute Working Papers on Law, Economics, and Evolutionary Biology*, 2(1), available at: http://www.bepress.com/giwp/default/vol2/iss1/art1

Castronova, E., 2005, *Synthetic Worlds: The Business and Culture of Online Games*, Chicago: The University of Chicago Press.

cDc (Cult of the Dead Cow), 2006, Congress Jerks Off, Gang of four Reach for Raincoats, Press Release, 15 Feb, available at: http://w3.cultdeadcow.com/cms/2006/02/congress-jerks.html

Cell Signs, 2008, Text Message Statistics, November, available at: http://www.cellsigns.com/industry.shtml

Chadwick, A. and May, C., 2003, Interaction Between States and Citizens in the Age of the Internet: 'e-government' in the United States, Britain and the European Union, *Governance: International Journal of Policy, Administration and Institutions*, 16(2): 271–300.

Chalaby, J., 1998, *The Invention of Journalism*, Basingstoke: Macmillan.

Choi, J.H., 2006, Living in Cyworld: Contextualising Cy-Ties in South Korea, in A. Bruns and J. Jacobs (eds), *Use of Blogs* (pp. 173–186), New York: Peter Lang.

Christensen, C.M., 1997, *The Innovator's Dilemma: When New Technologies Cause Great Firms to Fail*, Boston, MA: Harvard Business School Press.

Cnet, 2010, Video game sales explode in industry's best month ever, 14 January, available at: http://news.cnet.com/8301-13772_3-10435516-52.html#ixzz1FdjOOEGy

Cockburn, P., 2007, Stoning to death of girl provokes wave of killings, in *The Independent*, 7 May, available at: http://www.independent.co.uk/news/world/middle-east/stoning-to-death-of-girl-provokes-wave-of-killings-447813.html

Coleman, S., 2009, Making Parliamentary Democracy Visible, in A. Chadwick and P. Howard (eds), *Routledge Handbook of Internet Politics* (pp. 86–98), London and New York: Routledge.

Coleman, S. and Dyer-Witheford, N., 2007, Playing on the Digital Commons: Collectivities, Capital and Contestation in Videogame Culture, *Media, Culture and Society*, 29(6): 934–953.

Cornfield, M., Carson, J., Kalis, A. and Simon, E., 2005, Buzz, blogs, and beyond: The Internet and the national discourse in the fall of 2004, Pew Internet and American Life Project, available at: http://www.pewinternet.org/ppt/BUZZ_BLOGS_BEYOND_Final05-16-05.pdf

Cornfield, M., Rainie, L., and Horrigan, J., 2003, *Online Campaigners, Citizens and Portals in the 2002 Elections*, Pew Internet and American Life Project, available at: http://www.pewinternet.org/~/media//Files/Reports/2003/PIP_IPDI_Politics_Report.pdf

Couldry, N., 2008, Mediatization or Mediation? Alternative Understandings of the Emergent Space of Digital Storytelling, *New Media and Society*, 10(3): 373–391.

Couldry, N., Livingstone, S. and Markham, T., 2007, *Media Consumption and Public Engagement: Beyond the Presumption of Attention*, London: Palgrave Macmillan.

Curran, K., Concannon, K. and McKeever, S., 2008, Cyber Terrorism Attacks, in L. Janczewski and A. Colaric (eds), *Cyber Warfare and Cyber Terrorism* (pp. 1–7), Hershey, PA. and London: Information Science Reference.

Dahlberg, L., 2001, Computer-Mediated Communication and the Public Sphere: A Critical Analysis, *Journal of Computer-Mediated Communications*, 7(1), available at: http://www.ascusc.org/jcmc/vol7/issue1/dahlberg.html

Dahlberg, L., 2005, The Corporate Colonization of Online Attention and the Marginalization of Critical Communication?, *Journal of Communication Inquiry*, 29(2): 1–21.

Dahlberg, L., 2007, Rethinking the Fragmentation of the Cyber-Public: From Consensus to Contestation, *New Media and Society*, 9(5): 829–849.

Dahlberg, L. and Siapera, E., 2007, Tracing Radical Democracy and the Internet, in L. Dahlberg and E. Siapera (eds), *Radical Democracy and the Internet* (pp. 1–17), Basingstoke: Palgrave-Macmillan.

Dahlgren, P., 1996, Media Logic in Cyberspace: Repositioning Journalism and its Publics, *Javnost/The Public*, 3(3): 59–72.

Danet, B., 1998, Text as a Mask: Gender, Play and Performance in the Internet, in S. Jones (ed.), *Cybersociety 2.0: Revisiting Computer-Mediated Communication and Community* (pp. 129–158), Thousand Oaks, CA: Sage.

de Beauvoir, Simone, 1953, *The Second Sex*, London: Jonathan Cape.

Debord, G., 1967, *The Society of the Spectacle*, London: Rebel Press.

Deibert, R. and Rohozinski, R., 2009, Ottawa needs a strategy for cyberwar, in *National Post,* 30 June, available at: http://network.nationalpost.com/np/blogs/fullcomment/archive/2009/06/30/ottawa-needs-a-strategy-for-cyberwar.aspx

De Peuter, G. and Dyer-Witheford, N., 2005, A Playful Multitude? Mobilising and Counter-Mobilising Immaterial Game, *Fibreculture*, 5: np.

Derrida, J., 1974 (third edition 1997), *Of Grammatology,* trans. Gayatri Spivak, Baltimore, MD: Johns Hopkins University Press.

Derrida, J., 1991, *Of Spirit: Heidegger and the Question*, trans. Geoffrey Bennington and Rachel Bawlby, Chicago: Chicago University Press.

de Sola Pool, I., 1983, *Technologies of Freedom*, Cambridge, MA: Harvard University Press.

Deuze, M., 2006, Participation, Remediation, Bricolage: Considering Principal Components of a Digital Culture, *The Information Society*, 22(2): 63–75.

Deuze, M., Bowen Martin, C. and Allen, C., 2007, The Professional Identity of Gameworkers, *Convergence*, 13(4): 335–353.

Dibbell, J., 2006, *Play Money: Or How I Quit My Day Job and Struck It Rich in Virtual Loot Farming*, New York: Perseus.

Dibbell, J., 2007, The Life of the Chinese Goldfarmer, available at: http://www.nytimes.com/2007/06/17/magazine/17lootfarmers-t.html?_r=1

DiMaggio, P. and Hargittai E., 2001, From the 'Digital Divide' to 'Digital Inequality': Studying Internet Use As Penetration Increases, *Working Paper #15,* Summer 2001, available at: http://www.princeton.edu/~artspol/workpap15.html

Dimitrakopoulou, D., 2005, Time, Internet and Journalism, in Ch. Fragkonikolopoulos (ed.), *Media, Society and Politics*, Athens: Sideris Publications.

Donath, J. and boyd, d., 2004, Public Displays of Connection, *BT Technology Journal*, 22(4): 71–82.

Drezner, D. and Farrell, H., 2004, The Power and Politics of Blogs, Paper presented at the American Political Science Association, available at: http://www.utsc.utoronto.ca/~farrell/blogpaperfinal.pdf

Durkheim, E., 1972 [1933], Forms of Social Solidarity, in A. Giddens (ed.), *Emile Durkheim: Selected Writings* (pp. 123–140), Cambridge: Cambridge University Press.

Dutton, W.H., Helsper, E.J. and Gerber, M.M., 2009, *Oxford Internet Survey 2009 Report: The Internet in Britain*, Oxford: Oxford Internet Institute, University of Oxford.

Dyer-Witheford, N., 2003, Sim Capital: General Intellect, World Market, Species and the Video Game, in M. Bousquet and K. Wills (eds), *The Politics of Information: The Electronic Mediation of Social Change* (pp. 122–140), Alt-x press, available at: http://www.altx.com/ebooks/download.cfm/infopol.pdf#page=130

Dyer-Witheford, N. and de Peuter, G., 2009, Empire@Play: Virtual Games and Global Capitalism, in *CTheory*, available at: http://www.ctheory.net/articles.aspx?id=608

Dyer-Witheford, N. and Sharman, Z., 2005, The Political Economy of Canada's Video and Computer Game Industry, *Canadian Journal of Communication*, 30: 187–210.

Economist, 2010, Still Playing? 23 March.

Ellison, N.B., Steinfield, C. and Lampe, C., 2007, The Benefits of Facebook 'Friends': Social Capital and College Students' Use of Online Social Network Sites, *Journal of Computer-Mediated Communication*, 12(4): 1143–1168.

Emarketer, 2009, Social Network Ad Spending: 2010 Outlook, December, available at: http://www.emarketer.com/Reports/All/Emarketer_2000621.aspx

Enet, 2010, Parelasi Misous (Parade of Hate), 26 March, available at: http://www.enet.gr/?i=news.el.ellada&id=145379

Entertainment Retailers Association, 2009, UK Market Statistics, report by S. Redmond, available at: http://www.eraltd.org/_attachments/Resources/yearbook.pdf

Enzensberger, H.M., 1970, Constituents of a Theory of the Media, *New Left Review*, 64: 13–36.

Erdal, I.J., 2009, Repurposing of Content in Multi-Platform News Production: Towards a Typology of Cross-media Journalism, *Journalism Practice*, 3(2): 178–195.

Ernkvist, M. and Ström, P., 2008, Enmeshed in Games with the Government: Governmental Policies and the Development of the Chinese Online Game Industry, *Games and Culture*, 3(1): 98–126.

Eskelinen, M., 2001, The Gaming Situation, *Game Studies*, 1(1): np.

Etzioni, A. and Etzioni, O., 1999, Face-to-Face and Computer-Mediated Communities, A Comparative Analysis, *The Information Society*, 15(4): 241–248.

Fallows, D., 2005, *How Women and Men Use the Internet*, Pew Internet and American Life Project, available at: http://www.pewinternet.org/Reports/2005/How-Women-and-Men-Use-the-Internet.aspx

Feeley, J. and van Voris, B., 2010, Hacker Gets 20 Years in Largest Identity-Theft Case, in *Bloomberg*, 25 March, available at: http://www.bloomberg.com/apps/news?pid=20601103&sid=aCDo3co5A0Zk

Fenton, N. (ed.), 2009, *New Media, Old News: Journalism and Democracy in the Digital Age*, London: Sage.

Ferguson, C. and Kilburn, J., 2010, Much Ado About Nothing: The Misestimation and Overinterpretation of Violent Video Game Effects in Eastern and Western Nations: Comment on Anderson et al. (2010), *Psychological Bulletin*, 136(2): 151–173.

Flynn, B., 2001, Convergence: Never Mind the Technology, it's a People Thing, in Broadband, supplement, in *Broadcast*, 9 February.

Foucault, M., 1980, *Power/Knowledge: Selected Interviews and Other Writings, 1972–1977*, ed. Colin Gordon, London: Pantheon Books.

Foucault, M., 1988, Technologies of the Self, in L.H. Martin et al., *Technologies of the Self: A Seminar with Michel Foucault* (pp.16–49), London: Tavistock, available at: http://foucault.info/documents/foucault.technologiesOfSelf.en.html

Foucault, M., 1989 [1969], *The Archaeology of Knowledge*, London and New York: Routledge.

Foucault, M., 1995 [1975], *Discipline & Punish: The Birth of the Prison*, New York: Vintage Books.

Foucault, M., 2002 [1966], *The Order of Things*, London and New York: Routledge.

Franklin, M.I., 2007, Democracy, Postcolonialism, and Everyday Life: Contesting the 'Royal We' Online, in L. Dahlberg and E. Siapera (eds), *The Internet and Radical Democracy: Exploring Theory and Practice* (pp. 168–190), New York/London: Palgrave Macmillan.

Freeth, T., Bitsakis, Y., Moussas, X., Seiradakis, J., Tselikas, A., Mangou, H., Zafeiropoulou, M., Hadland, R., Bate, D. and Ramsey, A., 2006, Decoding the Ancient Greek Astronomical Calculator Known as the Antikythera Mechanism, *Nature*, 11/2006, 444: 587–591.

Frejes, F., 1981, Media Imperialism: An assessment, *Media, Culture and Society*, 3: 281–289.

Funk, J., Bechtoldt Baldacci, H., Pasold, T. and Baumgardner, J., 2004, Violence Exposure in Real-Life, Video Games, Television, Movies, and the Internet: Is There Desensitization?, *Journal of Adolescence*, 27: 23–39.

Gahran, A. (1998). Credibility in online media: seven voices from the news business, Contentious 1(3). Available at http://www.contentious.com/articles/1-3/qa1-3/qa1-3.html.

Galtung, J. and Ruge, M., 1965, The Structure of Foreign News: The Presentation of the Congo, Cuba and Cyprus Crises in Four Norwegian Newspapers, *Journal of International Peace Research*, 1: 64–91.

Gane, N., 2005, Radical Post-humanism: Friedrich Kittler and the Primacy of Technology, *Theory, Culture & Society*, 22(3): 25–41.

Gans, H., 1980, *Deciding What's News*, New York: Vintage Books.

Gans, H., 2003, *Democracy and the News*, Oxford: Oxford University Press.

Gareis, K., 2003, Home-based vs. Mobile Telework: The Interrelationship between Different Types of Telework, in B. Rapp and P. Jackson (eds), *Organisation and Work Beyond 2000* (pp. 171–185), Heidelberg and New York: Physica.

Geertz, C., 1973, *The Interpretation of Cultures: Selected Essays*, New York: Basic Books.

Gellner, E., 1983, *Nations and Nationalism*, Ithaca, NY: Cornell University Press.

Georgiou, M., 2002, Les Diasporas en Ligne: Une Expérience Concrète de Transnationalisme, *Hommes & Migrations,* 1240: 10–18.

Gergen, K., 2002, The Challenge of the Absent Presence, in J. Katz and M. Aakhus (eds), *Perpetual Contact: Mobile Communication, Private Talk, Public Performance* (pp. 227–241), Cambridge: Cambridge University Press.

Gibson, R.K. and Ward, S., 2003, Online and On Message? Candidate Websites in the 2001 General Election, *British Journal of Political Science and International Relations*, 5(2): 188–205.

Giddens, A., (ed.), 1972, *Emile Durkheim: Selected Writings*, Cambridge: Cambridge University Press.

Giddens, A., 1990, *The Consequences of Modernity*, Cambridge: Polity.

Giddens, A., 1991, *Modernity and Self-Identity*, Cambridge: Polity Press.

Giddens, A., 2003, *Runaway World: How Globalization is Reshaping our World*, London and New York: Routledge.

Giddens, A., 2006, *Sociology* (fifth edition), Cambridge: Polity Press.

Gill, R., 2002, Cool, Creative and Egalitarian?: Exploring Gender in Project-Based New Media Work in Europe, *Information, Communication and Society*, 5(1): 70–89.

Gillan, K. and Pickerill, J., 2008, Transnational Anti-war Activism: Solidarity, Diversity and the Internet in Australia, Britain and the United States after 9/11, *Australian Journal of Political Science*, 43(1): 59–78.

Gillmor, D., 2003, *We the Media: Grassroots Journalism by the People, for the People*, Sebastopol, CA: O'Reilly Media.

Gitlin, T., 2009, Journalism in Crisis, Keynote presentation at the Journalism in Crisis Conference, University of Westminster, 19 May, available at: http://www.westminsternews-online.com/wordpress/?p=1951

Gittell, R. and Vidal, A., 1998, *Community Organizing: Building Social Capital as a Development Strategy,* Thousand Oaks, CA: Sage.

Goggin, G., 2008, The Models and Politics of Mobile Media, *Fibreculture*, 12: np.

Golding, P., 2000, Forthcoming Features: Information and Communications Technologies and the Sociology of the Future, *Sociology*, 34(1): 165–184.

Golding, P. and Murdock, G., 1979, Ideology and the Mass Media: the Question of Determination, in M. Barrett, P. Corrigan, A. Kuhn and J. Wolff (eds), *Ideology and Cultural Production* (pp. 198–224), London: Croom Helm.

Googin, D., 2009, DDoS attack boots Kyrgyzstan from net, in *The Register*, 28 January, available at: http://www.theregister.co.uk/2009/01/28/kyrgyzstan_knocked_offline/

Gore, A., 1994, Speech to Academy of Television Arts & Sciences, UCLA, 11 January, available at: http://www.ibiblio.org/icky/speech2.html

Granovetter, M., 1973, The Strength of Weak Ties, *American Journal of Sociology*, 78: 1360–1380.

Granovetter, M., 1983, The Strength of Weak Ties: A Network Theory Revisited, *Sociological Theory*, 1: 201–233.

Grossman, L.K., 1995, *The Electronic Republic: Reshaping Democracy in the Information Age*, New York: Penguin.

Grossman, L., 2009, Iran Protests: Twitter, the Medium of the Movement, in *Time Magazine*, 17 June, available at: http://www.time.com/time/world/article/0,8599,1905125,00.html

Guardian, 2009, ABCs: National daily newspaper circulation August 2009, 11 September, available at: http://www.guardian.co.uk/media/table/2009/sep/11/abcs-pressandpublishing

Guardian, 2010, Ian Tomlinson family waits for answers one year on from G20 protests, 26 March, available at: http://www.guardian.co.uk/uk/2010/mar/26/ian-tomlinson-g20-protests-anniversary

Habermas, J., 1989 [1962], *The Structural Transformation of the Public Sphere*, Cambridge: Polity Press.

Habermas, 1996a, *Between Facts and Norms*, Cambridge: Polity Press.

Habermas, J., 1996b, Three Normative Models of Democracy, in S. Benhabib (ed.), *Democracy and Difference* (pp. 21–30), Princeton, NJ: Princeton University Press.

Haire, M., 2009, A Brief History of the Walkman, in *Time Magazine*, 1 July, available at: http://www.time.com/time/nation/article/0,8599,1907884,00.html

Hall, J., 2001, *Online Journalism: A Critical Primer*, London: Pluto Press.

Hampton, K.N. and Wellman, B., 1999, Netville on-line and off-line, *American Behavioral Scientist*, 43(3): 478–495.

Hands, J., 2010, *@ is for Activism*, London: Pluto Press.

Hands, J., 2011, Twitter Revolution? in Pluto Press Blog, http://plutopress.wordpress.com/2011/01/25/twitter-revolution/

Hansen, M., 2006, Media Theory, *Theory, Culture & Society*, 23 (2–3): 297–306.

Haraway, D., 1991, A Cyborg Manifesto: Science, Technology, and Socialist-Feminism in the Late Twentieth Century, in D. Haraway, *Simians, Cyborgs and Women: The Reinvention of Nature* (pp. 149–181), New York; Routledge, available at: http://www.stanford.edu/dept/HPS/Haraway/CyborgManifesto.html

Hardt, M. and Negri, A., 2000, *Empire*, Cambridge, MA: Harvard University Press.

Hargittai, E., 2002, Second-Level Digital Divide: Differences in People's Online Skills, *First Monday*, 7(4): np.

Hargittai, E., 2010. Digital Na(t)ives Variation in Internet Skills and Uses among Members of the 'Net Generation', *Sociological Inquiry*. 80(1): 92–113.

Hargittai, E. and Shafer, S., 2006, Differences in Actual and Perceived Online Skills: The Role of Gender, *Social Science Quarterly*, 87(2): 432–448.

Harris, J.L. and Taylor, P., 2005, Friedrich Kittler – Network 2000?, in J.L. Harris and P. Taylor, *Digital Matters: Theory and Culture of the Matrix* (pp. 66–86), Abingdon and New York: Routledge.

Heidegger, M., 1977, *The Question Concerning Technology and Other Essays*, trans. William Lovitt, New York: Harper and Row.

Held, D., 2003, Cosmopolitanism: Taming Globalization, in D. Held and A. McGrew (eds), *The Global Transformations Reader: An Introduction to the Globalization Debate*, Polity Press, Cambridge.

Held, D., 2006, *Models of Democracy*, Cambridge: Polity Press.

Held, D., McGrew, A., Goldblatt, D., and Perraton, J., 1999, Introduction, in ibid. (eds), *Global Transformations*, Stanford: Stanford University Press, pp 1–31.

Helsper, E., 2010, Gendered Internet Use Across Generations and Life Stages, *Communication Research*, 37(3): 352–374.

Herald Sun, 2010, Pornography fiends in sights, 15 March, available at: http://www.heraldsun.com.au/news/pornography-fiends-in-sights/story-e6frf7jo-1225840641430

Herman, E. and Chomsky, N., 1989, *Manufacturing Consent*, New York: Pantheon Books.

Hirschkind, C., 2010, New Media and Political Dissent in Egypt, *Revista de Dialectologia y Tradiciones Populares*, 65(1): 137–153.

Hirst, P. and Thompson, G., 1999, *Globalization in Question: The International Economy and the Possibilities of Governance*, Oxford: Wiley-Blackwell.

Hobsbawm, E. and Ranger, T. (eds), 1983, *The Invention of Tradition*, Cambridge: Cambridge University Press.

Hof, R., 2007, The End of Work as You Know It, in *Business Week*, available at: http://www.businessweek.com/magazine/content/07_34/b4047426.htm

Homeland Security Newswire, 2010a, What the Chinese attacks on Google mean for enterprise security, 20 January, available at: http://homelandsecuritynewswire.com/what-chinese-attacks-google-mean-enterprise-security

Homeland Security Newswire, 2010b, Google turns to NSA for assistance in thwarting Chinese cyberattacks, 5 February, available at: http://homelandsecuritynewswire.com/google-turns-nsa-assistance-thwarting-chinese-cyberattacks

Horrigan, J., 2006, *Online News: For many home broadband users, the internet is a primary news source*, Pew Internet and American Life Project, available at: http://www.pewinternet.org/Reports/2006/Online-News-For-many-home-broadband-users-the-internet-is-a-primary-news-source.aspx

Hoskins, A., Awan, A. and O'Loughlin, B., 2011, *Radicalisation and Media: Connectivity and Terrorism in the New Media Ecology*, London and NY: Routledge.

Howe, J., 2006, The Rise of Crowdsourcing, in *Wired*, 14 June, available at: http://www.wired.com/wired/archive/14.06/crowds.html

Howe, J., undated, Crowdsourcing: a Definition, available at: http://crowdsourcing.typepad.com/

Hughes, D., 2000, The Internet and Sex Industries: Partners in Global Sexual Exploitation, *IEEE Technology and Society Magazine*, 19: 35–42.

Hughes, D., 2002, The Use of New Communications and Information Technologies for Sexual Exploitation of Women and Children, *Hastings Women Law Journal*, 13(1): 129–148, available at: http://www.genderit.org/upload/ad6d215b74e2a8613f0cf5416c9f3865/Donna_HughesNewTech.pdf

Huizinga, J., 2003 [1938], *Homo Ludens: A Study of the Play-Element in Culture*, London and New York: Routledge.

Humphreys, S., 2009, Norrath: New Forms, Old Institutions, *Game Studies*, 9(1): np, available at: http://gamestudies.org/0901/articles/humphreys

IGDA (International Game Developers Association), 2004, Quality of Life in the Game Industry: Challenges and Best Practices, available at: www.igda.org.

Innis, H., 1950, *Empire and Communications*, Oxford: Clarendon Press.

Innis, H., 1951, *The Bias of Communication*, Toronto: University of Toronto Press.

Isenberg, D.S., 1999, Mother of All Disruptions. The Internet Combines Disruptive Technologies of Many Component Markets, *America's Network*, 15 July.

IT News Africa, 2009, Africa's High Mobile Penetration Sets the Stage for Internet Revolution, 2 July, available at: http://www.itnewsafrica.com/?p=2839

Ito, M., 2005, Mobile Phones, Japanese Youth, and the Re-Placement of Social Contact, in R. Ling and P. Pedersen (eds.), *Mobile Communications: Re-negotiation of the Social Sphere* (pp. 131–148), available at: http://www.itofisher.com/mito/archives/mobileyouth.pdf

Jackson, L.A., Zhao, Y., Kolenic III, A., Fitzgerald, H.E., Harold, R. and von Eye, A., 2008, Race, Gender and Information Technology (IT) Use: The New Digital Divide, *Cyberpsychology and Behavior*, 11(4): 437–442.

Jacobs, K., Janssen, M. and Pasquinelli, M. (eds), 2007, *C'Lick Me: A Netporn Studies Reader*, Amsterdam: Institute of Network Cultures, available at: http://www.networkcultures.org/_uploads/24.pdf

Janack, J., 2006, Mediated Citizenship and Digital Discipline: A Rhetoric of Control in a Campaign, *Social Semiotics*, 16(2): 283–301.

Jenkins, H., 1992, *Textual Poachers: Television Fans and Participatory Culture*, New York: Routledge.

Jenkins, H., 2001, Convergence? I Diverge, *Technology Review*, p. 93, MIT, available at: http://web.mit.edu/cms/People/henry3/converge.pdf

Jenkins, H., 2002, Interactive Audiences?: The 'Collective Intelligence' of Media Fans, in D. Harries (ed.), *The New Media Book*, London: British Film Institute, available at: http://web.mit.edu/cms/People/henry3/collective%20intelligence.html

Jenkins, H., 2006a, *Fans, Bloggers and Gamers: Explorations in Participatory Culture*, New York: New York University Press.

Jenkins, H., 2006b, *Convergence Culture: Where Old and New Media Collide*, New York: New York University Press.

Jenkins, H., 2007, Reality Bytes: Eight Myths About Video Games Debunked, in *PBS: The Video Game Revolution*, available at: http://www.pbs.org/kcts/videogamerevolution/impact/myths.html

Jenkins, H., Purushotma, R., Weigel, M., Clinton, K. and Robison, A., 2009, *Confronting the Challenges of Participatory Culture: Media Education for the 21st Century*, Cambridge, MA: MIT Press.

Jepperson, R.L., 1991, Institutions, Institutional Effects, and Institutionalism, in W.W. Powell and P. DiMaggio (eds), *The New Institutionalism in Organizational Analysis* (pp. 143–163), Chicago: University of Chicago Press.

Jin, Y.D. and Chee, F., 2008, Age of New Media Empire: A Critical Interpretation of the Korean Online Game Industry, *Games and Culture: A Journal of Interactive Media*, 3(1): 38–58.

JiWire, 2010, Wifi Finder Tool, available at: http://v4.jiwire.com/search-hotspot-locations.htm

Johne, M., 2006, Prize for Playing the Game: A Career, in *The Globe and Mail*, 26 April.

Johnson, B., 2010, Google China: Hacking bid that quickly grew into a clash of titans, in *Guardian*, 23 March, available at: http://www.guardian.co.uk/technology/2010/mar/23/google-china-hacking-bid-clash

Jones, S., and Fox S., 2009, *Generations Online 2009*, Pew Internet and American Life Project, available at: http://www.pewinternet.org/Reports/2009/Generations-Online-in-2009/Generational-Differences-in-Online-Activities/Generations-Explained.aspx?r=1

Jordan, T., 2007, Online Direct Action: Hacktivism and Radical Democracy, in L. Dahlberg and E. Siapera (eds), *Radical Democracy and the Internet: Interrogating Theory and Practice* (pp. 73–88), Basingstoke: Macmillan Palgrave.

Kahn, R. and Kellner, D., 2004, New Media and Internet Activism: From the 'Battle of Seattle' to Blogging, *New Media and Society*, 6(1): 87–95.

Kahn, R. and Kellner, D., 2007, Globalization, Technopolitics and Radical Democracy, in L. Dahlberg and E. Siapera (eds.), *Radical Democracy and the Internet: Interrogating Theory and Practice* (pp. 17–36), Basingstoke: Macmillan Palgrave.

Karatzogianni, A., 2004, The Politics of Cyberconflict, *Journal of Politics*, 24(1): 46–55.

Karatzogianni, A., 2006, *The Politics of Cyberconflict*, London and New York: Routledge.

Karatzogianni, A. (ed.), 2009, *Cyber Conflict and Global Politics*, London and New York: Routledge.

Katz, J. and Aakhus, M. (eds) 2002, *Perpetual Contact: Mobile Communication, Private Talk, Public Performance*, Cambridge, UK: Cambridge University Press.

Katz, J.E. and Rice, R.E., 2002, *Social Consequences of Internet Use: Access, Involvement and Expression*, Cambridge, MA: MIT Press.

Katz, J.E., Rice, R.E., Acord, S., Dasgupta, K. and David, K., 2004, Personal Mediated Communication and the Concept of Community in Theory and Practice, in P. Kalbfleisch (ed.), *Communication and Community, Communication Yearbook 28* (pp. 315–371), Mahwah, NJ: Erlbaum.

Keegan, V., 2000, Dial-a-fortune: Gordon Brown is making piles of cash, in the *Guardian*, 13 April, available at: http://www.guardian.co.uk/technology/2000/apr/13/mobilephones.victorkeegan

Keen, A., 2007, *The Cult of the Amateur: How Today's Internet is Killing our Culture*, London: Crown.

Kendall, L., 1996. MUDder? I Hardly Know HER!: Adventures of a Feminist MUDder, in L. Cherny and E. Reba Weise (eds), *Wired Women: Gender and New Realities in Cyberspace* (pp. 216–217), Seattle: Seal Press.

Kerbel, K. and Bloom, J., 2005, Blog for America and Civic Involvement, *The Harvard International Journal of Press/Politics*, 10(4): 3–27.

Kerr, A., 2006, *The Business and Culture of Digital Games: Gamework/Gameplay*, London: Sage.

King, D., 1997, *The Commissar Vanishes: The Falsification of Photographs and Art in Stalin's Russia*, New York: Metropolitan Books.

Kittler, F., 1992, *Discourse Networks 1800/1900*, Stanford, CA: Stanford University.

Kittler, F., 1997a, Protected Mode, in F. Kittler and J. Johnston, *Literature, Media, Information Systems: Essays* (pp. 156–168), Amsterdam, NL: OPA.

Kittler, F., 1997b, There is no software, in F. Kittler and J. Johnston, *Literature, Media, Information Systems: Essays* (pp. 147–155), Amsterdam, NL: OPA.

Kittler, F., 1999, *Gramophone, Film, Typewriter*, Stanford, CA: Stanford University.

Kittler, F. and Johnston, J., 1997, *Literature, Media, Information Systems: Essays*, Amsterdam, NL: OPA.

Kline, S., Dyer-Witheford, N. and De Peuter, G., 2003, *Digital Play: The Interaction of Technology, Culture, and Marketing*, Montreal: McGill-Queen's University Press.

Koman, R. and Auerbach, K., 2002, ICANN 'Out of Control', in *O'Reilly Media*, available at: http://www.oreillynet.com/pub/a/policy/2002/12/05/karl.html

Koselleck, R., 1998, *Critique and Crisis: Enlightenment and the Pathogenesis of Modern Society*, Cambridge, MA: MIT Press.

Kroker, A. and Lovink, G., undated, Data Trash: the theory of the Virtual Class, in conversation with Geert Lovink, available at: http://www.thing.desk.nl/bilwet/TXT/KROKER.INT.txt

Kroker, A. and Weinstein, M., 1994, *Data Trash: The Theory of the Virtual Class*, Montreal: New World Perspectives.

Kuipers, G., 2006, The Social Construction of Digital Danger: Debating, Defusing, and Inflating the Moral Dangers of Online Humor and Pornography in the Netherlands and the United States, *New Media and Society*, 8(3): 379–400.

Lacan, J., 1980 [1966], Écrits: a Selection, trans. Alan Sheridan, London: Tavistock Publications.

Lacohée, H., Wakeford, N. and Pearson, I., 2003, A Social History of the Mobile Telephone With a View of its Future, *BT Technology Journal*, 21(3): 203–211.

Lange, P.G., 2008, Publicly Private and Privately Public: Social Networking on YouTube, *Journal of Computer-Mediated Communication*, 13: 361–380.

Lasica, J.D., 2008, *Civic Engagement on the Move: How Mobile Media can Serve the Public Good*, Washington, DC: The Aspen Institute, available at: http://www.artesianmedia.com/seminar/reports/Civic-Engagement-Mobile-Media.pdf

Latzer, M., 2009, ICT Innovations: Radical & Disruptive? Vague Concepts – Delicate Choices – Conflicting Results, *New Media & Society*, 11(4): 599–619.

Lazzarato, M., 1996, Immaterial Labour, trans. Paul Colilli and Ed Emory, in Paolo Virno and Michael Hardt (eds), *Radical Thought in Italy* (pp. 132–146), Minneapolis: University of Minnesota Press, available at: http://www.generation-online.org/c/fcimmateriallabour3.htm

Lazzarato, M., 2004, From Capital-Labour to Capital-Life, *Ephemera*, 4(3): 187–208.

Lee, M[artin]., 1993, *Consumer Culture Reborn: The Cultural Politics of Consumption*, London: Routledge.

Lee, M[in]., 2007, China issues strict new rules for TV talent shows, in *The China Post*, 23 September, available at: http://www.chinapost.com.tw/asia/2007/09/23/123693/China-issues.htm

Leroi-Gourhan, A., 1993, *Gesture and Speech*, Cambridge, MA and London: MIT Press.

Leslie, J., 1993, Technology: MUDroom, in *Atlantic Monthly*, 272: 28–34.

Lessig, L., 1999, *Code and Other Laws of Cyberspace*, New York: Basic Books.

Lessig, L., 2001, *The Future of Ideas: The Fate of the Commons in a Connected World*, New York: Random House.

Levinson, P., 1999, *Digital McLuhan: A Guide to the Information Millennium*, New York: Routledge.

Levitt, M., 2002, The Political Economy of Middle East Terrorism, *Middle Eastern Review of International Affairs*, 6(4): np, available at: http://meria.idc.ac.il/journal/2002/issue4/jv6n4a3.html

Leyden, J., 2008, Bear prints found on Georgian cyber-attacks, in *The Register*, 14 August, available at: http://www.theregister.co.uk/2008/08/14/russia_georgia_cyberwar_latest/

Lievrouw, L., 2006, New Media Design and Development: Diffusion of Innovations Versus Social Shaping of Technology, in S. Livingstone and L. Lievrouw (eds), *Handbook of New Media* (pp. 246–265), London: Sage.

Lind, J., 2005, Ubiquitous Convergence: Market Redefinitions Generated by Technological Change and the Industry Life Cycle, Paper for the DRUID Academy Winter 2005 Conference, 27–29 January.

Liss, S., 2010, Social Media Growth in 2010 will be in Mobile Technology, in SunSentinel, 4 January, available at: http://articles.sun-sentinel.com/2010-01-04/news/fl-slcol-seth-social-media-growth-2010-20100104_1_social-media-mobile-technology-phones

Lister, M., Dovey, J., Giddings, S., Grant, I. and Kelly, K., 2009, *New Media: A Critical Introduction*, London and New York: Routledge.

Livingstone, S., 2009, On the Mediation of Everything, *Journal of Communication*, 59(1): 1–18.

Livingstone, S. and Helsper, E., 2007, Gradations in Digital Inclusion: Children, Young People and the Digital Divide, *New Media and Society*, 9(4): 671–696.

Longe, O., Ngwa, O., Wada, F. and Mbarika, V., 2009, Criminal Uses of Information & Communication Technologies in Sub-Saharan Africa: Trends, Concerns and Perspectives, *Journal of Information Technology Impact*, 9(3): 155–172.

Loomis, C. and McKinney, J., 2002, Introduction, in F. Tönnies, *Community and Society*, Devon: David and Charles.

LSE, Centre for Civil Society, 2004, What is Civil Society, available at: http://www.lse.ac.uk/collections/CCS/what_is_civil_society.htm

Ludwig, S., 2010, Don't Buy '4G' Phones for 4G Features – Yet, *PC Mag*, 24 March, available at: http://www.pcmag.com/article2/0,2817,2361765,00.asp

Lukacs, G., 1974 [1914], *The Theory of the Novel*, trans. Anna Bostock, Boston, MA: MIT Press.

Lutz, M., 2009, *The Social Pulpit: Barack Obama's Social Media Toolkit*, Edelman, available at: http://tinyurl.com/6x5rbzy

Lyon, D., 2001, *Surveillance Society: Monitoring Everyday Life*, Buckingham: Open University Press.

Lyon, D., 2003, *Surveillance as Social Sorting: Privacy, Risk and Digital Discrimination*, London and New York: Routledge.

Mabillot, D., 2007, User Generated Content: Web 2.0: Taking the Video Sector by Storm, Munich Personal RePEc Archive, available at: http://mpra.ub.uni-muenchen.de/4579/1/MPRA_paper_4579.pdf

Machin, D. and Suleiman, U., 2006, Arab and American Computer War Games: The Influence of Global Technology on Discourse, *Critical Discourse Studies*, 3(1): 1–22.

Machin, D. and van Leeuwen, T., 2005, Computer Games as Political Discourse: The Case of Black Hawk Down, *Journal of Language and Politics*, 4(1): 119–141.

Malaby, T., 2006, Parlaying Value: Forms of Capital In and Beyond Virtual Worlds, *Games & Culture*, 1(2): 141–162.

Malcolm, J., 2008, *Multi-Stakeholder Governance and the Internet Governance Forum*, Perth: Terminus Press.

Manovich, L., 2001, *The Language of New Media*, Cambridge, MA: MIT Press.

Mansell, R., 2004, Political Economy, Power and New Media, *New Media, Culture and Society*, 6(1): 74–83.

Margolis, M. and Resnick, D., *Politics as Usual: The 'Cyberspace Revolution'*, Thousand Oaks, CA: Sage.

Markoff, J., 2008, Before the Gunfire, Cyberattacks, *The New York Times*, 12 August, available at: http://www.nytimes.com/2008/08/13/technology/13cyber.html?_r=1&em

Marx, K., 1852, *The 18th Brumaire of Napoleon Bonaparte*, available at: http://www.marxists.org/archive/marx/works/1852/18th-brumaire/

Marx, K., 1959 [1844], *Economic and Philosophic Manuscripts of 1844*, Moscow: Progress Publishers, available at: http://www.marxists.org/archive/marx/works/1844/manuscripts/preface.htm

Marx, K., 1969, *Theories of Surplus-Value*, London: Lawrence & Wishart.

Marx, K. and Engels, F., 1969 [1848], *The Manifesto of the Communist Party,* in Marx/Engels *Selected Works*, *Vol. One*, Moscow: Progress Publishers (pp. 98–137), available at: http://www.marxists.org/archive/marx/works/1848/communist-manifesto/

Mashable, 2008, Cult of the Dead Cow Releases Exploit Search Engine Goolag, 22 Feb, available at: http://mashable.com/2008/02/22/goolag/

Maslow, A., 1954, *Motivation and Personality*, New York: Harper.

Maslow, A. and Lowery, R. (ed.), 1998, *Toward a Psychology of Being* (third edition), New York: Wiley & Sons.

Massey, B.L. and Levy, M.R., 1999, Interactive Online Journalism at English Language Web Newspapers in Asia, *International Communication Gazette*, 61(6): 523–538.

Mathiesen, T. , 1997, The Viewer Society: Michel Foucault's Panopticon revisited, *Theoretical Criminology,* 1(2): 215–334

Matsuda, M., 2005, Mobile Communication and Selective Sociality, in M. Ito, D. Okabe and M. Matsuda (eds), *Personal, Portable, Pedestrian: Mobile Phones in Japanese Life* (pp. 123–142), Cambridge, MA: The MIT Press.

Mayfield, A., 2007, What is Social Media? in Online Resource, available at: http://www.icrossing.co.uk/fileadmin/uploads/eBooks/What_is_Social_Media_iCrossing_ebook.pdf

McGuigan, J., 2005, Towards a Sociology of the Mobile Phone, *Human Technology* 1(1): 45–57, available at: http://www.humantechnology.jyu.fi/articles/volume1/2005/mcguigan.pdf

McLuhan, M., 1969, The Playboy Interview: Marshall McLuhan, in *Playboy Magazine*, March, pp. 53–74, available at: http://www.digitallantern.net/mcluhan/mcluhanplayboy.htm

McLuhan, M., 2001 [1964], *Understanding Media: The Extensions of Man*, London and New York: Routledge.

McLuhan, M., 2002 [1962], *The Guttenberg Galaxy*, Toronto: University of Toronto Press.

McMillan, R., 2010, Security Researcher IDs China Link in Google Hack, in *CSO Security and Risk*, 20 January, available at: http://www.csoonline.com/article/519013/Security_Researcher_IDs_China_Link_in_Google_Hack

McPherson, M., Smith-Lovin, L. and Cook, J., 2001, Birds of a Feather: Homophily in Social Networks, *Annual Review of Sociology*, 27: 415–444.

Meiksins Wood, E., *2002, The Origin of Capitalism: A Longer View*, London: Verso Books.

Mejias, U., 2011, The Twitter Revolution Must Die, in Ulises Mejias' Blog, available at: http://blog.ulisesmejias.com/2011/01/30/the-twitter-revolution-must-die/

Mesch, G.S., 2010, Together and Alone, the Use of SNS according to □Occupation in Israel, Paper presented at the Annual Conference of Organizational □Sociology, Haifa University, February, available at: http://gustavomesch.wordpress.com/2010/03/26/gender-and-occupational-uneven-distributions-in-sns-use/

Monfort, S., 2009, 21/12, Twitter's Search Agreements Provide a New Revenue Stream, in *Nasdaq,* available at: http://www.nasdaq.com/newscontent/20091221/Twitter's-search-agreements-provide-a-new-revenue-stream.aspx

Mosco, V., 1996, *The Political Economy of Communication: Rethinking and Renewal*, London and Thousand Oaks, CA: Sage.

Murdock, G. and Golding, P., 2001, Digital Possibilities and Market Realities: Contradictions of Communications Convergence, in L. Panitch and C. Leys (eds), *A World of Contradictions* (pp. 111–129), London: The Merlin Press.

Murray, A., 2009, The Reclassification of Extreme Pornographic Images, *Modern Law Review*, 72(1): 73–90, available at: http://works.bepress.com/cgi/viewcontent.cgi?article=1004&context=andrew_murray

Muthukumaraswamy, K., 2009, Games and journalism: Now that journalism is in trouble, why not play with it?, in Online Journalism Blog, available at: http://onlinejournalismblog.com/2009/04/16/games-and-journalism-now-that-journalism-is-in-trouble-why-not-play-with-it/

Nakamura, L., 2002, *Cybertypes: Race, Ethnicity, and Identity on the Internet,* London and New York: Routledge.

Negroponte, N., 1995, *Being Digital*, New York: Alfred A. Knopf.

Newhagen, J. and Rafaeli, S., 1996, Why Communication Researchers Should Study the Internet, *Journal of Computer Mediated Communication*, 1(4): np.

Nielsen, 2009, Global Faces, Networked Places, available at: http://blog.nielsen.com/nielsenwire/wp-content/uploads/2009/03/nielsen_globalfaces_mar09.pdf

Nolan, S., 2003, *Journalism Online: the Search for Narrative Form in a Multilinear World,* Paper presented at Fifth Annual Digital Arts and Culture Conference, available at: http://hypertext.rmit.edu.au/dac/papers/Nolan.pdf

Norris, P., 2003, Preaching to the Converted? Pluralism, Participation and Party Websites, *Party Politics*, 9(1): 21–45.

O'Brien, J., 1999, Writing in the Body: Gender (Re)production in Online Interaction, in M. Smith and P. Kollock (eds), *Communities in Cyberspace*, London: Routledge.

O'Reilly, T., 2005, What is Web 2.0, available at: http://oreilly.com/web2/archive/what-is-web-20.html

O'Reilly, T. and Wales, J., 2007, Draft Blogger's Code of Conduct, in O'Reilly Radar, available at: http://radar.oreilly.com/archives/2007/04/draft_bloggers_1.html

OECD, 2005, Digital Broadband Content: The online computer and video game industry, available at: http://www.oecd.org/dataoecd/19/5/34884414.pdf

Ohmae, K., 1995, *The End of the Nation State: The Rise of Regional Economies*, New York: Free Press.

Ortiz, C.E., 2008, Worldwide and US mobile subscriber penetration (December), available at: http://weblog.cenriqueortiz.com/mobility/2008/12/29/worldwide-and-us-mobile-sub-scriber-penetration-dec-2008/

Ostrow, A., 2010, YouTube Revenue Approaching $1 Billion Per Year, in *Mashable,* 5 March, available at: http://mashable.com/2010/03/05/youtube-revenue-2010/

Paasonen, S., 2010, Online Pornography: Ubiquitous and Effaced, in M. Consalvo, R. Burnett and C. Hess (eds), *The Handbook of Internet Studies* (pp. 424–440), Malden, MA and Oxford: Wiley-Blackwell.

Paczkowski, J., 2009, Credit Suisse Far Better at Analyzing Derivatives than YouTube Infrastructure Costs, *Digital Daily,* 17 June, available at: http://tiny.cc/NulVg

Papacharissi, Z., 2002, The Virtual Sphere: The Internet as a Public Sphere, *New Media & Society*, 4(1): 9–27.

Papacharissi, Z. and Rubin, A.M., 2000, Predictors of Internet Use, *Journal of Broadcasting & Electronic Media*, 44: 175–196.

Parker, D. and Song, M., 2007, Inclusion, Participation and the Emergence of British Chinese Websites, *Journal of Ethnic and Migration Studies*, 33(7): 1043–1061.

Patelis, K., 2000, The Political Economy of the Internet, in James Curran (ed.), *Media Organizations and Society* (pp. 84–106), London: Arnold.

Paulussen, S., 2004, Online News Production in Flanders, *Journal of Computer Mediated Communication*, 9(4): np, available at: http://jcmc.indiana.edu/vol9/issue4/paulussen.html

Pavlik, J.V., 2001, *Journalism and New Media*, New York: Columbia University Press.

Pew Hispanic Center, 2009, *Latinos Online, 2006–2008: Narrowing the Gap*, report by G. Livingston, K. Parker and S. Fox, available at: http://pewhispanic.org/files/reports/119.pdf

Pew Project for Excellence in Journalism, 2009, *The State of the News Media*, available at: http://www.stateofthemedia.org/2009/index.htm

Pew Research Center for the People and the Press, 2008, *Key News Audiences Now Blend Online and Traditional Sources: Audience Segments in a Changing News Environment*, available at: http://people-press.org/report/444/news-media

Plant, S., 1998, *Zeros and Ones: Digital Women and the New Technoculture*, London: Fourth Estate.

Polanyi, K., 1944, *The Great Transformation*, Boston, MA: Beacon Press.

Poole, S., 2000, *Trigger Happy: The Inner Life of Videogames*, London: Fourth Estate.

Poole, S., 2008, *Working for the Man: Against the Employment Paradigm in Videogames*, available at: http://stevenpoole.net/trigger-happy/working-for-the-man/

Poster, M., 1995, *The Second Media Age*, Cambridge: Polity Press.

Poster, M., 2007, Internet Piracy as Radical Democracy? in L. Dalhberg and E. Siapera (eds), *Radical Democracy and the Internet* (pp. 207–225), Basingstoke, Macmillan-Palgrave.

Pryor, L., 2002, An Explanation of 'Immersive news', in *Online Journalism Review*, available at: http://www.ojr.org/ojr/technology/1017962897.php

Putnam, R., 1995, Bowling Alone: America's Declining Social Capital, *Journal of Democracy*, 6: 65–78.

Putnam, R., 2000, *Bowling Alone: The Collapse and Revival of American Community*, New York: Simon and Schuster.

Raessens, J., 2006, Playful Identities, or the Ludification of Culture, *Games and Culture*, 1: 52.

Rainie, L., 2005, *iPods and MP3 Players storm the Market*, available at: http://www.pewinternet.org/Commentary/2005/February/iPods-and-MP3-Players-storm-the-market.aspx

Rash, W., 1997, *Politics on the Nets: Wiring the Political Process*, New York: W.H. Freeman and Co.

Raynes-Goldie, K., 2010, Aliases, Creeping, and Wall Cleaning: Understanding Privacy in the Age of Facebook, *First Monday*, 15(1).

Reagle, 1998, Why the Internet is Good: Community Governance that Works Well, Berkman Center Draft, available at: http://cyber.law.harvard.edu/archived_content/people/reagle/regulation-19990326.html

Reed, A., 2005, 'My Blog is Me': Texts and Persons in UK Online Journal Culture (and Anthropology), *Ethnos*, 70(2): 220–242.

Resnick, D., 1998, Politics on the Internet: Normalization and the Public Sphere, in C. Touluse and W.T. Luke (eds), *The Politics of Cyber-space* (pp. 48–68), London: Routledge.

Rheingold, H., 1993, *The Virtual Community: Homesteading on the Electronic Frontier*, Reading, MA: Addison-Wesley, 1998 edition available at: http://www.rheingold.com/vc/book/

Rheingold, H., 2002, *Smart Mobs: The Next Social Revolution*, Cambridge, MA: Perseus.

Rolandson, R., 1992, *Globalization: Social Theory and Global Culture*, London: Sage.

Rodino, M., 1997, Breaking out of Binaries: Reconceptualizing Gender and its Relationship to Language in Computer-Mediated Communication, *Journal of Computer-Mediated Communication*, 3(3): np, available at: http://www.ascusc.org/jcmc/vol3/issue3/rodino.html

Rogers, E.M., 2003, *Diffusion of Innovations* (fifth edition), New York: Free Press.

Rosen, J., 2006, The People Formerly Known as the Audience, in PressThink, 27 June, available at: http://journalism.nyu.edu/pubzone/weblogs/pressthink/2006/06/27/ppl_frmr.html

Ruffin, O., 2009, More from Oxblood Ruffin, in *Tech Radar*, 14 July, available at: http://www.techradar.com/news/world-of-tech/more-from-oxblood-ruffin-615932

Salmon, G., 2002, *E-tivities: the key to active only learning*. Sterling, VA: Stylus Publishing.

Saltzis, K. and Dickinson, R., 2008, Inside the Changing Newsroom: Journalists' Responses to Media Convergence, *Aslib Proceedings*, 60(3): 216–228.

Schiller, D., 2007, *How to Think about Information*, Urbana and Chicago: University of Illinois Press.

Schumpeter, J., 1991, *The Economics and Sociology of Capitalism*, ed. Richard Swedber, Princeton: Princeton University Press.

Segan, S., 2010, WiMAX vs. HSPA+: The Hands-On Test, *PC Mag*, 14 February, available at: http://www.pcmag.com/article2/0,2817,2359139,00.asp

Selwyn, N., 2004, Reconsidering Political and Popular Understandings of the Digital Divide, *New Media & Society*, 6(3): 341–362.

Siapera, E., 2004, Asylum Politics, the Internet and the Public Sphere, *Javnost/The Public*, 11(1): 79–100.

Siapera, E., 2005, Minority Activism on the Web: Between Deliberation and Multiculturalism, *Journal of Ethnic and Migration Studies*, 31(3): 499–519.

Siapera, E., 2007a, Transnational Islam and the Internet, in M. Georgiou, O. Guedes-Bailey and R. Harindranath (eds), *Reimagining Diasporas: Transnational Lives and the Media*, Basingstoke: Macmillan Palgrave.

Siapera, E., 2007b, Multicultural Radical Democracy and Online Islam, in L. Dahlberg and E. Siapera (eds), *Radical Democracy and the Internet* (pp. 148–167), Basingstoke: Macmillan Palgrave.

Siapera, E., 2008, The Subject of Political Blogs, Special Issue on Blogs, Governance and Democracy, *Information Polity*, 13(1–2): 97–110.

Siapera, E., 2010, *Cultural Diversity and Global Media*, Oxford: Wiley-Blackwell.

Sihvonen, T., 2009, *Players Unleashed! Modding The Sims and the Culture of Gaming*, Doctoral dissertation, University of Turku.

Silverstone, R., 2005, The Sociology of Mediation and Communication, in C. Calhoun, C. Rojeck and B. Turner (eds), *The Sage Handbook of Sociology*, London: Sage.

Silverstone, R., 2006, *Media and Morality*, Cambridge: Polity Press.

Sklair, L., 1999, Competing Conceptions of Globalization, *Journal of World-Systems Research*, V(2): 143–163.

Skrbis, Z., 1999, *Long-distance Nationalism: Diasporas, Homelands and Identities*, Aldershot: Ashgate.

Smith, A., Lehman Schlozman, K., Verba S., and Brady, H., 2009, *The Internet and Civic Engagement*, Pew Internet and American Life Project, available at: http://www.pewinternet.org/~/media//Files/Reports/2009/The%20Internet%20and%20Civic%20Engagement.pdf

Smith, D., 2009, Africa calling: mobile phone usage sees record rise after huge investment, in the *Guardian*, 22 October, available at: http://www.guardian.co.uk/technology/2009/oct/22/africa-mobile-phones-usage-rise

Smith, M., Borash, V., Getoor, L. and Lauw, H., 2008, Leveraging Social Context for Searching Social Media, *Proceedings of the 2008 ACM Workshop on Search in Social Media*, New York.

Smythe, D.W., 1981, *Dependency Road: Communications, Capitalism, Consciousness and Canada*, Norwood, NJ: Ablex Publishing.

Solum, L., 2008, Models of Internet Governance, in *Illinois Public Law Research Paper No. 07–25*, available at: http://papers.ssrn.com/sol3/papers.cfm?abstract_id=1136825

Sorensen, C., 2006, Continuous Conversations, in Mobile Life, (ed.), *The Mobile Life Report 2006: How Mobile Phones Change the Way we Live* (pp. 35–39), London: The Carphone Warehouse.

Spangler, T., 2009, YouTube May Lose $470 million, in Multichannel News, 4 March, available at: http://www.multichannel.com/article/191223-YouTube_May_Lose_470_Million_In_2009_Analysts.php

Steuer, J., 1992, Defining Virtual Reality: Dimensions Determining Telepresence, *Journal of Communication*, 42(4): 73–93.

Stiegler, B., 1998, *Technics and Time, 1: The Fault of Epimetheus*, Stanford, CA: Stanford University Press.

Stiegler, B., 2006, Anamnesis and Hypomnesis: The Memories of Desire, in L. Armand and A. Bradley (eds), *Technicity* (pp. 15–41), Prague: Litteraria Pragensia.

Stiegler, B., 2007, Individuation, Hypomnemata and Grammatisation, in *Second Moscow Biennale, Philosophy symposium*, available at: http://2nd.moscowbiennale.ru/en/stiegler_report_en/

Stiglitz, J., 2003, *Globalization and its Discontents*, New York: WW Norton and Co.

Stump, R., Gong, W. and Li, Z, 2008, Exploring the Digital Divide in Mobile Phone Adoption Levels across Countries, *Journal of Macromarketing*, 28(4): 397–412.

Subramanian, L., Surana, S., Patra, R., Nedevschi, S., Ho, M., Brewer, E. and Sheth, A., 2006, Rethinking Wireless for the Developing World, paper presented at the Hotnets-V Workshop, University of California at Irvine, available at: http://conferences.sigcomm.org/hotnets/2006/subramanian06rethinking.pdf

Sunstein, C., 2001, *Republic.com*, Princeton, NJ: Princeton University Press.

Sunstein, C., 2007, *Republic.com 2.0*, Princeton, NJ: Princeton University Press.

Szendro Bok, M., 2009, The Mega-merger of Comcast and NBC: a lethal marriage, in *New Media Rights*, available at: http://www.newmediarights.org/nmr/mega_merger_comcast_and_nbc_lethal_marriage

Tajfel, H., 1981, *Human Groups and Social Categories: Studies in Social Psychology*, Cambridge: Cambridge University Press.

Tarì, M. and Vanni, I., 2005, On the Life and Deeds of San Precario, Patron Saint of Precarious Workers and Lives, in *Fibreculture*, 5, available at: http://five.fibreculture journal.org/fcj-023-on-the-life-and-deeds-of-san-precario-patron-saint-of-precarious-workers-and-lives/

Taylor, F., 1911, *Principles of Scientific Management*, New York and London: Harper.

Taylor, T. L., 2006a, *Play Between Words: Exploring Online Game Culture*, Cambridge, MA: MIT Press.

Taylor, T.L., 2006b, Does WoW change everything? How a PvP Server, Multinational Player Base, and Surveillance Mod Scene Caused Me Pause, *Games and Culture*, 1(4): 318–337.

Technorati, 2009, State of the Blogosphere 2009, available at: http://technorati.com/blogging/article/state-of-the-blogosphere-2009-introduction/

The Daily Telegraph Newsroom, 2007, Multimedia Newsroom Integration, available at: http://www.youtube.com/watch?v=2yXT_1pvDv4&NR=1

Thompson, J.B., 2005, The New Visibility, *Theory, Culture and Society*, 22(6): 31–51.

Thurlow, C. and Brown, A., 2003, Generation Txt? The Sociolinguistics of Young People's Text-messaging, *Online Discourse Analysis,* available at: http://extra.shu.ac.uk/daol/articles/v1/n1/a3/thurlow2002003-paper.htm

Tilly, C., 2004, *Social Movements, 1768–2004*, Boulder, CO: Paradigm Publishers.

Time Magazine, 2009, The 10 Most Endangered Newspapers in America, 9 March, available at: http://www.time.com/time/business/article/0,8599,1883785,00.html

Toffler, A., 1970, *Future Shock*, New York: Bantam Books.

Tomlinson, J., 1991, *Cultural Imperialism: A Critical Introduction*, Baltimore, MD: Johns Hopkins University Press.

Tomlinson, J., 1999, *Globalization and Culture*, Chicago: University of Chicago Press.

Tönnies, F., 2001 [1887], *Community and Civil Society*, trans. J. Harris and M. Hollis, Cambridge: Cambridge University Press.

Touraine, A., 1971, *The Post-Industrial Society. Tomorrow's Social History: Classes, Conflicts and Culture in the Programmed Society*, New York: Random House.

Tsagarousianou, R., Tambini, D. and Bryan, C. (eds), 1998, *Cyberdemocracy: Technology, Cities and Civic Networks*, London: Routledge.

Tunstall, J., 1977, *The Media are American*, London: Constable.

Turkle, S., 1995, *Life on the Screen*, Cambridge, MA: MIT Press.

Universal McCann, 2008, Social Media Tracker, Wave 3, available at: http://ia700303.us.archive.org/12/items/UniversalMccannWave3PowerToThePeople/Wave3.pdf

Vaccari, A. and Barnet, B., 2009, Prolegomena to a Future Robot History: Stiegler, Epiphylogenesis and Technical Evolution, *Transformations*, 17, available at: http://www.transformationsjournal.org/journal/issue_17/article_09.shtml

van Doorn, N., van Zoonen, L. and Wyatt, S., 2007, Writing from Experience: Presentation of Gender Identity on Weblogs, *European Journal of Women's Studies*, 14(2): 143–159.

von Tunzelmann, G.N., 1995, *Technology and Industrial Progress: The Foundations of Economic Growth*, Aldershot, Hants: Edward Elgar.

Wajcman, J., 2010, Feminist Theories of Technology, *Cambridge Journal of Economics*, 34(1): 143–152.

Wallerstein, I., 2005 [1974], *The Modern World-System, Vol. I: Capitalist Agriculture and the Origins of the European World-Economy in the Sixteenth Century*, New York and London: Academic Press.

Wark, M., 2006, *Gamer Theory*, Cambridge, MA: Harvard University Press.

Warnick, B., 2002, *Critical Literacy in a Digital Era: Technology, Rhetoric, and the Public Interest*, Mahwah, NJ: Lawrence Erlbaum.

Washington Post, 1999, Shooter Pair Mixed Fantasy, Reality, 22 April, available at: http://www. washingtonpost.com/wp-srv/national/daily/april99/suspects042299.htm

Waters, M., 1995, *Globalization*, London: Routledge.

Weber, M., 1958, *The Protestant Ethic and the Spirit of Capitalism*, trans. Talcott Parsons, New York: Scribners.

Webster, F., 1995 (second edition 2002), *Theories of the Information Society*, London: Routledge.

Weintraub J., and Kumar, K. (eds.), 1997, *Public and Private in Thought and Practice*, Chicago: Chicago University Press.

Wellman, B., 1988, Structural Analysis: From Method and Metaphor to Theory and Substance, in B. Wellman and S.D. Berkowitz (eds), *Social Structures: a Network Approach* (pp. 19–61), Cambridge, Cambridge University Press.

Wellman, B., 1999, The Network Community: An Introduction, in B. Wellman (ed.), *Networks in the Global Village*, Boulder, CO: Westview, available at: http://homes.chass.utoronto. ca/~wellman/publications/globalvillage/in.htm

Wellman, B., 2001a, Computer Networks as Social Networks, *Science*, 293(5537): 2031–2034.

Wellman, B., 2001b, Physical Place and CyberPlace: The Rise of Personalized Networking, *International Journal of Urban and Regional Research*, 25: 227–252.

Wellman, B., 2002, Little Boxes, Glocalization, and Networked Individualism, in M. Tanabe, P. van den Besselaar and T. Ishida (eds), *Digital Cities II: Computational and Sociological Approaches* (pp. 10–25), Berlin: Springer-Verlag.

Wellman, B. and Gulia, M., 1999, Net-Surfers Don't Ride Alone: Virtual Communities as Communities, in B. Wellman (ed.), *Networks in the Global Village: Life in Contemporary Communities* (pp. 72–86), Boulder, CO: Westview.

Wellman, B., Quan-Hasse, A., Boase, J., Chen, W., Hampton, K., de Diaz, I.I., et al., 2003, The Social Affordances of the Internet for Networked Individualism, *Journal of Computer-Mediated Communication*, 8(3).

Wellman, B., Quan-Haase, A., Witte, J. and Hampton, K., 2001, Does the Internet Increase, Decrease, or Supplement Social Capital? Social Networks, Participation, and Community Commitment, *American Behavioral Scientist*, 45(3): 437–456.

Willson, M., 2010, The Possibilities of Network Sociality, in J. Hunsinger, L. Klastrap and M. Allen (eds), *International Handbook of Internet Research* (pp. 493–506), Dordrecht: Springer.

Winthrop-Young, G., 2006, Implosion and Intoxication: Kittler, a German Classic, and Pink Floyd, *Theory, Culture & Society*, 23(7–8): 75–91.

Winthrop-Young, G. and Wutz, M., 1999, Translators' Introduction: Friedrich Kittler and Media Discourse Analysis, in F. Kittler, *Gramaphone, Film, Typewriter* (pp. xx–xxi), trans. G. Winthrop-Young and M. Wutz, Stanford, CA: Stanford University Press.

Wolf, M., 2001, Genre and the Video Game, in M. Wolf (ed.), *The Medium of the Video Game* (pp. 113–134), Austin: University of Texas Press.

Wolfsfeld, G., 1997, *Media and Political Conflict: News From the Middle East*, Cambridge: Cambridge University Press.

World Internet Project, 2010, World Internet Project Report Finds Large Percentages of Non-Users, and Significant Gender Disparities in Going Online, Press Release, available at: http://www.digitalcenter.org/WIP2010/wip2010_long_press_release_v2.pdf

Wu, T., Dyson, E., Froomkin, A.M. and Gross, D.A, 2007, On the Future of Internet Governance, in *American Society of International Law, Proceedings of the Annual Meeting*, 101, available at SSRN: http://ssrn.com/abstract=992805

Wynn E. and Katz, J. E., 1998, Hyperbole over cyberspace: self-presentation and social boundaries in Internet home pages and discourse, *The Information Society*, 13(4): 297–328.

Yoon, K., 2003, Retraditionalizing the Mobile Phone, *European Journal of Cultural Studies*, 6(3): 327–343.

Young, I.M., 1996, Communication and the Other: Beyond Deliberative Democracy, in S. Benhabib (ed.), *Democracy and Difference* (pp. 120–136), Princeton, NJ: Princeton University Press.

INDEX